Teaching the Moderately and Severely Handicapped

Volume II
Second Edition

Author's Note

The curriculum is published in three volumes. Volume I contains objectives and activities in the areas of self-care, gross motor, fine motor skills, and prevocational and household management. Volume II contains objectives and activities in communication, interpersonal skills, sex education, drug education, and leisure skills. Following consultation with educators, the authors concluded that a three-volume format would organize the extensive amount of information contained within the curriculum into a manageable form suitable for use in instructional situations.

While the complete curriculum is meant specifically for use by the teacher, the material in Volume I is of special interest to other professionals such as physical therapists, psychologists, and nurses. The material in Volume II is of particular interest to professionals such as speech, language, and hearing therapists, recreational and music therapists. Volume III is a valuable resource for those teaching functional academics to the mildly and moderately handicapped and those who are teaching the areas of prereadiness and readiness skills to nonhandicapped students as well. Each volume is organized to meet many different learning needs in a variety of educational and habilitative settings. With such diversity of use in mind, the authors have designed each volume as a self-sustaining unit, and teachers may use each one independently of the others, according to the specific interests, needs, and abilities of their students.

Volume I *Functional Curriculum for Self-Care, Motor Skills, and Household Management*

Contents

Introduction and Curriculum Overview
Self-Care Skills
Gross Motor Skills
Fine Motor and Prevocational Skills
Household Management and Living Skills

Volume III *Functional Academics for the Mildly and Moderately Handicapped*

Contents

Introduction
Curriculum
Functional Academics
Functional Reading
Functional Writing
Functional Arithmetic
- **Numerals**
- **Money**
- **Measurement**
- **Time**

Consumer Skills

Volume II
Second Edition

Teaching the Moderately and Severely Handicapped

A Functional Curriculum for Communication and Socialization

Peter J. Valletutti

Michael Bender

pro-ed
5341 Industrial Oaks Blvd.
Austin, Texas 78735

Printed in the United States of America.

Library of Congress Cataloging in Publication Data
(Revised for vol. 2)

Bender, Michael, 1943-
Teaching the moderately and severely handicapped.

On v. 2 Peter J. Valletutti's name appears first.
Contents: v. 1. A functional curriculum for self-care, motor skills, and household management—v. 2. A functional curriculum for communication and socialization.
1. Handicapped children—Education. 2. Handicapped children—Education—Curricula. 3. Handicapped—Life skills guides. I. Valletutti, Peter J. II. Title.
LC4015.B37 1985 371.9 84-22861
ISBN 0-936104-52-X (v. 1)
ISBN 0-936104-53-8 (v. 2)

pro-ed
5341 Industrial Oaks Blvd.
Austin, Texas 78735

10 9 8 7 6 5 4 3 2 1 84 85 86 87

Dedication

to my sister-in-law, Lynne Mayrsohn and my special sister-in-law Madeleine Valletutti, then, now, and always.

P. J. V.

to all the Benders, Morrises, and Mushinskis with all my love, and especially to Richie so he knows we are thinking of him.

M. B.

Contents

Preface / ix

Acknowledgments / xi

1 Introduction and Curriculum Overview / 1

2 Nonverbal Communication Skills / 25

3 Verbal Communication Skills / 85

4 Interpersonal Skills / 183

5 Sex Education / 227

6 Drug Education / 259

7 Leisure Skills / 287

Preface

This new edition of the curriculum provides functional educational goals designed to assist teachers, other professionals, and parents in facilitating the performance of moderately and severely handicapped students in the full variety of life situations and environmental contexts.

This book is *not* a methods book nor does it contain presentations and/or charts of task analyses. It presumes a basic understanding of teaching methods and a fundamental level of expertise in analyzing educational tasks so that they may be used as a framework for evaluation and as a means of focusing on discrete behaviors requiring remedial or instructional attention. A task analysis approach to instructing moderately and severely handicapped learners is insufficient for teaching within a functional framework because it is too atomized to be of significant value in preparing students for life's reality contexts. Real situations involve diverse and interrelated cognitive judgments as well as varied environmental settings. Reality contexts can only be effectively simulated in a classroom setting if the entire behavior is demonstrated with all its applicable dimensions (psychomotor, affective, and cognitive) expressed as a total, integrated act. A task analysis approach is also inadequate, from a functional perspective, whenever small steps are tangibly reinforced because such frequency of reinforcement does not occur naturally in the environment.

Although specific objectives have generally been placed in their developmental sequence, known sequences have only been considered if they make functional sense. Developmental milestones have been deemphasized if the specific behavior does not contribute to the functional success of moderately and severely handicapped students (e.g., drawing a geometric shape or matching wooden blocks of different colors).

The curriculum is not intended as a model one for profoundly handicapped individuals; in fact, many high level goals are purposely included to encourage program implementers not to have a restricted and limiting view because there are many mildly handicapped students who are functioning at a lower than expected level and would benefit appreciably from the activities in this curriculum. Further, it is to be remembered that there are many moderately and severely handicapped students who are not primarily cognitively restricted but rather are physically, emotionally, and/or language impaired.

This new edition of the curriculum has been developed as a guide to preservice and inservice teachers and other professionals who work with moderately and severely handicapped students.

Parents, surrogate parents, and other family members as well as house parents in group homes/apartments or other alternate living arrangements will find this curriculum valuable as they interact with and instruct the handicapped individuals with whom they work and/or live.

This curriculum is designed, in addition, to serve as a text for students taking courses in curriculum development and teaching methods in special education at undergraduate and graduate levels.

The Suggested Readings appended to each curriculum section not only contain recent publications but some of the older, classic materials as well. These classic materials have been included because they have maintained their immediacy and, therefore, should not be automatically dismissed out of a passion for newness.

The Materials Lists attached to each curriculum section are deliberately brief because the materials of a functional curriculum are ordinary materials invariably found in the home, school, and community and because teacher-made materials are usually more appropriate, better focused, and more motivating to students.

The area of safety education has been eliminated from this new edition of the curriculum because safety factors must be diligently addressed in meeting *each* of the other identified objectives and in implementing *all* suggested motivational activities. Safety considerations are of such great importance that they must be integrated into the total curriculum and not treated as a separate curricular entity.

Finally, this curriculum does not address all the dimensions of a functional curriculum because that is neither practical nor possible. It does not provide all the possible instructional activities that are interesting or applicable to individual students; it simply provides a structure out of which a creative professional can extrapolate additional objectives and activities and provide answers to the challenging questions that arise from the actual implementation of the curriculum.

Acknowledgments

The material for this revised curriculum has been developed over a period of years. It has been developed by the authors from their deep conviction that a functional curriculum is critical to the development of handicapped learners. Functional materials and approaches are valued not only for their sake as the end goals of educational programming for moderately and severely handicapped persons but also because they result in greater learner interest and involvement. Developing functional learning experiences is not an easy task, primarily because we have all been conditioned to think in traditional educational ways by virtue of the mistakes of our own schooling. Therefore, it was necessary to seek the help of others. We wish to thank those individuals who helped us complete this work. We are deeply grateful to:

Gail McGregor, Shelley Hammerman, Edith Garrett, Anne Smith, and Candice Suggars, who teach and/or work with moderately and severely handicapped individuals.

Susan Harryman, Director of Physical Therapy, and Lana Warren, Director of Occupational Therapy, at the John F. Kennedy Institute.

We especially wish to thank Irene Gray for her understanding, commitment, and tireless efforts in typing and retyping the manuscript. The quality of her work and advice is greatly appreciated.

1 Introduction and Curriculum Overview

When establishing curricula for students who are nonhandicapped or mildly handicapped, the range of skills that must be included is much narrower than that for a population of students with moderate and severe handicaps. It is axiomatic that the greater the handicap the greater the educational need, and, thus, the more comprehensive the curriculum must be. The skills needed by moderately and severely handicapped students continue to expand as society becomes more complex. The curriculum must encompass all of the functional domains, including: self-care, gross motor, fine motor, and prevocational skills; household management and living skills; and communication, interpersonal, sex education, drug education, and leisure skills.

For the past 7 years, the first edition of this curriculum has been used extensively by educators and other human service professionals working with the moderately and severely handicapped. Feedback provided by "hands-on" users of the curriculum, including parents, and by college and university professors, coupled with input from the authors' own teaching experiences, has resulted in modifications and refinements that have been incorporated into this new edition.

A Functional Orientation

A functional orientation to curricula for handicapped students can be readily accommodated while operating in a subject-oriented structure and setting. For example, a traditional way of teaching color concepts is to introduce young children to various colored shapes, beads, and blocks. A functional approach, on the other hand, involves the learner with objects he or she will come into contact with while functioning in real-life situations and activities. For example:

1. In the dressing area, show the learner a blue shirt, and ask him to find a pair of socks of the same color on a mock store counter. Tell him that the socks he wants may not always be on display, and he may have to ask the store clerk for them. For example, he may say, "Do you have a pair of blue woolen socks, size twelve?"
2. Give the learner a swatch of cloth from her "new" dress, and ask her to match it to the shoes on display in a glass case. Tell her to ask the clerk for help in locating a pair of red shoes to match her new red dress.
3. In the food area, show the learner a green banana, a yellow banana, and a brown, overripe one. Ask him which one is ready to be eaten. Ask him which one is not ripe yet and which one is overripe.
4. In the community, show the learner a traffic light. Tell him that he is going to visit his Aunt Rose. While walking or cycling to his aunt's house, he will come to four corners where there are traffic signals. Show him the color green and tell him he can walk when the light is green if it is safe. Remind him not to cross when it is red. Role play and practice.
5. Show the learners a map of a stadium where sections are color coded. Tell them to find their seats using color clues.
6. In a simulated work experience, give the learner a wiring task in which wires of the same color have to be properly connected or the system will not work. Ask him to perform the wiring task.
7. In a consumer setting, send the learner to the "store" to buy red apples, green grapes, blueberries, and/or oranges.
8. In a school setting, tell the learner to get a workbook (e.g., the orange book on the top shelf).
9. Discuss the fish in the aquarium. Tell the learner to describe any unusual identifying characteristics. Then, ask him to describe the fish in terms of their colors.
10. As part of a leisure experience, take the learner on a nature walk, and ask him to note nature's colors: the green of the grass, the blue of the sky, and the red of the sunset.
11. Play games that involve moving markers along colored paths. Encourage the learner to take turns along the colored path as designated by spinners or game card directions. Tell him to select his game marker by the color of his choice.

Teaching colors from a functional perspective makes them come alive because you have infused them with reality. A functional approach is much more motivating than the more traditional unidimensional approaches.

The holistic nature of a functional curriculum requires that it be taught within the context of its functional reality. A skill must be taught in its total context. For example, it is unwise to teach the motor skill of turning on water faucets unless water is drawn for a real purpose (e.g., filling an ice cube tray or a pet's water bowl or washing one's hands) and then used for that purpose—the ice cube tray must be carried to the freezer with any spillage cleaned up; the pet's water bowl must be put in its customary spot; the washed hands must be ready for a nutritious snack or meal. A functional approach to curriculum development and implementation reflects the demands of living independently in society.

Developing a Functional Curriculum

The development of a functional curriculum is not an esoteric task. A functional curriculum is based on the total life events of people as they meet the challenges and demands that are an integral part of functioning in their society. Therefore, looking at life from a "reality" perspective is all that is needed to begin to design a curriculum that is functional because it is natural.

Curriculum Steps

The first step is *to conceptualize those general behaviors that are critical to successful independent functioning*. These general behaviors become the focus and framework of a functional curriculum. They are written as general objectives (i.e., those long-range objectives that when acquired will enable individuals to lead a more productive, satisfying, and enriching life). General objectives, because they are long range, may be written in nonbehavioral terms, since their total acquisition is an ideal toward which the individual is striving. However, the identification of general objectives is not an idle process, because it provides the basic framework of the curriculum from which all other structures evolve.

Once the general objectives of a functional curriculum are identified, the second task is *to articulate those specific objectives that will contribute to the realization of each of the identified general objectives*. Thus, all of the specific objectives subsumed under each general objective address those behaviors that will enable the learner to realize more closely the ideal that is implicit in the words of the general objective. Specific objectives are stated in behavioral terms because they describe skills that are to be demonstrated by the individual learner, whenever possible, in natural settings and in real-life contexts.

Once the specific objectives are identified, the next step is *to explore possible functional activities that will lead to their acquisition*. The authors have identified three functional settings: the *school*, the *home*, and the *community*. Suggested activities for the home and the community are meant to be communicated by teachers as they form partnerships with parents and utilize the natural settings of the home and the community to structure and reinforce learning. Suggested activities for the school are meant to stimulate teacher creativity while utilizing the natural environment of the classroom, the school building, and its immediate surroundings.

It is expected that as readers carry out the curriculum they will continue to find new bits of the universe of skills, will reject some suggested activities, and will create others. These modifications are encouraged because professional educators must not be automatons who blindly and unthinkingly follow any guide. Rather, they must be creative, dynamic leaders who, through judicious educational evaluation and a creative spirit, design learning experiences that will enrich the lives of the handicapped students they teach, no matter where that learning takes place. A learning area is not the physical setting itself but the nature of the human interaction. Readers no doubt will find gaps in the curriculum. A recurrent nightmare is that something vital has been left out. If gaps are found, *then fill them.*

As an aid to brainstorming for possible instructional activities, *functional emphases are identified* because they are the keys to creating instructional experiences that are reality based and are not divorced from the world in which we expect individuals to function. Failure to observe the functional elements of a learning experience renders the instructional act as disfunctional as the more traditional disconnected approaches common to subject-oriented curricula.

Developing Instructional Plans

Once the sequence and scope of general (or unit) objectives and their supporting specific objectives are charted, the structure for educational evaluation and programming is present. These objectives serve as the framework for systematically observing and assessing the student's performance in terms of both processes and products. Evaluation occurs as the learner functions on a daily basis in natural settings and responds to structured and simulated activities presented by parents, instructors, instructional aides, and other human service professionals. These observations aid in determining those general and specific objectives appropriate for the individual. Once these decisions are made, planning can commence as follows:

1. The design of a specific instructional plan begins with the articulation of a general objective that represents a major curriculum segment, followed by identification of a relevant specific objective.
2. Following the selection of a specific objective, a pertinent instructional objective is then constructed. The instructional objective, like the specific objective, is student oriented and has the dual purpose of: (a) structuring the instructional sequence and (b) suggesting the assessment strategy and assigned performance criterion levels. Toward these ends, an instructional objective has three elements:

a. The definition of the stimulus situation or conditions (e.g., "When given . . ." or "After being shown . . .").
b. The specification of the desired response (e.g., "The learner will . . .").
c. The establishment of a mastery level (e.g., "The learner will do so in 4 out of 5 trials," or "He will do so correctly within 5 minutes.").

3. Next, materials and equipment are listed. The instructional segment is placed early in the plan for ease in reading as one skims the written plan prior to its implementation.
4. Individualized reinforcement and reinforcement schedules are then identified in recognition of: (a) the different reward preferences and needs of individuals and (b) their varying response rates.
5. The motivating activity is then stated. For many, this is a challenging task, because it may be difficult to specify age-appropriate motivating activities that will capture the attention, imagination, and interest of those individuals for whom the instruction is designed.
6. Instructional procedures are then enumerated. They are instructor oriented and are sequenced in logical steps from initial motivation to assessment. Attention must be paid throughout to instructional steps that illuminate the teaching-learning process. Evidence that some teaching is taking place must be included. Demonstrations, assistance, and problem-solving challenges must be an integral part of explaining the instructional procedure.
7. The assessment strategy to be used is then specified. This strategy reflects the desired response and mastery criterion or criteria stated in the instructional objective. It is instructor oriented and includes record-keeping requirements.
8. At this point, a proposed follow-up activity or objective is written to ensure that the sequence of instruction is observed. A follow-up objective is specified when the instructor believes that the specific objective will be mastered and that the learner will then be ready to proceed to a new functional context, the next specific objective, or, at times, to a new general objective. If the learner, despite the best laid plans, fails to meet criteria, then a new plan must be written on an ad hoc basis to meet the specific problem demonstrated by the learner. A remedial instructional experience is likely to concentrate only on a cognitive dimension, a psychomotor aspect, or a health and safety factor.

   For example, an individual learner may have failed to meet mastery criteria in making a bed because he was unable to select new linen in the right size. In this case, remediation is then pursued through an instructional design and experience that concentrates solely on developing this skill. As a further example, the learner may not meet performance criterion because he was unable to put on new pillowcases. In this case, remediation is then pursued through an instructional experience that concentrates on developing the skill of putting on pillowcases. As a final example, the learner may not select clean linen to make up the bed;

therefore, attention must be paid to developing the awareness that clean linen is needed to make a bed.

9. Recommended instructional resources are identified next. These suggested readings and resources are meant to support the instructional design and to provide relevant information to readers and implementers of the instructional plan. It should be noted that they are not materials used during the implementation of the plan. They are simply the materials used in the design process.
10. Finally, a concluding section is appended for the purpose of recording observations and their programming implications for later reference and for use in completing checklists, writing progress reports, and designing individualized educational programs (IEPs). For educational and treatment purposes, the instructor should schedule a time for recording observations that provide special insights into the individual's learning characteristics and interests. Certainly, this is the place where relevant observations are recorded that specify program modifications, especially when the learner fails to meet criteria.

A final note relevant to the final presentation of the instructional plan should be heeded. Introductory information at the beginning of the plan should include basic organizational details, such as:

The topic area
The proposed date of instruction
The plan designer and primary instructor
The names of the individual or group members for whom the plan is designed
The time allotted or recommended
Special notes or precautions, including general health and safety factors and individual needs and concerns

A sample instructional plan is presented in Chapter Appendix A to further clarify the elements identified above.

Developing the Functional Curriculum

Education of moderately and severely handicapped persons is viewed as a lifelong endeavor that continually strives to add more and more skills to the student's repertoire and eternally seeks to reinforce previously acquired behaviors. All the objectives in the curriculum have been included because they are expected to facilitate the individual student's accommodation to society on the one hand and society's acceptance of the handicapped individual on the other. This socially functional orientation demands a lifetime effort. Therefore, artificial and arbitrary upper age limits are primitive and must be removed if this population of citizens is to be served educationally.

Some of the skills and their accompanying activities may appear to be scaled at too *high* a level for moderately and severely handicapped students. They are included *deliberately*, to reinforce the concept of lifelong education, to establish higher horizons for this population, and to suggest appropriate educational goals for mildly handicapped students and perhaps even for nonhandicapped students.

The functional curriculum has been designed for handicapped students without designating traditional diagnostic labels. This approach was taken because it is clearly recognized that categorical labels such as "mentally retarded" and "autistic" are nonproductive for educational programming purposes. A specific label does not suggest a specific educational program; what is of concern is the student's unique profile of abilities and disabilities. Knowledge that a student is retarded avails little, but an appraisal of what the student can and cannot do provides key evaluative/diagnostic information.

Parent Involvement

Parents can be most helpful in reinforcing learning that has taken place in the school, acting as carry-over agents, and offering suggestions about motivating materials and activities. Therefore, the curriculum is also meant for parents and other adults who have primary responsibility for and/or will want to facilitate learning in children and adults with moderate and severe handicaps. Parents must play a critical role in the education of their handicapped children, especially when the natural setting for learning is in the home environment and when they can more effectively and consistently use the community as an instructional setting.

Teaching Strategies and Programming Considerations

Success in educating moderately and severely handicapped students requires extensive knowledge, a broad range of professional skills, and a positive attitude. Primary among the skills needed to teach moderately and severely handicapped persons is the understanding and use of a variety of effective and proven teaching strategies. As with their nonhandicapped peers, teaching moderately and severely handicapped students requires individualization. What is a successful approach on one day might be the antecedent for a behavioral problem on another. It is therefore important to have in one's instructional repertoire a variety of teaching strategies.

Listed below are instructional, programming, and organizational strategies that have been used successfully by classroom teachers of moderately and severely handicapped learners. These strategies are also appropriate for teachers of nonhandicapped students who have looked to special education for innovative ways to manage behavior, organize classrooms, and personalize instruction.

Normalization Considerations

Age Appropriateness Always select instructional materials and activities that would be considered suitable for nonhandicapped individuals of the same age.

Appearance Program, at all times, to help the student behave and look as appropriate as possible. If the student looks and behaves in deviant ways, he will be stigmatized by others.

Avoidance of Stereotypic Judgments Do not assume that a handicapped person is unable to perform certain skills and participate in specific activities and events just because he is handicapped.

Cultural Background Choose materials and activities that reflect the student's cultural and ethnic background and expose him to new cultures that reflect the cultural diversity of his society.

Nonhandicapped Peers Involve the student, whenever possible, in activities with nonhandicapped peers. The handicapped student can usually participate in some way.

Peer Interest Encourage the student's interest in the welfare of his friends and peers (e.g., make him aware of a friend's/peer's illness and the need to send a get-well card). Match students with different skills so that they can assist each other.

Privacy Remember to respect the student's privacy. For example, respect his privacy when teaching self-care skills such as toileting and bathing. However, do not sacrifice safety for privacy.

Teacher Behavior

Communication Use your voice as a means of communicating your feelings and wants to the student, especially with the nonverbal student who does not comprehend oral language. Be aware that monotonous voice patterns turn a student off. It is also important to supplement vocal communication with gestures whenever possible to optimize the student's understanding of your message and to facilitate his comprehension of total communication.

Control Remain calm and poised no matter what happens. A student often will react negatively to a teacher who is losing or has lost control.

Cooperation Seek the cooperation of other teachers, professionals, and support staff. Bus drivers, school custodians, and community helpers can assist immeasurably in normalizing the lives of your students.

Enthusiasm Show enthusiasm when a student progresses or attempts to comply with your requests. Remember that what may seem to you like very little progress may be a giant step for the student.

Expression of Affection Express sincere affection for the student. React to the human qualities in the student no matter how handicapped he is. Your warmth, interest, and love will elicit positive responses. Do not express affection by touching, hugging, and kissing the student too much; this will provide a poor model of behavior if carried into his adult years. Also, do not infantilize the student by mothering him too much.

Flexibility Demonstrate flexibility in carrying out lesson plans. If an unexpected negative behavior occurs that requires immediate action on your part, change your schedule. For example, suppose a student begins to eat someone else's food during lunch. Stop the student immediately, and work on the idea of "my food" versus "not my food," even if you had previously scheduled an outdoor event or another activity. Always keep your priorities in mind. *Seize the moment* to teach, because you might not get a good opportunity for a long time. Do not wait to create an artificial situation; react when the real situation occurs.

Humor A sense of humor that is not hostile or sarcastic always helps.

Modeling At all times serve as a model of behavior in the way you look, act, talk, walk, eat, etc. Verbalize models of behavior. For example, "Other people like to be near a person who smells pleasant."

Materials

Assistive Devices Become familiar with assistive devices. If you can operate these devices yourself, you will be more likely to use them properly in instructional situations. The use of walkers and hearing aids is an important skill for the teacher to master.

Diversity Discover and use exciting materials and activities from other disciplines. Music, art, dance, and physical education activities can serve to stimulate different students. Do not be restricted by a narrow view of educational programming and goals.

Familiarity Use familiar games and songs in activities. Do not waste time searching for educational games or special songs when there are familiar ones available. Keep in mind ethnic, cultural, and geographic preferences.

Progress Charts Construct charts that graphically demonstrate student progress. For example, draw a picture of a stopwatch or clock face to show the time it took the student to run a specified distance. Encourage the student to try harder. Chart his progress and urge him to chart his own progress, when feasible.

Relevancy Use current materials, toys, games, television shows, and records to motivate the student. Dancing to a current favorite top tune usually will be more stimulating than dancing to the *Nutcracker* Suite. However, remember that some old favorites have lasting appeal.

Reminder Charts Construct charts that will help the student keep track of required behaviors (e.g., a Shopping List Chart that the student uses to match food on hand with the pictures on the chart). When he has less food at home than is pictured on the chart, he will know that he needs to go food shopping.

Variety Vary activities and materials whenever possible; take advantage of the motivating effects of surprise, suspense, and novelty. For example, a personal computer can bring magic to a class session.

Instructional Considerations

Activity Alternation Alternate quiet activities with activities involving gross motor actions. This alternating of activities acts as a motivating factor and as an aid to classroom management.

Changing Activities Activities should be changed frequently enough so that students do not have time to become disinterested. There also should be opportunities for the student to select alternate activities, including a non-participatory one.

Consistency Students need to continually know what is expected of them and what the consequences of their actions will be. Consistency is one of the most important assets in a well-managed classroom.

Developmental Learning Plan your learning experiences so that they are developmental. Always keep in mind the hierarchical arrangement of skills. Consult other members of the team before you teach a skill that does not follow the usual developmental sequence.

Disturbing Behaviors Program, at all times, to reduce inappropriate and disturbing behaviors. If these behaviors persist, they will interfere with attempts to successfully normalize the lives of handicapped persons.

Goal Planning Be realistic in planning goals. Do not develop objectives at so high a level that you and the student become frustrated. Also, do not develop objectives and activities that are too low in level. Review your objectives, and, if their levels are too high or too low, modify them.

Imitation Tell the student to imitate your actions after he has observed you. For example, tell the student to watch you as you wash your hands. Next, tell the student to do what you just did. Praise the student for approximating or imitating the task. Use peer models whenever practical. Verbalize the peer's behavior and reward that behavior.

Individualized Instruction Individualize instruction, because there is such wide diversity in handicapped populations that personalizing instruction is essential. Remember that individual programs can be implemented and be successful within a group setting.

Instructional Grouping Although one-to-one instruction may be necessary, overuse of this procedure is often impractical in most classrooms and minimizes the natural opportunities to learn from others.

Instructional Programming Set up your instructional program in small steps so that the student is likely to be successful. Use successful experiences to encourage the student to attempt more advanced steps. If possible, end each activity with student success.

Lifelong Skill Sequences When selecting instructional targets, it is important to keep in mind where a child may be functioning in the future. Instructional time should be directed to those skill areas that will ultimately be most functional. Minimize the amount of time spent on relatively unimportant skills.

Model Demonstration Demonstrate the finished product whenever possible. For example, when the student is expected to assemble a wooden puzzle, show him the complete puzzle before you ask him to assemble the pieces. In an arts and crafts project, show him the completed project. For example, when making Halloween masks, show him a sample mask so that he has a model available to refer to as he is working. The model also may act as motivation.

Music Incorporate music into activities whenever possible. As an example, you can play a tune on an autoharp and sing the instructions appropriate to an activity, such as, "Johnny, line up, line up, line up."

Nutrition Serve nutritious snacks instead of junk foods and other non-nutritional foods that may be unhealthy for the students. Foods and beverages such as candy, cookies, cake, pretzels, potato chips, and soda have little nutritive value. Do not offer these foods to students as rewards, for snacks, at mealtimes, or at parties. Nutritious snacks such as fresh fruit, raisins, nuts, sunflower and pumpkin seeds, milk, and pure fruit juices are liked by students and are healthy. Also, avoid food reinforcers whenever possible.

Pantomimed Instruction Use pantomime to demonstrate a skill. For example, in pantomime show the student how to thread a needle and sew on a button. This approach helps to isolate the required movements; it also is an enjoyable activity.

Past Experience Inquire about the experiences the student has had whenever possible. Talk to his parents, guardians, or past teachers. References to these experiences often will provide the needed motivation for lessons.

Peer Tutoring Organize your lessons in such a way as to take advantage of the benefits of peer tutoring and buddy systems. The student may learn a skill more readily when it is demonstrated by a peer.

Physical Prompting Physically guide the student through an activity whenever he is unable to do the activity himself. For example, if the student is unable to cut with scissors, use a pair of training scissors and guide him through the activity. In writing activities hold the student's hand and the pencil, and move his hand in the desired pattern. Whenever you physically guide a student through an action or series of actions, encourage him to remember how his body feels when he moves it in a specific way.

Practice Practice a task often. Even after you are convinced that the student has mastered a particular skill, practice and reinforce it periodically. Schedule practice sessions. Vary the activities as much as possible to maintain student interest and to promote generalization.

Resource People Seek the help of resource people who can enrich the educational program. Store managers, bus drivers, police officers, and road repair people not only can provide interesting demonstrations and lectures, but also may allow you the use of their facilities so that the student can have first-hand experiences. For example, a bus driver can provide you with the use of an empty bus to practice getting on and off.

Reverse Programming Program in reverse when working on some motor skills that consist of a series of separate motor events. For example, the *backward chaining* approach is helpful in teaching the tying of shoelaces. Starting in the middle of a sequence may also be appropriate for some students.

Role Play Use role playing, puppet play, and creative dramatics to simulate real experiences and to practice skills.

Routines in Learning When dealing with an activity that has several steps, establish a routine for the student to follow. "First you do this, then this, then this . . .," etc. Practice the steps in sequence.

Seasonal Activities Program activities appropriate to the seasons. Plan for those activities, such as shoveling snow and planting seeds, to coincide with the seasons. Outdoor recreation and camping activities should be planned according to the weather.

Skill Demonstration Demonstrate the skill you are attempting to facilitate. Explain what you are doing as you are doing it. For example, say, "Look at me as I button my shirt. I take the button between my thumb and index finger of one hand; look. Then I take the buttonhole with the same fingers of my other hand; look. And then, I push the button through; look. Now let's do it together."

Skill Instruction Teach a skill at the time of its functional use (i.e., when it occurs naturally). For example, show the student how to wash his hands after he has gone to the toilet. Also, schedule practice sessions at times of functional application. When the student has developed skills in the use of eating utensils, plan parties, invite guests for dinner, and practice during snack and cafeteria times. Schedule practice sessions often.

Task Analysis Use a task analysis approach whenever possible. For example, teaching the brushing of teeth may have to be broken down into holding a tube of toothpaste, unscrewing the cap, and placing the toothpaste on the brush. While teaching the individual steps, do not lose sight of the total task.

Teaching Environment Always consider the environment in which teaching activities should be presented (i.e., the home, the school, and/or the community).

Understanding Objectives Let the student know the specific objective on which you are working and why it is necessary. Tell him, "You must know how to regulate the water in the sink so that you can wash your hands and face without burning yourself. Together we'll work on it. First you . . ."

Useful Skills Do not waste time teaching a skill that can be circumvented by modern styles or modern technology. For example, if a student has inordinate difficulty in telling time using a regular watch or clock, teach him how to tell time with a digital watch or clock. If a student has excessive difficulty in tying shoes, encourage him to wear loafers.

Visual Monitoring Use mirrors for visual monitoring so that the student can see how he is doing a task while he is doing it. Mirrors are especially valuable in observing the movements required to make speech sounds. (Remember to use unbreakable mirrors.)

Classroom Management

Activity Substitution Substitute a constructive activity whenever a student is engaged in a maladaptive behavior such as a destructive or self-stimulatory activity. For example, if the student is waving his fingers and hands in a perseverative manner, provide him with something to do with his hands, such as modeling clay or playing with a toy with movable parts. Demonstrate how to use these objects appropriately.

Appropriate Assistance A teacher should provide only enough assistance to allow the student to participate in or complete a task he is not able to do independently.

Correction If a student is behaving or performing inappropriately or incorrectly, correct him in a positive manner. Say, "This is the way to play the game" and simultaneously demonstrate the desired behavior.

Directions Be explicit in your directions and commands. Be sure the student knows exactly what behaviors are expected. Classroom organization, behavioral management, and success of student performance are, to a large degree, dependent on the instructor's explicitness.

Ignoring Behavior Ignore inappropriate behavior whenever possible. For example, the student who continually talks out, if ignored, will not be reinforced for this behavior. As with other strategies, ignoring should not be overused, or it will lose its effectiveness.

Reprimands Use reprimands whenever necessary. Reprimands are not punishment and can be effectively used in the structuring of behaviors. For example, say, "No," if you want to discourage a student from taking someone else's food or materials.

Responsibility Assign the student a classroom responsibility no matter how severe his handicap and no matter how small the task. Program responsibility from the beginning. Use class assignments as rewards.

Timeout Remove a student who is disruptive from the class or learning area and place him in social isolation for a short period of time. Make sure that you explain to him the reason for his removal. It is important that the student not be returned to the exact milieu he left when the timeout period is completed. It is advisable to place him near other students, right next to you, or in a new activity when he returns.

Reinforcement

Appropriate Reinforcement Be reinforcing at appropriate times, but do not overreinforce or it will lose its effectiveness. For example, you may praise the student for being quiet during quiet time by saying, "I'm glad you're being quiet." However, if this is repeated too many times, the student may feel this is an automatic response and will not accept it as reinforcement. Always use age-appropriate reinforcers.

Carry-Over Agents Train and encourage teacher aides, parents, foster parents, foster grandparents, and house parents, to be effective carry-over and practice agents. If the significant persons who interact with the student are consistent in reinforcing desired behaviors, the program will be more successful in a shorter period of time and will facilitate generalization of skills to the natural environment. Make sure you are consistent too.

Immediate Feedback Provide the student with immediate feedback of results (i.e., reward him as soon as possible after he has attempted, approximated, or achieved a task). Also, if a student is performing a task inappropriately or incorrectly, stop him from continuing the task, and indicate your disapproval in any way that he will understand. Demonstrate the acceptable behavior.

Inappropriate Reinforcement Never reinforce any behavior that, if it persists, will cause the student problems later in life. For example, when teaching handshaking, encourage the student to shake hands only when a new acquaintance offers his or her hand first. Do not reinforce the student if he continually initiates handshaking. This behavior, if it persists and is abused, might prove to be annoying and/or might accentuate the student's handicap. Do not overly encourage a young student to clap his hands in glee when a peer does well. This behavior may be carried over into his adult years, and he may clap whenever he is pleased or happy. Although clapping is viewed by many as acceptable behavior for the young, it may be inappropriate in older students. Always try to reinforce the student during naturally occurring situations.

Interests Find out what the student's interests are. Knowledge of a favored toy, a favorite person, a special game, and a preferred food can mean the difference between success and failure in an activity. Keep a list of these preferences for each student and continually update it.

Peer Reinforcement Show the student's peers how to behave in reinforcing ways. Encourage them to reward the student's desirable behaviors.

Reinforcement Preferences Discover the student's reinforcement preferences. What might be reinforcing to you or to other students you have taught might not be reinforcing to a specific student. You may have to search for a reinforcer.

Token Economies A token economy may be an effective management strategy on an individual, classroom, or school-wide basis. Assigning units of value or tokens for particular behaviors enables a teacher to reward behaviors as they occur or at a later time when they are "cashed" in.

Environmental Considerations

Community Resources Become familiar with community resources, and use them as learning environments. Make the entire community your classroom. For example, the neighborhood supermarket is the best place to facilitate learning in the purchase of foods. The office building and the department store offer opportunities in learning how to use elevators, revolving doors, and automatic doors.

Ecology Behave in an ecologically minded way (e.g., when teaching a student how to cut up newspapers to make paper designs, use old papers). Become a model for conservation and pollution control whenever possible.

Geographic Area Take into consideration the geographic area in which the student lives and its impact on the program. Lessons designed to facilitate locomotion skills in the use of a subway only make sense when subway travel is part of the student's environment.

Learning Area Make your learning area as attractive and pleasant as possible. However, beware of the dangers of overstimulation. Make your room interesting with plants, animals, books, toys, and games that are motivating.

Safety Hazards Be aware of potential safety hazards in all activities. For example, do not use sharp tools with the student who is destructive, and do not use miniature objects with the student who puts nonedible objects into his mouth.

Work Displays Display the student's work on bulletin boards, in display cases, and at school exhibits. The joy and pride of displayed work are reinforcing.

Evaluation

Assessment Instruction should always be preceded by assessment. This will provide the teacher with a general profile of a student's skills as well as identifying areas for future instruction.

Continuousness Evaluation should be a continuous process. It is important to develop criteria to assess how effective a particular technique or activity is in achieving a desired goal.

Self-monitoring Some students react positively when they are actively involved in keeping track of their own performance. Whenever possible, and when appropriate, this type of monitoring should be encouraged.

Evaluating Individual Performance and Progress

Teachers who fully appreciate the essential role of educational evaluation in designing instructional programs are aware that learners continually provide diagnostic information as they interact or fail to interact with people and objects in their environment. Strategies for observing and recording performance and progress are necessary to a systematic evaluation process; in addition, a framework must be provided that will structure and formalize observations.

The scope and sequence of curriculum objectives provide that needed framework, because learners should be evaluated in terms of the tasks you require of them. Therefore, a suggested companion to any curriculum is a complementary checklist that mirrors the objectives stated there.

A sample completed checklist is provided in Chapter Appendix B to clarify its composition and use. A response legend accompanies the checklist to illuminate the nature of possible responses and, when applicable, the types of assistance employed to obtain the desired responses.

Chapter Appendix A: Sample Instructional Plan

Topic Area:	Interpersonal Skills
Date:	December 3, 1985
Designed by:	Ms. Niguchi
Students Involved:	T. Lane, L. Mayrsohn, R. Parrish, G. Lee, E. Patterson, L. Fishman, C. Bennett, T. Shaw, and R. Brown

Special Notes or Precautions

1. General Health and Safety Factors

   Make sure the students use a wet sponge to seal the envelopes and wet the stamps.

2. Individual Needs and Concerns

   L. Mayrsohn is overly reliant on the approval of other people. Encourage her to self-evaluate when she seeks the praise and confirmation of others. T. Shaw has experienced difficulty in the past with writing too large for the space. Monitor him closely to make certain he doesn't ruin the envelopes. C. Bennett may need help in placing the stamp.

General Objective I*

The student will function as optimally as possible in social and interpersonal relationships.

Specific Objective KK*

The student communicates with friends, relatives, neighbors, and acquaintances with cards and letters at appropriate times.

*Refers to Specific Objective I, KK in Chapter 4, Interpersonal Skills, Volume II.

Instructional Objective

When asked to select, prepare, and send holiday cards to five relatives and friends, the students will select five appropriate cards, purchase five stamps, pay for the purchase, prepare the cards for mailing, and then mail the cards at the mailbox closest to the school. They will do so without any errors.

Materials and Equipment

1. boxes of assorted cards
2. boxes of Christmas and Hanukkah cards
3. boxes of birthday cards
4. boxes of get-well cards
5. books of stamps
6. wet sponges
7. the personal directories of the students
8. a specially prepared map of the school and its vicinity, showing all nearby mailboxes

Individualized Reinforcement and Reinforcement Schedules

L. Mayrsohn should be only occasionally reinforced since she is overly dependent on the approval of others. Give each student a holiday greeting card addressed to him or her as a personal holiday greeting from you.

Motivating Activity

Prepare the students in advance to be certain they wish to participate and to make certain they bring their personal telephone directories (previously prepared) and money for cards and stamps. Show the student three collages. Explain that you made them from old Christmas or Hanukkah cards. One collage should be a Christmas collage, the second a Hanukkah collage, and the third an interdenominational holiday collage.

Instructional Procedures

1. Show the students the specially prepared map of the school and its vicinity with all of its nearby mailboxes. Assist them in identifying the nearest one.
2. Show the students the boxes of cards. Ask them to find holiday cards for five of their relatives or friends. Demonstrate the process. Make sure to explain why you rejected specific cards. For example, "This is not a Christmas card; it is a birthday card." And "This is a Christmas card. My friend Sylvia is Jewish. I'll find a Hanukkah card instead."

3. Discuss the health factor of using the wet sponge to seal envelopes and put on the stamps. Practice with old Christmas and other seals.
4. Tell them to select the cards and pay for the cards and stamps needed. Remind them to verify change.
5. Monitor the mail preparation process.
6. Ask them to take you to the nearest mailbox.

Assessment Strategy

Check to see whether the students have:

1. selected the cards appropriate to the occasion
2. selected the cards appropriate to the persons to whom they are being sent
3. selected the correct number of cards
4. paid the correct amount for cards and stamps and then verified change received
5. correctly prepared the cards for mailing
6. located the nearest mailbox and mailed the cards

Record the performance of each student on his or her "Interpersonal Skills Checklist."

Follow-Up Activity or Objective

If the students achieve the instructional objective, proceed to a learning experience involving the sending of special occasion cards.

Recommended Instructional Resources

Bender, M., & Valletutti, P. J. (1982). *Teaching Functional Academics: A Curriculum Guide for Adolescents and Adults with Learning Problems.* Austin: PRO-ED.

SRA Manuscript Handwriting. Chicago: SRA, Inc., 1977

Cartledge, G., & Milburn, J. F. (Eds.). (1980). *Teaching social skills to children: Innovative approaches.* New York: Pergamon Press.

Observations and Their Programming Implications

Chapter Appendix B: Sample Completed Checklist

Individual's Name: Peter Michaels

General Objective: Communication Skills—Nonverbal

III. The student will respond to and use facial expressions in a manner that allows him to function optimally.

Special Physical Restrictions/Conditions (if any):

Evaluator(s):

Mr. Parham, teacher

Ms. Chapman, foster mother

Ms. Rao, psychologist

Specific Objectives	Response[a]	Number of observations/ by whom[a]	Dates	Observations and their programming implications
The student:				
A. responds to a smile by smiling in turn	IF	4/P and T	10/23/85 11/02/85 12/03/85 01/08/86	
B. responds to a smile by continuing an activity	DFS	4/T and P	09/08/85 09/16/85 09/23/85 10/02/85	Peter often looks for approval when playing with a favored toy. When smiled at, he resumes the activity 100% of the time.
C. smiles when receiving a favored object or upon seeing a favorite person	PP	3/T	11/03/85 11/10/85 11/17/85	Peter always smiles when given a favored object. At this point he only smiles when he sees his foster mother and classroom teacher. Work on greeting other school staff members.

Specific Objectives	Response[a]	Number of observations/ by whom[a]	Dates	Observations and their programming implications
D. smiles when told good news	NR	4/P and T	12/18/85 11/06/86 11/12/86 11/15/86	Peter does not yet appear to comprehend the verbal message. Work on the "good news" that he is going to receive a reward.
E. responds to the facial expression of sadness by comforting the individual expressing it	CAR (P)	3/T and OTM psychologist play therapy	02/26/86 03/03/86 03/05/86	Peter will comfort a person role playing sadness if physically guided to stroke that person's hand. Work on a more consistent response.
F. makes a sad face when told disappointing or sad news	N/R	4/P and T	12/18/85 01/06/86 01/12/86 01/15/86	Peter does not, as yet, appear to comprehend the verbal message. Work on the "sad news" that playtime is over.
G. ceases a destructive activity when a significant person expresses anger	N/A			Peter does not demonstrate destructive behavior.
H. identifies when a significant person in his environment is frightened, removes the frightening stimulus, and then comforts the person	N/ATT			
I. expresses fear (with or without words) when confronted with a fear-evoking situation	PP	3/P	09/17/85 10/18/85 11/19/85	Peter, according to his foster mother, expresses fear when he sees feathers and small animals, including stuffed toys. He does not, as yet, respond with words to these feared objects. He does not show fear in legitimately fearful situations.

[a]Response legend: N/A—not applicable; NR—no response; N/ATT—not attempted; PP—partial performance; CAR—completed/assistance required; P—physical guidance; G—gestural prompts; V—verbal cues; IF—independent functioning; DFS—demonstrated in functional situation; T—teacher; P/SP—parent/surrogate parent; OTM—other team member (specify).

2 Nonverbal Communication Skills

The development of communication skills cannot be effectively promoted unless consideration is given to the total communication act, including nonverbal as well as verbal elements. Verbal communication disorders/disabilities of a psycholinguistic nature and their fundamental auditory and visual processes have long received the attention of teachers of the handicapped. Particular attention has been directed toward the teaching of reading in patent disregard of the primacy of oral language in social interaction and of its critical precursor function in the development of the higher-level skills of written language comprehension and expression. Cursory attention has been paid to the development of oral language skills; even less attention has been directed to the perception and expression of nonverbal communication, despite the fact that a substantial amount of beginning communication is nonverbal (Valletutti, 1983).

The ability to comprehend and use facial expressions, gestures, and other body language cues (kinesics) is vital to skilled interpersonal communication and to effective participation in the life of the community. The ability to interpret and to appropriately express the nonword communicative elements of the vocalization process (paralanguage) is also critical to communication. Nonverbal communication includes distance between speaker and listener (proxemics), how they look at each other, clothes and makeup worn (artifactual cues), and physical attributes (Weiss & Lillywhite, 1981). It has been suggested that up to 93% of a message's content is communicated nonverbally (Egolf & Chester, 1973). Krauss, Apple, Morency, Wenzel, and Winton (1981) disagree. Their study of judgments of affect found no support for the assumption that nonverbal channels form the primary basis for the communication of affect. This apparent difference in opinion may simply be a function of the degree of explicitness of the message (i.e., the greater the ambiguity of the verbal message, the greater the attention paid to nonverbal components).

As with verbal communication, nonverbal communication exists within a situational context (Spignesi & Shor, 1981). Social kinesis refers to the role and meaning of different bodily movements within a social context (Devito, 1978). Ekman and Friesen (1969) first distinguished five classes of nonverbal movements based on the origins, functions, and coding of the behavior: *emblems, illustrators, affect displays, regulators,* and *adaptors. Emblems* are nonverbal behaviors that directly translate words or meaning units (e.g., the "goodbye" gesture). *Illustrators* accompany, clarify, and illuminate the verbal message. *Affect displays* refer to those facial movements that communicate emotional content. *Regulators* control the speech of others. *Adaptors* refer to those nonverbal actions that serve basic communicative needs. The ability to receive and process relevant communicative stimuli, nonverbal as well as verbal, coupled with the ability to read social situations (Johnson & Myklebust, 1967), is essential to effective social performance (Morrison & Bellack, 1981).

The paucity of data on developmental sequences in nonverbal communication has made the organized sequencing of curricular objectives and educational tasks relevant to the comprehension and use of gestural language particularly difficult. For many students, natural gestures (gestures that indicate the language idea) represent the first language modality through which contact with the environment is possible (Sternberg, Battle, & Hill, 1980). For these individuals, in their later development of oral language skills, the use of natural gestures complements and verifies oral messages and thus becomes an integral part of the total communication act (Harris, 1978). For others, gestural language in combination with other nonverbal communication may represent the primary means through which the instructor is able to facilitate language and other learning in their beginning stages. In other cases, gestures may be the only form of language comprehension and/or expression that the student is able to master. Gestures will serve as that individual's principal means of communicating his needs, desires, and thoughts.

In the absence of definitive developmental guidelines, the sequencing of gestural language skills became an arduous task that required the precise and continuous observation of many young students as they communicated or attempted to communicate with their peers and others. Considerable time was spent in recording the natural gestures employed by handicapped and nonhandicapped students as they communicated in natural contexts. From these observations, a list of specific teaching objectives for gestural language was constructed and recorded in order of apparent acquisition and/or usefulness. Those natural gestures, most frequently used by teachers working with nonverbal, normal-hearing students, were then incorporated into the list, according to their frequency of use and utility in the school environment.

A curriculum objective dealing with alternative means of communication is also included. When the reader examines the possible alternate methods, it should become obvious that several have been included because of their applicability to moderately and severely physically handicapped students who, despite sufficient intelligence, are prohibited from speaking by marked neuromuscular dysfunction (Harris, 1982).

The exciting possibilities of technological advances and the promise of decreasing costs of personal computers and their peripherals, especially the development of increasingly natural voice synthesizers, promise to free many severely and profoundly neuromuscularly handicapped students from their cruel silence. The identified alternate means of communication are also of special interest to those working with students who are severely restricted intellectually. This section is included because of the rewarding educational programming with many nonoral students who no longer are being denied an opportunity to influence and/or control their environment because they lack speech (Calculator & Dollaghan, 1982; Jones, 1980).

It is hoped that for some nonoral students, an alternate mode of communication will be merely a first language from which oral language skills will later emerge. Certainly, General Objective IV of this chapter should be omitted when a student possesses or has the potential to develop adequate oral language skills. For those students, however, who require an alternate means of communication, attention then must be directed to developing those language elements subsumed under General Objectives II and III of Verbal Communication Skills (see Chapter 3). Just as the oral student requires diverse linguistic structures, so does the student who uses an alternate communication mode. Teachers, therefore, must select a meaningful vocabulary and develop syntactical communication units based on their functional relevance, frequency of usage, emotional intensity, and social utility (Carlson, 1981).

The nonverbal skills included under facial expression and vocal tones are included because of those moderately and severely handicapped students who, although they may possess other language skills, experience problems in interpreting and/or using these nonverbal communication systems. Comprehension of body language (kinesics) and paralinguistic (vocal tones) clues are particularly important in those situational contexts when an oral message is negated by more subtle nonverbal cues that modify or contradict the surface communication (Krauss, Apple, Morency, Wenzel, & Winton, 1981). For many moderately and severely handicapped students, the lack of vocal affect and variety distinguishes their speech from nonhandicapped persons, thus exacerbating the social penalties that come from being, looking, and/or sounding different.

The Suggested Readings/References at the end of this chapter provide information on nonverbal communication skills. The reader should decide which material and information are applicable to a specific student or students being taught.

General Objectives of the Unit

I. The student will respond to and use natural or commonly accepted gestures in a manner that allows him to function optimally.
II. The student will respond to and use vocal tone patterns in a manner that allows him to function optimally.
III. The student will respond to and use facial expressions in a manner that allows him to function optimally.
IV. The student who is unable to comunicate through speech and/or natural gestures will use an alternate method of communication.

General Objective I

The student will respond to and use natural or commonly accepted gestures in a manner that allows him to function optimally.

Specific Objectives

The student:

A. responds by looking at an individual who is waving his hand and/or arm for attention.
B. who is unable to speak gains a person's attention by waving his hand or arm or gesturing in some other way.
C. responds to the warning signal of a shaking finger by stopping an activity.
D. responds to the "no" headshake by stopping an activity.
E. looks at an object or person pointed to.
F. who is unable to speak points to a desired object or location.
G. who is unable to speak and cannot take care of his toilet needs unassisted indicates that he has to go to the bathroom by making an agreed-upon sign that is socially appropriate.
H. who is unable to speak and cannot obtain food unassisted indicates that he is hungry by directing a flexed finger or fingers toward and then away from his slightly opened mouth.
I. who is unable to speak and cannot obtain a beverage unassisted indicates that he is thirsty by gesturing with the hand, imitating drinking out of a glass or cup.
J. who is unable to speak and cannot get to a resting or sleeping area unassisted indicates that he is tired or sleepy by tilting his head and resting his cheek against his hands held in the praying position.

K. waves goodbye in response to the goodbye wave of a departing individual.
L. waves goodbye when he is leaving someone to go to a different location.
M. who is unable to speak and cannot obtain a desired object indicates "Give me" by extending his arm and hand toward the desired object and, if possible, also alternately flexing his fingers.
N. who is unable to speak shakes his head when he does not want an object or does not wish something to happen.
O. who is unable to speak indicates that he is not feeling well by rubbing or pointing to the part of his body that hurts while expressing a pained facial expression.
P. who is unable to speak encourages people to approach him by gesturing "Come here" (bending of the index finger).
Q. responds to the "Sh" gesture and sound by becoming quiet.
R. indicates "Be quiet" by using the "Sh" gesture and/or sound.
S. responds to the "shooing" gesture by moving out of the way of the person who is making the gesture.
T. who is unable to speak indicates "Get away from me" by using the "shooing" gesture.
U. stops an activity when gestured to stop (hand raised with the palm facing the person to be stopped).
V. resumes an activity when given the "Go ahead" gesture (sweeping motion of the hand).
W. responds to the "Leave" or "Get away" gesture by moving away.
X. responds to someone nodding his/her head by continuing an approved activity.
Y. who is unable to speak nods his head to indicate that he wants an object or that he approves of a suggested activity.
Z. responds to the "Hi" or "Hello" gesture by gesturing "Hi" in return.
AA. shakes hands when a person extends his/her hand when greeting him or when saying goodbye.
BB. who is unable to speak, indicates that he is cold by using the "I am cold" gesture (holding his elbows while hugging himself and engaging in mock shivering).
CC. who is unable to speak indicates that he is hot by using the "I am hot" gesture (wiping the brow or simulating fanning his face).
DD. responds by standing up when signaled to do so.
EE. responds by sitting down when signaled to do so.
FF. selects an object by size when gestures are used that indicate an object is big or little (hands or fingers are held parallel to each other at differing distances (i.e., close = little and far apart = big).
GG. who is unable to speak indicates the size of a desired object by using the size gesture that indicates big or little.
HH. responds to the finger gesture that indicates the number of objects desired (one through ten) by selecting the correct number of objects.
II. who is unable to speak indicates the number of objects desired by holding up the appropriate number of fingers (one through ten).

There are other gestures that you may wish to include in your instructional program. This is especially true for gestures that are needed for simple pantomimes—the rubbing of hands together to indicate "Wash your hands" and the moving of the hand from front to back several times over the head to indicate "Comb your hair." The use of gestures and pantomimes may be a vital part of your instructional program with the nonverbal student and also in the beginning stages of oral language development.

Specific Objective A

The student responds by looking at an individual who is waving his hand and/or arm for attention.

Functional Settings and Suggested Instructional Activities

School

1. Wait for the student to be engrossed in an activity. Wave your hand directly in the student's line of vision until his eyes either fix on your hand or he looks at your face. If he looks at your face, reward him by giving him a favorite toy or food. If he looks at your hand, direct his eyes to an interesting, colorful, and favorite toy. Then move this object up to your face and smile at him. Remove the toy from his view. If necessary, stop him from following the path of the toy. Reward him for looking at your face. While he is looking at your face, sing or chant a favorite song or rhyme. Practice.
2. Engage in a play activity that includes puppets. Move one puppet in an attempt to gain another puppet's attention by waving its arm and/or hand. While waving the arm of the puppet, simultaneously say, "When I wave my arm and hand, that means I want your attention. Please look at me." When the other puppet looks up, manipulate both puppets in such a way that they begin to play a game such as bean bag in which one puppet throws the bean bag to the other.

Home

1. Ask the parents to wait until their child is intent on a particular activity and they wish to gain their child's attention for feeding, play, or other important activity. Tell them to attempt to attract their child's attention by the hand/arm wave gesture. Tell them to reward their child if he responds to the gesture.
2. Ask the parents to role play a scene in which they are engaged in a pretend situation with a doll or stuffed animal. Encourage them to act pleased ("That's a good dolly. You looked at me when I waved to you."). Then repeat the role play with their child who is to play the part of the doll/stuffed animal.

Functional Emphases In designing your own instructional activities and plans, emphasize the following elements:

1. Establishment of eye contact subsequent to the student's response to the hand/arm wave.
2. Communication of a variety of play and work activities subsequent to the student's response to the hand/arm wave.
3. Use of age-appropriate materials.

Specific Objective B

The student who is unable to speak gains a person's attention by waving his hand or arm or gesturing in some other way.

Functional Settings and Suggested Instructional Activities

School

1. Stand in front of a mirror with the student. Make the "attention-getting" wave. Assist the student in imitating your movements while standing. When he has approximated this movement, tell him that the gesture he has just practiced will help him get the attention of others. Play the part of a preoccupied person. If the student waves, give him your attention and show obvious delight with his accomplishment.
2. Sit in front of the student and play with an interesting toy. Carry on excitedly with it while totally ignoring the student. If the student makes physical contact, move away without looking at her. If she attempts or succeeds with making the hand wave, look at her and share the toy with her. If the student makes no attempt to gain your attention, take her hand and lead her through the gesture. Follow this with a play activity.
3. Point out to the student a peer who is preoccupied, and then attempt to attract the peer's attention by waving. Whenever a peer reacts appropriately to this gesture (you should have a reason for interrupting him), give him a toy or a nutritious treat.

Home

1. Ask the parents to pretend to be preoccupied at crucial times (e.g., when their child is likely to be hungry or want attention because he has soiled himself). Tell them to respond only if he indicates in a socially acceptable way that he wants their attention.
2. Remind the parents that they must not respond to the student if he grabs them or touches them to get attention. Tell them they should, at the most, remove his hand, reprimand him, and go back to their previous activity or behavior.

Functional Emphases In designing your own instructional activities and plans, emphasize the following elements:

1. Avoidance of touching or grabbing as an attention-getting device.
2. Utilization of the attention-getting gesture only when attention is reasonable.
3. Use of age-appropriate toys or objects when implementing activities.

Specific Objective C

The student responds to the warning signal of a shaking finger by stopping an activity.

Functional Settings and Suggested Instructional Activities

School

1. Wait for the student to be engaged in a noisy or destructive activity. Approach him and shake your finger at him. Immediately either cover his mouth gently or stop him from continuing his activity. Release him. If he resumes the noisy or destructive activity, repeat the silencing or restraining gesture. When you release him, reward him if he does not resume the activity.
2. When a peer is engaged in a noisy or destructive activity, follow the procedure outlined in Activity 1. Make sure the student observes you as you warn the peer. Tell her that her peer was doing something unacceptable and that the shaking of your index finger means "Stop!" Ask the student to imitate your actions.

Home and Community

1. Ask the parents to use the finger-shaking gesture along with other warning gestures such as the headshake and vocal utterances ("Uh-Uh") whenever their child engages in a socially unacceptable activity.
2. Take a walk in the community. If the student behaves in a socially unacceptable way, warn him by shaking your finger and immediately stop him from continuing that behavior.

Functional Emphases In designing your own instructional activities and plans, emphasize the following elements:

1. Incorporation of the finger-shaking gesture in a total comunication pattern including facial expressions, other gestures, and words.
2. Elimination of the finger-shaking gesture when the student comprehends the word "no."

Specific Objective D

The student responds to the "no" headshake by stopping an activity.

Functional Settings and Suggested Instructional Activities

School

1. Repeat the activities in Nonverbal Communication Skills, I, C, School Activities 1 and 2. Use both gestures (the shaking finger and the "no" headshake)

simultaneously. Remember to reward the student when he stops the undesired activity.

2. Repeat the activities in Nonverbal Communication Skills I, C, School Activities 1 and 2. This time use the "no" headshake instead of the shaking finger.

Home and Community

1. Ask the parents to use the "no" headshake along with other warning gestures, vocal utterances, and the word "no" whenever their child behaves in an unsafe or socially unacceptable way.
2. Ask the parents to use the "no" headshake whenever their child behaves in a way that interferes with the smooth operation of the household or when the child misbehaves in the community.

Functional Emphases In designing your own instructional activities and plans, emphasize the following elements:

1. Elimination of the "no" headshake as soon as the student understands the word "no."
2. Reduction in communicating "no" as the student becomes more skilled in his behavior and mastery of his environment.

Specific Objective E

The student looks at an object or person pointed to.

Functional Settings and Suggested Instructional Activities

School

1. Place other students around the room. Play a game of "Point and Give." Hand an object to the student and point to another student. Assist the student in giving the object to the selected student. Play the game of "Point and Give" so that each student has a turn.
2. Place various interesting objects on the student's desk or work area. Point to an object and encourage the student to pick up and play with that object.
3. Play a game in which everyone is expected to do something when he is pointed to (e.g., doing a dance step, sounding a rhythm instrument, or clapping hands). Point to the student. Praise her if she responds appropriately.

Home and Community

1. Ask the parents to place objects that interest their child around the house. Tell them to point to one of the objects and reward him when he looks at it. Tell them to point to each of the objects.
2. Ask the parents to show their child pictures of family members and close friends. Tell them to point to each picture and comment on the person in the photograph.

3. Take a trip into the community. Point out various natural sights, including trees, birds, squirrels, trees, dogs, and cats. When the student looks at the object, name and describe the object.
4. Take a trip into the community. Point out various man-made features, including buildings, architectural features, sculpture, store decorations, and posters/graphics.

Functional Emphases In designing your own instructional activities and plans, emphasize the following elements:

1. Incorporation of the word for objects pointed to and elimination of the gesture when the student comprehends the word.
2. Utilization of the environment as a means of stimulating language development.

Specific Objective F

The student who is unable to speak points to a desired object or location.

Functional Settings and Suggested Instructional Activities

School

1. Tell the student he can play a game with one or more of his peers. Ask him to point to the game and to the peer(s) with whom he wishes to play. Provide him with the game.
2. Return a book or toy to a storage shelf. Give the student a similar book or toy; then ask her to point to the shelf where it is usually kept. Practice using a variety of toys and objects.
3. Ask the student if he wants to stay in the playroom or to go outside to the playground. Show him how to indicate a desired location or area by pointing in the direction of that spot.

Home and Community

1. Ask the parents to place favorite objects in front of and within the line of vision of their child. Tell them to encourage him to point to the object he wants and reward him by giving him the object he points to.
2. Ask the parents to place desired foods in front of and within the line of vision of their child. Tell them to continue as in Activity 1.
3. Take the student on a shopping trip. Ask him to indicate objects he would like you to purchase by pointing to them. Purchase these items when they are reasonable requests.

Functional Emphases In designing your own instructional activities and plans, emphasize the following elements:

1. Elimination of the pointing gesture when the student is able to speak or to vocalize in such a way that her wants are understood.

2. Avoidance of pointing when the student wishes to indicate or refer to a favorite person unless there is no alternate means available.
3. Substitution of "eye" pointing for finger pointing when the student has a significant motor problem.

Specific Objective G

The student who is unable to speak and cannot take care of his toilet needs unassisted indicates that he has to go to the bathroom by making an agreed-upon sign that is socially appropriate.

Functional Settings and Suggested Instructional Activities

School

1. If there is no established time already set, set a specific time or times during the school day (e.g., before recess or during free time) when the student is free to go to the bathroom. Check to see if the student uses the agreed-upon gesture to let you know that he has to go to the bathroom.
2. Be alert to any behaviors of the student that indicate a need to go to the bathroom. Very often the student will get very quiet, will begin to fidget, will stare into space, will make facial grimaces, or will make some other repeated behavior just before he begins to void. When signals occur that indicate the student has a need to void or to evacuate, tell him that he should let you know if he needs help and that one way of doing so is by using the bathroom gesture explained in Activity 1. Demonstrate the appropriate gesture and remind the student to use this gesture each time he needs help in toileting. Assist him to the bathroom.

Home and Community

1. Ask the parents if they notice when their child is consistently wet. Tell them to ask their child to indicate whether she has to go to the bathroom ten to fifteen minutes before these times occur.
2. When possible, go for a walk through the student's immediate community or go to a community event (e.g., a ball game, the movies, or a puppet show). Encourage the student to gesture appropriately when he has to go to the bathroom. Assist him in finding a public restroom.

Functional Emphases In designing your own instructional activities and plans, emphasize the following elements:

1. Use of a gesture that is socially acceptable.
2. Use of a gesture that is as widely recognized as possible.
3. Use of an appropriate gesture in an unobtrusive way (i.e., the student does not wave his hand frantically or interrupt others unnecessarily).
4. Termination of requesting assistance when he is able to function independently.

Specific Objective H

The student who is unable to speak and cannot obtain food unassisted indicates that he is hungry by directing a flexed finger or fingers toward and then away from his slightly opened mouth.

Functional Settings and Suggested Instructional Activities

School

1. Deliberately overlook feeding the student while providing food for the other students. If he gestures appropriately, apologize for forgetting him, and give him food. If he does not gesture, after a short time, role play pretending to notice that he has not been given his food. Tell the student that he should have let you know by gesturing that he was hungry.
2. Praise the student's peers for indicating their hunger. Then supply them with food. Make sure that the student is eating sensibly. She may be using the "I am hungry" gesture to gain attention or out of gluttony. Impress upon the student that she should only use the "I am hungry" gesture when absolutely necessary.

Home and Community

1. Ask the parents to role play a tea party. As part of the role play, encourage the parents to tell their child if he wants something more to "ask" for it, using the "hungry" gesture.
2. Take the student for a field trip for which the group has "brown-bagged it." Tell him to let you know when he is hungry so you can go back to the bus to get lunch.

Functional Emphases In designing your own instructional activities and plans, emphasize the following elements:

1. Elimination of the gesture when he is able to indicate orally that he is hungry.
2. Avoidance of this gesture as a stimulus to overeating.
3. Identification of foods that should be avoided because of special diet regimens.

Specific Objective I

The student who is unable to speak and cannot obtain a beverage unassisted indicates that he is thirsty by gesturing with the hand, imitating drinking out of a glass or cup.

Functional Settings and Suggested Instructional Activities

School

1. Encourage the student to imitate the "I am thirsty" gesture. As a preliminary step, use a paper cup to help the student make the gesture.

2. After an active game or other strenuous physical activity, tell the student that if he is thirsty and needs help in obtaining a beverage, it is his responsibility to let you know. Assist him with the gesture if necessary. Help him to get a drink.
3. Give the student a daily snack that includes a beverage. On occasion, omit the beverage. Encourage her to remind you that she needs something to drink by using the "I am thirsty" gesture.

Home and Community

1. Ask the parents to tell their child that he may want a drink when he is thirsty, when he wishes to drink water for health purposes, and when he must take pills. Tell them to give him pills and not the water and then say, "Show me what's missing." Or tell them to omit the milk for his afternoon snack and say, "Show me what I forgot."
2. Take the student for a walk where there are public drinking fountains. Point out these fountains. Tell the student to indicate if he is thirsty so you can help him find a fountain.

Functional Emphases In designing your own instructional activities and plans, emphasize the following elements:

1. Elimination of the "thirsty" gesture as soon as the student is able to communicate his needs unassisted.
2. Elimination of the "thirsty" gesture as soon as the student is able to obtain a desired beverage without assistance.

Specific Objective J

The student who is unable to speak and cannot get to a resting or sleeping area unassisted indicates that he is tired or sleepy by tilting his head and resting his cheek against his hands held in the praying position.

Functional Settings and Suggested Instructional Activities

School

1. Whenever the student behaves in a way that suggests fatigue, assist him in using the appropriate gesture. Depending upon his age, place him in a comfortable and attractive cot, bed, or carriage. Tell him that everybody needs rest and sleep and that being tired or sleepy means your body needs rest.
2. Pantomime the story *Goldilocks and the Three Bears*. Ask the student to play the part of Goldilocks and to make the "sleepy" gesture before going to sleep in the baby bear's bed. Use a sequence from *Rip Van Winkle* for the older student.

Home and Community

1. Ask the parents to demonstrate the "tired" gesture while yawning. Tell them to explain that he will get sleepy and tired at times and that, if he needs help in getting to a bed or cot, making the "I am tired" gesture is a good way of letting people know this. Tell them to use a mirror to assist him in acquiring this gesture.
2. Role play a situation in which you and the student are tired after a busy day touring your or a nearby community. Tell her to show you that she is tired.

Functional Emphases In designing your own instructional activities and plans, emphasize the following elements:

1. Elimination of this gesture when the student can substitute a yawn and stretching gesture.
2. Observation of the social skill of covering one's mouth when yawning.
3. Elimination of the gesture as soon as the student is able to indicate his wants orally.

Specific Objective K

The student waves goodbye in response to the goodbye wave of a departing individual.

Functional Settings and Suggested Instructional Activities

School

1. Announce to the student in a role play situation that you will be gone for awhile and that a substitute teacher will be in the class. Start to leave the room, and suddenly stop, turn, and say that you forgot to wave goodbye.
2. Sing the song "So Long, It's Been Good To Know You." Wave goodbye in time to the music.

Home and Community

1. Ask the parents to demonstrate how to wave goodbye. Tell them to assist the student in waving goodbye in its functional context.
2. Take the student for a walk in the community. When you return, say and wave goodbye to him as he boards the school bus.

Functional Emphases In designing your own instructional activities and plans, emphasize the following elements:

1. Differentiation of the goodbye gesture from other gestures.
2. Maintenance of the waving gesture for a suitable duration.

Specific Objective L

The student waves goodbye when she is leaving someone to go to a different location.

Functional Settings and Suggested Instructional Activities

School

1. When the student leaves the learning area for the day, assist him in waving goodbye to you and to his peers who remain in the area. Insist that he do this every day as he leaves.
2. If the student is going on a field trip, encourage her to wave goodbye to peers and staff members who remain.

Home and Community

1. Ask the parents to sing the song or play the record of "So Long, It's Been Good To Know You" and pantomime leaving while waving goodbye. Then tell them to encourage their child to conduct the pantomime to their singing or the record.
2. After a field trip, encourage the student to wave goodbye to the bus driver.

Functional Emphases In designing your own instructional activities and plans, emphasize the following elements:

1. Avoidance of waving goodbye when he is leaving one area to go to another area but will be returning shortly.
2. Maintenance of the gesture long enough to communicate the idea but not long enough to draw undue attention to the student.

Specific Objective M

The student who is unable to speak and cannot obtain a desired object indicates "Give me" by extending his arm and hand toward the desired object and, if possible, also alternately flexing his fingers.

Functional Settings and Suggested Instructional Activities

School

1. Play the "Guess Which Hand" game. Show the student a small object. Then put your hands behind your back, hiding the object in one of your closed hands. If the student gestures "Give me," open up your closed fist and give him the object.
2. Place the student in a large circle with his peers. Play the "Give Me–Pass It" game. Tell each student that he must gesture "Give me" before the object is

passed to him. Tell the student to wait for the "Give me" gesture before passing the object to the next student in the circle.

Home and Community

1. Ask the parents to place a desired object in front of but out of the reach of their child. Tell them not to give their child the object unless he approximates or makes the "Give me" gesture. If necessary, tell them to demonstrate the gesture and assist their child as she makes it and reward her for attempting or making the gesture.
2. Take the student on an outing such as a picnic where toys are displayed as part of the day's recreational activities. Encourage the student to ask for an out-of-reach toy by using the "Give me" gesture.

Functional Emphases In designing your own instructional activities and plans, emphasize the following elements:

1. Discouragement of the overuse of the "Give me" gesture.
2. Elimination of the gesture when the student is able to indicate his wants orally.

Specific Objective N

The student who is unable to speak shakes his head when he does not want an object or does not wish something to happen.

Functional Settings and Suggested Instructional Activities

School

1. Place a favorite object and a disliked object in front of the student. Attempt to give him the disliked object. While doing this, speak as if you were speaking for the student (e.g., "(Student's name) does not want the furry animal. No (while shaking the student's head from side to side). He wants the car." Then ask him the question "Do you want the furry animal?" If he does not shake his head, say "no" and move his head from side to side.
2. Determine whether a student dislikes a particular game or activity. Initiate this activity with a peer. Ask the student if he wants to join in the activity. If he indicates by grimacing or moving away that he does not want to participate, say, "Oh, you do not want to play. If so, shake your head to let me know that your answer is no. If the student follows these directions, play a game he likes.

Home and Community

1. Ask the parents to place a favored food and a disliked food in front of their child and offer her the disliked food. Tell them to help her to shake her head. When she does so, tell them to reward her by giving her the favored food.

2. Take a trip to a community playground. If the student does not like a particular playground activity or piece of equipment, invite him to join the activity or play with the equipment. Reward him for rejecting the activity with a headshake by praising him and allowing him to engage in a desired activity.

Functional Emphases In designing your own instructional activities and plans, emphasize the following elements:

1. Elimination of the headshake when she can indicate a negative response orally.
2. Willingness to participate in activities or to try unliked or untasted foods and not automatically indicate "no."

Specific Objective O

The student who is unable to speak indicates that he is not feeling well by rubbing or pointing to the part of his body that hurts while expressing a pained facial expression.

Functional Settings and Suggested Instructional Activities

School

1. Play a "Let's Pretend" game. Ask the student to pretend that he has a headache. Then ask him to show you, through gestures, that his head aches. Pretend the following: (a) toothache, (b) stomach ache, (c) sore finger, (d) sore toe, and (e) stomach cramps.
2. Tell the student to try not to cry or whimper when he has a pain but instead to show you where it hurts. Tell him that sometimes he will have to tell a doctor where it hurts him. Reward the student for indicating where it hurts.
3. If a student begins to cry or whine, ask him if he is crying because something hurts. If he indicates that this is so, remind him that he is the only one who can show you where it hurts. If he does not do so, ask him a series of questions, such as "Does your head hurt?" Once you discover where it hurts, tell the student that he would have received help sooner if he had rubbed gently the part of his body that hurt.

Home and Community

1. Ask the parents to role play being hurt and to place oversized bandaids or bandages on different parts of their body. Tell them to rub the bandaged area gently and say to their child, "When some part of my body hurts, I sometimes rub it gently. That is a good way to tell people it hurts."
2. Role play a picnic at which the student pretends to get a stomach ache from overeating. Reward her for rubbing his stomach and expressing a pained expression.

Functional Emphases In designing your own instructional activities and plans, emphasize the following elements:

1. Elimination of the gesture when he is able to communicate orally.
2. Avoidance of the tendency to "cry wolf" or to use this gesture to gain sympathy.

Specific Objective P

The student who is unable to speak encourages people to approach him by gesturing "Come here" (bending of the index finger).

Functional Settings and Suggested Instructional Activities

School

1. Give the student a task to complete that requires help. Tell him to use a gesture in order to get a peer to help him. Demonstrate the appropriate gesture to the student and assist him in making the gesture. Make sure the peer is one who will respond to the "Come here" gesture.
2. Wait for a situation in which the student requires assistance. Provide help only if she signals "Come here."

Home and Community

1. Tell the parents to explain to their child that he will sometimes need help and that he should use the "Come here" gesture when he needs assistance. Tell them to explain that he may have to wait for a response when they are busy.
2. Take the student on a trip to a museum or to another exhibit. Find an exciting exhibit and gesture to the student to "Come here." Share your enjoyment with him. Encourage him to share something in the same way.

Functional Emphases In designing your own instructional activities and plans, emphasize the following elements:

1. Elimination of the "Come here" gesture when he is able to communicate this request orally.
2. Utilization of this gesture only when necessary and discouragement of using this gesture to manipulate or control others.

Specific Objective Q

The student responds to the "Sh" gesture and sound by becoming quiet.

Functional Settings and Suggested Instructional Activities

School

1. Whenever the student is noisy, indicate "Sh."

2. Gesture "Sh" to a noisy peer. Explain to the student that when you make this gesture, it means "Be quiet!"

Home and Community

1. Ask the parents to wait for their child to be engaged in a noisy activity. Tell them to approach him, and indicate "Sh" by putting their index finger in front of their pursed lips and then immediately close his lips gently and/or stop him gently from his noise-making actions. Tell them to shake their finger and their head in the "no" gesture. Tell them to include the shushing sound as part of the gesture and to repeat this activity until the student stops making noise without being restrained and without the finger- and/or head-shaking. Tell them to reward him for responding to the "Sh" gesture alone.
2. Take the student to a public library. Tell her that one must be quiet so readers are not disturbed. Use the "Sh" gesture to emphasize your point.

Functional Emphases In designing your own instructional activities and plans, emphasize the following elements:

1. Utilization of the "Sh" gesture to indicate "Be quiet" or to indicate that this is a place or situation in which quiet is necessary.
2. Identification of different settings where quiet is important (e.g., a library, a hospital, a sick room, and a church or temple).

Specific Objective R

The student indicates "Be quiet" by using the "Sh" gesture and/or sound.

Functional Settings and Suggested Instructional Activities

School

1. Wait for a noisy situation to arise and ask the student to join you in telling the noisy peer to be quiet. Encourage the student to imitate your behavior.
2. Play a record and increase the volume to an uncomfortable level. Encourage the student to use the "Sh" gesture to indicate that the volume should be lowered.
3. Role play with the student. Pretend he is sleeping. Ask people to be quiet. Stage some noise. When he gestures "Sh," stop making the noise.

Home and Community

1. Ask the parents to sing "Rock-a-Bye Baby" or some other lullaby. Tell them to pretend a doll has fallen asleep, look around, gesture "Sh," and say "Be quiet!" Tell them to ask their child to help in gesturing everybody to be quiet so that the baby will not be awakened.
2. Role play being in a movie or theater and pretend to be noisy. Reward the student for telling you to be quiet as long as he does it nicely.

Functional Emphases In designing your own instructional activities and plans, emphasize the following elements:

1. Elimination of this gesture when the student can indicate "please be quiet," orally.
2. Identification of when it is appropriate to tell someone to be quiet.
3. Identification of when it might be dangerous to tell someone to be quiet (e.g., when people are arguing).

Specific Objective S

The student responds to the "shooing" gesture by moving out of the way of the person who is making the gesture.

Functional Settings and Suggested Instructional Activities

School

1. Pretend that a fly is bothering you. You may use a plastic or rubberized fly or bug. Move the fly near your face and shoo it away by waving your hand back and forth. Tell the students to imitate your actions.
2. Arrange several students in a circle. Sing and dance to "Shoo Fly, Don't Bother Me." Shoo a student, and reward him for moving out of the way and then back into the circle of dancers. Ask each student to take a turn shooing his peers as they dance to "Shoo Fly, Don't Bother Me."

Home and Community

1. Ask the parents to warn their child away from an obstacle in his path by using the "shooing" gesture.
2. Take the student for a walk into the community. When you arrive at heavily trafficked intersections, shoo the student away from the curb if he gets too close.

Functional Emphases In designing your own instructional activities and plans, emphasize the following elements:

1. Identification of the "shooing" gesture as a warning to get away and stay away.
2. Differentiation of the "shooing" gesture from the goodbye wave and the stop/resume gesture sequence.

Specific Objective T

The student who is unable to speak indicates "Get away from me!" by using the "shooing" gesture.

Functional Settings and Suggested Instructional Activities

School

1. Use a plastic bug or fly. Encourage the student to shoo it away. Play the song "Tarantella" (Italian for tarantula) and, while dancing, approach the student from different angles with the bug. Assist him, if necessary, as he shoos the bug away. Make it clear that this dance should only be played during play time and only if everyone agrees to join in. This dance might be too frightening for some students. Also, it might provide a mischievous student with a way to torment his peers.
2. If an actual situation arises (e.g., a fly or bug bothers the student), help and/or remind her to shoo it away.

Home and Community

1. Tell the parents to discuss the "shooing" gesture whenever they need to shoo away an insect or to chase away a pet (e.g., a cat or dog).
2. Take a trip to an outdoor recreation area where there are likely to be flying insects. Show the student how to shoo the insect away.
3. Role play a scene in which a stray animal becomes bothersome. Show him how to safely shoo the animal away.

Functional Emphases In designing your own instructional activities and plans, emphasize the following elements:

1. Application of the "shooing" gesture only when it is absolutely necessary because it can become an obnoxious trait.
2. Elimination of this gesture when the student can say "Pardon me" or "Excuse me" to persons in his path.

Specific Objective U

The student stops an activity when gestured to stop (hand raised with the palm facing the person to be stopped).

Functional Settings and Suggested Instructional Activities

School

1. Pour juice into a cup, and gesture or say "Stop" when the cup is sufficiently full.
2. When walking to classes or to the cafeteria, gesture "Stop" whenever you wish the student to stop.
3. During gross motor activities, assign the student to lead exercises.
4. Arrange for a timed activity. Set a hand timer and when it goes off, say "Stop!"

Home and Community

1. Ask the parents to play a march on a stereo or a phonograph. Tell them to march with him until the music stops and they say "Stop!" Tell them to say "Stop" first and then stop the music.

2. When at a community playground, play "Red Light." This game requires the student to run and then to stop at the command "Stop!"

Functional Emphases In designing your own instructional activities and plans, emphasize the following elements:

1. Judgment as to whether he should always obey the command to stop, differentiating between the need to stop and the wisdom of ignoring a command.
2. Observation of this gesture when used by police officers and crossing guards and when depicted in safety posters and signs.

Specific Objective V

The student resumes an activity when given the "Go ahead" gesture (sweeping motion of the hand).

Functional Settings and Suggested Instructional Activities

School

1. March the student around the room. Guide her, and at various points signal her to "Stop" and then to "Go ahead."
2. Play a variation of "Musical Chairs" in which the impetus for movement is the "Go ahead" gesture and the signal to sit down is the "Stop" gesture.

Home and Community

1. Ask the parent to use the "Go ahead" gesture whenever the student is waiting to do something new until he finishes what he is doing (e.g., he can go watch television now that he has finished his dinner).
2. Role play the situation of a pedestrian wanting to cross the street and being helped by a police officer or crossing guard. Stop the student with the "Stop" gesture. Pretend to look for traffic, indicate that the street is clear, make the "Go ahead" gesture, and help the student to cross the street.

Functional Emphases In designing your own instructional activities and plans, emphasize the following elements:

1. Identification of the "Go ahead" gesture when used by crossing guards in his home and school communities.
2. Differentiation of the "Go ahead" gesture from the goodbye wave and the "shooing" gesture.

Specific Objective W

The student responds to the "Leave" or "Get away" gesture by moving away.

Functional Settings and Suggested Instructional Activities

School

1. Role play a situation in which a peer is misbehaving. Gesture to him to leave the room. Rehearse the peer well so that he will pretend misbehavior, leave the room, ask to come back with an apology, and then return to his work. Use a puppet if no peer capable of this complicated role-play activity is available.
2. Set up special sections of the learning area that are designated for specific activities. If a student goes to one of these areas at the wrong time, gesture her to leave the area and tell her she must leave. At first, combine the gesture with its verbal counterpart. Eventually use only the gesture.

Home and Community

1. Ask the parents to use this gesture whenever their child is legitimately in their way. Remind them always to say the words when they use a gesture.
2. Take a trip in the community. When you come across an unsafe place, indicate that it is off limits by making the "Get away" gesture.

Functional Emphases In designing your own instructional activities and plans, emphasize the following elements:

1. Use of this gesture to warn the student of unsafe places.
2. Use of this gesture to indicate that the time has arrived to go to a new setting.

Specific Objective X

The student responds to someone nodding his/her head by continuing an approved activity.

Functional Settings and Suggested Instructional Activities

School

1. Place two objects in front of the student. Gesture, "Give me," and place your hand in a position midway between the objects. If the student chooses the object you like, nod your head and accept it gratefully. If he chooses the disliked object, shake your head and reject it.
2. If the student is misbehaving, indicate "no" by shaking your head. Substitute a constructive activity while simultaneously nodding your head and smiling.

Home and Community

1. Tell the parents that when their child is involved in a constructive or benign activity, they should go to him and nod their head in approval. Tell them to show pleasure if he resumes or continues the activity.
2. Role play a situation in which you pretend you are asking an usher in a theater or sports stadium whether you are in the right aisle. When he nods "yes," walk

to your seat. Then encourage the student to show the usher her ticket and wait for the nod of approval before continuing.

Functional Emphases In designing your own instructional activities and plans, emphasize the following elements:

1. Appreciation of the fact that people indicate approval in a variety of ways, including nodding, smiling, and/or with verbal praise.
2. Judgment as to what people in her environment she should seek approval from.

Specific Objective Y

The student who is unable to speak nods his head to indicate that he wants an object or that he approves of a suggested activity.

Functional Settings and Suggested Instructional Activities

School

1. Place a favored object and a disliked object in front of the student. Attempt to give him the disliked object. If he indicates "no," with a head shake, hesitantly offer him the desired object instead. Assist him in nodding his head "yes" in response to the desired object. When he does so, give him the desired object.
2. Place boys' and girls' articles of clothing in front of a male student. Hand him an article of boys' clothing. Reward him if he nods his head "yes." Hand him an article of girls' clothing. Enjoy the mistake with him if he realizes the joke and indicates "no" by shaking his head. Reverse the activity with a female student.

Home and Community

1. Ask the parents to show their child a favored food and ask him whether he wants it. Tell them to help him nod his head, if necessary, before giving him the food.
2. Ask the parents to suggest a preferred activity. Tell them to help him nod his head in approval, if necessary, before allowing him to participate in or before joining him in the activity.
3. Give the student a choice of community activities. Tell him to indicate his preference by nodding.

Functional Emphases In designing your own instructional activities and plans, emphasize the following elements:

1. Elimination of this gesture when the student is able to communicate orally.
2. Maintenance of this gesture (even after the student is able to communicate approval orally) at times when quiet is required (library, hospital, or classroom).

Specific Objective Z

The student responds to the "Hi" or "Hello" gesture by gesturing "Hi" in return.

Functional Settings and Suggested Instructional Activities

School

1. Greet the student each day with the "Hi" gesture. Encourage the student to imitate you. Assist him if necessary.
2. Use a doll with eyes that close when the doll is laid down. Lay the doll down for a short period and then sit the doll up. When the eyes open, say and gesture "Hi," while raising the student's hand in the "Hi" gesture.

Home and Community

1. Ask the parents to play a variation of the game "Peek-A-Boo." Tell them that when they uncover their eyes to gesture "Hi." Then tell them to ask the student to play "Peek-A-Boo" and to gesture "Hi" when he uncovers his eyes.
2. Take a walk in the neighborhood and gesture "Hi" to crossing guards, storekeepers, police officers, and friends. Before the trip, explain to community people that you are working on the "Hi" gesture and would appreciate their signaling "Hi" when they see you and the student.

Functional Emphases In designing your own instructional activities and plans, emphasize the following elements:

1. Incorporation of the "Hi" gesture along with the oral greeting when the student is able to speak.
2. Identification of when it is not appropriate to greet someone who might be dangerous (e.g., a stranger in a dimly lit area and a person who is acting in a bizarre fashion).

Specific Objective AA

The student shakes hands when a person extends his/her hand when greeting him or when saying goodbye.

Functional Settings and Suggested Instructional Activities

School

1. Modify the song "If You're Happy and You Know It" to include the activity of handshaking.
2. Sing the song "How Do You Do, My Partner" and ask the students to shake hands when meeting their partners.
3. When a new peer enters the school, introduce him to the student and encourage the student to shake his hand in greeting. Explain that we shake hands when

we first meet someone new or when we greet someone we have not seen for a long while.

Home and Community

1. Ask the parents to encourage visitors to the home to shake their child's hand in greeting. Tell the parents that in the beginning stages they may have to show their child how to shake hands in a role play.
2. Arrange to meet friends in the community. Tell them in advance to extend their hands in the handshake gesture when you and the student arrive.

Functional Emphases In designing your own instructional activities and plans, emphasize the following elements:

1. Recognition of the need to use the right hand in this custom, unless the right hand is dysfunctional.
2. Awareness of the need to remove a glove if she is wearing a glove on her right hand.

Specific Objective BB

The student who is unable to speak indicates that he is cold by using the "I am cold" gesture (holding his elbows while hugging himself and engaging in mock shivering).

Functional Settings and Suggested Instructional Activities

School

1. Wait for a cool or cold day. Turn the classroom thermostat to a lower temperature than usual (60°) so the room will be a little chilly. When you feel cold, gesture that you are cold by crossing your arms and rubbing the outside of your upper arms while shrugging your shoulders and shaking the upper part of your body. Simulate shivering from the cold. After the gesture, put on a sweater or jacket. Tell the student that if he grows cold and needs help, he should make the "I am cold" gesture. Show him how to make the gesture, and encourage imitation.
2. If the student has been swimming and appears to be cold, ask him whether he is cold. If he indicates "yes" by nodding his head, tell him he should have let you know this by making the "I am cold" gesture. Help him to towel-dry himself and encourage him to change into dry clothes (see Volume I, Self-Care, for dressing and undressing activities).

Home and Community

1. Ask the parents to urge their child to make the "I am cold" gesture when they see signs that he might be getting cold (e.g., when the air conditioner has cooled the room down or when he is not feeling well).

2. If the weather becomes cooler while you are out on a trip in the community, make the "I am cold" gesture and either bundle up or seek shelter.

Functional Emphases In designing your own instructional activities and plans, emphasize the following elements:

1. Identification of ways to avoid becoming chilled or cold.
2. Identification of steps to follow when he becomes cold.

Specific Objective CC

The student who is unable to speak indicates he is hot by using the "I am hot" gesture (wiping the brow or simulating fanning his face).

Functional Settings and Suggested Instructional Activities

School

1. On a hot day, show the student that you are hot by wiping your brow. Follow up by doing something to cool yourself, such as opening a window and/or door, removing a jacket, drinking a cold glass of water, and/or rinsing your face and hands with cold water. After you have done one or more of these activities, tell the student that you are not hot anymore. Encourage him to imitate your actions.
2. Wait for a hot day and ask the question "Are you hot?" If the student nods "yes," tell her she should have let you know by making the "I am hot" gesture. Encourage the student to cool herself by using one of the suggestions in Activity 1.

Home and Community

1. Ask the parents to urge their child to make the "I am hot" gesture when they see signs that he is getting hot. Signs include perspiring and flushing.
2. If while on a trip in the community you enter a place that is not air conditioned on a hot day or whose air conditioner is not working properly, say, "Wow, it is hot in here!" and make the "I am hot" gesture.

Functional Emphases In designing your own instructional activities and plans, emphasize the following elements:

1. Identification of ways to avoid becoming overheated.
2. Identification of steps to take when he becomes too hot.

Specific Objective DD

The student responds by standing up when signaled to do so.

Functional Settings and Suggested Instructional Activities

School

1. Call the student's name and issue the command to stand up. Make the appropriate gesture and help him to stand up if necessary.
2. Point to the student and make the "Stand up" gesture. (Gesture is to place your hand in front of you, palm up, and raise it slowly to indicate "Stand up!").
3. Physically assist the student to stand up whenever he does not respond appropriately to the command. Employ time-out procedures if necessary.
4. Use the Hap Palmer record, "Parade of Colors." Assign a color to each student and ask each one to stand whenever his color is asked to stand up on the record.
5. Practice standing up for such activities as the pledge to the flag, lining up and waiting for the bus, and returning trays to the cafeteria.

Home and Community

1. Ask the parents to play school in which they play the part of the teacher. As part of the role play, tell them to gesture to the student (their child) to stand up to move to a new activity.
2. Role play a trip in the community in which you have sat down on a park bench because you have become tired. Then say, "Time to go," and then gesture to the student to stand up.
3. Role play sitting in a movie theater while someone wishes to pass the seated student to get to his seat. Gesture to the student to stand up if he does not do so automatically.

Functional Emphases In designing your own instructional activities and plans, emphasize the following elements:

1. Awareness that there are formal situations when one is expected to stand up (the playing of the national anthem).
2. Awareness that there are social situations when one is expected to stand up (e.g., when greeting a woman).

Specific Objective EE

The student responds by sitting down when signaled to do so.

Functional Settings and Suggested Instructional Activities

School

1. Demonstrate sitting in response to the command "Sit down." Use a peer as a model. Ask the peer to sit when commanded, and ask the student to watch as you reward the peer for following the command. Repeat the activity with the student.
2. As the students arrive in the classroom after lunch, physical education, and work study, ask them to stand by their chairs. Appoint a student as "teacher." His job is to signal his peers to sit. He should simultaneously say "Sit down"

and hold his hands in front of himself and lower them to indicate "Sit down." Do this whenever the students need to be seated (e.g., in the bus, in the cafeteria, or in the classroom).

Home and Community

1. Tell the parents to play "Musical Chairs" and to say "Sit down" when the music stops.
2. Role play a trip in the community where you are traveling on a bus, subway, or train. Indicate that there is an empty seat and gesture to the student to sit down.

Functional Emphases In designing your own instructional activities and plans, emphasize the following elements:

1. Recognition of the need to sit down in a public place to avoid blocking the view of spectators sitting behind you.
2. Identification of the proper way of sitting for health reasons.
3. Identification of the proper way of sitting for social reasons (e.g., when she's wearing a dress or skirt, a female student should make certain she does not expose her thighs or undergarments).

Specific Objective FF

The student selects an object by size when gestures are used that indicate an object is big or little (hands or fingers are held parallel to each other at differing distances, i.e., close = little and far apart = big).

Functional Settings and Suggested Instructional Activities

School

1. Carry out Home Activities 1 and 2, using objects found in the classroom.
2. Hide objects in the classroom. Make a size gesture and ask the student to find the object it matches. Continue in this way until all objects are found.

Home

1. Ask the parents to obtain two sizes of a toy (e.g., a toy car) and place them in front of their child. Tell them to say and gesture "Give me" and follow up by making one of the size gestures. Tell them to explain through speech and pantomime that the size of the object corresponds to the size indicated by the gesture.
2. Tell the parents to ask their child to match a variety of household items (e.g., different-size food cans and boxes) to the space made by their use of the size gesture.

Functional Emphases In designing your own instructional activities and plans, emphasize the following elements:

1. Selection of appropriate size objects that meet the desired objective (e.g., the right-size ball for a particular ball game or the right-size can of tomatoes for the recipe).
2. Relationship of this gesture and other gestures to the idea to be communicated.

Specific Objective GG

The student who is unable to speak indicates the size of a desired object by using the size gesture that indicates big or little.

Functional Settings and Suggested Instructional Activities

School

1. Give the student various objects to measure with his hands. Ask him first to measure the object and then to repeat the size gesture after you have removed the object from his view.
2. Place two objects of different size in front of the student. Point to each object and encourage her to make the "Give me" gesture. If she points to the bigger object, demonstrate the appropriate size gesture. Do the same if she indicates the smaller object. Practice.
3. Repeat Activity 2 using several pairs of objects.

Home and Community

1. Ask the parents to place two sizes of the same toy in front of their child so that he can gauge their size. Tell them to remove them and ask him, "Which one do you want?" Tell them to tell him to use the size gesture.
2. Make up a shopping list in preparation for a shopping trip. Indicate the size of the item by scaled drawings (e.g., peas or milk) where the desired size is circled. When you get to the store, give the student the list and ask him to make the gesture to let you know the size you need so you can go to get the item. Sometimes bring back the correct size and sometimes make an error. Praise him for correcting you by shaking his head "no" whenever appropriate.

Functional Emphases In designing your own instructional activities and plans, emphasize the following elements:

1. Utilization of this gesture to control the environment (i.e., to influence the actions of others to obtain the desired results).
2. Relationship of this gesture as well as other gestures to the idea to be communicated.

Specific Objective HH

The student responds to the finger gesture that indicates the number of objects desired (one through ten) by selecting the correct number of objects.

Functional Settings and Suggested Instructional Activities

School

1. Carry out the Home Activities 1 through 3 using objects available in the classroom.
2. Sing finger plays and counting songs (e.g., "Ten Little Indian Boys and Girls" and "This Old Man").

Home

1. Ask the parents to hold up one object and one finger. Tell them to tap the object with that finger. Then tell them to hold up one finger and encourage their child to pick up the object.
2. Ask the parents to repeat Activity 1; this time, tell them to have a group of objects (all the same) in front of their child.
3. Tell them to repeat Activities 1 and 2 with different groups of objects (e.g., buttons, beads, and clothespins) until he responds to the number of fingers up to ten.

Functional Emphases In designing your own instructional activities and plans, emphasize the following elements:

1. Comprehension of one-to-one correspondence.
2. Relationship of this skill to later oral counting skills.

Specific Objective II

The student who is unable to speak indicates the number of objects desired by holding up the appropriate number of fingers (one through ten).

Functional Settings and Suggested Instructional Activities

School

1. Place several different objects (such as pencils, toothbrushes, or paint brushes) that should be used one at a time on a desk or table. Assist the student in holding up one finger to indicate that he needs or wants just one of a group. Reward him by giving him the object.
2. Place several groups of paired objects such as cymbals, shoes, and drumsticks on a desk or table. Assist the student in using two fingers to indicate that he wants or needs two of each group. Reward her by allowing her to play with the pair of objects she selects.

3. Place favorite objects such as stars, peanuts, and small toy cars on a desk or table. Tell the student that he may have as many as he wants if he shows you the number he wants with his fingers. Tell him to count how many there are before showing his fingers. Use different numbers for each item (e.g., three cars, four stars, and five peanuts).

Home and Community

1. Ask the parents to teach their child finger plays and counting songs (see School Activity 2 in Specific Objective HH directly above). Tell them to sing, chant, or say the words while their child does the pantomime.
2. Tell the parents that they should expect their child to indicate desired amounts by using his fingers to indicate quantity.
3. Take the student to a baseball game. Ask him the following questions: "What inning is it?" "How many balls and strikes?" and "What's the score?" (*Note*: You will have to teach him the zero gesture—the thumb and index finger forming a circle.) Repeat with appropriate questions at other scored sports events (e.g., soccer and hockey).

Functional Emphases In designing your own instructional activities and plans, emphasize the following elements:

1. Application of one-to-one correspondence.
2. Relationship of this skill to later oral counting skills.
3. Elimination of finger counting when the student is able to communicate numbers orally.
4. Appreciation for the frequent need to communicate information involving numbers and quantity.

General Objective II

The student will respond to and use vocal tone patterns in a manner that allows him to function optimally.

Specific Objectives

The student:

A. responds to the vocal utterance of happiness or pleasure (with or without words) by continuing the activity in which he is engaged.
B. responds to the vocal utterance of happiness or pleasure (with or without words) by smiling.
C. expresses happiness or pleasure vocally (with or without words) upon receiving a favorite object or seeing a favorite person and whenever something joyful occurs.

D. expresses happiness or pleasure vocally (with or without words) upon hearing that he is going to participate in a favorite activity.
E. responds to the vocal expression of sadness (with or without words) by comforting the individual expressing sorrow.
F. vocalizes sadness (with or without words) when denied participation in a favorite activity or whenever something unhappy occurs.
G. ceases an activity when presented with a vocal pattern (with or without words) that indicates anger.
H. upon hearing an angry utterance (with or without words), coupled with threatening behaviors, leaves the area or backs away from the individual and, if possible, signals for help.
I. expresses anger vocally (with or without words) when aggressively interfered with by others.
J. expresses fear vocally (with or without words) when confronted with a fear-evoking situation.

Specific Objective A

The student responds to the vocal utterance of happiness or pleasure (with or without words) by continuing the activity in which he is engaged.

Functional Settings and Suggested Instructional Activities

School

1. Carry out the Home Activities 1 and 2.
2. Sing the song "If You're Happy and You Know It." Add the element of laughing out loud to the series of actions.
3. Sing the song "Everybody's Got a Laughin' Place" from Walt Disney's *Tales of Uncle Remus* or some other happy children's song. Sometimes sing a happy song with its words and sometimes without the words while vocalizing "Ha-Ha-Ha."

Home

1. Ask the parents to wait until their child is engaged in a constructive activity and demonstrate approval by vocalizing happiness. Tell them to do this sometimes with and sometimes without words. Tell them it may be necessary to practice vocalizing happiness without words before working with their child. Tell them if their child has sufficient speech comprehension to use words when praising him for the activity. Tell them to encourage him to continue his activity, nod their heads in approval, and reward him for continuing the activity. Tell them to indicate periodically their satisfaction with his work by vocalizing happiness and to combine the vocalization with a reassuring pat on his hand and a smile.

2. Tell them to repeat Activity 1. This time, however, tell them to vocalize their happiness from other parts of the room so their child will be responding only to their words and/or sounds of happiness or pleasure and not to any body-language clues.

Functional Emphases In designing your own instructional activities and plans, emphasize the following elements:

1. Differentiation of the vocalization of happiness/pleasure from other paralinguistic patterns.
2. Identification of the total affective expression of happiness/pleasure, including the vocal utterance, the facial expression of smiling, and the relaxed skeletomuscular system.

Specific Objective B

The student responds to the vocal utterance of happiness or pleasure (with or without words) by smiling.

Functional Settings and Suggested Instructional Activities

School

1. Present learning activities that typically evoke happiness, such as playing a game, singing, dancing, or playing with a favorite toy. A favorite toy need not be a commercial product. Many students, especially the young, enjoy playing with household items (e.g., pots and pans, lids, empty margarine tubs, paper towel tubes, strainers, and spoons). Discover for yourself the inexpensive "toys" around you that are fun for young students to play with. Punctuate the activity with laughter and other utterances of happiness. Smile. Tell the student how much you are enjoying yourself and that when you are happy, you laugh and smile. Tell him to look at your smile and to see how the smile makes your face look. Smile at the student in a mirror. Show him a frown and tell him that it is not a smile. Smile at the student again and encourage him to imitate your actions. If necessary, manipulate the student's lips into a smiling position and tell him that is what he must do with his lips and cheeks to make a happy smile.
2. Present activities producing happiness/pleasure several times a day, especially after periods of intensive work. Repeat the activities in 1 until the student begins to smile without assistance when he hears words or sounds of laughter/pleasure/happiness.

Home

1. Ask the parents to engage in play activities (e.g., dancing to a bouncy tune) that their child enjoys in front of a mirror. Tell them to smile and laugh at this activity while vocalizing their happiness. Tell them if their child smiles

spontaneously that they should show her his smile and comment that she is smiling and happy.

2. Ask the parents to play "Pat-A-Cake," "Peek-A-Boo," or some other game that stimulates spontaneous smiling. Tell them to explain to their child that when people are happy and they express it, they like to see others joining them in their happiness. Tell the parents to explain that a smile is one way a person shows happiness.

Functional Emphases In designing your own instructional activities and plans, emphasize the following elements:

1. Differentiation of the vocalization of happiness/pleasure from other paralinguistic patterns.
2. Identification of the total affective expression of happiness/pleasure, including the vocal utterance, the facial expression of smiling, and the relaxed skeletomuscular system.

Specific Objective C

The student expresses happiness or pleasure vocally (with or without words) upon receiving a favorite object or seeing a favorite person and whenever something joyful occurs.

Functional Settings and Suggested Instructional Activities

School

1. Collect comical pictures. Make them into slides. Show them to the student and laugh at them. Encourage the student to join in the fun.
2. Wait for the student to express happiness or pleasure spontaneously. Encourage the student to vocalize his happiness/pleasure. Stroking the student's throat may help to get across the idea that you want him to vocalize, especially if you are vocalizing at the same time. Reward the student if he vocalizes.
3. Play "Peek-A-Boo" and reward the student when she vocalizes her happiness or pleasure.
4. Dance, sing, pantomime, and play with games and toys. Express your pleasure/enjoyment/happiness freely. Reward the student for doing so.
5. Ask a favorite person to enter the room at a previously specified time. When the person comes into the room, show great pleasure in seeing him. Indicate this in your words, vocal tones, and facial expressions. Encourage the student to do the same.

Home

1. Ask the parents to sing the song "Little Brown Jug" and to encourage their child to join in the chorus of "Ha-Ha-Ha."

2. Ask the parents to put on silly hats and then to put one on their child. Tell them to laugh and encourage their child to laugh along with them. Tell them to use tickling to stimulate laughter if necessary.

Functional Emphases In designing your own instructional activities and plans, emphasize the following elements:

1. Expression of laughter at appropriate times.
2. Suppression of laughter whenever it is inappropriate, including the reading of the mood of others with whom the student is interacting.
3. Congruence of happy vocal tones with the message and purpose of the communication when the child has speech.

Specific Objective D

The student expresses happiness or pleasure vocally (with or without words) upon hearing that he is going to participate in a favorite activity.

Functional Settings and Suggested Instructional Activities

School

1. At various times during the day, give the student a choice between two activities. Ask the student to indicate his preference by vocalizing his happiness/pleasure at the activity of his choice. Practice, offering a variety of activities.
2. Introduce each new activity by demonstrating it to the student. Encourage the student to indicate that he wants to participate in the activity by vocalizing happiness or pleasure with or without words.

Home

1. Ask the parents to give their child a choice of activities at free-play times during the day. Tell them to encourage him to indicate his choice by vocalizing pleasure with or without words.
2. Ask the parents to plan a favorite activity and tell their child that they have a surprise activity for him. Tell the parents to tell their child that he can show his happiness with the activity by vocalizing his pleasure.

Functional Emphases In designing your own instructional activities and plans, emphasize the following elements:

1. Expression of laughter at appropriate times.
2. Suppression of laughter whenever it is inappropriate, including the reading of the mood of others with whom the student is interacting.
3. Congruence of happy vocal tones with the message and purpose of the communication when the child has speech.

Specific Objective E

The student responds to the vocal expression of sadness (with or without words) by comforting the individual expressing sorrow.

Functional Settings and Suggested Instructional Activities

School

1. Whenever another student becomes sad and expresses sadness vocally, take the student to his peer and together comfort him by holding his hand.
2. Reward the student if, on his own, he comforts individuals who express sadness. Make sure that comforting behaviors are gentle and are not overdone. Also make sure that the person wants to be comforted.

Home

1. Ask the parents to cradle a doll that makes crying sounds in their arms. Tell them to rock it back and forth gently and give a similar doll to their child. Tell them to encourage imitation while chanting, "Ah-ah, baby."
2. If there is a younger sibling in the home who becomes sad, tell the parents to demonstrate how to comfort a saddened youngster.

Functional Emphases In designing your own instructional activities and plans, emphasize the following elements:

1. Discrimination as to whether a person wishes to be comforted.
2. Identification of occurrences that are likely to result in someone becoming sad.
3. Realization as to when comforting behaviors should be terminated.

Specific Objective F

The student vocalizes sadness (with or without words) when denied participation in a favorite activity or whenever something unhappy occurs.

Functional Settings and Suggested Instructional Activities

School

1. Engage the student in vocal play. Vary the sounds articulated and your vocal tones. Then show the student a picture of a sad clown, a crying child, or a sad situation. Vocalize sadness and encourage the student to model your tones. Reward the student for successfully imitating your tones.
2. Engage in vocal play. Vary the sounds articulated and your vocal tones. Play a sad record. Vocalize along with the sad music by using sad tones. Encourage the student to imitate you.
3. Wait for the student to express sadness spontaneously in some way, such as by making a sad face or by drooping his shoulders. Encourage the student to

vocalize his sadness. Gently stroking the student's throat may help express the idea that you want him to vocalize, especially if you are vocalizing at the same time. Reward the student if he vocalizes.
4. Tell the student that a favorite activity of his may have to be canceled. Tell him that if this makes him feel unhappy or sad, he should let you know by using his voice. Change your mind about canceling the activity if he vocalizes sadness with or without words.

Home

1. Tell the parents that when situations occur that sadden their child, they should encourage him to express his sadness vocally. Urge them at these times to comfort him and attempt to correct or change the situation.
2. Tell the parents to express their sadness vocally, both with and without words, if rain or snow has forced them to cancel a trip, an outdoor activity, or other favorite event. Tell them to urge their child to express his sadness (with or without words) if he shares their disappointment.

Functional Emphases In designing your own instructional activities and plans, emphasize the following elements:

1. Appreciation of the problems of "crying wolf" or trying to manipulate others.
2. Congruence between vocal tone and the words expressed when the student has speech.
3. Realization of the need to express sadness as a means of reducing stress.

Specific Objective G

The student ceases an activity when presented with a vocal pattern (with or without words) that indicates anger.

Functional Settings and Suggested Instructional Activities

School

1. When you are outside the visual range of the student and the student is engaged in a destructive or nonproductive activity, vocalize anger. If the student fails to respond, approach him and gently stop him. If the student stops of his own accord, reward him.
2. With the student who has speech comprehension, use appropriate words of anger in order to stop the undesired behavior, both within and out of his visual field. If the behavior does not stop, approach her and gently stop her. If the student stops of her own accord, reward her.

Home

1. Tell the parents to wait until their child engages in a destructive or nonproductive activity. Tell them first to vocalize anger, while shaking their

heads and using the warning gesture of the shaking finger. Tell them to prevent the undesired behavior and to provide the student with an alternate and constructive activity.

2. Tell the parents to explain that they will become angry at times when he is misbehaving or doing something he should not do. Tell them to clarify that the sound of people's voices as well as the words they say when they are angry are clues to stopping an activity and changing behavior.

Functional Emphases In designing your own instructional activities and plans, emphasize the following elements:

1. Appreciation for the vocal expression of anger, especially when the oral message is ambiguous (e.g., "Oh, you're at it again!").
2. Awareness that expressed anger will be dissipated at a later time and identification of signs that a person's anger has gone and the mood is again positive.

Specific Objective H

The student upon hearing an angry utterance (with or without words), coupled with threatening behaviors, leaves the area or backs away from the individual and, if possible, signals for help.

Functional Settings and Suggested Instructional Activities

School

1. Wait for a conflict to arise between the student and an angry peer who is vocally expressing anger. First, prevent the students from continuing the conflict, and then move the student away and out of the range of the angry peer. Whenever a similar situation occurs, move the student away. When the student moves away of his own accord, reward him.
2. Select a signal within the student's repertoire of signaling, such as stamping his feet, tapping the table, or vocalizing. When a conflict arises between the student and a peer who is expressing anger vocally, make the designated signal and encourage the student to imitate you. Whenever the student makes the attention-getting signal in an appropriate situation, go to his aid. Explain that he has been practicing a sound that he should make only under special circumstances (e.g., when other people aggressively interfere with him).

Home

1. Ask the parents to play a scene in which two puppets engage in an argument. When one puppet picks up a stick (as is traditional in a *Punch and Judy* show), tell them to move the other puppet out of range.
2. Ask the parents to role play a scene in which they and their child come across a threatening person. Tell the parents to emphasize retreating together from the potentially dangerous situation.

Functional Emphases In designing your own instructional activities and plans, emphasize the following elements:

1. Differentiation between anger that is part of a potentially dangerous situation from anger that is nonthreatening.
2. Awareness of the role he might play in causing others to lose their temper.
3. Identification of signs that indicate that someone is close to losing his/her temper.
4. Awareness of the diverse ways that people express their anger.

Specific Objective I

The student expresses anger vocally (with or without words) when aggressively interfered with by others.

Functional Settings and Suggested Instructional Activities

School

1. Role play anger-producing situations. Express anger vocally. Encourage the student to express his anger vocally by imitating your vocalizations.
2. Wait for a peer to interfere forcefully with the student when he is at rest, play, or otherwise engaged in a suitable activity. Approach and vocalize anger at the offending peer. Encourage the student to imitate your behavior. Reward the student for expressing his anger in appropriate situations.
3. Stage role-playing scenes in which the expression of anger is an appropriate response to a situation (e.g., a peer steals the student's food). Encourage the student to express anger. Reward him when he can successfully vocalize anger without resorting to overly aggressive behavior. Reward him for expressing anger only in appropriate situations.

Home

1. Ask the parents to act out a folk tale or fairy tale that has an angry character such as the giant in *Jack and the Beanstalk*. Tell them to encourage their child to join them in making the angry sounds of the giant.
2. Tell the parents to explain to their child that he has been practicing a sound that he should make only under special circumstances (e.g., when other people aggressively interfere with him). Tell them to role play each of these identified situations.

Functional Emphases In designing your own instructional activities and plans, emphasize the following elements:

1. Appropriate expression of anger without resorting to physical measures except in self-defense.
2. Awareness of the appropriate way to express anger and the taking of steps to dissipate anger and to resolve the situation or conflict.

Specific Objective J

The student expresses fear vocally (with or without words) when confronted with a fear-evoking situation.

Functional Settings and Suggested Instructional Activities

School

1. Wait for a fearful situation to arise. Vocalize fear and encourage the student to imitate you. When he imitates you, comfort and reassure him that things will be all right. Remove the fearful stimulus. Many handicapped individuals will show unexpected and inordinate fear toward such stimuli as a furry animal, a feather, or Santa Claus played at a Christmas party, which might not be threatening to others. Although it may be necessary to remove these stimuli, it may also be useful gradually to desensitize the student by setting up an educational program that gradually introduces these stimuli into the student's life. For example, a Santa Claus cutout doll may be placed on the bulletin board away from the student but still near enough to be seen. After a while, the student should be moved closer and closer to the picture. Then use three-dimensional pictures and statues. Gradually introduce a real, dressed-up version of Santa Claus.
2. Stage role-playing situations in which fear is an appropriate response for most people (e.g., a sudden loud noise or being lost). Encourage the frightened student to express fear vocally with or without words and then to seek help.

Home

1. Ask the parents to tell their child that sometimes we become frightened and that it sometimes helps to let someone else know that you are frightened so that you can get needed help or comfort. Tell them to let their child know they will help him to make sounds that are sounds of being afraid. Encourage him to make these sounds.
2. Tell the parents to role play functional situations that are fear-producing (e.g., being lost or having the electricity go off). Express your fear vocally, and encourage the student to imitate your vocalizations.

Functional Emphases In designing your own instructional activities and plans, emphasize the following elements:

1. Avoidance of vocalizing fear when the student does not need the intervention of others.
2. Avoidance of vocalizing fear when the student has sufficient speech skills to deal with the fear-evoking situation.
3. Observation of behaviors that will prevent fearful situations from arising.

General Objective III

The student will respond to and use facial expressions in a manner that allows him to function optimally.

Specific Objectives

The student:

A. responds to a smile by smiling in turn.
B. responds to a smile by continuing an activity.
C. smiles when receiving a favored object or upon seeing a favorite person.
D. smiles when told good news.
E. responds to the facial expression of sadness by comforting the individual expressing it.
F. makes a sad face when told disappointing or sad news.
G. ceases a destructive activity when a significant person expresses anger.
H. identifies when a significant person in his environment is frightened and removes the frightening stimulus and/or comforts the person.
I. expresses fear (with or without words) when confronted with a fear-evoking situation.

Specific Objective A

The student responds to a smile by smiling in return.

Functional Settings and Suggested Instructional Activities

School

1. Present classroom activities that usually evoke happiness/pleasure, such as participating in a game, playing with toys, hearing music, and being at birthday or holiday parties. Periodically smile and encourage the student to smile by using a mirror and by manipulating his mouth. Smile at appropriate times and reward the student when he smiles in response.
2. Show the student pictures of smiling faces. Encourage her to imitate these faces.
3. Play "Simon Says" using facial expressions.
4. Show the student pictures of smiling and nonsmiling faces. Ask him to separate them into two piles. Then ask him to smile back at the smiling faces.

Home and Community

1. Ask the parents to smile whenever they greet their child. Tell them to explain to him that a smile is part of a happy greeting. Tell them to role play happy greetings.
2. Visit a community park or playground. Join the student in play activities. Smile to show your enjoyment and encourage the student to smile in return.

Functional Emphases In designing your own instructional activities and plans, emphasize the following elements:

1. Appreciation for the fact that a well-timed smile can be an effective reinforcer of others and, thus, a way to exercise control of others.
2. Differentiation of when it is not appropriate to smile as part of a greeting (e.g., when greeting someone at a wake or funeral).
3. Recognition that it may not always be appropriate to smile in response to a smile (e.g., when it is a sarcastic smile and the student must "read" the total situation).

Specific Objective B

The student responds to a smile by continuing an activity.

Functional Settings and Suggested Instructional Activities

School

1. Wait until the student is engaged in a pleasant, constructive activity. Demonstrate your approval by smiling. Reward him with something tangible as well. Intermittently reward him with just the smile.
2. Give the student a "smiling" sticker for participating in a cooperative activity. Paste it on his chart or notebook. Reward him with a prize for getting a certain number of stickers. Use "smiling" pictures in the likeness of a parent, one of his peers, or the student himself for variety.

Home and Community

1. Ask the parents to smile whenever their child is engaged in a suitable or productive activity. Tell them to explain that their smiles show they are pleased with what he is doing and that he should continue what he is doing.
2. If the student behaves appropriately on a trip to the community, smile to show that you approve of his traveling behavior.

Functional Emphases In designing your own instructional activities and plans, emphasize the following elements:

1. Discrimination of a smile of approval from a sarcastic smile that signals disapproval.
2. Realization that he can get others to continue an activity by smiling at them.

Specific Objective C

The student smiles when receiving a favored object or upon seeing a favorite person.

Functional Settings and Suggested Instructional Activities

School

1. Collect a variety of objects. Tell the student he may choose one. Allow him to play with the object he selects only if he smiles at the one of his choice.
2. Arrange for a favorite person to visit the classroom. When the person enters the room, greet him cheerfully and remember to smile. Encourage the student to smile when greeting the individual.

Home and Community

1. Ask the parents to determine their child's favorite toys, playthings, and foods. Ask them to share this information with you. Tell them to demonstrate that they smile when they receive something they like (e.g., a hug from their child, a picture he has drawn, and a favored snack). Tell them to tell him that a "thank you" smile is a good way to show appreciation.
2. While on a shopping trip in the community, purchase a desired object and give it to the student. Remind the student to smile his thanks.

Functional Emphases In designing your own instructional activities and plans, emphasize the following elements:

1. Appreciation for the fact that showing gratitude is more likely to result in further favors.
2. Awareness of the variety of ways one can indicate thanks.
3. Awareness of the various situations in which an expression of thanks is expected.

Specific Objective D

The student smiles when told good news.

Functional Settings and Suggested Instructional Activities

School

1. Tell the student a happy story. Smile broadly at the happy ending. Encourage the student to smile at the climax of a happy story.
2. Read news stories from the media that tell of happy or good news. Smile at appropriate times. Encourage the student to imitate your behavior.
3. Tell the student that a favorite person is coming to visit the classroom. Urge her to smile if she likes the news.

4. When the student has a favorite sports team and that team has won a game, announce the happy results. Urge him to smile if he is happy.
5. If you are able to obtain tickets to an enjoyable recreational event, announce the news to the student.

Home

1. Ask the parents to inform their child that he is going to engage in a favorite activity such as going out to play, dancing to records, or watching movies. Tell the parents to make it clear that if he wants to engage in the activity, he must let them know by smiling. Tell them that if he smiles, they should proceed with the activity.
2. Ask the parents periodically to give their child a choice of activities. Tell them to encourage him to indicate his choice by smiling.

Functional Emphases In designing your own instructional activities and plans, emphasize the following elements:

1. Appreciation of the fact that he can show various feelings merely by changing his facial expression.
2. Awareness that a smile is reinforcing to a person who shares good news.

Specific Objective E

The student responds to the facial expression of sadness by comforting the individual expressing it.

Functional Settings and Suggested Instructional Activities

School

1. Wait for a sad situation to occur, such as a broken toy or spilled milk. Facially express your sorrow and comfort the student by holding his hand.
2. Role play sad situations. Encourage the student to comfort the actor who is facially expressing his sadness.
3. When a peer is expressing sadness with his face and with other body language, encourage the student to comfort him in a suitable manner.
4. Reward the student for independently comforting a sad individual.
5. Make sure you indicate in some way that not every sad person wants to be comforted. Help the student to identify body language that means "Stay away from me."

Home

1. Ask the parents to obtain a crying doll. Tell them to role play comforting the doll and urge them to encourage their child to comfort the doll as well.
2. Ask the parents to tell their child when they are sad or upset and need to be comforted. Tell them to show her how to comfort her parents.

Functional Emphases In designing your own instructional activities and plans, emphasize the following elements:

1. Identification of an acceptable way to comfort others.
2. Identification of people whom it is appropriate for him to comfort.
3. Recognition of signs that he should discontinue his comforting behavior.
4. Awareness that there are individuals who do not wish to be comforted and perception of those body language signs that discourage comforting behavior.

Specific Objective F

The student makes a sad face when told disappointing or sad news.

Functional Settings and Suggested Instructional Activities

School

1. When an actual situation arises in which a change of plan is necessary (e.g., rain canceling out an activity), encourage the student to express his disappointment by making the appropriate facial expression.
2. Read news that tells of sad occurrences. Make a sad face. Encourage the student to imitate your behavior.

Home

1. Ask the parents to avoid protecting their child from disappointing and even sad news unless they believe it would be too devastating. Tell them to explain that it is the natural thing to look sad when we are disappointed or sad.
2. Tell them to role play sad or disappointing news (e.g., a trip has been canceled, a visit from a favorite friend has been postponed, or a family pet has to be put to sleep).

Functional Emphases In designing your own instructional activities and plans, emphasize the following elements:

1. Appreciation for the fact that there are many disappointments and moments of sadness in life.
2. Realization that the facial expression of sadness is the socially acceptable and expected response to sad or disappointing news.

Specific Objective G

The student ceases a destructive activity when a significant person expresses anger.

Functional Settings and Suggested Instructional Activities

School

1. If the student is engaged in an activity that causes him to come into conflict with an angry peer, first prevent the students from entering into physical conflict and then move the student out of the way of the angry peer. Explain to the student why his behavior was inappropriate and why it angered his classmate. Engineer a positive interaction between the two students.
2. Interrupt undesirable behaviors by showing the student photographs or sketches of angry faces. Reward the student for stopping the activity and for substituting a productive activity.

Home

1. If the child engages in destructive activity (including aggression toward others, property, and self), tell the parents to shake their heads, use the warning gesture of the shaking finger, and facially show their anger. (*Note*: Controlled anger, appropriately expressed and legitimately aroused, is acceptable. Tell them always to involve their child in a constructive activity after stopping a destructive one.)
2. Ask the parents to take pictures of themselves demonstrating sadness, happiness, and anger. Then tell them to present hypothetical situations to their child that deal with his behavior. (The nature of the activity involves the child pointing to the correct photograph that matches the situation.) For example, "You are helping Mommy dust the furniture; show me how I would look." "Grandma is sick. Show me how Mommy would look." "You have thrown your dish on the floor. Show me how Daddy would look."

Functional Emphases In designing your own instructional activities and plans, emphasize the following elements:

1. Awareness that the anger of another may be due to her own behavior.
2. Acquisition of an attention-getting signal so that he may signal for help if needed when someone is angry and he is physically threatened.

Specific Objective H

The student identifies when a significant person in his environment is frightened and removes the frightening stimulus and/or comforts the person.

Functional Settings and Suggested Instructional Activities

School

1. Wait for a peer to express fear facially in a nonemergency situation. First, approach the frightened peer and reassure him by holding his hand. Encourage the student to join you in comforting his frightened peer.
2. Reward the student for independently comforting a frightened peer at appropriate times and in an appropriate way.

3. Give the student a collection of pictures showing happy, frightened, angry, and sad faces. Reward the student for separating them into groups.

Home

1. Ask the parents to demonstrate what their faces look like when they are frightened. Then tell them to role play situations in which they pretend to be frightened. (*Note*: Make sure they do not overreact or overact.) Tell them to encourage their child to remove the frightening stimulus and/or comfort them.
2. If there is a younger sibling in the home, ask the parents to explain that there might be a time when the sibling is frightened. If such a situation arises, ask the parents to demonstrate how to handle the situation successfully.

Functional Emphases In designing your own instructional activities and plans, emphasize the following elements:

1. Identification of a fear response and matching the response to a specific stimulus.
2. Awareness of the appropriate way to comfort a person.
3. Recognition of when to stop comforting a person who has been frightened.
4. Awareness of signs that indicate a person does not wish to be comforted.

Specific Objective I

The student expresses fear (with or without words) when confronted with a fear-evoking situation.

Functional Settings and Suggested Instructional Activities

School

1. Sit the student down in front of a mirror. Practice making sad, happy, and fearful faces. For each face appropriately made, match it with a real situation that could cause the expression.
2. If the student expresses fear of an object, thing, or situation which should not evoke such a response, desensitize the object or situation.

Home

1. Ask the parents to identify objects and things that frighten their child. Tell them how to desensitize this fear by gradually introducing these objects in a nonthreatening way to their child.
2. Tell the parents to help their child distinguish between situations that evoke fear but are not truly dangerous and those that should be feared, avoided, or cautiously approached.

Functional Emphases In designing your own instructional activities and plans, emphasize the following elements:

1. Discrimination between those situations that should be avoided, feared, or cautiously approached from those that are harmless.
2. Employment of a total communication act in which the student expresses fear so that the facial expression matches the oral message.

General Objective IV

The student who is unable to communicate through speech and/or natural gestures will use an alternate method of communication.

Specific Objectives

The student uses one of the following:

A. a form of sign language to communicate his needs, thoughts, and feelings.
B. a nonspeech symbol system to communicate his needs, thoughts, and feelings.
C. a picture communication board to communicate her needs, thoughts, and feelings.
D. a word communication board to communicate his needs, thoughts, and feelings.
E. a letter communication board or typewriter to communicate his needs, thoughts, and feelings.
F. a picture, word, or letter communication board in combination with other systems, including: his own vocalizations; hand, arm, foot, leg, and eye movements; electronic equipment; and a typewriter to communicate his needs, thoughts, and feelings.
G. a personal computer system, including a voice synthesizer and graphics and other video displays to communicate her needs, thoughts and feelings.

Specific Objective A

The student uses a form of sign language to communicate his needs, thoughts, and feelings.

Functional Settings and Suggested Instructional Activities

School

1. When working with a student who is unable to communicate through speech and/or natural gestures, instruct the student in a sign-language form of communication. Observe the student as he interacts with his environment. From your observations, select those words for which you will introduce signs.

Learn how to make these signs with facility and clarity. Then introduce these signs as they relate to situations, incidents, and tasks that occur in the student's learning area and living quarters. Once you are sure that the student comprehends a sign, assist the student in imitating it. Once the student develops skill in producing a sign, encourage him to use each acquired sign for the meaningful expression of his needs, thoughts, and feelings. Always speak while you are using the manual system.
2. Select sign words that represent words you have selected as being important to the student's functioning in life situations. It probably will be advantageous to begin with those sign words that resemble or suggest the concept or idea of the words themselves. Do not attempt to instruct the student in the use of sign markers (i.e., gestures that signal structural changes in word form). In special cases, however, you may decide to include several sign markers that signal verb tense and noun plurality. Do this only when a particular student demonstrates special proficiency.
3. Review the use of Signed English and American Sign Language to determine whether either one is appropriate for use with a particular student. Whatever form of sign language you select for your educational program, present it with spoken English.

Home

1. Ask the parents to join you in learning the sign language system to be used with their child. (If possible, set up a sign language class for parents.) Ask the parents to help you identify those signs that will have greatest functional value to their child. Ask the parents to communicate with you on a regular basis so that signs can be developed, on a continuing basis, that meet their child's communicative needs and interests.
2. Ask the parents to practice daily with their child so that you and the parents together are reinforcing active communication and the acquisition of pertinent skills.

Functional Emphases In designing your own instructional activities and plans, emphasize the following elements:

1. Comprehension of spoken language through the use of a total communication system.
2. Facilitation of oral language usage whenever the student is able to develop relevant mechanical and structural speech skills.

Specific Objective B

The student uses a nonspeech symbol system to communicate his needs, thoughts, and feelings.

Functional Settings and Suggested Instructional Activities

School

1. When working with a student who is unable to communicate through speech and/or natural gestures, instruct the student in the use of a nonspeech symbol system. Observe the student as she interacts with her environment. From your many observations, select the words for which you will introduce nonspeech symbols.
2. Use Bliss Symbols as a nonspeech communication system. This communication system was designed, developed, and implemented at the Ontario Crippled Children's Centre. It involves the use of abstract symbols (idio- and pictographic) that are arranged on a board. The student communicates by pointing to one symbol or a combination of symbols. Begin by posting Bliss Symbols in learning areas and living quarters. Decide on a basic introductory set of symbols for working with the student. Next, introduce each symbol by pointing to the symbol and naming its concept. Then encourage the student to imitate your pointing behavior and engage in symbol discrimination activities. Once the student has attained some degree of mastery in discriminating and identifying the introductory set of symbols, use these symbols to "talk" to him. Encourage the student to use these symbols to express his needs, thoughts, and feelings. For example, the symbol for feel is a heart, and the symbol for up is an arrow pointing upward. Happiness is communicated by pointing to a symbol that combines the heart and upward-pointing arrow. Once the student is successful at comprehending and expressing himself using the introductory set of symbols, gradually increase his vocabulary by providing instruction in the use of new symbols that reflect his functional needs. Encourage him to use his board or boards to communicate his needs, thoughts, and feelings.
3. Develop a nonspeech communication board using rebus symbols alone or in combination with other nonvocal systems.

Home

1. Ask the parents to help you identify a nonspeech symbol system that is likely to be most successful with their child, provided that they believe a nonspeech symbol system is preferable to other alternate means of communication.
2. Once you and the parents have decided on the basic symbol system to be used, ask them to help you develop the basic vocabulary list and to make decisions on adding words to the system.

Functional Emphases In designing your own instructional activities and plans, emphasize the following elements:

1. Development of a system that has the greatest communicative value (i.e., is most likely to be understood by others).
2. Development of a system that is as portable as possible (i.e., it can be moved from location to location).
3. Incorporation of computer software (i.e., Bliss software, whenever appropriate).

Specific Objective C

The student uses a picture communication board to communicate his needs, thoughts, and feelings.

Functional Settings and Suggested Instructional Activities

School

1. Take an inventory of the vocabulary needed by the student. Observe him as he functions daily and as others interact with him. On the basis of these interactions, construct a list of basic words and make simple drawings, obtain simple pictures, and/or take photographs of favored objects and people.
2. Begin with photographs of favored objects. Put the photograph of one of his favorite objects, such as a toy, in front of the student. Ask him to point to the picture of the toy. Assist him if necessary. If he succeeds, indicate in some way that he will now be able to let you or anybody else know when he wants the toy by pointing to its photograph if the toy is not within view or reach. Place the photograph on the student's communication board. Put the board in a place that is within the student's reach or is accessible to the student in some other way (e.g., with the use of a pointer or a flashlight). As the student successfully identifies each photograph, add it to his board. Periodically review the pictures on the board to make sure that the student is able to identify each of the photographs. Arrange daily activities during which the student is expected to indicate his wants or thoughts by pointing to photographs on his communication board.
3. Proceed as in Activity 2; this time present the student with simple drawings or pictures of favorite foods and beverages. Follow up with other foods and beverages.
4. Proceed as in Activity 2; this time present the student with photographs of favorite persons. Then add photographs of other persons who play significant roles in the student's life. Next, add pictures of types of people who might play a part in his life (e.g., a police officer, a nurse, and a mail carrier).
5. Proceed as in Activity 2; this time present the student with simple drawings of places to which she may want or need to go (e.g., a bathroom).
6. Once the student has mastered the use of his communication board with its various pictures, drawings, and photographs of objects, people, and places, add drawings and pictures that depict favorite activities. Later, add pictures that illustrate activities the student may need to perform as he functions in life.
7. Use the communication board to "tell" the student to perform an activity. Use the communication board to "tell" the student to go to an activity or place.
8. Add prepositions to the board by using rebus drawings. If the student is not successful with the rebuses, attempt to draw or find pictures that illustrate prepositions (e.g., a picture of a book *in* an open drawer, a picture of the same book *on* the table, a picture of the same book *under* a table, and a picture of the same book *next to* a magazine).

9. Add pictures, drawings, and photographs that illustrate feelings such as happiness, sadness, anger, fear, illness, and pain. Considerable time may need to be spent on aiding the student in discriminating between and among facial expressions that signal different feelings. Practice.
10. Add rebuses that represent question markers: where, when, what, how, and how many. For example, a clock face followed by a question mark for when, arrows pointing in four directions for where, a question mark for what, a picture of two hands for how, and several numbers separated by question marks for how many (1?2?3?). Use these question markers to ask the student questions. Encourage him to use these words to ask questions of you and other significant persons.
11. Make sure that the student has some way of expressing his opinion or attitude. The indication of "yes" or "no" and of "like" and "not like" can be accomplished in several ways (e.g., a headshake/nod, a smile/frown, one tap of a foot/two taps, a look up/look down, a look to the right/to the left, a smack of the lips/no movement, or one sound/two sounds).

Home

1. Ask the parents to help you identify words that should be added to their child's communication board. Ask them to assist you in obtaining pictures and photographs of these words.
2. Ask the parents to practice, on a daily basis, communicating with their child. Tell them to arrange interactions that increase their child's comprehension of spoken language and practice his use of the picture communication board to express his needs, thoughts, and feelings. Assist the parents in designing "conversations" that give their child sufficient practice in active communication.

Functional Emphases In designing your own instructional activities and plans, emphasize the following elements:

1. Development of a system that has the greatest communicative value (i.e., is most likely to be understood by others).
2. Development of a system that is as portable as possible (i.e., it can be moved from location to location).
3. Development of a system that has parts that can easily be replaced.
4. Development of a system that is cost effective.

Specific Objective D

The student uses a word communication board to communicate his needs, thoughts, and feelings.

Functional Settings and Suggested Instructional Activities

School

1. There may be some physically handicapped students who will be unable to speak and/or use gestures because of the severity of their motor handicaps, but who might have sufficient reading skill to use a communication board with printed words rather than pictures or in combination with pictures. If so, proceed as in Nonverbal Communication Skills, IV, C, School Activities 1 to 11, using words instead of pictures. It may well be necessary to initiate the program by using pictures coupled with printed words before eliminating the pictures.
2. Provide the student with a means of indicating the words he wishes to communicate. This means should be determined on the basis of his physical skills. Consult with occupational and physical therapists. Such means might include a look, a flashlight, or a light attached to a band around his head.

Home

1. Ask the parents to help you identify words that should be added to their child's communication board. Ask them to assist you in obtaining words.
2. Ask the parents to practice, on a daily basis, communicating with their child. Tell them to arrange interactions that increase their child's comprehension of spoken language and practice his use of the word communication board to express his needs, thoughts, and feelings. Assist the parents in designing "conversations" that give their child sufficient practice in active communication.

Functional Emphases In designing your own instructional activities and plans, emphasize the following elements:

1. Development of a system that has the greatest communicative value (i.e., is most likely to be understood by others).
2. Development of a system that is as portable as possible (i.e., it can be moved from location to location).
3. Development of a system that has parts that can easily be replaced.
4. Development of a system that is cost effective.

Specific Objective E

The student uses a letter communication board or typewriter to communicate his needs, thoughts, and feelings.

Functional Settings and Suggested Instructional Activities

School

1. There may be some physically handicapped students who will be unable to speak and/or use gestures because of the severity of their motor handicaps, but who might have sufficient writing/spelling skills to use a communication board made up of letters and numerals and/or to use a typewriter. If so, take an

inventory of the student's basic vocabulary needs and assist him in first identifying and then writing these words using his board or typewriter. Encourage him to use his board or typewriter to tell you what he wants and what he is thinking.

2. Consult with occupational therapists in order to provide the student with the most convenient way to use her board or typewriter. They may also assist in providing specially designed equipment and other aids to help the student communicate as effectively and efficiently as possible.

Home

Use Home activities 1 and 2 for Specific Objective C, substituting the use of letters or a typewriter. The goal is to obtain the active involvement of the parents to increase the likelihood of programmatic success.

Functional Emphases In designing your own instructional activities and plans, emphasize the following elements:

1. Development of a system that has the greatest communicative value (i.e., is most likely to be understood by others).
2. Development of a system that is as portable as possible (i.e., it can be moved from location to location).
3. Development of a system that has parts that can easily be replaced.
4. Development of a system that is cost effective.

Specific Objective F

The student uses a picture, word, or letter communication board in combination with other systems, including: his own vocalizations; hand, arm, foot, leg, and eye movements; electronic equipment; and a typewriter to communicate his needs, thoughts, and feelings.

Functional Settings and Suggested Instructional Activities

School

1. Determine the physical and vocal skills of students who are unable to speak and/or use gestures. Incorporate these vocalizations and movements as the student uses his particular communication board (e.g., the student might tap his foot a certain number of times to indicate the number of the panel on his board that he wants you to look at, or he might vocalize one sound to indicate a negative response and two sounds (or a different sound) to indicate a positive response).
2. It is possible to set up a letter board electronically so that when the student touches or types a letter, that letter will then appear on a television screen or be typed electronically on a nearby typewriter. Check with rehabilitation and habilitation agencies that may allow you to borrow this equipment.

Encourage the student to self-monitor as he observes the video screen and/or typewriter. Reward him.

Functional Emphases In designing your own instructional activities and plans, emphasize the following elements:

1. Development of a system that has the greatest communicative value (i.e., is most likely to be understood by others).
2. Development of a system that is as portable as possible (i.e., it can be moved from location to location).
3. Development of a system that has parts that can easily be replaced.
4. Development of a system that is cost effective.

Specific Objective G

The student uses a personal computer system, including a voice synthesizer and graphics and other video displays to communicate his needs, thoughts, and feelings. (Note: A variety of personal computers currently on the market are adaptable for use as a communication system. It is important, however, that the parent and teacher work with a computer consultant who is knowledgeable in working with the handicapped.)

Functional Settings and Suggested Instructional Activities

School

1. Provide the student with access to a personal computer. Contact consultants or individuals who are knowledgeable in the computer field to work with you and the student initially in developing some basic vocabulary understanding or picture identification. Involve the parents at all stages so they can reinforce what is being taught.
2. Include graphics and voice synthesizers for students who can benefit from these types of modifications. Develop a program that includes daily attainable goals so the student can be reinforced on a regular basis.
3. Use computer games as reinforcement and as another way of developing motivation to become familiar with the system initially. Games, however, should be kept to a minimum, and those that are selected should be of an educational nature.

Home See School Activities.

Functional Emphases In designing your own instructional activities and plans, emphasize the following elements:

1. Selection of a system that is cost effective.
2. Selection of a system that is portable and has parts which are easily replaced.
3. Avoidance of sophisticated software that is expensive and provides little content.

4. Avoidance of computer game software that does little to teach the student.
5. Selection of hardware and software from a reputable firm that provides ongoing service and repair.
6. Use of computer consultants whenever available.

Special Materials List—Nonverbal Communication Skills

Record(s)

Parade of Colors, Hap Palmer Record Library, Educational Activities, Inc., P. O. Box 392, Freeport, NY 11520.

Suggested Readings/References—Nonverbal Communication Skills

Archer, L. A. (1977). Blissymbolics—A nonverbal communication system. *Journal of Speech and Hearing Disorders*, *42*, 568–579.

Bernard-Opitz, V. (1982). Pragmatic analysis of the communicative behavior of an autistic child. *Journal of Speech and Hearing Disorders*, *47*, 99–108.

Bigge, G. L., & O'Donnell, P. A. (1979). *Teaching individuals with physical and multiple disabilities.* Columbus, OH: Charles E. Merrill.

Bjorling, B. (Ed.) (1977). *Language and communication.* Lansing, MI: Midwest Regional Center for Services to Deaf-Blind Children.

Bricker, D. D. (1972). Imitative sign training as a facilitator of word-object association with low-functioning children. *American Journal of Mental Deficiency*, *76*, 509–516.

Calculator, S., & D'Altilio Lucho, C. (1983). Evaluating the effectiveness of a communication board training program. *Journal of Speech and Hearing Disorders*, *48*, 185–191.

Calculator, S., & Dollaghan, C. (1982). The use of communication boards in a residential setting: An evaluation. *Journal of Speech and Hearing Disorders*, *47*, 281–287.

Carlson, F. (1981). A format for selecting vocabulary for the non-speaking child. *Language, Speech and Hearing Services in the Schools*, *12*, 240–245.

Carrier, J. K., Jr. (1974). Nonspeech noun usage training with severely and profoundly retarded children. *Journal of Speech and Hearing Research*, *17*, 510–517.

Chapman, R., & Miller, J. (1980). Analyzing language and communication in the child. In R. Schiefelbusch (Ed.), *Nonspeech language and communication analysis and intervention.* Baltimore: University Park Press.

Coleman, C. L., Cook, A. M., & Meyers, L. S. (1980). Assessing non-oral clients for assistive communication devices. *Journal of Speech and Hearing Disorders*, *45*, 515–526.

Curtis, C. (Ed.) 1978. *A prelanguage curriculum guide for the multihandicapped.* Denver: Mountain Plains Regional Center for Services to Deaf-Blind Children.

Deich, R. E., & Hodges, P. M. (1977). *Language without speech.* New York: Brunner/Mazel.

Dennis, R., Reichle, S., Williams, W., & Vogelsberg, R. T. (1982). Motoric factors influencing the selection of vocabulary for sign production programs. *Journal of the Association for the Severely Handicapped*, *7*, 20–32.

Devito, J. A. (1978). *Communicology: An introduction to the study of communication.* New York: Harper & Row.

DuBose, R. F. (1978). Development of communication in nonverbal children. *Education and Training of the Mentally Retarded, 13,* 37–41.

Egolf, D., & Chester, S. (1973). Nonverbal communication and the disorders of language. *ASHA, 15,* 511–518.

Ekman, P., & Friesen, W. V. (1969). The repertoire of nonverbal behavior: Categories, origin, usage, and coding. *Semiotica, 1,* 49–98.

Fant, L. J., Jr. (1972). *Ameslan, An Introduction to American Sign Language.* Silver Spring, MD: National Association of the Deaf.

Faw, A., Reid, D., Schepis, M., Fitzgerald, J., & Welty, P. (1981). Involving institutional staff in the development and maintenance of sign language skills with profoundly retarded persons. *Journal of Applied Behavior Analysis, 14,* 411–424.

Fristoe, M., & Lloyd, L. (1978). A survey of the use of non-speech systems with the severely communication impaired. *Mental Retardation, 16,* 99–103.

Fristoe, J., & Lloyd, L. (1980). Planning an initial expressive sign lexicon for persons with severe communication impairment. *Journal of Speech and Hearing Disorders, 45,* 170–180.

Gallender, D. (1980). *Symbol communication for the severely handicapped.* Springfield, IL: Charles C Thomas.

Goodman, L., Wilson, P., & Borenstein, H. (1978). Results of the national survey of sign language programs in special education. *Mental Retardation, 16,* 104–106.

Griffith, P. L., & Robinson, J. H. (1980). Influence of iconicity and phonological similarity on sign learning by mentally retarded children. *American Journal of Mental Deficiency, 85,* 291–298.

Harris, D. (1982). Communicative interaction process involving nonvocal physically handicapped children. *Topics in Language Disorders, 2,* 21–37.

Harris, T. L. (1978). The language spectrum: Using total communication with the severely handicapped. *Education and Treatment of the Mentally Retarded, 13,* 85–89.

Harris-Vanderheiden, D., & Vanderheiden, G. C. (1977). Basic considerations in the development of communicative and interactive skills for non-vocal severely handicapped children. In E. Sontag, J. Smith, & N. Certo (Eds.), *Educational programming for the severely and profoundly handicapped,* Reston, VA: Council for Exceptional Children.

Hollis, J., & Carrier, J. (1978). Intervention strategies for nonspeech children. In R. Schiefelbusch (Ed.), *Language intervention strategies.* Baltimore University Park Press.

Johnson, D. J., & Myklebust, H. R. (1967). *Learning disabilities: Educational principles and practices.* New York: Grune & Stratton.

Jones, T. W. (1980). Is it necessary to decide whether to use a nonvocal communication system with retarded children? *Education and Training of the Mentally Retarded, 15,* 157–160.

Kahn, J. V. (1981). A comparison of sign and verbal language training with mute and retarded children. *Journal of Speech and Hearing Research, 24,* 113–119.

Kirschner, A., Algozzine, B., & Abbott, T. B. (1979). Manual communication systems: A comparison and its implications. *Educcation and Training of the Mentally Retarded, 14,* 5–10.

Knapp, M. (1980). *Essentials of nonverbal communication.* New York: Holt, Rinehart & Winston.

Kohl, R., Karlan, G., & Heal, L. (1979). Effects of pairing manual signs with verbal cues upon the acquisition of instruction—following behaviors and the generalization to expressive language with severely handicapped students. *AAESPH Review, 4,* 291–300.

Kohl, F., Wilcox, B. L., & Karlan, G. R. (1978). Effects of training conditions on the generalization of manual signs with moderately handicapped students. *Education and Training of the Mentally Retarded, 13,* 327–335.

Krauss, R. M., Apple, W., Morency, N., Wenzel, C., & Winton, W. (1981). Verbal, vocal, and visible factors in judgments of another's affect. *Journal of Personality and Social Psychology, 14,* 15–19.

Kriegsmann, E., Gallagher, J. C., & Meyers, A. (1982). Sign programs with non-verbal hearing children. *Exceptional Children, 48,* 436–445.

Lloyd, L. L. (1980). Unaided nonspeech communication for severely handicapped individuals. An extensive bibliography. *Education and Training of the Mentally Retarded, 15,* 15–34.

McLean, L., & McLean, J. (1978). A language training program for non-verbal autistic children. *Journal of Speech and Hearing Disorders, 39,* 186–193.

Minskoff, E. H. (1980). Teaching approach for developing nonverbal communication skills in students with social perception deficits, Part 1. *Journal of Learning Disabilities, 13,* 118–124.

Minskoff, E. H. (1980). Teaching approach for developing nonverbal communication skills in students with social perception deficits, Part 2. *Journal of Learning Disabilities, 13,* 203–208.

Morrison, R. L., & Bellack, A. S. (1981). The role of social perception in social skill. *Behavior Therapy, 12,* 69–79.

Nietupski, J., & Hamre-Nietupski, S. (1979). Teaching auxiliary communication skills to severely handicapped students. *AAESPH Review, 4,* 107–124.

Oliver, C., & Halle, J. (1982). Language training in the everyday environment: Teaching functional sign use to a retarded child. *Journal of the Association for the Severely Handicapped, 7,* 50–62.

Poulton, K. T., & Algozzine, B. (1980). Manual communication and mental retardation: A review of research and implications. *American Journal of Mental Deficiency, 85,* 145–152.

Provisional Dictionary. (1975). Ontario, Canada: Blissymbolics Communication Foundation.

Reich, R. (1978). Gestural facilitation of expressive language in moderately/severely retarded preschoolers. *Mental Retardation, 16,* 113–117.

Reichle, J., Williams, W., & Ryan, S. (1981). Selecting signs for the formulation of an augmentative communicative modality. *Journal of the Association for the Severely Handicapped, 6,* 48–56.

Salisbury, C., Wambold, C., & Walter, G. (1978). Manual communication for the severely handicapped: An assessment and instructional strategy. *Education and Training of the Mentally Retarded, 13,* 393–397.

Schaeffer, B., Musil, A., & Kollinzas, G. (1980). *Total communication: A signed speech program for nonverbal children.* Champaign, IL: Research Press.

Schiefelbusch, R. L. (Ed.) (1980). *Nonspeech language and communication analysis and intervention.* Baltimore: University Park Press.

Silverman, F. (1980). *Communication for the speechless.* Englewood Cliffs, NJ: Prentice–Hall.

Silverman, H., McNaughton, S., & Kates, B. (1979). *Handbook of blissymbolics for instructors, users, parents, and administrators.* Toronto: Blissymbolics Communication Institute.

Spignesi, A., & Shor, R. E. (1981). The judgment of facial expressions, contexts, and their combination. *Journal of General Psychology, 104,* 41–58.

Sternberg, L., Battle, C., & Hill, J. (1980). Prelanguage communication programming for the severely and profoundly handicapped. *Journal of the Association for the Severely Handicapped*, 5, 224–233.

Stokoe, W. (1980). The study and use of sign language. In R. Schiefelbusch (Ed.), *Nonspeech language and communication: Analysis and intervention.* Baltimore: University Park Press.

Syntax Supplement No. 1. (1975). Toronto: Blissymbolics Communication Foundation.

Valletutti, P. (1983). The social and emotional problems of children with learning disabilities. *Learning Disabilities*, 2, 17–29.

Van Biervliet, A. (1977). Establishing words and objects as functionally equivalent through manual sign training. *American Journal of Mental Deficiency*, *82*, 178–186.

Vanderheiden, D. H., Brown, W. P., MacKenzie, P., Reinen, S., & Scheibel, C. (1975). Symbol communication for the mentally handicapped. *Mental Retardation*, *13*, 34–37.

Vanderheiden, G., & Grilley, K. (1978). *Non-vocal communication techniques and aids for the severely physically handicapped.* Austin: PRO-ED.

Van Kleech, A., & Frankel, T. L. (1981). Discourse devices used by language disordered children: A preliminary investigation. *Journal of Speech and Hearing Disorders*, *46*, 250–257.

Weiss, C. E., & Lillywhite, H. S. (1981). *Communication Disorders*, 2nd edition. St. Louis: C. V. Mosby.

Weller, E. L., & Mahoney, G. J. (1983). A comparison of oral and total communication modalities on the language training of young mentally handicapped children. *Education and Training of the Mentally Retarded*, *18*, 103–110.

Wendt, E., Sprague, H. J., & Marquis, J. (1975). Communication without speech. *Teaching Exceptional Children*, *8*, 38–42.

Wilbur, R. B. (1983). Where do we go from here? In J. Miller, D. Yoder & R. Schiefelbusch (Eds.), *Contemporary issues in language intervention.* Rockville, MD: ASHA Reports 12.

Williams, S. G., Lombardo, L. J., MacDonald, J. D., & Owens, R. E. (1982). Total communication: Clinical report on a parent-based language training program. *Education and Training of the Mentally Retarded*, *17*, 293–298.

3 Verbal Communication Skills

The functional communication skills important to skilled interpersonal interaction and necessary to cognitive, social, and emotional development can be separated into verbal and nonverbal domains. This chapter deals with the verbal aspect of human communication (see Chapter 2 for the nonverbal area). Although verbal skills include oral and written language comprehension and expression, this section of the curriculum deals solely with auditory-oral language skills because of their more immediate relevancy to moderately and severely handicapped students.

Three major general or long-term objectives have been identified and serve as the framework for the articulation of specific, short-term instructional goals. The first of these general objectives is concerned with the prelinguistic skills of vocalic and articulatory production as well as those involved in auditory awareness and responsiveness, essential precursors that facilitate later oral language comprehension and speech. The second general objective involves the comprehension of auditory language (i.e., the assignment of meaning to phonemic, morphemic, and linguistic units) (Rees & Shulman, 1978; Wiig & Semel, 1980). The third objective attends to the development of oral expressive language skills, including phonological (articulated sounds), morphological (patterns of word formation), syntactic (sentence structure), prosodic (features of pitch, stress, and juncture), pragmatic (intent and social context), and semantic (meaning) components (Eisenson & Ogilvie, 1983).

Whenever possible, the general and specific curricular objectives have been placed in generally accepted developmental sequences. Although developmental milestones supply a logical organization to curricular design, it must be remembered that they reflect general patterns that are not always individually applicable. Program implementers must be able to ignore developmental sequences whenever they are not pertinent to a given student. For example, a given student, for inexplicable or even obvious physiological reasons (neurological involvement of the lips), might be unable to satisfactorily articulate the developmentally early labials (/p/, /b/, and /m/) while being able to make the /s/ (a developmentally late phoneme) in isolation. Certainly in this case the teacher or therapist should assist the student in incorporating the /s/ into words and into his connected speech before expending inordinate time or effort on the articulation of the labials. Teachers and therapists should work with students where they find them and assist them in progressing to newer (not necessarily higher) levels of functioning that logically arise from the pupil's idiosyncratic developmental pattern. With this caveat in mind, the reader then can more successfully program for the identified curricular objectives that have been sequenced based upon the abundance of information available on the normative development of oral language (Benedict, 1978; Bloom & Lahey, 1978; Caramazza & Zurif, 1978; Casby & Ruder, 1983; Chomsky, 1969; Eisenson & Ogilvie, 1983; Halliday, 1977; Hillenbrand, 1983; Hutton, 1980; Kent, 1981; Lodge & Leach, 1975; McCarthy, 1954; Moerk, 1977; Piaget, 1974; Wiig & Semel, 1980).

In implementing a communication skills curriculum, the unifying principle should be the success of the communication—how well the student understands and responds to the spoken language of others (Eisenson & Ogilvie, 1983) and how successfully he communicates his needs, wants, feelings, and thoughts to others (Bloodstein, 1984). Accuracy of articulation, for example, should not be the program emphasis; rather, articulation should be considered only from the perspective of its contribution to the intelligibility of the speaker's message (Flowers, 1974; Goetz, Schuler, & Sailor, 1979; Greer, Anderson, & Davis, 1976). Speech intelligibility and speaker intent within the social context (pragmatics) should receive the major prescriptive attention (Bedrosian & Prutting, 1978; Berry & Marshall, 1978; Curtiss, Prutting, & Lowell, 1979; Damico & Oller, 1980; Goetz, Schuler, & Sailor, 1979; Guess, Sailor, & Baer, 1978; Halliday, 1977; Higginbotham & Yoder, 1982; James & Seebach, 1982; Lucas, 1980; Moerk, 1977; Platt, 1979; Shuy & Griffin, 1978).

Halliday (1977) has identified the various pragmatic aspects of functional communication. These include: instrumental, regulatory, interactional, personal, heuristic, imaginative, and informative communicative intents. In the creation of activities designed to meet the curricular objectives enumerated in this chapter, teachers and therapists should make these diverse functional dimensions the framework for improving and enhancing phonologic, morphologic, prosodic, syntactic, and semantic aspects of oral language comprehension and expression. Moreover, the individual using this curriculum must appreciate the primacy of oral language skills and their importance in the implementation of the total curriculum. Oral language is the medium through which most other skills, knowledge, and concepts are mastered. Language is used for controlling one's own behavior as well as the behavior of others (Weiss & Lillywhite, 1981). Cognitive development is enhanced by the acquisition of oral language as people codify the cognitive processes of thought, memory, learning, and problem-solving activities through language (Eisenson & Ogilvie, 1983).

The Suggested Readings/References and Special Materials List at the end of this chapter provide information on verbal communication skills. The reader should decide which material and information are applicable to a specific student or students being taught.

General Objectives of the Unit

I. The student will develop skills that facilitate the development of language.
II. The student will respond to spoken language in a manner that allows him to function optimally.
III. The student will speak in such a manner that his needs and thoughts are readily understood by listeners.

General Objective I

The student will develop skills that facilitate the development of language.

Specific Objectives

The student:

A. responds to sound.
B. makes gurgling and growling sounds.
C. coos and chuckles.
D. becomes quiet at the sound of humming, singing, chanting, or talking.
E. turns his eyes and head in the direction of someone vocalizing or speaking.
F. turns his head and shoulders in the direction of noise.
G. turns his head and shoulders in the direction of someone vocalizing or speaking.
H. responds vocally to others who approach him.
I. vocalizes in response to the vocalization of others.
J. vocalizes "m" and other single consonants.
K. babbles or vocalizes two (duplicated) syllables.
L. initiates vocal play with toys.
M. vocalizes in self-initiated sound play.
N. babbles or vocalizes two or more different syllables.
O. vocalizes displeasure when a favorite or needed object is withdrawn.
P. vocalizes pleasure or satisfaction upon obtaining a desired or favorite object.
Q. responds differentially to friendly and angry talking.
R. initiates vocal play with people.
S. vocalizes to music.

T. discriminates among the sounds of his language, including individual sounds and blends, by articulating diverse consonant-vowel, vowel-consonant, and consonant-vowel-consonant combinations.
U. echoes words and phrases in songs and rhymes.
V. echoes individual words and phrases spoken by others.

Specific Objective A

The student responds to sound.

Functional Settings and Suggested Instructional Activities

School

1. Play a game in which pieces are moved on a game board. Take your turn after you ring a bell (a desk bell, perhaps). Tell him to take his turn only after you have finished your turn and the bell has been rung again.
2. Obtain a teletrainer and pick up the telephone when it rings.
3. Give the student a noisemaker identical to the one you have. Communicate in some way to the student that she should play her noisemaker when you play yours. Play it out of her sight. Vary this activity by using several different toy noisemakers.

Home

1. Ask the parents to play stimulus-response games (i.e., sound leads to a definite action). For example, tell them to turn on music and immediately start dancing. Tell them to play music again; this time they should immediately take their child's hands and dance with him to the music. Tell them to stop when the music stops.
2. Ask the parents to set a timer to indicate "Stop" when they want their child to shift to a new activity. Tell them to pantomime hearing the timer and then stop the activity in which they are engaged.

Functional Emphases In designing your own instructional activities and plans, emphasize the following elements:

1. Awareness that sound is a sign to which an individual should respond in diverse ways.
2. Appreciation that sound can provide pleasurable experiences.
3. Realization that sounds provide clues to what is occurring.

Specific Objective B

The student makes gurgling and growling sounds.

Functional Settings and Suggested Instructional Activities

School

1. Provide the student with a variety of playthings and assist him as he touches, manipulates, sees, and hears them. As you participate in play activities with him, make vocal playing an integral part of all play activities.
2. Use a toy or a hand-puppet dog. Make growling sounds as you manipulate the toy or puppet. Give the student the toy or puppet and encourage her to imitate your behavior.

Home

1. Tell the parents to give their child a favorite food. Tell them that, as soon as he has eaten, they should make gurgling sounds while simultaneously stroking his neck in the area of his throat while moving their hand back to front under his jaw. Tell them to tape record these gurgling sounds as they are made by the child. Tell the parents to play the tape or cassette of their child's gurgling sounds during their child's quiet times.
2. Tell the parents that whenever they play with their child, they should include vocal play as an integral part of the activities.

Functional Emphases In designing your own instructional activities and plans, emphasize the following elements:

1. Bombardment of the student with pleasurable sounds.
2. Association of sound with pleasurable experiences.

Specific Objective C

The student coos and chuckles

Functional Settings and Suggested Instructional Activities

School

1. Play with the student. During the play make cooing and chuckling sounds. Make these sounds with obvious enjoyment. Make these sounds an integral part of all play activities.
2. With the very young student, hold and hug him while you are vocalizing, chanting, singing, and speaking.

Home

1. Tell the parents to tickle their young child gently to elicit chuckling or cooing sounds. Tell them to tape record these cooing and chuckling sounds as they are made by the child.

2. Tell them to play tapes of chuckling and cooing sounds, especially the ones he has made himself. Tell them to play these tapes during their child's quiet times.

Functional Emphases In designing your own instructional activities and plans, emphasize the following elements:

1. Bombardment of the student with pleasurable sounds.
2. Association of sound with pleasurable experiences.

Specific Objective D

The student becomes quiet at the sound of humming, singing, chanting, or talking.

Functional Settings and Suggested Instructional Activities

School Carry out the same activities in the classroom that the parent is doing at home.

Home

1. Tell the parents that when their child is involved in a noisy activity, they should vocalize within his visual field and indicate "Be Quiet" by closing his lips and/or making the "Sh" gesture.
2. Tell the parents to place their child in movable furniture such as a rocking chair, a crib, a bed with wheels, or a movable apparatus such as a swing, rocking horse, stroller, or teeter-totter. Tell them to vocalize within his visual field and then keep time with the vocal play by moving the furniture. Remind them to say "Sh," make the appropriate gesture, and continue their vocalizing only if their child becomes quiet and remains quiet.
3. Tell them to repeat Activities 1 and 2. This time, however, hum a simple tune such as "Bah, Bah, Black Sheep."
4. Tell them to repeat Activities 1 and 2. This time, however, have them sing a simple tune such as "Mary Had a Little Lamb."
5. Tell them to repeat Activities 1 and 2. This time, however, have them chant a simple chant often used with young children, such as "Aah-aah, Baby."

Functional Emphases In designing your own instructional activities and plans, emphasize the following elements:

1. Surrounding of the student with pleasurable sounds.
2. Association of sound with pleasurable experiences.

Specific Objective E

The student turns his eyes and head in the direction of someone vocalizing or speaking.

Functional Settings and Suggested Instructional Activities

School

1. Use a hand puppet to run through the same activities as outlined in Home Activities 1 through 3 above.
2. Place an object of interest in front of the student. Move it to one side and then to the other. If the student follows the object visually, repeat the activity. This time, however, accompany the movement with vocalization. Repeat this activity by vocalizing without an object. Reward the student for turning his eyes and head in the direction of the vocal sound.

Home

1. Tell the parents to vocalize by humming, singing, chanting, and speaking. Tell them to make sure their child is looking at them. Tell them to stand to one side of him and vocalize once again. Tell them if their child does not respond, they should lean over and turn his head in the direction from which the sound came. Tell them to hold his head in place, if necessary, while they vocalize over and over again. Tell them to release his head and make the sound once again and encourage him to turn toward them.
2. Tell them to repeat Activity 1, this time while standing on the other side of the child.
3. Tell them to repeat Activities 1 and 2. This time, however, tell them to continue vocalizing only if the child turns and hold her head in the position facing them.

Functional Emphases In designing your own instructional activities and plans, emphasize the following elements:

1. Maintenance of attention once the student has turned to the sound source and the subsequent development of other skills during these times.
2. Localization of sound from a variety of directions and the appropriate behavior when the sound stimulus suggests a definitive response.

Specific Objective F

The student turns his head and shoulders in the direction of noise.

Functional Settings and Suggested Instructional Activities

School

1. Start to make the noise, lean over, and touch only one of the student's shoulders. Continue to make the noise only if he turns his head and shoulder in the direction of the noise. Do this over again; this time, touch his other shoulder.
2. Engage in Home Activities 1 and 2.

Home

1. Tell the parents to stand behind the child and make a noise with a noisemaker. When he turns his eyes and head in the direction of the noise, tell them to assist him by moving the upper part of his body. Tell them to stand to the side and behind the child the next time they make the noise. Tell them to make sure they vary their position so that he must turn his shoulders and upper torso to see from where the noise is coming.
2. Tell the parents to place a noisemaker in front of the child. Then, using the noisemaker, have them make a noise and simultaneously make an arc with the noisemaker. Tell them to go to one side and then the other. Tell them to finish up by putting the noisemaker behind him so that he must move his head and shoulders to see it.

Functional Emphases In designing your own instructional activities and plans, emphasize the following elements:

1. Development of awareness of sound.
2. Development of skill in the localization of sound.

Specific Objective G

The student turns his head and shoulders in the direction of someone vocalizing or speaking.

Suggested Instructional Activities Use the activities listed for Specific Objective F, substituting vocalization and speech for the noisemaker and other noise sources.

Specific Objective H

The student responds vocally to others who approach him.

Functional Settings and Suggested Instructional Activities

School

1. Vocalize greetings whenever a student enters the room in the morning. Also, vocalize greetings whenever someone visits the classroom.
2. Sing the song "Hi-Lilli-Hi-Lilli-Hi Lo" as part of a greeting pantomime and song. Seek out other songs that are greeting songs, such as "How Do You Do, My Partner."

Home

1. Ask the parents to vocalize or speak greetings every time they approach the child in an effort to stimulate her to vocalize a greeting.

2. Ask the parents to vocalize every time they are approached by someone else to demonstrate the reciprocity of greetings.

Functional Emphases In designing your own instructional activities and plans, emphasize the following elements:

1. Identification of sounds and sound patterns the student is able to vocalize.
2. Awareness of the need to greet others and the enjoyment that comes from vocal play.

Specific Objective I

The student vocalizes in response to the vocalization of others.

Functional Settings and Suggested Instructional Activities

School

1. Perform simple motor acts such as clapping hands and tapping a hand on a desk. Set up a series of motor imitations that may lead to the imitation of speech sounds. Gradually lead up to motor acts that involve the speech mechanism, such as smacking the lips, throwing a kiss, and making a "brr-rr" sound.
2. Say the single-consonant-plus-vowel sounds: "da," "ba," "ma." While vocalizing, manipulate and stroke the peripheral speech mechanism, (the lips, jaws, and throat) of the student. Place the student's hands on your face, nose, lips, and throat while you are vocalizing.
3. Vocalize consonant-vowel combinations while playing a tune on a toy piano or xylophone. Encourage the student to join in the vocalizing.
4. Use a hand puppet. Vocalize as you manipulate the puppet. Give the student his own hand puppet and encourage him to vocalize as he manipulates his puppet.
5. Vocalize while using a toy telephone. Encourage the student to vocalize into her own toy telephone.
6. Play with a doll or toy animal. Vocalize to the doll while playing with it. Give the student his own doll or toy animal and encourage him to vocalize while playing with it.

Home

1. Tell the parents to vocalize with their lips against an inflated balloon. Tell them to place the child's hands on the balloon so that he can feel the vibrations as they vocalize with their lips against it. Tell them to encourage him to imitate their vocalizations.
2. Tell the parents to vocalize while engaging in a rhythmic activity. Tell them to encourage the child to do the same. Clapping hands and vocalizing can be particularly successful.

Functional Emphases In designing your own instructional activities and plans, emphasize the following elements:

1. Facilitation of vocal play as a precursor of gaining control over the speech mechanism.
2. Facilitation of vocal play as a precursor of sound imitation.

Specific Objective J

The student vocalizes "m" and other single consonants.

Functional Settings and Suggested Instructional Activities

School

1. Make the "m" sound, and simultaneously press the student's lips together and then apart. Do this while playing melodic music.
2. Make all of the individual consonant sounds as you play and work with the student. Encourage him to join the vocalizing. Repeat this activity frequently.
3. Pair individual consonant sounds with words the student might need as he functions daily (e.g., "p" for "Push me on the swing," and "k" for "car").
4. Sit in front of a mirror with the student; direct her attention to your face as you make all the consonant sounds.

Home

1. Tell the parents to sing the "Campbell Soup" jingle while encouraging the child to join in the chorus of "mm-mm-good."
2. Tell the parents to make all of the individual consonant sounds plus consonant and vowel combinations as they play and work with the child. Tell them to encourage him to join them in vocalizing. Tell them to repeat this play frequently.

Functional Emphases In designing your own instructional activities and plans, emphasize the following elements:

1. Facilitation of the imitation of the various sounds of the language.
2. Awareness of the relationship between various movements and the sounds created.
3. Association of individual consonant sounds with high interest words and activities.

Specific Objective K

The student babbles or vocalizes two (duplicated) syllables.

Functional Settings and Suggested Instructional Activities

School

1. Encourage the student to imitate motor patterns consisting of one action repeated twice (e.g., clapping hands twice or tapping a foot twice). Encourage the student to make sounds with noisemakers in the pattern of one action repeated twice. Give the student a variety of noisemakers and assist him as he beats a drum twice, rings a bell twice, and strikes sticks together twice.
2. Place a large mirror in front of the student. Direct him to look in the mirror and to look at your mouth as it is reflected in the mirror. Mouth the duplicated consonant-vowel combinations without making the sounds. Encourage the student to imitate your behavior. Then repeat, this time making the sounds.
3. Engage in quiet play with toys. Do this in front of a large full-length wall mirror. Give the student duplicates of the toys and ask him to play. Vocalize duplicated consonant-vowel combinations during play activities. Encourage him to watch you and himself in the mirror and to imitate your actions.

Home

1. Ask the parents to make a tape of duplicated consonant-vowel combinations (e.g., "Ma-Ma," "Da-Da," and "Bye-Bye"). Tell them to play the tape as background "music" during the child's quiet times.
2. Tell the parents to sing nursery rhymes and other simple tunes in which they repeat the duplicated syllables to the melody. Tell them to begin with the melody of "Mary Had a Little Lamb" or "Jack and Jill."

Functional Emphases In designing your own instructional activities and plans, emphasize the following elements:

1. Development of a repertoire of duplicated syllables that includes all the possible consonant-vowel combinations.
2. Encouragement of vocalization as a pleasurable activity.
3. Encouragement of vocalization as an attention-getting device.

Specific Objective L

The student initiates vocal play with toys.

Functional Settings and Suggested Instructional Activities

School

1. Using a doll or toy animal, vocalize to it using vowels, cooing, chuckling, and growling sounds. Talk to it. Give the student an exact duplicate of the toy being used and ask him to imitate your actions. Sit in front of a large full-length mirror so the student can watch you and himself as you are vocalizing. Repeat the activity using puppets and other toys.
2. Engage the student in free-play activities while playing tapes of children vocalizing in the background. Reward the student if she begins to vocalize.

Home

1. Tell the parents to play with favored toys of the child. Tell them to talk to the mobile hanging over his bed, vocalize to his favorite teddy bear, and answer the rattling noise of his rattle. Tell them to hand the toy to the child immediately after they have vocalized to it while encouraging him to imitate them. Tell them to repeat this activity until he responds.
2. Tell them to observe the child and, if he begins to vocalize while playing with a toy, to join him excitedly and reward him in other ways.

Functional Emphases In designing your own instructional activities and plans, emphasize the following elements:

1. Facilitation of vocal play as an enjoyable activity independent of playing with toys.
2. Facilitation of vocal play in response to people.

Specific Objective M

The student vocalizes in self-initiated sound play.

Functional Settings and Suggested Instructional Activities

School

1. See Home Activities 1 and 2.
2. If the student engages in self-initiated sound play, reward him in some way. Join him in vocalizing if it brings him pleasure.

Home

1. Ask the parents to model vocalizing as an acceptable form of self-stimulation. Tell them to sing as they do housework or engage in a one-person game such as solitaire or a jigsaw puzzle.
2. Ask the parents to sing nursery rhymes and simple songs as they look out the window on a rainy day (or other kind of day) to model vocalizing as a quiet form of pleasure.

Functional Emphases In designing your own instructional activities and plans, emphasize the following elements:

1. Encouragement of self-initiated vocal play as an appropriate form of self-stimulation.
2. Encouragement of self-initiated vocal play as a pleasurable accompaniment to motor and quiet activities, providing it is not disturbing or distracting to others.

Specific Objective N

The student babbles or vocalizes two or more different syllables. (*Note*: See Specific Objective K. This time, however, encourage the vocalization of two or more syllables in which the consonant and/or vowel elements are different, such as "ta-kuh," "bah-me," "la-de-dah," and "ma-moo." You do not have to deal only with nonsense syllables; po-ny, ra-di-o, and other real words can also be part of the fun without attempting to build comprehension, except incidentally.)

Specific Objective O

The student vocalizes displeasure when a favorite or needed object is withdrawn.

Functional Settings and Suggested Instructional Activities

School

1. Conduct the role plays in Home Activities 1 and 2, making them appropriate to the classroom setting.
2. Reward a nonverbal peer for appropriately voicing his/her displeasure when a needed or favorite object is withdrawn. Show your displeasure if the peer fails to react or expresses anger or in some other way overreacts.

Home

1. Ask the parents to role play a situation in which a friend or a member of the household removes an object with which they are playing. Tell her to model displeasure or annoyance without expressing anger.
2. Ask the parents to role play another situation in which a needed object (for a household project) is withdrawn by somebody. Tell them to model displeasure without overreacting or expressing anger.

Functional Emphases In designing your own instructional activities and plans, emphasize the following elements:

1. Awareness that vocal tones are important ways of communicating.
2. Establishment of congruence of vocal tones (paralanguage) with body language (kinesics).

Specific Objective P

The student vocalizes pleasure or satisfaction upon obtaining a desired or favorite object.

Functional Settings and Suggested Instructional Activities

School

1. See Home Activities 1 and 2. Modify them for the classroom setting.
2. Reward the student for independently vocalizing pleasure. Tell him that his vocal tone and facial expression told you he was pleased and that people do not always need to use words to communicate their feelings.

Home

1. Ask the parents to role play a situation in which they are given a favorite object (e.g., flowers) by a friend or family. Tell them to voice their pleasure.
2. Ask the parents to stage a scene in which they ask a friend or family member for a desired object and that person follows through. Tell them to model vocalizing their pleasure.

Functional Emphases In designing your own instructional activities and plans, emphasize the following elements:

1. Awareness that vocal tones are important ways of communicating.
2. Establishment of congruence of vocal tones (paralanguage) with body language (kinesics).

Specific Objective Q

The student responds differentially to friendly and angry talking.

Functional Settings and Suggested Instructional Activities

School

1. Encourage the student to join them when classmates are engaged in talking. Demonstrate effective joining skills.
2. Discourage the student from joining classmates who are quarreling.

Home

1. Ask the parents to role play a scene in which they engage in a friendly exchange with a family member or friend. Tell them to indicate to the child that she can join them if she wishes.
2. Tell the parents that if it doesn't frighten the child and if it is clear that it is only make-believe, to engage in an angry exchange with a family member or friend. Tell them to indicate to the child that he is to stay away from the quarrel.

Functional Emphases In designing your own instructional activities and plans, emphasize the following elements:

1. Discrimination of vocal affect.
2. Awareness of when to approach people and when to stay away or retreat.
3. Comprehension and practice of appropriate joining skills.

Specific Objective R

The student initiates vocal play with people.

Functional Settings and Suggested Instructional Activities

School

1. See Home Activities 1 and 2 below. Modify them for the classroom.
2. Create play situations that encourage the student to initiate vocal play with his peers and you (e.g., play a game that requires the student to ask for things). Accept any vocalization attempts. Later on, refine the game so that a specific sound or sound combination is required.

Home

1. Ask the parents to hold conversations with family members and/or friends with the child in the midst of the group. Tell them to include him in the exchange even if it is just for a smile, a head nod, or a gesture. Tell them that if he vocalizes, they should show their happiness and pleasure as graphically as possible.
2. Ask the parents to reward siblings and any of the child's playmates if they initiate vocal play in appropriate ways and at appropriate times.

Functional Emphases In designing your own instructional activities and plans, emphasize the following elements:

1. Encouragement of vocal play initiated by the student in appropriate ways and at appropriate times.
2. Refinement of vocal play so that the student begins to acquire increasing control over his production of individual sounds and sound patterns.

Specific Objective S

The student vocalizes to music.

Functional Settings and Suggested Instructional Activities

School

1. Discover a song or songs that the student enjoys listening to. Play them during rest periods. Quietly vocalize to these melodies. Encourage the student to join you in the song.
2. Role play putting a child (doll or puppet) to sleep. Sing it a lullaby. Encourage the student to be the "daddy" and sing his baby to sleep.

Home

1. Ask the parents to play background music to which they hum, vocalize, and/or sing along. Tell them to encourage the child to join in the "song fest."
2. Tell the parents to encourage family members and/or friends to join in a group or community sing at gatherings and parties. Tell them to include him in the activity and to encourage his participation.

Functional Emphases In designing your own instructional activities and plans, emphasize the following elements:

1. Appreciation for the relaxing effect of vocalizing to music.
2. Awareness of the enjoyment and leisure-time benefits of group singing.

Specific Objective T

The student discriminates among the sounds of his language, including individual sounds and blends, by articulating diverse consonant-vowel, vowel-consonant, and consonant-vowel-consonant combinations.

Functional Settings and Suggested Instructional Activities

School

1. During the student's quiet times, play tapes of various consonant-vowel combinations. Make these tapes of yourself, the student's favorite person, or peers.
2. Engage in a variety of play activities with the student. As you and she play, vocalize various consonant-vowel combinations. Encourage the student to imitate your behavior. Reward self-initiated sounds.
3. Engage the student in games and songs in which he must imitate such motor activities as clapping hands, stamping feet, and waving arms. Gradually lead up to motor activities involving the peripheral speech mechanism, activities such as opening and closing the mouth and sticking the tongue out and back in. Finally, say various consonant-vowel combinations.
4. Hold the hand of the student while you vocalize various consonant-vowel combinations. Encourage imitation. The gentle touch of another person may stimulate vocalization.
5. Play simple tunes on the piano, autoharp, or zither, and play recordings of simple tunes without words. Vocalize consonant-vowel combinations as you follow the melody. Encourage the student to vocalize as he sings along. Follow up by asking him to lead the sing-along.

Home

1. Tell the parents to vocalize the various consonant-vowel combinations during play. Tell them to encourage the child to listen and look at them as they make the various sound patterns. Tell them to reward him for imitating these patterns.

Tell them to reward him especially when he makes these sounds without imitation.

2. Tell the parents to encourage the child who is having difficulty imitating particular sound patterns to look in the mirror as they make the sound patterns. Tell them to give him clues to what he must do with his lips, tongue, jaw, and teeth to make the sounds. Tell them to give him further help by putting his hands on their face, nose, and throat as appropriate to the sound or sounds.

Functional Emphases In designing your own instructional activities and plans, emphasize the following elements:

1. Articulation of all the possible consonant or consonant blend + vowel patterns of the language.
2. Articulation of all the possible vowel + consonant or consonant blend patterns of the language.
3. Articulation of all the possible consonant or consonant blend + vowel + consonant or consonant blend patterns of the language.
4. Facilitation of auditory discrimination and sound recalling skill in the echoing of words and phrases (see Specific Objectives U and V).

Specific Objective U

The student echoes words and phrases in songs and rhymes.

Functional Settings and Suggested Instructional Activities

School

1. Sing nursery rhymes that appeal to the student. Clap hands in time to the music. Assist the student in clapping his hands. Also, hold his hands and sway to the music. After you have repeated a rhyme several times, stop at the end of the line that contains the rhyming word. Wait for the student to supply it:

   Mary had a little lamb
   Its fleece was white as snow
   And everywhere that Mary went
   The lamb was sure to ____ .

   Indicate by pointing to the student that he should finish the rhyme. Other ways of indicating this are to tap his hand, stop the clapping or swaying, and then look at him with anticipation. Reward him for filling in the rhyming words. Repeat the activity often, using a variety of rhymes.
2. Sing currently popular commercials and proceed as outlined in Activity 1. Reward the student for filling in the missing words.
3. Sing currently popular songs that have simple rhyme, melodic, and rhythmic patterns. Proceed as outlined in Activity 1. Reward the student for filling in the missing words.

Home

1. Ask the parents to sing simple rhymes to the child. Tell them to accompany the singing with dancing. Dancing and swaying to the music will encourage participation. Tell the parents to stop the dancing and singing at the end of a rhyming pattern while encouraging him to fill in the missing words before they resume the dancing and singing.
2. Tell the parents to engage in hand clapping and other finger-play poems and songs. Tell them to repeat these activities until the child begins to sing along and/or fills in missing words.

Functional Emphases In designing your own instructional activities and plans, emphasize the following elements:

1. Facilitation of imitation skills in diverse psychomotor activities.
2. Facilitation of imitation skills as related to the movements involved in speech production.
3. Development of leisure-time interests in singing and movement activities.

Specific Objective V

The student echoes individual words and phrases spoken by others.

Functional Settings and Suggested Instructional Activities

School

1. Every day, when you first see the student, repeat the same greeting, "Good morning. Good morning. How are you today?" When the student leaves, repeat the same farewell, "So long. So long for now. I will see you tomorrow."
2. For every possible occasion, establish a particular word, phrase, or sentence with which the student can associate a specific situation or act.

Home

1. Tell the parents to engage in a repetitive act while repeating a preselected phrase or sentence over and over. For example, if they play a game of rolling a ball back and forth, they should repeat, "I am rolling the ball."
2. Tell the parents that whenever they engage in behavior that is carried on regularly, they should repeat a preselected phrase or sentence each time the activity takes place. For example, every day, as they assist their child in dressing, they should say, "Put on the shoes," or "On go the shoes."

Functional Emphases In designing your own instructional activities and plans, emphasize the following elements:

1. Facilitation of imitation skills related to speech production.
2. Encouragement of the use of those words he frequently echoes in meaningful communication.

General Objective II

The student will respond to spoken language in a manner that allows him to function optimally.

Specific Objectives

The student:

A. looks at an object that has been named.
B. looks at a person who has been named.
C. turns to and/or looks at the speaker when his name is called.
D. terminates a behavior when told "No!"
E. carries out the command "Show me the ________" by pointing to the object named.
F. carries out the command "Give me the ________" and "Get the ________" by giving or getting the object named.
G. points in response to the simple question "Where is the (object)?" when objects are named.
H. points in response to the simple question "Where is the (object)?" when pictures pictures of objects are named.
I. points to the main parts of his face and body upon request.
J. carries out simple one-part commands or directions containing verbs.
K. carries out simple one-part commands or directions containing adjectives that denote differences in visual, auditory, gustatory, proprioceptive, and tactile qualities.
L. carries out simple one-part commands or directions containing adjectives that denote color, shape, space, time, distance, and seriation.
M. carries out simple one-part commands or directions containing comparative and superlative adjectives.
N. carries out simple one-part commands or directions containing adverbs that end in *ly*.
O. carries out simple one-part commands or directions containing situation-bound definite adverbs ("here" and "there") and situation-bound indefinite adverbs ("anyplace" and "somewhere").
P. carries out simple one-part commands or directions containing prepositions that denote specific locations or times.
Q. carries out simple one-part commands or directions containing indefinite and instrumental prepositions.
R. carries out simple one-part commands or directions containing personal pronouns.
S. carries out simple one-part commands or directions containing demonstrative pronouns ("this," "that," "these," and "those").

T. carries out a sequence of two or more commands or directions.
U. indicates in some way the answer to function questions (e.g., "Which one do you cut with?").
V. indicates in some way comprehension of the details of simple stories.
W. carries out commands or directions involving the comprehension of number words.
X. responds differentially to common words that have multiple meanings.
Y. carries out commands or directions involving his left and right side (e.g., "Show me your left ________!").
Z. carries out directional commands (e.g., "Put your left hand on your right shoulder!").
AA. carries out commands and directions containing idiomatic, colloquial, and figurative speech.

Specific Objective A

The student looks at an object that has been named.

Functional Settings and Suggested Instructional Activities

School

1. Determine what objects are of interest to the student. Find out what objects he plays with, what objects he looks at for a long time, and what objects attract his attention when they come into his view or when he hears them. Once you have catalogued these objects, set up a program in which you say an object's name simultaneously with its presentation. For example, turn on the light. When the student looks at the light, say, "Light." Repetition of this behavior will help the student to make the connection between the spoken word and the object it represents.
2. Place a favorite food in front of the student and simultaneously say its name. Gently cover his eyes and then say the name again. Remove your hand from his eyes and reward the student by giving him the food if he looks at it. Attempt to establish this pattern: I say the name, you look, and then you get the reward.
3. Using favorite toys, repeat the activity described in Activity 2. Once you have established the pattern of the student looking at the object when he hears the word, place two favorite objects in front of him. Begin by showing each object in turn to the student. As you hold up each object, say its name. Pause and once again say its name. Hand the object to the student. Encourage him to touch and to manipulate the object. As he is manipulating the object, point to it once or twice and then repeat its name. Then take the object back and place it on a table or desk out of the student's reach. Next, hold up the other object and proceed as you did with the first object. Gently cover the student's eyes with your hand and say the name of one of the objects. If the student looks at the object named, reward him by giving him the object to hold. If the student does not look at either object, gently turn his head and eyes so

that he sees the object named; or hold the object directly in his line of vision and say its name while nodding "Yes." If, on the other hand, the student looks at the unnamed object, shake your head "No" and turn his eyes and head so that he sees the correct object. Continue in this way until the student looks at the named object 100% of the time.

4. Once the student successfully responds when given the choice of two objects, introduce a new object so that she must now look at one of three objects named. You may increase the number to four, five, six, or more, depending upon the student's skills and needs.
5. Repeat the activities described in Activity 3. This time, cover the objects after they have been thoroughly introduced. Reward the student if he looks at the location where the object is, despite the fact that it is under cover. Remove the cover and tell him to play with the object that has been named.
6. Continue introducing new objects, especially those that are commonly found in the student's environment.

Home

1. Ask the parents to surround the child with the names of objects found in the home. Tell them to say each object's name as they handle or point to it. Tell them to turn the child's head to look at the object, if necessary, or hold it directly in his line of vision. Tell them to reward him for looking at the object that has been named.
2. Ask the parents to play a game with the child in which they place several objects in front of him and then pretend they do not know where one of the objects is by saying, "Where is the apple? Where did it go? It was here a minute ago!" These words must be said with the appropriate vocal inflections, shaking of the head, shrugging of the shoulders, and other relevant body-language cues. Tell the parents to thank the child if he helps them find the object by looking at it.

Functional Emphases In designing your own instructional activities and plans, emphasize the following elements:

1. Establishment of a large comprehension vocabulary, depending on the most frequently occurring objects and those that are of greatest interest to the student.
2. Use of the eyes to indicate a desired object as an expressive sequel to oral comprehension.

Specific Objective B

The student looks at a person who has been named.

Functional Settings and Suggested Instructional Activities

School

1. Identify the people who are favorites of the student. Determine the name, nickname, or relationship label by which each one is generally called. Introduce each person to the student by saying his or her name. Do not use carrier phrases such as "This is __________ ." Say the person's name and reward the student for looking at the person named.
2. Introduce two persons to the student. Reward her for looking at the person who has been named. Locate these two people at opposite sides of the room so that the student's responses are more easily evaluated. Say the name of one of the persons. When the student looks at the person who has been named, that person should react to the student's recognition with great enthusiasm.
3. Take pictures of the people you are introducing to the student. Display these pictures in prominent places so that he can look at them freely. Also say the names of persons in these pictures and reward the student if he looks at the right photograph.

Home

1. Ask the parents to introduce each person in the household by either his/her first name (siblings) or by his/her relationship to the child (Daddy, Grandpa, or Aunt Helen). Tell them to play the game of "Where is __________?" Tell them to reward the child if he looks at the person who has been named.
2. Ask the parents to repeat Activity 1, this time with relatives and friends who are frequent visitors to the home. With adult visitors, tell them to use "Mr.," "Mrs.," "Ms.," or "Miss" as appropriate.

Functional Emphases In designing your own instructional activities and plans, emphasize the following elements:

1. Use of the eyes to indicate that he wishes the attention of a favorite person as an expressive sequel to oral comprehension.
2. Comprehension of relationship words as well as names, (e.g., the word "brother" for male siblings and the word "sister" for female ones).

Specific Objective C

The student turns to and/or looks at the speaker when his name is called.

Functional Settings and Suggested Instructional Activities

School

1. When the student is engaged in an activity, approach him and call his name. If he fails to respond, lift his head and turn it in your direction. While the student is facing you, call his name again, point to him, and smile.
2. Show the student a favorite object and then move away. Call his name a few moments later. If he turns and looks at you, reward him with the object. Make

the task more difficult by calling out the names of peers and other individuals. If the student responds to the name of someone else, say, "No!" Repeat his name and praise him for responding to it.

3. Ask peers with good speech to gain the student's attention by calling his name. Make sure each person calls the student by the same name. Nicknames and middle names used in addition to the student's first name may unnecessarily confuse him.
4. Include the student in a small group activity in which the group takes turns performing certain tasks such as jumping, clapping hands, and hopping. Make sure that the student is capable of performing the task. Explain that each person should take his turn when his name is called. The other participants in the group activity should be capable of responding to their names.
5. Sing an action song (e.g., "The Eensy Weensy Spider") or act out a finger play or action poem (e.g., "There Was a Little Turtle"). Ask the student to imitate your movements and gestures after his name is called.

Home

1. Ask the parents to refrain from using a nickname for the child since it might be confusing later when he is called by his correct name in school and other settings. Tell them to use his correct name whenever they seek his attention.
2. Ask the parents to play a game with the child and other members of the household or visitors in which each person takes a turn only when her name is called.

Functional Emphases In designing your own instructional activities and plans, emphasize the following elements:

1. Differentiation of the student's name from other words commonly used in the home and classroom.
2. Identification of the student's photograph from photographs of others and association of his name with the photograph.
3. Identification of a life-size drawing of the student and association of his name with that drawing.

Specific Objective D

The student terminates a behavior when told "No."

Functional Settings and Suggested Instructional Activities

School

1. Place several objects in front of the student. Name one of the objects and ask him to show it to you (by pointing) or to give it to you. If he selects the wrong object or engages in the wrong activity, say, "No!" while simultaneously stopping the student's movement. Then help the student select the right object

or activity. At first, while you are saying "No!" simultaneously shake your head and finger. Gradually reduce the gesture and body-language clues until the student responds to the "No!" alone.
2. Whenever the student or one of his peers engages in a destructive or disruptive behavior, indicate your displeasure by saying "No!" and restrain him from continuing the behavior.
3. Whenever the student is involved in an inappropriate activity, say "No!" Reward him for stopping the behavior and assist him in substituting a more appropriate behavior.

Home

1. Ask the parents to use the word "No" whenever the child is behaving inappropriately. Tell them to take their time in showing their displeasure vocally and facially. Tell them to reward him whenever he discontinues an activity in response to the "No."
2. Ask the parents to demonstrate that an area is forbidden or off limits (e.g., the door leading to the basement) by using the word "No" with its accompanying facial expression, shaking of the head, and warning shake of the finger.

Functional Emphases In designing your own instructional activities and plans, emphasize the following elements:

1. Termination of undesirable behaviors.
2. Development of an appropriate response to a "No" when the student is not looking at the speaker.
3. Substitution of appropriate behaviors in response to the "No" signal.
4. Identification of unsafe objects, areas, and behaviors.

Specific Objective E

The student carries out the command "Show me the ________" by pointing to the object named.

Functional Settings and Suggested Instructional Activities

School

1. Take the objects with which the student has already worked (see Specific Objective A, School Activities 1 through 6) and place them in front of the student. Pick up her hand and form it into the pointing gesture (see Chapter 2). Then hold her hand so that the pointing position is maintained. Next, say the name of one of the objects and point to it. Repeat this several times, making sure that you show sufficient enthusiasm when the student's pointing finger touches or approaches the object named. Continue in this way until the student is able to point without assistance.

2. Place your desk and chair next to the student's desk and chair. Put a number of objects on your table and duplicates on the student's table. Name one of the objects and point to it on your table. Encourage the student to imitate your behavior.
3. Take the student on a walk around the classroom. Do this daily until he is able to point to the main pieces of furniture, equipment, and accessories in response to the command "Show me the ________ !"

Home and Community

1. Ask the parents to take the child on a tour of the house or apartment. Tell them to do this daily until the child is able to point to or gesture in the direction of objects, furniture, equipment, and accessories in response to the command "Show me the ________ !"
2. Ask the parents to place several small objects on a table in front of the child. Tell them to practice with the child identifying each of the objects in response to the command "Show me the ________ !" Tell them gradually to expand the child's repertoire, beginning with familiar objects.
3. Take the student on a walk or sightseeing trip in his community. Do this frequently until the student is able to point out the major attractions in response to the command "Show me the ________ !"

Functional Emphases In designing your own instructional activities and plans, emphasize the following elements:

1. Extension of the pointing gesture to expressive usage to obtain desired objects, at first through gesture and then through speech.
2. Development of an extensive oral comprehension vocabulary as a precursor of expressive language usage.

Specific Objective F

The student carries out the command "Give me the ________ " and "Get the ________ " by giving or getting the object named.

Functional Settings and Suggested Instructional Activities

School

1. Engage in a cooperative activity such as making a mural. Ask the student to give you such needed equipment as scissors, a paintbrush, or a crayon.
2. Play the game of "Barter" (i.e., "If I give you my car, will you give me your wagon?"). Reward the student for giving you the requested object.

Functional Emphases In designing your own instructional activities and plans, emphasize the following elements:

1. Development of a broad oral comprehension vocabulary, starting with familiar objects.
2. Development of oral comprehension vocabulary as a first step in facilitating oral expressive usage.

Specific Objective G

The student points in response to the simple question "Where is the (object)?" when objects are named.

Functional Settings and Suggested Instructional Activities

School

1. Give the student objects to hide somewhere in the room. Once he has hidden the objects, search for them. Pretend not to find them and to give up. Then ask him the "where" question. When he leads you to the hiding place, praise him for remembering where he hid the objects and for hiding them so well.
2. Take the student for a walk or sightseeing tour around the classroom. Do this daily until the student is able to point to the main pieces of furniture, equipment, and accessories in response to the question "Where is the ________?"
3. Sing the song "Where is Thumbkin?"

Home and Community

1. Ask the parents to place several familiar objects in front of the child. Tell them to ask the "where" question and, if she fails to respond, to help her point to the object named.
2. Ask the parents to play a game of "Treasure Hunt." In this version, however, they should hide the objects so that he can see where they are hiding them. Tell them to ask him the "where" question. If he points to the spot where the object is hidden, tell them to join him in retrieving it.
3. Take the student for a walk or sightseeing trip in his community. Do this frequently until the student is able to point out the major attractions in response to the question "Where is the ________?"

Functional Emphases In designing your own instructional activities and plans, emphasize the following elements:

1. Development of a broad oral language comprehension vocabulary.
2. Identification of objects as a precursor of their use in oral expression and in the expression of the "where" question.

Specific Objective H

The student points in response to the simple question "Where is the (object)?" when pictures of objects are named.

Functional Settings and Suggested Instructional Activities

School

1. Play a matching game. This game involves matching an actual object to a picture of the object. At first, exact duplicates or actual photographs of the objects should be used. Gradually increase the dissimilarity of the picture to the object until the student can match pictures to objects that are markedly dissimilar but still represent a match (e.g., different colors of blocks, different styles of chairs, or different models of cars).
2. Place pictures of several familiar objects on a table in front of the student. Ask the question "Where is the ________ ?" If the student responds, reward her. If not, help her point to the picture of the object named.

Home

1. Ask the parents to read children's dictionaries and simple storybooks with interesting and colorful photographs. Tell them to name each object and ask the child to point to it. Tell them to follow up with the "where" question.
2. If the child is able to identify photographs, ask the parents to read simple storybooks and children's dictionaries with interesting and clear illustrations. Tell them to name each object and ask the child to point to it. Tell them to follow up with the "where" question.

Functional Emphases In designing your own instructional activities and plans, emphasize the following elements:

1. Association of photographs with objects they depict.
2. Association of illustrations with objects they depict, including color illustrations, sketches, and drawings with missing elements requiring visual closure.

Specific Objective I

The student points to the main parts of his face and body upon request.

Functional Settings and Suggested Instructional Activities

School

1. Play the game "Simon Says," in which the student is asked to show or point to his feet, arms, legs, hands, fingers, nose, ears, eyes, and mouth.
2. Show the student mannequins, asking him to point to a part of the body or face on the mannequin and then himself. Repeat using photographs and drawings.

Home

1. Ask the parents to sit the child in front of a mirror and point out the eyes, ears, nose, mouth, and hair.

2. Ask the parents to point out their arms, hands, fingers, stomach, legs, and feet.

Functional Emphases In designing your own instructional activities and plans, emphasize the following elements:

1. Comprehension of the major parts of the face and body.
2. Comprehension of the other parts of the face (e.g., eyebrows, eyelashes, forehead, cheeks, chin, and jaw).
3. Comprehension of other parts of the body (e.g., ankles, wrists, elbows, chest, waist, hips, and shoulders).
4. Comprehension of the appropriate words for the genitals.

Specific Objective J

The student carries out simple one-part commands or directions containing verbs.

Functional Settings and Suggested Instructional Activities

School

1. Take an inventory of the student's fine and gross motor skills (see Volume I, Fine and Gross Motor Skills). Once you have determined what motor behaviors the student can perform, incorporate them into one-part commands like (a) "Jump up and down!" (b) "Clap your hands!" (c) "Roll over!" (d) "Close the door!" and (e) "Pick up the pencil!"
2. Use these commands as part of your program for developing gross motor and/or fine motor skills (see Volume I, Fine and Gross Motor Skills for additional activities).
3. Demonstrate a motor behavior, telling the student what you are doing as you do it (e.g., "I am touching my toes."). Once the student demonstrates the ability to perform a specific behavior, issue the command (e.g., "Touch your toes!") and assist the student in complying with it. At first, join him in carrying out the command. After a while, however, indicate that he is to carry out the command by himself.
4. During a small group activity, give a separate command to the student and each of her peers. Call the student's name and follow it with a command. Reward each participant for carrying out the command given.
5. Sing and act out songs such as "If You're Happy and You Know It" and "Row, Row, Row Your Boat." These action songs all involve commands that the student is expected to carry out. (*Note*: For the student with minimal motor skills, it will be necessary for you to modify the above activities so that he can demonstrate his comprehension of the command in an alternate way. Perhaps you can issue the command to a peer. If the peer carries it out correctly, the student could indicate his approval in some way. Another way might involve the use of pictures of someone performing the activity. In this case, the student would point or look at a picture that depicts the command.

Home

1. Tell the parents to ask the child to perform, during play activities, those motor activities he is capable of performing (e.g., "Drive the car," "Rock the baby," "Clap your hands," and "Put the bead on the string.").
2. Tell the parent to ask the child to perform those functional household tasks he is capable of performing (e.g., "Wipe the table," "Pick up the paper," and "Put the pot away.").
3. Tell the parent to ask the child to perform those self-care skills he is capable of performing (e.g., "Wash your hands," "Blow your nose," "Button your shirt," and "Tie your shoes.").

Functional Emphases In designing your own instructional activities and plans, emphasize the following elements:

1. Development of a broad comprehension vocabulary of action verbs, especially those that are commonly used.
2. Utilization of oral language comprehension activities as a means of stimulating speech.

Specific Objective K

The student carries out simple one-part commands or directions containing adjectives that denote differences in visual, auditory, gustatory, proprioceptive, and tactile qualities.

Functional Settings and Suggested Instructional Activities

School

1. Give the student two toy cars of different sizes to play with. After he has played with these toys, pick up the bigger car. Say, "This is a big car." Immediately place it next to the small car and show the student how much bigger the first car is by using your hands. Repeat your statement while making the size gesture. Put the car down and ask the student to give you the big car. Reward him for picking up and giving you the correct car. After continued success with this activity, provide the student with several pairs of familiar objects. Repeat the activity, each time asking for the big one of the pair. Once the student identifies the bigger object with a high degree of accuracy, repeat the procedure, this time picking up the small one. Say, "This is a small car." Immediately place it next to the big car and show the student the difference in size by using a size gesture. Put the car down and ask the student to give you the small car. Reward him for picking up and giving you the small car. After continued success, provide the student with several pairs of familiar objects. Repeat the activity, each time asking for the small one of the pair. In the last stages, ask for the small or big one in random order. (*Note*: Because there are a number of synonyms for "small," you may want to use one, such

as "little." Whatever word you choose, use it exclusively until the student develops the concept of size.)

2. Make a happy face for the student (see Chapter 2). Say to him, "Make a happy face." Use a mirror if necessary. Once the student is able to make a happy face, make a sad face and ask him to imitate you. Once the student is able to imitate both a happy and a sad face, say to him, "Make a (happy, sad) face." Reward him for making the happy or sad face as commanded. Also use pictures of sad and happy faces, and say to the student, "Show me the (happy, sad) face."
3. Show the student a new toy. Place it next to an old and broken toy. Pick up the new toy and say, "This is a new car. The old one is broken." Point to the old broken car as you say the second part. Ask the student to give you the new car. Reward her. Collect other pairs of new/old objects. Ask the student to bring her new sneakers to you. When an old item is beyond repair or further use, ask her to throw the old item away.
4. Put a glass of iced tea and a cup of warm tea in front of the student. For safety reasons, do not use tea that is too hot. Touch the glass and say, "This is cold tea." Take the student's hand and touch it to the glass of iced tea. Say, "Feel how cold it is. The ice cubes help to make it cold." Say, "Ice cubes are cold. Tea with ice cubes in it feels cold!" Touch the glass again. Then touch the outside of the cup. Say, "This is hot tea. It feels hot." Take the student's hand and touch the cup of tea. Say, "It is hot tea. It feels hot. It is hot because I used hot water to make it." Show him how you heat water. Use chocolate milk as a variation. Ask the student for hot or cold chocolate milk. Reward him for touching or giving you the item requested. Remember to use safety precautions when handling hot liquids. When serving food to the student, ask him if he wants hot or cold versions of the same dish.
5. Give the student a piece of silk and say "smooth" as you feel it and urge him to feel it. Then give him a piece of sandpaper and say "rough" as you feel it and urge him to feel it. Next, ask him to give you something that feels smooth or rough.
6. Put both a thin and a thick slice of cheese in front of the student. Use the size gesture made with the thumb and index finger parallel at varying distances from each other. Make the gesture that represents thin and hold it next to the thin slice. Then ask the student to give you the thin slice of cheese. Show the student a variety of thin/thick pairs such as sandwiches, books, slices of bread, and luncheon meat. Ask the student to give you the thin one. Once he demonstrates that he understands the concept of thin, repeat the activity. This time, however, ask for the thick item. Once the student does this successfully, show him a variety of thin/thick objects. This time ask for a thick piece. In the last stages, repeat the activity asking for thin and thick slices in varying order.
7. Wet a wash cloth or towel slightly. Put it next to a dry one. Pick up the wet one, touch it, hand it to the student, and say, "Wet towel." Then pick up the dry one, touch it and say, "Dry towel." Hand it to the student and repeat, "Dry towel." Do this several times. Then gently cover the student's eyes and

place one of the towels in his hand. Reward him for saying whether the towel is wet or dry. Ask him to give you the wet one first and then the dry one. Repeat the activity, asking for the towels in varying order.

8. Show the student a noisemaker such as a drum. Beat the drum loudly and say, "Loud." Take his hand and assist him in making a loud noise on the drum. Repeat the word "loud." Then beat the drum softly and say, "Soft." Take the student's hands and assist him in making soft sounds. After sufficient practice, ask the student to make loud or soft sounds in varying order.
9. Give the student a grape or other sweet fruit and say "sweet" while showing facially that you enjoy eating it. Then take a piece of a lemon and show its sourness facially while repeating the word "sour." Ask the student to point to sweet and sour items.
10. Show the student a heavy and a light paperweight. Say the word "heavy" as you pick up the heavy one. Demonstrate its heaviness by the way you hold and move your hand and arm. Then pick up the light one. Next, ask the student to give you the light or heavy one. Practice.

Home

1. Explain to the parents the relationship of some adjectives to sensory differences in objects and things. Help them draw up pairs of adjectives that describe sensory qualities. For example:
   Visual: big-little, happy-sad, and long-short
   Auditory: loud-soft and high-low
   Gustatory: sweet-sour
   Proprioceptive: light-heavy
   Tactile: smooth-rough, cold-warm, and hard-soft
   Then tell them to provide the child with experiences in comparing objects at both ends of the scale (e.g., "Give me the big car. Now, give me the little car.").
2. Tell the parents to collect pictures that demonstrate different qualities. Tell them to ask the child to point to different parts of the picture (e.g., "Show me the thick sandwich!" and "Point to the happy person!").

Functional Emphases In designing your own instructional activities and plans, emphasize the following elements:

1. Differentiation of objects, people, and things by demonstrated qualities.
2. Comprehension of the comparative nature of adjectives (e.g., someone is tall because he/she is taller than a standard size, or a line is long because it is being compared to a nearby short line).

Specific Objective L

The student carries out simple one-part commands or directions containing adjectives that denote color, shape, space, time, distance, and seriation.

Functional Settings and Suggested Instructional Activities

School

1. Give the student several objects of the same primary color: red, blue, or yellow. Pick up each item and name it. Then pick up each item and say its color. After this, pick up each item once again and say its color followed by its name (e.g., red car).
2. Give the student the same items used in Activity 1. This time add several objects of another primary color. Assist the student in separating the objects by color into two groups. Pick up each item belonging to the group used in Activity 1 and call it by its color. Then pick up the items in the second group and, first, identify the object by name and, second, by color. Last, pick up each item and say its color followed by its name (e.g., blue car).
3. Place two similar objects in front of the student. One object should be the color used in Activity 1 and the other object the color used in Activity 2. Ask the student to give you the red car and then the blue car. Place two of several objects on the table in front of the student. Ask her to give you an item by its color designation.
4. If successful, add items of the third primary color. Introduce the last color as in Activities 1 through 3. Once this has been accomplished, ask the student to get for you and give to you objects of the different primary colors: blue, red, and yellow.
5. Introduce the secondary colors green, violet, and orange.
6. Introduce the colors brown, purple, and gray.
7. Introduce the special colors black and white.
8. Use food coloring and water. Drop food colors into the water. As the water becomes colored, enthusiastically say its color. Students particularly enjoy this activity.
9. Show the student a map of a stadium where sections are color-coded. Tell him to find his seats using color clues.
10. Play games that involve moving markers along colored paths. Assign the student a marker. Reward him for picking up the correct one.
11. Ask the student to give you a round, square, and triangular block. Place these blocks in a shape formboard.
12. Show the student a bookcase, file cabinet, refrigerator, closet with shelves, and furniture with drawers. For each of these items, point to the top shelf or drawer and say, "Top (shelf) (drawer)." Take the student to each of the objects and repeat "top (shelf) (drawer)." Once the student demonstrates that he can locate the top drawer or shelf, introduce, in the same way, the bottom drawer or shelf. Once he is able to locate the bottom drawer or shelf, ask him to point to the top shelf, put something on the bottom shelf, open the bottom drawer, and get something off a shelf. Ask him to point to the top and bottom buttons on his shirt.
13. Ask the student to place objects near to or far from places in the classroom.
14. Show the student pictures of morning and late scenes. Ask him to show you "Where is it early?" "Where is it late?"

15. Move a toy car slowly across the table. Say, "This is a slow car." Then move the toy car fast across the table. Now say, "This is a fast car." Then say, "Show me a fast car. Show me a slow car."

Home

1. Assist the parents in identifying these commonly used adjectives:
    Color: Primary (red, yellow, and blue); Secondary (green, violet, and orange)
    Shape: Round and square
    Space: Top, middle and bottom, deep and shallow
    Time: Fast and slow, early and late
    Distance: Near and far
    Seriation: First, second, third, and last

   Then tell them to provide the child with experiences involving these adjectives.
2. Tell the parents to collect photographs and pictures that demonstrate the adjectives worked on in Activity 1 above. Tell them to ask the child to point out the adjectives as demonstrated in the photographs and pictures.

Functional Emphases In designing your own instructional activities and plans, emphasize the following elements:

1. Development of a diverse comprehension vocabulary of adjectives that denote color, shape, space, time, distance, and seriation, especially as they relate to functioning in the home, school, and in the community, in both worker and consumer roles.
2. Stimulation of speech as a sequel to the development of oral language comprehension.

Specific Objective M

The student carries out simple one-part commands or directions containing comparative and superlative adjectives.

Functional Settings and Suggested Instructional Activities

School

1. Put two different-size books on the table and ask the student to give you the bigger and then the smaller one. Engage in this basic type of activity with common, everyday adjectives that form the comparative form by adding *er* to the root word.
2. Put three identical objects of different weights on the student's desk and ask him to give you the heaviest and then the lightest one. Engage in this basic type of activity with common, everyday adjectives that form the superlative by adding *est* to the root word.

Home

1. Tell the parents to work with those adjectives developed in Specific Objectives K and L. This time, tell them to use two objects that are similar except in one dimension. Tell them to ask the child to give them the bigger, heavier, smaller, or thinner one.
2. Tell the parents to work with those objectives developed in Specific Objectives K and L. This time, tell them to use three objects that are similar except in one dimension. Tell them to ask the child to give them the smallest, thickest, largest, and shortest one.

Functional Emphases In designing your own instructional activities and plans, emphasize the following elements:

1. Comprehension of as many adjectives as possible along with the understanding of the relativity of adjectival use and the clarity or specificity it gives to communication.
2. Stimulation of speech as a sequel to the development of oral language comprehension.

Specific Objective N

The student carries out simple one-part commands or directions containing adverbs that end in "ly."

Functional Settings and Suggested Instructional Activities

School

1. Ask the student to carry out various classroom activities (e.g., "Put your crayons away quickly" and "Walk slowly").
2. Play a variation of the game "Simon Says" in which the student is asked to march slowly or quickly, clap her hands softly or loudly, and stamp her feet heavily or lightly.

Home

1. Ask the parents to give instructions to the child as he performs self-care activities (e.g., "Wash your hands thoroughly or completely," and "Slow down," "Button your shirt slowly").
2. Ask the parents to give instructions to the child as he performs various household chores (e.g., "Be neat in making your bed. Do it neatly." "Be careful carrying the dish. Carry it carefully.").

Functional Emphases In designing your own instructional activities and plans, emphasize the following elements:

1. Comprehension of commonly used adverbs that refer to modifications in required behavior.
2. Stimulation of speech through the comprehension of oral language.

Specific Objective O

The student carries out simple one-part commands or directions containing situation-bound definite adverbs ("here" and "there") and situation-bound indefinite adverbs ("anyplace" and "somewhere").

Functional Settings and Suggested Instructional Activities

School

1. Show the student where things belong in the classroom. Then tell him to put it here or there, depending on the place's distance from you (e.g., "Put the book there." "Put it down here.").
2. Plan activities in which the student has a choice of places to put or do something (e.g., "Sit anywhere for your playtime activity." "Find somewhere to put it.").

Home

1. Ask the parents to give instructions to the child, specifying a definite place to put or do something.
2. Ask the parents to give instructions to the child, specifying that he can put or do something anyplace or somewhere, providing that it is an appropriate behavior.

Functional Emphases In designing your own instructional activities and plans, emphasize the following elements:

1. Comprehension of the spatial relationships that distinguish "here" from "there."
2. Comprehension of the difference between definite and indefinite situation-bound adverbs.
3. Development of speech as a sequel to the development of oral comprehension.

Specific Objective P

The student carries out simple one-part commands or directions containing prepositions that denote specific locations or times.

Functional Settings and Suggested Instructional Activities

School

1. Demonstrate putting an object in various positions relative to a stationary point (e.g., on the table, over the table, under the table, or in the table drawer), telling the student what you are doing as you do it. Ask the student to put an object in various positions relative to a stationary point. Practice.
2. Ask the student to put something in his pocket, in his desk drawer, in his bank, and in his closet. Practice.

3. Ask the student to put things away as part of tidying up his learning area. Ask him to put the broom in the closet, the books in the desk, his clothing in the wardrobe, and his crayons in the box.
4. Ask the student to put on various articles of clothing.
5. Ask the student to place various items such as packages of food, canned goods, and decorative and utilitarian items on shelves, on table tops, on furniture tops.
6. Ask the student to put the cover over the typewriter, to put the cover over the bird cage, to step over an obstacle, to jump over a stick, to hop over a line, to put his hands over his eyes or mouth, and to fly a toy plane over a building made of blocks.
7. During a small group activity, demonstrate the meaning of the preposition "to." Have a preselected toy for the student and each of his peers. Give each a toy to play with and say, "I am giving the car to Tom. I am giving the ball to Mary. I am giving the dog to Robert." Ask the student to give his object to a peer.
8. Ask the student to walk or to move his wheelchair to different parts of the room. Assist him, if necessary, in carrying out the command. Vary the commands. "Walk to the door, to the closet, or to the desk." "Jump" and "Skip" may be used if the student has the prerequisite skills. Remember to intersperse these commands with others involving prepositions and to include previous learning.
9. Give the student four different toys to play with. After he has played with them, take two of the toys and put them next to each other. Say, "I am putting the cowboy and the horse next to each other. You put the car and the truck next to each other." Reward the student for carrying out the commands. Put all four objects together again. This time, put the cowboy and horse next to each other again, but in the reverse order because next to can be on either side. Say, "I have put the horse next to the cowboy." Then rearrange them and say, "The horse and the cowboy are still next to each other." Then ask the student to put the car and truck next to each other. If he does, ask him to put them next to each other in a different way.
10. Ask the student to stand or to sit next to you or a peer, first on one side and then on the other.
11. Demonstrate the difference between "behind" and "in front of." Line the student up in front of a favorite peer. Say, "John is standing in front of James." Then reverse the position of the students and say, "James is now standing in front of John." Repeat this activity with another favorite peer.
12. Put various objects in a line (e.g., a toy car and a toy bus) and say, "The car is in front of the bus." Ask the student to put the bus in front of the car. Repeat this activity using a variety of objects. Once the student demonstrates that he can put objects in front of other objects, introduce the concept "behind" in the same way you introduced the concept "in front of." For instance, put the student in front of his friend James and say, "John is in front of his friend James, but James is behind John." Then ask John to stand behind James. If the student does well with this activity, review "next to," "in front of," and

"behind." Use different objects, and vary the position of the objects and people in relation to the student.

Home

1. Ask the parents to introduce various prepositions in relationship to household chores (e.g., "Put your underwear in the drawer," "Put your books on your desk," and "Put the bucket under the sink.").
2. Ask the parents to introduce various prepositions in relationship to self-care activities, (e.g., "Put your shirttail in your pants," "Put on your socks before you put on your shoes.").

Functional Emphases In designing your own instructional activities and plans, emphasize the following elements:

1. Comprehension of the antonym pairs of various spatial and temporal prepositions (in-out, on-off, up-down, above-below, over-under, and in front of-in back of).
2. Facilitation of speech as a sequel to the oral comprehension of prepositional modifiers.

Specific Objective Q

The student carries out simple one-part commands or directions containing indefinite and instrumental prepositions

Functional Settings and Suggested Instructional Activities

School

1. Demonstrate the concept of "near," "by," and "at." Then ask the student to carry out directions involving those prepositions (e.g., "Put it near the science table," "Place it at the door").
2. Demonstrate doing something with and without objects, things, and people. Then ask the student to carry out directions involving those prepositions (e.g., "Come to my desk without your notebook," "Come with Mary").

Home

1. Ask the parents to provide the child with experiences involving comprehending instructions involving putting things nearby or at someplace.
2. Ask the parents to provide the child with experiences involving the prepositions "with" and "without" (e.g., "Come without your umbrella," "Take your toy with you").

Functional Emphases In designing your own instructional activities and plans, emphasize the following elements:

1. Development of comprehension of a variety of prepositional modifiers.
2. Stimulation of speech as a sequel to oral language comprehension.

Specific Objective R

The student carries out simple one-part commands or directions containing personal pronouns.

Functional Settings and Suggested Instructional Activities

School

1. Place the student in a small group consisting of two peers—one male and one female. Give each student in the group a preselected toy. Say, "I am giving the car to Paul. I am giving it to him." Then say, "I am giving the ball to Mary. I am giving it to her." Repeat these statements several times. Then point to the male peer and say, "Him." Point to the female peer and say, "Her." Ask the student to give the toy to him and then to her. Practice these two pronouns using a variety of objects.
2. Place an object, such as a piece of chalk, in front of the student. Point to yourself and say, "Me." Then make the "Give me" gesture and say to the student, "Give me the piece of chalk." Reward the student if he does so.
3. Place a variety of objects (e.g., car, ball, and crayon) in front of a small group of students. Prepare a list of commands using the pronouns "him," "her," and "me." Then give the student and each of his peers a separate command such as "Give the car to him. Give the ball to her. Give the crayon to me."
4. Include the student in a small group of several peers, both male and female. Collect material or equipment belonging to the student and each of the peers. Say, "I am giving a book to her. I am giving a book to him." Next, touch the male peer and say, "Him." Touch the female peer and say, "Her." Touch both of them together and say, "Them." Say to the student, "Give the book to him. Give the book to her. Give the crayons to them." Reward the student when he does so.
5. Use the same group as above. This time, however, gather one item, such as an apple, for the student, his peers, and yourself. Give each person an apple and, as you are doing so, say, "I am giving an apple to him. I am giving an apple to her. I am giving an apple to you. I am taking an apple. It is for me. I gave an apple to each of us." Say to the student, "Give a napkin to each of us." Reward him. Practice, using a variety of objects.
6. Show the student one of his own belongings. Say, "This is John's hat. This is your hat." Then put in front of him another one of his possessions plus a possession of one of his peers. Say, "Pick up your sweater." Practice this activity with a variety of objects belonging to the student.
7. Show the student an object that belongs to you. Say, "This is Miss (name)'s book. It is my book." Put the book down and say, "This is my book. I want my book." Then gesture "Give me." Practice with several items belonging to you.

8. Show the student an object that belongs to a male peer. Say, "This is James' lunch box. It is his lunch box. Give James his lunch box." Practice with several different male peers, singly and in groups.
9. Show the student an object that belongs to a female peer. Say, "This is Mary's scarf. It is her scarf. Give Mary her scarf. Give it to her." Practice with several different female peers, singly and in groups.

Home

1. Explain the various forms of the seven personal pronouns: I, you, he, she, it, we, and they. Tell the parents to use each one in all its forms (e.g., "I own this book. It is my book. It is mine. Give it to me."). Tell them if there is a sibling in the house, they should practice in the sibling's presence (e.g., "This is Sally's hat. She owns the hat. It is her book. It is hers. Give it to her.").
2. Tell the parents to describe different occurrences: "It is raining." "They are playing ball." "We are having fun." "Our hands are dirty." "My feet are tired." "Her hat is pretty."

Functional Emphases In designing your own instructional activities and plans, emphasize the following elements:

1. Experience with all the forms of the personal pronouns (i.e., subjective, objective, possessive, and possessive-replacement).
2. Development of speech as a natural sequel to oral comprehension.

Specific Objective S

The student carries out simple one-part commands or directions containing demonstrative pronouns ("this," "that," "these," and "those").

Functional Settings and Suggested Instructional Activities

School

1. Demonstrate the spatial relationships involved in distinguishing between "this" and "that." Use materials and equipment found in the classroom.
2. Demonstrate the spatial and number relationships involved in distinguishing between "these" and "those." Use materials and equipment found in the classroom and in the school building.

Home

1. Ask the parents to provide the child with experiences with these pronouns in terms of their spatial relationships (e.g., "I have two pots. This one is near me. That one is there."). Tell them to relate "this" to the adverb "here" and "that" to the adverb "there."
2. Ask the parents to place several cans of food near them on a table and to say, "These cans have to be put away." Then tell them they should put the cans

in the closet and walk back to the table and then say, "Those cans will be used for dinner tomorrow." Then tell them to put some books on the table and some on the shelf and instruct the child to "put these books away and bring those books to me."

Functional Emphases In designing your own instructional activities and plans, emphasize the following elements:

1. Facilitation of oral expressive language skills as a sequel to the development of oral language comprehension.
2. Association of here with the words "this" and "these."
3. Association of there with the words "that" and "those."

Specific Objective T

The student carries out a sequence of two or more commands or directions.

Functional Settings and Suggested Instructional Activities

School

1. Play the "Teacher's Aide" game. Give the student two or more commands involving classroom chores and activities. After the student performs them, thank him for being a good helper or aide. Requests might include: "Please collect the books and put them on the top shelf of the bookcase."
2. Play a modified version of "Simon Says," using two-part commands.
3. Engage in calisthenics involving two activities performed one after the other (e.g., "Touch your shoulders and then touch the floor.").
4. After the student has successfully carried out a variety of two-part commands, introduce three-part commands.

Home

1. Ask the parents to review all types of simple one-part commands. Then tell them to continue by asking the child to carry out more complex single commands such as: "Open the big box." "Give the big box to Mary." "Give the little box to him." "Put the little box here." "Give him the yellow stars." "Give him the little red car." "Give him the big round blue beads."
2. Tell the parents to give the child two-part commands. Tell them to first demonstrate the actions involved and/or ask another member of the household to carry out the two-part command. Tell them to make sure the behaviors are within his motoric capabilities.

Functional Emphases In designing your own instructional activities and plans, emphasize the following elements:

1. Expansion of his comprehension repertoire to include increasingly more complex single commands as well as multiple-part commands.

2. Development of comprehension for multiple modifiers including several adjectives and a variety of prepositional and adverbial modifiers (e.g., "Walk slowly to the small red chair and pick up the heavy box next to it.").

Specific Objective U

The student indicates in some way the answer to function questions (e.g., "Which one do you cut with?").

Functional Settings and Suggested Instructional Activities

School

1. Demonstrate the various equipment and materials found in the classroom. Then ask the student to point to each item in response to a function question (such as "Which one do you use to write on the blackboard?" "Which one do I use to sharpen pencils?" "Which one do I use to fasten papers to the bulletin board?").
2. Show the student photographs and pictures of equipment and appliances used in a variety of settings (e.g., a typewriter, a drill press, an iron, a dishwasher, and a computer).

Home

1. Ask the parents to discuss the function of appliances and materials the child uses in his self-care activities (e.g., his toothbrush, comb, and hair dryer). Then tell them to ask him questions such as "Which one do you need to brush your teeth?" "Which one dries your hair?" "Which one do you use to untangle your hair?"
2. Ask the parents to discuss the function of appliances, utensils, and equipment found in the home (e.g., the stove, knives, a vacuum cleaner, and a towel). Then tell them to ask him questions such as "Which one do you cut with?" "Which one do you dry your face and hands with?" "Which one do you use to cook and bake?" "Which one do you use to clean the rugs?"

Functional Emphases In designing your own instructional activities and plans, emphasize the following elements:

1. Comprehension of the function of a wide variety of tools, utensils, apparatus, appliances, and equipment.
2. Facilitation of speech skills based upon the development of oral language comprehension.

Specific Objective V

The student indicates in some way comprehension of the details of simple stories.

Functional Settings and Suggested Instructional Activities

School

1. Read storybooks to the student and engage the student in various pantomimes and actions that illustrate the story (e.g., knocking on the table when a door is knocked on in a story).
2. Tell the student simple stories and carry out creative dramatic activities in which the story is acted out by you, the student, and several of his peers.

Home

1. Ask the parents to read simple stories to the child from picture books and to point out relevant illustrations at appropriate points in the story. Tell them to ask him to respond to pertinent questions about story details and relationships by pointing to pictures and indicating "Yes" or "No" in some way.
2. Ask the parents to tell the child simple stories. Then tell them to ask her questions that require "Yes" or "No" responses.

Functional Emphases In designing your own instructional activities and plans, emphasize the following elements:

1. Development of active listening skills in which the student participates in the telling/reading of a story and/or its retelling or enactment.
2. Facilitation of speech skills.
3. Exploration of the creative arts in relation to story telling.

Specific Objective W

The student carries out commands or directions involving the comprehension of number words.

Functional Settings and Suggested Instructional Activities

School

1. Ask the student to get a required number of paper drinking cups that need to be passed out to the class for a tooth brushing activity.
2. Carry out a cooking activity and ask the student to get you the required number of eggs, cups of milk, or teaspoons of salt.
3. Carry out a workshop activity in which the student is expected to count out a predetermined number of objects and place them in a container.

Home

1. Ask the parents to give the child directions that involve the child in household chores that require the comprehension of number words (e.g., "Get me two cans of corn from the closet," "Get three napkins," "Bring me three clothespins.").

2. Tell the parents to involve the child with quantity determinations, preferably up to five. Tell them to proceed to ten if at all possible. Tell them to show him how to use his fingers to show numbers up to ten.

Functional Emphases In designing your own instructional activities and plans, emphasize the following elements:

1. Development of one-to-one correspondence.
2. Facilitation of counting by twos, once meaningful counting by ones is accomplished.
3. Facilitation of associating spoken numbers with written numerals.

Specific Objective X

The student responds differentially to common words that have multiple meanings.

Functional Settings and Suggested Instructional Activities

School

1. Give the student experiences in which he must respond differentially to a word (e.g., "Show me the picture of someone building. Now show me a building." "Show me the picture of a light. Now show me the light color.").
2. Check basic word lists to determine which ones have multiple meanings. Use these words in classroom language activities.

Home

1. Ask the parents to provide the child with experience with words that have multiple meanings as in words such as "run" and "building," which are verbs as well as nouns.
2. Explain to the parents that words with multiple meanings have multiple listings in the dictionary. Give them a list of basic words that have multiple meanings and ask them to review the different meanings with the child.

Functional Emphases In designing your own instructional activities and plans, emphasize the following elements:

1. Comprehension of the multiple meaning of words from their semantic context.
2. Facilitation of speech as a sequel to oral language comprehension.

Specific Objective Y

The student carries out commands or directions involving his left and right side (e.g., "Show me your left ________ !").

Functional Settings and Suggested Instructional Activities

School

1. Sing and act out the song "Hokey Pokey."
2. Review the parts of the face. Work on the eyes and ears. Ask the student to point to his right eye and ear and then to his left eye and ear.

Home

1. Ask the parents to show the child where his preferred hand is (i.e., if he is left-handed, they should show him his left hand and say, "This is your left hand!"). Then tell them they should ask him to raise his left hand and stamp his left foot.
2. Tell the parents that once the child is able to identify her preferred hand and corresponding foot, they should work on the hand and foot of the other side.

Functional Emphases In designing your own instructional activities and plans, emphasize the following elements:

1. Identification of the right and left sides of his body.
2. Identification of the right and left side of his body when someone he is facing, as in a game, dance, or song, is identifying the right and left sides of his/her body.

Specific Objective Z

The student carries out directional commands (e.g., "Put your left hand on your right shoulder!").

Functional Settings and Suggested Instructional Activities

School

1. Give the student directions to a hidden treasure in the classroom that involve moving and turning in different directions.
2. Give the student directions to an important place in the school (e.g., "John, go to the principal's office. Turn right as you leave this room and walk to the end of the corridor. Turn left and go to the third door on your left.").

Home

1. Ask the parents to include in their directional games and commands involving movement in space (e.g., "Take three steps to your left, turn right, and walk straight ahead.").
2. Ask the parents to play "Simon Says" in which the child is expected, for example, to "Put his right hand on his left knee."

Functional Emphases In designing your own instructional activities and plans, emphasize the following elements:

1. Movement in space.

2. Use of gestures and pantomime skills in giving directions to others.
3. Facilitation of speech skills in which the student indicates directions to others.

Specific Objective AA

The student carries out commands and directions containing idiomatic, colloquial, and figurative speech.

Functional Settings and Suggested Instructional Activities

School

1. List some idiomatic expressions found in American English. Use them in your conversations and in your commands to the student.
2. Use figurative language such as similes, metaphors, personification, and hyperbole whenever appropriate in your conversations with the student. Use them in commands, if possible.
3. Show the student pictures of different situations that can be described using figurative speech (e.g., "That boy is really brave. He is as brave as a bull.").

Home

1. Discuss with the parents the problems that arise from idiomatic expressions. Ask them to use common idioms in their commands and explain their meaning to the child (e.g., Show him a picture of someone who is angry and say, "He is angry. He is going to hit the roof. Show me the angry man!").
2. Ask the parents to refrain from using colloquial speech unless it is currently in use by the child's peers and significant adults in his environment.

Functional Emphases In designing your own instructional activities and plans, emphasize the following elements:

1. Comprehension of a wide range of semantic transformations.
2. Facilitation of the usage of commonly used figurative speech in the student's communicative speech.

General Objective III

The student will speak in such a manner that his needs and thoughts are readily understood by listeners.

Specific Objectives

The student:

A. says a first word with meaning.
B. says the names of common objects.
C. answers in response to the question "What is this?" by naming the object.
D. indicates his wants and thoughts by using nouns (i.e., by naming a desired object).
E. identifies and names the actions of people by using verbs.
F. names the action capabilities of common objects and toys by using verbs.
G. uses adjectives to describe people, places, and things.
H. refers to himself by his first name (or nickname).
I. identifies and names objects when shown pictures of them.
J. asks for food and water (or another beverage) when desired.
K. combines two words in noun/verb combinations.
L. refers to others by their first name and/or by their familial relationship.
M. combines two words in adjective/noun combinations.
N. identifies and names the parts of his face and the principal parts of his body.
O. uses personal pronouns in his connected speech.
P. uses prepositions to describe the position and direction of people and things.
Q. uses pivot words such as *a*, *my*, and *that*.
R. indicates his wants and thoughts by using plural nouns.
S. indicates a desired amount by saying the numbers one through five.
T. uses the present progressive form ("ing") of verbs in his connected speech.
U. uses the past tense of regular verbs in his connected speech.
V. uses nouns in the possessive form in his connected speech.
W. uses the third person singular of verbs in his connected speech.
X. says several nursery rhymes or sings simple television or radio commercials.
Y. uses adverbs in his conversational speech.
Z. uses demonstrative pronouns to indicate specific objects.
AA. indicates his wants and thoughts by saying a variety of simple declarative sentences.
BB. asks questions beginning with "what," "where," "when," "whose," and "who."
CC. transforms kernel sentences (subject + verb + direct object) into questions and asks unsolicited questions.
DD. uses negative statements to communicate his disapproval or wish not to comply with a request.
EE. uses simple language courtesies.
FF. uses indefinite and negative pronouns.
GG. responds appropriately to questions beginning with the question markers "who," "what," "whose," "how," "where," and "how many."
HH. names the primary colors and uses them to describe objects.
II. identifies the time of day (i.e., day or night).
JJ. identifies and names objects in terms of their use.
KK. uses categorical nouns in his speech.
LL. says her age and the month and date of his birthday.
MM. says his home address and telephone number when appropriate.
NN. says the days of the week with meaning.

OO. says the date by giving the month and the day.
PP. describes pictures in detail, using a variety of sentences.
QQ. relates the details of stories told or read to him.
RR. relates experiences and describes activities.
SS. carries out simple conversations, including telephone conversations, on a one-to-one basis.
TT. participates in group conversations and discussions.
UU. indicates comparative relationships.
VV. asks "how" and "why" questions.
WW. uses compound structures and compound sentences in his speech.
XX. uses complex sentences in his speech.
YY. uses idiomatic and figurative expressions in his speech.
ZZ. speaks in the patterns of acceptable adult speech and does so with intelligible articulation.

Specific Objective A

The student says a first word with meaning.

Functional Settings and Suggested Instructional Activities

School

1. Observe the student carefully so that you can select one or more words having high emotional content for him that might become his first word/words. Select a word or words whose sounds are well established in his vocal play. If one or more of the words are objects, introduce the words in the following manner. Show the student the object and say its name. Tell the student to look at you and to listen to you as you say the name. Tell him to do what you are doing with your mouth and to say what you are saying. Give the student the object to touch and to manipulate. As he does so, repeat its name several times. Then pick up the object, feel it, manipulate it, and once again repeat its name. Offer it to the student and point to his mouth to indicate that he must make a sound. Use a peer (or teaching aide) who will say its name. Give the object to the peer who names it. If someone other than the student names the object, praise that person and allow him to play with it for awhile. Then ask the other person for the object by simply saying its name. Set up a pattern of name-it-and-get-it. After using this pattern of name-it-and-get-it, turn back to the student and offer him the object once again. If he attempts to speak, reward him. Introduce other objects of high interest in the same manner. Do this several times a day. Vary the activity by placing the object or objects on a shelf and saying to the student, "Tell me what you want." If the student points or gestures, say, "I know that you want something, but tell me with your mouth what you want." Arrange for an aide to come up at this point (when the student has not responded in speech) and to ask for the object. Gladly hand it over to the individual who asked for it. Then turn to the student and say, "I gave it to

him because he named it. If you want something, you have to name it." Then resume the pattern of name-it-and-get-it.

2. Show the student a desired object and then hide it. Look around the room in mock confusion, suddenly say the word, and pretend to discover the object. Hide it once again and encourage the student to say the word. If he does so, take the object from its hiding place and give it to him to hold or play with it.
3. If one of the selected words with high emotional content is the name of a favorite person, such as "Momma" or "Dadda," ask that person to join you in the learning area. Say that person's name and ask the person to reward you in some way. Encourage the student to say the person's name. If the student approximates or says the word, ask the favorite person to reward the student in some way.

Home

1. Ask the parents to show the child a favorite toy. Tell them to indicate in some way to him that if he wants to play with it, he has to say it. Tell them if there is a sibling or other person available they should ask the individual to say its name and then give the toy to him/her.
2. Ask the parents to show the child a favored snack or food. Tell them to say its name and take a piece. Tell them to then offer him the food and to tell him if he wants a taste, he has to say its name. Tell them to reward attempts and approximations as well as whole words.

Functional Emphases In designing your own instructional activities and plans, emphasize the following elements:

1. Stimulation of first words that have high interest and high emotional content.
2. Stimulation of first words that have functional utility in helping the student obtain desired objects.

Specific Objective B

The student says the name of common objects.

Repeat the activities in Specific Objective A until the individual uses several words meaningfully and functionally. Review and introduce new words as the individual demonstrates interest in specific objects and persons.

Specific Objective C

The student answers in response to the question "What is this?" by naming the object.

Functional Settings and Suggested Instructional Activities

School

1. Put objects that the student can name into a surprise box. Remove one object at a time and ask the question "What is this?" Reward the student for an appropriate response. If the student does not respond appropriately, say, "This is a ______." Repeat the activity.
2. Ask the student to close his eyes and to open his hand. Then place a familiar object in his hand and ask, "What is in your hand?" If the student is unable to name the object, say the name of the object a few times and repeat the activity.
3. Hide objects in your pockets and in the drawers of your desk. Play the part of a magician by pulling one object out at a time and asking the student, "What is this?" If the student is unable to name the object, say the name of the object a few times and repeat the activity.

Home and Community

1. Tell the parents to place familiar objects of high interest in front of the child and ask him, "What is this?" Tell them to reward him if he names the object. Tell them that if he fails to do so, they should ask a family member or friend to name the object and praise the individual. Then they should turn to the child and ask him the question "What is this?" once again and answer, "This is a ______." Tell them to repeat this exchange for each object displayed.
2. Tell the parents to take the child for a walk around the house. Tell them to point to different objects and ask him the question, "What is this?" Tell them to reward him for responding appropriately. If the student does not respond appropriately, tell them to say, "This is a ______" and to repeat the activity frequently.
3. Take the student on a trip in his community. Point to different objects and ask her the question "What is this?" Reward her for answering appropriately. If the student does not respond appropriately, say, "This is a ______." Repeat the activity.

Functional Emphases In designing your own instructional activities and plans, emphasize the following elements:

1. Identification of objects that the student is likely to name in functional situations.
2. Identification of objects in which the student is interested, has experience with, and that have emotional power.

Specific Objective D

The student indicates his wants and thoughts by using nouns (i.e., by naming a desired object).

Functional Settings and Suggested Instructional Activities

School

1. Place several nutritious treats or snacks in front of the student. Tell him he can have one of the snacks if he asks for it. Ask an aide or a peer who can speak if he wants something to eat. When he asks for the treat, give it to him. Encourage the student to take his turn and reward him with the treat. Repeat the activity often.
2. Frequently tell the student the things you want or need. Reward him for giving you what you requested. Then ask him what he wants. Encourage him to answer. Try to establish a pattern of ask and then receive.

Home and Community

1. Ask the parents to select several objects of high interest to the child. Tell them they should inform him that he may have one of the objects if he asks for it. Tell them to let you know what he/she wants to play with by saying its name. When that individual says a name, tell them to give him/her the object named. Tell them to encourage him to take his turn in asking for a toy. Tell them to repeat the activity often.
2. Take the student to a supermarket or grocery store. Tell him to tell you what he wants you to buy for a class activity.

Functional Emphases In designing your own instructional activities and plans, emphasize the following elements:

1. Provision of a substantial amount of experience with as many different objects and things as possible.
2. Development of a wide vocabulary of names for significant persons, places, and things.

Specific Objective E

The student identifies and names the actions of people by using verbs.

Functional Settings and Suggested Instructional Activities

School

1. Draw up a list of motor activities that you can easily perform in the classroom. Name the action as you demonstrate it. Perform each action several times. For example, repeatedly open and close a door in the room. Encourage the student to join in the action and in saying the action word.
2. Sing action songs such as "The Animal Fair." Encourage the student to join in the action and to sing the lyrics that describe the action.
3. Act out action poems and stories such as "The Turtle." Encourage the student to perform the actions and to recite the action words.
4. Schedule daily calisthenics. Encourage the student to join you in calling out the action words.

5. Encourage the student to play the leader in a game of "Simon Says" and to call out commands such as dance, jump, hop, skip, march, throw, and catch.
6. Collect a group of action pictures and shuffle them. Look at each one and use noun/verb combinations to describe the action. Shuffle the pictures again and ask the student to look at each one and to name its action.

Home

1. Ask the parents to perform an action such as standing up, sitting down, running, and jumping. Tell them to encourage the child to imitate the action. Tell them to repeat the action and say the appropriate verb simultaneously (e.g., saying "jump" as they jump). Tell them to do this several times and to add new actions as soon as the child has acquired a new verb. Tell them to point to the moving parts of their bodies if the action is small.
2. Tell the parents to vary Activity 1 by telling the child to say, "I am now going to pretend to open a door. Watch me as I do it." After they go through the pantomime, tell them to describe what one has to do with one's body to open the door. Tell them to encourage the child to imitate their actions.

Functional Emphases In designing your own instructional activities and plans, emphasize the following elements:

1. Development of an action verb vocabulary.
2. Identification of implied actions in photographs and pictures.

Specific Objective F

The student names the action capabilities of common objects and toys by using verbs.

Functional Settings and Suggested Instructional Activities

School

1. Engage in activities with objects that are found in the classroom while saying the appropriate word (e.g., "clean" while erasing or washing the chalkboard, "cut" while using scissors, and "paint" while using finger paints).
2. Engage in a wide variety of role plays involving actions that you name. Pantomime or actually carry out the actions (e.g., ironing clothes, sewing a button, and picking flowers).

Home

1. Ask the parents to pantomime or engage in actions that are typically engaged in within the home while saying the appropriate verb (e.g., "drink" while pretending to drink a beverage, "eat" while pretending to eat something, and "wash" when pantomiming washing their hands).

2. Ask the parents to pantomime or engage in actions with toys found in the home while saying the appropriate verb (e.g., "drive" while playing with a toy car and "turn" while playing with a top).

Functional Emphases In designing your own instructional activities and plans, emphasize the following elements:

1. Development of a large vocabulary of action verbs for common action capabilities.
2. Association of verbs with common nouns for objects found in the student's environment.

Specific Objective G

The student uses adjectives to describe people, places, and things.

Functional Settings and Suggested Instructional Activities

School

1. See Home Activities 1 and 2.
2. Give the student pairs of items and encourage him to name them, then examine them, and last identify a distinguishing quality. Start with the positive or more frequently identified attribute (i.e., happy before sad, big before small, old before new, heavy before light, and hot before cold).

Home

1. Once the child has begun to name common objects in his environment, ask the parents to begin to identify an interesting dimension of that object (e.g., "Doll—*pretty* doll," "Doggy—*nice* doggy," "Soup—*hot* soup," and "Car—*big* car").
2. Tell the parents that, whenever possible, they should introduce dimensions of things by presenting contrasting pairs (e.g., pantomime "Mommy—*sad* Mommy. Mommy is *sad*," followed by a contrasting pantomime, "Mommy—*happy* Mommy. Mommy is *happy*," and "Book—*heavy* book. Book is *heavy*," then "Book—*light* book. Book is *light*.").

Functional Emphases In designing your own instructional activities and plans, emphasize the following elements:

1. Comprehension of adjectival clarifiers.
2. Use of adjectives to specify particular objects desired.
3. Use of adjectives to describe facial expressions and other body language and feelings (e.g., sick, sleepy, tired, and hungry).

Specific Objective H

The student refers to himself by his first name (or nickname).

Functional Settings and Suggested Instructional Activities

School

1. Show the student pictures of himself, his family members, yourself, and other significant individuals in his environment. Then place these pictures face down on a desk. Turn each one over and refer to the person by name. When you turn over the picture of the student, pause and say his name. Repeat the activity; this time, ask the student to turn each one over until he comes to his own picture. When he does so, encourage him to refer to the picture by saying his name.
2. Show the student an article of clothing or a toy that belongs to him. Identify each object by its name and then put the student's name in front of it while saying the possessive form (e.g., "John's ________ ."). Collect objects that belong to the student and other objects that belong to a peer. Encourage the student to say his own name when he picks up a garment or a toy that belongs to him.
3. Play the "Introduction" game. Say, "Hello, my name is ________ . What is yours?" Encourage the student to respond by saying, "Hello, my name is ________ ."

Home

1. Ask the parents to sit in front of a mirror with the child. Tell them to point to themselves and say "Mommy" and *then* point to her and say her name. Tell them to then ask her to imitate them.
2. Tell the parents to show the child a family scrapbook. Tell them to name each person. Tell them to indicate to him that he is to point to his picture and say his name.

Functional Emphases In designing your own instructional activities and plans, emphasize the following elements:

1. Comprehension of his name when it is said by others.
2. Identification of his belongings.

Specific Objective I

The student identifies and names objects when shown pictures of them.

Functional Settings and Suggested Instructional Activities

School

1. Set up a "Treasure Chest" of favorite pictures for the student. Use a folding accordion file or a shoebox for storage. Add a picture each time he identifies and names one correctly.

2. Read aloud to the student from a picture storybook. At appropriate times during the story, point to a picture and encourage the student to name the picture before you continue reading the story.
3. Assist the student in making his very own scrapbook of pictures. As you assist him in choosing and pasting the pictures, encourage him to name the picture.
4. Show pictures on a screen with a filmstrip projector. Ask the student to name the pictures. Proceed only when the student has successfully named the object shown. If the student is unable to name the picture, say the name a few times and ask the student to repeat it. Repeat the activity.
5. Paste or draw pictures of familiar objects on Language Master cards and record the names of the objects on the card. As the card goes through the Language Master and names the picture, tell the student to repeat it.

Home

1. Ask the parents to make a list of nouns that the child says in his usual speaking patterns. Tell them to locate a corresponding picture for each of these objects. Tell them to make sure that these pictures are clear representations of the objects. Color pictures are preferable. Tell them to show him the familiar object and ask him to name it. Then tell them to show him the corresponding pictures, which he must match to each object. When he has matched all the pictures and objects, they should hold up each picture/object pair. First tell them to name the object and then the picture and encourage him to imitate their actions. Repeat the activity; this time, tell them to ask the student to name the picture first and then imitate him if he has named it correctly. Tell them to repeat the activity, using a variety of objects and pictures.
2. Tell the parents to show the child a scrapbook of pictures of familiar objects. Tell them to encourage him to turn one page at a time and that he can turn each page only if he names the picture correctly.

Functional Emphases In designing your own instructional activities and plans, emphasize the following elements:

1. Identification of pictures of objects, persons, and things that are commonly found in the student's environment.
2. Identification of pictures of objects, persons, and things that are not commonly found in the student's environment.

Specific Objective J

The student asks for food and water (or other beverage) when desired.

Functional Settings and Suggested Instructional Activities

School

1. Engage the student in planning classroom snacks. Encourage him in his participation by asking him to name desired foods.
2. Role play asking to be taken to a school water fountain. Ask the student to join you in the role play and to indicate when he really wants the water.

Home and Community

1. Ask the parents to encourage the child to ask for a drink of water when he is thirsty, overheated, or when he needs it to take medication.
2. Ask the parents to encourage the child to ask for snacks and parts of meals when she is hungry and when they are planning meals.
3. Take the student on an outing in which he can buy his lunch. Encourage him to tell you what he wants to order.
4. Take the student to a playground or park where he engages in strenuous exercise and play activities and is likely to ask for a drink. Tell him to tell you when he is thirsty and you will take him to a drinking fountain or to a refreshment stand for a cold drink.

Functional Emphases In designing your own instructional activities and plans, emphasize the following elements:

1. Expansion of this skill to include a wide variety of foods and beverages.
2. Expansion of this skill to include asking for all other basic materials, including articles of clothing and grooming articles.

Specific Objective K

The student combines two words in noun/verb combinations.

Functional Settings and Suggested Instructional Activities

School

1. Reward any two-word combinations said meaningfully, whether they are noun/verb combinations or not. Although the objective is to get the student to use noun/verb combinations, the underlying objective is to stimulate the student to speak in word combinations.
2. Give the student objects such as toys that can be easily manipulated (e.g., a ball, a baby doll, or a stringed puppet). Perform an action with the object and simultaneously name the activity (i.e., "roll ball," "puppet dance," "baby cry"). Encourage the student to perform the same activity and to say the same word. Reward him for doing so.
3. Show the student an object, and indicate in some way that you are waiting to be given directions. Encourage the student to give you directions. Reward him for giving you two-word directions (e.g., "roll ball" and "hair comb").

Home

1. Ask the parents to make a list of the nouns that the child uses to indicate his wants. Tell them to then identify the verbs that logically pair with these nouns (e.g., milk-drink, door-open, and ball-play). Once the child is using nouns as one-word sentences (i.e., to express the idea of what he wants), tell the parents to attempt to get the child to use two-word combinations in everyday speech patterns: milk-drink, door-open, and ball-play. Tell them that when the child uses a noun/verb combination, indicate that they should understand what he is saying by using the noun/verb combination in a sentence (e.g., when he says milk-drink, they should say "Do you want a drink of milk?").
2. Tell them that when they have compiled the list of nouns and verbs as described in Activity 1, they should gather objects representing each of the nouns on the list. Tell them to introduce one object at a time by first pointing to it and by identifying it by saying its name. Then tell them to encourage him to say its name. After he has said its name, they should pick up the object and demonstrate the action with which they have paired it. (For example, pick up a piece of fruit and start to eat it. Point to their chewing teeth and say "Eat." Continue chewing the fruit, point to the fruit once again, and then point to their chewing teeth. Simultaneously say "fruit-eat."). Then tell them to offer a piece of fruit to the child. Tell them to give it to him only if he approximates or says "fruit-eat." Tell them that once he begins to use a specific noun/verb combination, they should introduce a new combination. Tell them to continue in this manner until he is using two-word combinations as part of his functional speech.

Functional Emphases In designing your own instructional activities and plans, emphasize the following elements:

1. Utilization of two-word combinations to further gain control or mastery of his environment.
2. Development of other two-word combinations including adjective/noun combinations.

Specific Objective L

The student refers to others by their first names and/or by their familial relationships.

Functional Settings and Suggested Instructional Activities

School

1. Include the student in a small group for at least one period a day. Take one of her peers out of the group and place her out of sight. Call the peer's name. Encourage the student to join you in calling the peer's name. Do this with each of the peers in the group.

2. Assign the student a partner for a specific activity. Encourage the student and his partner to call each other by their first names. Repeat the activity after giving the student an opportunity to learn the names of a variety of partners.
3. Give the student and a small group of peers an object to hold. Ask the student, "Where is the ________ ? Who has it?" Encourage the student to name the person who has the object.
4. Show the student pictures of his family members, yourself, and other significant individuals in his environment. Place these pictures face down on a desk. Turn each picture over and refer to the person by name. Repeat the activity; this time, however, ask the student to turn over each picture and to name each person. Practice until the student is able to name correctly the persons in the picture.
5. Make a bulletin board or wall display of the student's "favorite people." Periodically, ask the student to name the people whose pictures are on display.

Home

1. Ask the parents to help the child associate each significant family member with the appropriate title of address, including the name when appropriate. Tell them to make certain that they emphasize the form of address when the individual is present. (e.g., "This is Aunt Anna. Say 'Hello' to Aunt Anna.").
2. Ask the parents to organize a family scrapbook and ask the child to name family members.
3. Ask the parents to help the child associate each significant adult friend with the appropriate title of address and name. Tell them to make certain that they emphasize the form of address when the individual is present (e.g., "This is my friend, Ms. Hanlin. Say 'Hello' to Ms. Hanlin.").
4. Ask the parents to help the child associate each same-age friend with her name. name.

Functional Emphases In designing your own instructional activities and plans, emphasize the following elements:

1. Identification of people by familial relationships.
2. Identification of adults by Mr., Ms., Miss, or Mrs. as appropriate.
3. Association of people with their first and second names.

Specific Objective M

The student combines two words in adjective/noun combinations.

Functional Settings and Suggested Instructional Activities

School

1. Give the student two toy cars of different sizes to play with. After he has played with them for a while, ask for them back. Then say, "Ask for the car that

you want. If you want the big car (point to the big one), say, 'big car'; if you want the small car, say 'small car.'" Encourage the student to ask for the car he wants before you give it to him. Once he has accomplished this, provide him with several pairs of familiar objects. In each case, encourage him to ask for the one he wants by size.

2. Give the student a choice of an old teddy bear (or other toy) or a new teddy bear. Only give him the toy if he indicates it by using the adjective "new" or "old." To make sure he gets practice in using the word "old," use old toys that the student prefers to the new ones.
3. Give the student a choice of cold chocolate milk or hot chocolate. Only give him the beverage if he asks for it by stating "hot" or "cold." Do the same with hot and cold vegetables, hot and cold meats, and hot and cold cereals.
4. Give the student a choice of a wet cloth (sponge) or dry cloth to clean the table. Encourage him to ask for the wet cloth (sponge). Give the student a choice of a dry dustcloth or a wet dustcloth to dust the furniture. Encourage him to ask for the dry cloth.
5. Make a list of the student's possessions. Select adjectives that describe and differentiate these objects from each other. Avoid color designators at this point. Use only adjectives that are polar (i.e., those that have opposites). For each possession, describe it by pairing the noun with an adjective. Whenever possible, compare two of the same object (e.g., "This is your heavy sweater, and this one is your light sweater. This is your fat doll, and this is your thin doll. And this is your tall puppet, and this is your short puppet."). Encourage him to ask for his possessions by using descriptive adjectives. Practice.
6. Collect pairs of pictures that show opposite qualities. Show the student these pictures and assist her in describing them (e.g., a happy clown and a sad clown, a long snake and a short snake, and a tall building and a short building).
7. Give the student different textures to feel and assist him in describing them (e.g., rough sandpaper and smooth silk).
8. Give the student different foods to taste and assist him in describing them (e.g., a sour pickle and a salty peanut).
9. Give the student different things he can smell and assist him in describing them (e.g., pretty flowers or perfume).
10. Give the student different things to weigh with his hand and assist him in describing them (e.g., a heavy book and light paper).
11. Make sounds for the student to listen to and assist him in describing them (e.g., a soft whisper and a loud bang).

Home and Community

1. Ask the parents to describe items found in the household that can be compared (e.g., "This is the big chair and this is the small one." "This is a hot cereal and this is a cold cereal."). Tell them to point out the comparisons at appropriate times during the day.
2. Take the student for a tour around the building, outside of the building, into the community, and into the country. Describe the objects, people, and animals

you see. Encourage the student to describe them. Return to these places, and encourage the student to begin the describing activity.

Functional Emphases In designing your own instructional activities and plans, emphasize the following elements:

1. Development of oral language skills, especially the increase in the length of her responses and spontaneous expressions.
2. Facilitation of greater specificity in his speech.

Specific Objective N

The student identifies and names the parts of his face and the principal parts of his body.

Functional Settings and Suggested Instructional Activities

School

1. Give the student a favored doll or plush toy such as a teddy bear. Point to the eyes and say "Eyes." Point to your eyes and then point to the student's eyes. Each time, repeat the word "Eyes." Look in a mirror, point to the student's eyes and then to your eyes. Open and close your eyes and ask the student to open and close his eyes. Ask the student to point to his eyes and encourage him to say "Eyes."
2. Show the student large-size color pictures of faces. Point to the eyes and encourage the student to say "Eyes."
3. Once the student learns to identify eyes, proceed in a similar fashion (as in Activities 1 and 2) with nose, mouth, and ears.
4. Once the student is able to identify and to name the parts of the face on a favorite doll or plush toy, encourage him to name the parts of your face.
5. Place the student in front of a mirror and encourage him to name the parts of his face. Then move him away from the mirror and encourage him to name from memory the parts of his face. Repeat this activity frequently.
6. Point to the parts of the student's face and encourage him to name the parts of his face as you point to them. If this is not successful, point to the parts of the face of a large, life-size doll or mannequin. Practice.
7. Point to the various parts of your face and body and name them. Immediately after you name a part of your body, move it in some way. Encourage the student to name the parts of his face and body as you point to them. Ask him to move each part in some way. Repeat the activity often.

Home

1. Ask the parents to seat the child in front of a mirror and point to the parts of their and the child's face. Tell them that it may be necessary for the child to point to and touch the parts of their faces before he can identify and name his own.

2. Ask the parents to stand in front of a full-length mirror and point out various parts of their bodies, including the hands, arms, feet, and legs. Tell them to urge her to move and say the name of the movable parts of his body.

Functional Emphases In designing your own instructional activities and plans, emphasize the following elements:

1. Identification of the parts of his body to indicate problems such as pains and aches.
2. Identification of bodily and facial parts in pictures.

Specific Objective O

The student uses personal pronouns in his connected speech.

Functional Settings and Suggested Instructional Activities

School See Home Activities 1 through 4 below. Repeat them in role plays and in simulated situations in the classroom.

Home

1. Ask the parents to help the child acquire the subjective pronouns (I, you, he, she, it, we, and they). Tell them to set up situations in which the child talks about himself ("I"), directly to a listener ("you"), about a male other person ("he"), a female other person ("she"), about more than one person ("they"), about a nonperson ("it"), and about himself and others combined ("we").
2. Ask the parents to help the child acquire the objective pronouns (me, you, him, her, it, us, and them). Tell them to set up situations in which the child tells someone to give or do something to or with one or more persons or something.
3. Ask the parents to help the child acquire the possessive pronouns (my, your, his, her, its, our, and their). Tell them to set up situations in which the child associates objects with their owners (e.g., "This is his book." "This is her game." "This is my car." "This is your blouse." "This is its (the dog's) bone." "This is our radio." "This is their house.").
4. Ask the parents to help the child acquire the possessive-replacive pronouns (mine, yours, his, hers, its, ours, and theirs). Tell them to set up situations in which the child associates objects with their owners without mentioning the object (i.e., "This is mine" instead of "This is my car").
(*Note*: In all of the above activities, the child is encouraged to supply the missing pronoun while the parents say the carrier phrase.).

Functional Emphases In designing your own instructional activities and plans, emphasize the following elements:

1. Use of pronouns in functional situations as replacements for nouns the student understands and uses.
2. Development of skill in using these pronouns correctly in terms of case, sex, and number.

Specific Objective P

The student uses prepositions to describe the position and direction of people and things.

Functional Settings and Suggested Instructional Activities

School

1. Ask the student to move an object into various positions relative to a stationary point (on the table, over the table, and under the table). Once he has successfully done so, ask him to tell you where he has placed the object.
2. Ask the student to move an object into various positions relative to another object or objects (next to, behind, in front of, and between). Once he has successfully done so, ask him to tell you where he has placed the object.
3. Place objects in various positions, and ask the student to describe the position of each. Then change the position, and ask him to describe the new position.
4. Show the student a group of preselected pictures that show animals and objects in varying positions (e.g., a gift under the tree or snow on the roof). Ask the questions "Where is the dog?" and "Where is the snow?" Reward the student for each correct answer.
5. See the list of prepositions in Home Activity 2 to design additional activities.

Home

1. Ask the parents to tour the home with the child. Tell them to say, "Look, that table is next to the sofa." "The table pads are stored behind the drapes." "The table is between the beds." After they have described the position of furniture and accessories, they should ask the child to tell where each item is.
2. Tell the parents to introduce and encourage the child to use the following prepositions: in, on, under, above, below, on top of, underneath, beneath, in front of, behind, between, over, into, out of, up, down, to the right, to the left, at, by, beside, next to, around, to, from, toward, and away from.

Functional Emphases In designing your own instructional activities and plans, emphasize the following elements:

1. Utilization of a wide range of prepositions in the student's speech in order to indicate location.
2. Utilization of a wide range of prepositions in the student's speech in order to indicate direction.

Specific Objective Q

The student uses pivot words such as a, my, *and* that.

Functional Settings and Suggested Instructional Activities

School See Home Activities 1 and 2 below.

Home

1. Ask the parents to begin to use pivot words once the child is using single words and noun/verb and adjective/noun combinations. Ask them to say sentences such as "See the cat," "This is my book," and "Give me that" while using appropriate objects. Then tell them to encourage him to use these words in his communication.
2. Ask the parents to encourage the use of pivot words in all of the child's simple conversations and interactions.

Functional Emphases In designing your own instructional activities and plans, emphasize the following elements:

1. Expansion of the student's expressive vocabulary to include pivot words.
2. Utilization of pivot words to clarify communications.

Specific Objective R

The student indicates his wants and thoughts by using plural nouns.

Functional Settings and Suggested Instructional Activities

School

1. Review the objects whose names the student uses in her usual speech patterns. Gather together two or more samples of the same object. Pick up one sample of the object and refer to it by using the singular form of the noun. Then pick up two or more samples of the same object and use the plural form. Encourage the student.
2. Whenever a situation arises in which the student needs to use plural nouns, encourage him to do so and reward him (e.g., when he wants his shoes, two pieces of meat, or several crayons). Correct him if he uses the singular form, or only give him one of the item. Refuse to give him more unless he uses the plural form.

Home and Community

1. Ask the parents to show the child around the house and point out items that occur in units of more than one (e.g., canned goods, chairs, books, lamps, and spoons).
2. Take the student to a shopping center and look at the puppies in a pet shop, the books in the bookstore window, and the shoes in a shoe store. Ask the student to tell you what he sees.

Functional Emphases In designing your own instructional activities and plans, emphasize the following elements:

1. Development of skill in forming plurals that are not formed by adding "s."
2. Development of skill in counting more than one of an item.

Specific Objective S

The student indicates a desired amount by saying the numbers one through five.

Functional Settings and Suggested Instructional Activities

School

1. Place an object in front of the student. Ask him to say "One ________." Place two objects in front of the student and encourage him to say "Two ________." Continue in this manner until he is able to identify one and two successfully. Introduce three in the same manner. Continue with four and five.
2. Place varying amounts of different objects in front of the student. Ask him to identify each object by number and name (e.g., one car, two crayons, three raisins, four grapes, and five stars). Reward the student by giving him the objects that he successfully names.
3. Chant the numbers one through five. Encourage the student to join the chant as he counts various objects.
4. Count objects found in the classroom (e.g., one toy fire engine, two closets, three pictures of trees, four chairs, and five windows). Encourage him to do the same.

Home and Community

1. Ask the parents to count items found in the home (four chairs, two lamps, one sofa, three cans of peas, and five forks). Tell them to encourage the child to join them in counting items in and near the house.
2. Ask the parents to play finger games with the child and join the child in counting the fingers of one hand and the toes on one foot.
3. Take the student for a walk in the community and count the natural objects such as trees, flowers, and rocks.
4. Take the student for a walk in the community and count human-made objects found there (telephone poles, passing cars, houses, and street lights).

Functional Emphases In designing your own instructional activities and plans, emphasize the following elements:

1. Use of numbers to indicate desired amounts of objects.
2. Expansion of the number concept beyond five as appropriate to the student.
3. Utilization of counting as a precursor of calculating using small numbers.

Specific Objective T

The student uses the present progressive form ("ing") of verbs in his connected speech.

Functional Settings and Suggested Instructional Activities

School See Home Activities 1 and 2 below.

Home

1. Ask the parents to model the use of the present progressive form of verbs (e.g., "I am cooking dinner now." "We are going for a walk." "Look at Daddy. He is dancing." "Are you playing with your toy?").
2. Tell the parents to ask the child questions that lead to responses that require the use of the present progressive (e.g., "What are you doing?" "What is he/she making?" "Where are you going?").

Functional Emphases In designing your own instructional activities and plans, emphasize the following elements:

1. Utilization of this verb form to describe action that is taking place or that is soon going to take place.
2. Utilization of this verb form to ask what, where, when, and why questions.

Specific Objective U

The student uses the past tense of regular verbs in his connected speech.

Functional Settings and Suggested Instructional Activities

School

1. Ask the student to perform an activity and then say what he did (e.g., "I jumped over the stick." "I clapped my hands." "I hopped up and down.").
2. Engage in an activity and then lead a discussion about what took place.

Home

1. Tell the parents to ask the child questions that involve communication using the past tense (e.g., "What did sister do?" "She jumped rope.").
2. Tell the parents to relive a previous day's experience with the child, (e.g., "Remember yesterday when we walked to the zoo? The monkey climbed on the tree. The elephant moved its trunk.").

Functional Emphases In designing your own instructional activities and plans, emphasize the following elements:

1. Utilization of verbs that form the past tense with an "ed" in the student's connected speech.
2. Development of skill in using verbs that are irregular in the past tense, especially those that occur frequently.

Specific Objective V

The student uses nouns in the possessive form in his connected speech.

Functional Settings and Suggested Instructional Activities

School

1. Identify objects that belong to different children in the class. Ask the student to identify each object by naming its owner and the object (e.g., "Bob's pen," "Albert's book," and "Tanya's crayons").
2. Show the student pictures of various people and their possessions. Ask him to tell what he sees (e.g., "The man's suitcase," "The woman's dog," and "The girl's toy.").

Home

1. Ask the parents to show the child objects that belong to different people (e.g., brother's shoes, Mary's dog, Daddy's hat, and Aunt Helen's watch). Tell them they should then show him the item and ask him, "Whose ________ is this?").
2. Ask the parents to show the child pictures of various people and discuss their clothing and accessories (e.g., "This is a clown. These are the clown's shoes, the clown's hat, and the clown's floppy flower.").

Functional Emphases In designing your own instructional activities and plans, emphasize the following elements:

1. Use of the possessive form of people's first names.
2. Use of the possessive form of status words such as "boy," "girl," "man," and "woman."

Specific Objective W

The student uses the third person singular of verbs in his connected speech.

Functional Settings and Suggested Instructional Activities

School See Home Activities 1 and 2 below.

Home

1. Ask the parents to model the third person singular of verbs in discussing the behavior of males and females in his family and environment.

2. Tell the parents that, when the child uses the third person singular of verbs in positive statements, they should model the use of the third person singular in negative statements and negative questions.

Functional Emphases In designing your own instructional activities and plans, emphasize the following elements:

1. Utilization of the third person singular of verbs in the present and past tenses of regular verbs.
2. Utilization of the third person singular of verbs in the present and past tenses of irregular verbs.

Specific Objective X

The student says several nursery rhymes or sings simple television or radio commercials.

Functional Settings and Suggested Instructional Activities

School

1. Act out, with gestures and other body actions, familiar nursery rhymes, songs, or poems. Encourage the student to join you. Encourage him to sing, say, or chant these rhymes and songs by himself.
2. Using a tape recorder, play the game of "Radio" in which the student sings a short song or says a rhyme into the tape recorder's microphone. Play the tape back.

Home

1. Ask the parents to read and/or recite nursery rhymes on a regular basis to the child and to encourage him to join them or to say parts of the rhyme by himself, especially the rhyming ends of lines.
2. Ask the parents to sing familiar and catchy commercial jingles often played on radio and television. Tell them to encourage the child to join in or to sing the song by himself.

Functional Emphases In designing your own instructional activities and plans, emphasize the following elements:

1. Development of a repertoire of simple rhymes and poems that the student can recite as a leisure-time activity.
2. Development of a repertoire of chants, jingles, and simple songs that the student can recite as a leisure-time activity.

Specific Objective Y

The student uses adverbs in his conversational speech.

Functional Settings and Suggested Instructional Activities

School See Home Activities 1 and 2 below.

Home

1. Ask the parents to model the use of common adverbs that end in "ly," as in "slowly," "quickly," "smoothly," "softly," and "loudly." Tell them to encourage the child to use these words correctly.
2. Ask the parents to model the use of situationally bound adverbs such as "here," "there," "somewhere," and "anywhere." Tell them to encourage the child to use these words correctly.

Functional Emphases In designing your own instructional activities and plans, emphasize the following elements:

1. Utilization of the words "here" and "there" to specify definite places.
2. Utilization of the words "somewhere" and "anywhere" to specify indefinite places.
3. Association of adverbs that end in "ly" with the adjectives from which they are derived.

Specific Objective Z

The student uses demonstrative pronouns to indicate specific objects.

Functional Settings and Suggested Instructional Activities

School

1. Demonstrate the use of "this" and "these" in relationship to objects found in the classroom.
2. Demonstrate the use of "that" and "those" in relationship to objects that can be seen from the classroom windows.

Home

1. Ask the parents to demonstrate the use of "this" and "these" to indicate objects close to them. Then tell them to encourage their child to talk about single and multiple items that are close to him (e.g., "This car is big." "These books are heavy.").
2. Ask the parents to demonstrate the use of "that" and "those" to indicate objects at a distance from them. Then tell them to encourage their child to talk about items that are at a distance from him (e.g., "That plant is pretty." "Those pillows are attractive.").

Functional Emphases In designing your own instructional activities and plans, emphasize the following elements:

1. Utilization of the demonstrative pronouns to indicate specific objects desired.
2. Utilization of the demonstrative pronouns to indicate specific objects the student wishes to discuss.

Specific Objective AA

The student indicates his wants and thoughts by saying a variety of simple declarative sentences.

Functional Settings and Suggested Instructional Activities

School

1. Take an inventory of the phrases the student uses in his conversational speech. Once you have identified these phrases, you have a frame of reference from which to build sentences. For example, if a student says "Give apple," use this skill to develop the sentence "Give me an apple, please." When the student says a two- or three-word combination, say the appropriate sentence for him and encourage him to imitate your speech. Stage events that will naturally evoke phrases within the student's repertoire. Supply the student with appropriate sentences.
2. Place a variety of objects on a table in front of the student. Pick up each item and say the sentence pattern "This is a ________ ." Encourage the student to repeat the sentence.
3. Place a variety of objects on a table in front of the student. Pick up each item and say the sentence pattern "Here is a ________ ." Encourage the student to repeat the sentence.
4. Place a variety of objects at a distance from you and the student. Point to each item and then say the sentence pattern "There is a ________ ." Encourage the student to repeat the sentence.
5. Ask a peer to perform a variety of actions. Describe the peer's action by saying "Robert is eating the strawberries. Robert is climbing the stairs. Robert is throwing the ball." Encourage the student to repeat these sentences.
6. Show the student action pictures. Describe the action by saying, "The boy is painting the fence. The woman is driving the car. The girl is feeding the dog." Encourage the student to repeat these sentences.
7. Place pairs of objects with opposite qualities on a table in front of the student. Pick up each member of the pair and say, "This is a big car. This is a small car," or "This is a happy clown. This is a sad clown." Encourage the student to repeat these sentences. Vary this activity using pictures.
8. Ask male and female adults and male and female students to assist you in the next activity. These individuals should be known to the student by name. Say, "________ is a girl. ________ is a boy. Mr. ________ is a man. Mrs. ________ is a woman." Encourage the student to repeat these sentences.

Home

1. Ask the parents to model speaking in complete sentences.
2. Tell the parents to speak in various sentence patterns while encouraging the child to use similar structures.

Functional Emphases In designing your own instructional activities and plans, emphasize the following elements:

1. Utilization of sentences to clarify and specify meanings in conversations.
2. Utilization of sentences to clarify and specify meanings in diverse play, work, and social interactions.

Specific Objective BB

The student asks questions beginning with "what," "where," "when," "whose," and "who."

Functional Settings and Suggested Instructional Activities

School

1. Hide a toy that the student enjoys playing with. Provide her with the question form "Where is the ________ ?" Encourage the student to ask the question before you give her the toy.
2. Collect various objects and place them in a sack or a box. Place your hand in the box and say, "What is this?" Ask the student to do the same. Reward him for asking the question.
3. As part of a small group activity, collect personal objects that belong to the student and his peers. Ask the student to pick up one object at a time and encourage him to ask the question "Whose ________ is this?" "Whose ________ are these?"
4. Tell the student to cover his eyes. Ask a peer to tap him on the shoulder. Encourage the student to ask the question "Who is it?" before the peer tells his name.
5. Whenever a situation arises in which the student needs to ask a question, assist him by providing him with the model and encourage his imitation. Do not accept pointing, quizzical looks, or other body language as substitutes if the student has the potential for asking the questions.

Home

1. Ask the parents to hold a treasure hunt in which the child can find the object by asking the "where" question.
2. Ask the parents to role play the part of a child while he plays the part of a teacher or parent and shows pictures of objects and asks the "what" question."
3. Ask the parents to play a "Guess Who" game in which the child is expected to ask the "whose" question to determine to whom an object belongs.

4. Ask the parents to play a "Mystery Game" in which the child is expected to find out who did something by asking the "who" question (e.g., "Who ate the apple?").
5. Ask the parents to play a "Guess When" game in which the child is expected to ask the "when" question to find out when daily and special events are to take place.

Functional Emphases In designing your own instructional activities and plans, emphasize the following elements:

1. Utilization of these types of questions to participate in conversations.
2. Expression of these kinds of questions to obtain needed information.

Specific Objective CC

The student transforms kernel sentences (subject + verb + direct object) into questions and asks unsolicited questions.

Functional Settings and Suggested Instructional Activities

School

1. Tell the student that you are going to tell a peer to do something (i.e., to comb his hair or clap his hands). Model asking the questions "Are you going to clap your hands?" or "Will you be combing your hair?" Then ask the student to do the questioning.
2. Play a game of "I've Got a Secret" in which the student is expected to guess something you and/or a peer is holding or has in a pocket. Model asking the questions "Has he a toy car?" "Have you a balloon?" "Are you holding a feather?" and "Do you have a thimble?"

Home

1. Ask the parents to model transforming kernel sentences into questions (e.g., "The boy bought new shoes." "Did the boy buy new shoes?" "Yes, the boy bought new shoes."). Tell them to then say a kernel sentence and encourage the child to ask a question (e.g., *Parent*: "The girl played basketball." *Child*: "Did the girl play basketball?").
2. Tell the parents to pantomime different actions and encourage the child to ask questions about the pantomime during and after the gestures (e.g., "Did you brush your teeth?" and "Are you ironing your shirt?").

Functional Emphases In designing your own instructional activities and plans, emphasize the following elements:

1. Expression of question transformations as part of conversational interactions.
2. Expression of question transformations to obtain needed information.

Specific Objective DD

The student uses negative statements to communicate his disapproval or wish not to comply with a request.

Functional Settings and Suggested Instructional Activities

School

1. Put a selection of items on a table in front of the student. Some of these should be disliked toys or other objects. Pick up a disliked toy and ask "Do you want to play with this toy?" Encourage him to say, "No, I don't want that." Reward him by joining him in playing with a favorite toy.
2. Ask the student if he wants to participate in a disliked activity (e.g., "Do you want to play hopscotch?"). Encourage him to say, "I don't like hopscotch." Then join him in a favorite activity.

Home

1. Ask the parents to model negative statements to show that they do not approve (e.g., "I don't want you to play with that!"). Tell them to supply the child with negative statements whenever he wants to show his disapproval (e.g., "I don't want that.").
2. Ask the parents to model negative statements to communicate their wish not to comply with a request (e.g., "No, I don't want to go to the movies."). Tell them to supply the child with negative statements whenever he needs help in voicing his desire not to comply.

Functional Emphases In designing your own instructional activities and plans, emphasize the following elements:

1. Development of the negative form of statements to express her disapproval or wish to not comply in a variety of social interactions.
2. Utilization of the negative form of statements in leisure-time interactions.

Specific Objective EE

The student uses simple language courtesies.

Functional Settings and Suggested Instructional Activities

School

1. Use language courtesies appropriately and with consistency. Reward the student for modeling your use of these courtesies.
2. Review patterns of conversation appropriate to given situations. Use language courtesies in these conversational patterns (e.g., "Good morning. How are you? How is your mother?") Practice these conversations in various role-playing

situations. Encourage the student's participation. Practice greetings such as "Good morning," "Good afternoon," "Good evening," "Hello," and "Goodbye." Practice several different ways of asking how someone is feeling. Encourage the student to respond to these questions and then to ask the same question in return.

3. Practice language courtesies in greetings and farewells in simulated and real telephone conversations.
4. Set up the pattern of saying, "please" when asking for a favor. Engage in role playing in which you and the student take turns asking for a favor. Practice saying "Thank you" upon receiving the favor and "You're welcome" in response to the "Thank you." Schedule puppet shows, tea parties, and other play activities during which language courtesies should be used. Reward the student for using them.

Home

1. Ask the parents to model language courtesies in all their appropriate contexts (e.g., "I'm sorry," "Excuse me," "Pardon me," and "God Bless You.").
2. Ask the parents to role play simple conversations including greetings and farewells.

Functional Emphases In designing your own instructional activities and plans, emphasize the following elements:

1. Use of language courtesies in greetings and farewells.
2. Use of language courtesies when social errors or mistakes are made.
3. Use of language courtesies to negotiate space and movement patterns.
4. Use of language courtesies to express concern when someone sneezes.

Specific Objective FF

The student uses indefinite and negative pronouns.

Functional Settings and Suggested Instructional Activities

School See Home Activities 1 through 5 below and modify the activities as appropriate to the classroom.

Home

1. Ask the parents to model the use of indefinite pronouns such as "any," "anyone," "anybody," and "anything" in their speech. Tell them to encourage the child in the correct use of these words.
2. Ask the parents to model the use of indefinite pronouns such as "some," "someone," "somebody," and "anything" in their speech. Tell them to encourage the child in the correct use of these words.

3. Ask the parents to model the use of negative pronouns such as "no one," "nobody," and "nothing." Tell them to encourage the child in the correct use of these words.
4. Ask the parents to model the use of the indefinite pronouns such as "every," "everyone," "everybody," and "everything." Tell them to encourage the child in the correct use of these words.
5. Ask the parents to model the use of the indefinite pronouns such as "few," "couple," "several," and "most." Tell them to encourage the child in the correct use of these words.

Functional Emphases In designing your own instructional activities and plans, emphasize the following elements:

1. Use of indefinite pronouns with as much precision as possible.
2. Use of negative pronouns with as much precision as possible.

Specific Objective GG

The student responds appropriately to questions beginning with the question markers "who," "what," "whose," "how," "where," and "how many."

Functional Settings and Suggested Instructional Activities

School

1. In a small group, play a game of "Questions and Answers." Ask a question and tell the student and his peers to take turns in answering the question. Use questions that will review previously developed language skills (e.g., "What color is this?" "How many fingers am I holding up?").
2. Role play diverse conversations in which questions and answers are integral parts of these conversations. Reward the student for responding appropriately and for assuming conversational responsibility.

Home

1. Tell the parents that, whenever appropriate, they should ask the child pertinent questions relevant to his behavior (e.g., "What are you doing? Where are you going? What is that you have in your hand? How old are you? What is your name? Who are you going to play with? Whose toy is this? When are you going to finish playing that game? How many crayons do you want?"). Tell them to reward the child when he responds appropriately.
2. Tell the parents to ask the child questions about her environment (e.g., "Who is that man (Santa)?" "What is that (a squirrel)?" and "How many windows are there?").

Functional Emphases In designing your own instructional activities and plans, emphasize the following elements:

1. Comprehension of questions so that the student may participate in simple conversations.
2. Comprehension of questions so that the student may provide required information in a clear and accurate way.

Specific Objective HH

The student names the primary colors and uses them to describe objects.

Functional Settings and Suggested Instructional Activities

School

1. Provide the student with samples of objects, all of which are red. Pick up each item and name it. Then pick up each object and say "Red." Encourage the student to repeat the word.
2. If the student succeeds in Activity 1, pick up each item and say, "This is red." Encourage the student to repeat the phrase.
3. Provide the student with samples of objects, all of which are another color, such as yellow. Proceed as in Activities 1 and 2.
4. In random order, place on a table all of the red and yellow objects used in Activities 1 through 3. Ask the student to give you the object you have designated by its color ("Give me the red car."). Repeat this activity. Then indicate to the student that he is to do the same (i.e., ask for an item by designating its color).
5. Take a tour around the classroom and playground. Find objects that are red and yellow. Ask the student to name them by color (e.g., a red leaf and a yellow paper towel).
6. Provide the student with the type of objects used in Activities 1 and 3. This time, they should all be blue. Proceed as in Activities 1 and 2.
7. Give the student items such as buttons, beads, and blocks. Ask him to sort them by color: red, yellow, or blue. Once the student has satisfactorily grouped the objects by color, ask him to name the color of each of the groups.
8. Obtain bottles of red, yellow, and blue food coloring. Fill three jars with water and pour a few drops of each color into each of the jars. Encourage the student to name the color as it spreads through the water.

Home

1. Ask the parents to take the child around the house and point out objects that are red, yellow, and blue.
2. Ask the parents to purchase colored blocks, colored beads, and other colorful playthings designed especially for the beginning learner. Tell them to encourage the child to identify each item by its color.

Functional Emphases In designing your own instructional activities and plans, emphasize the following elements:

1. Use of color designations to clarify and make communications more explicit.
2. Development of comprehension for and the meaningful expression of secondary colors and other commonly occurring colors.

Specific Objective II

The student identifies the time of day (i.e., day or night).

Functional Settings and Suggested Instructional Activities

School

1. See Home Activities 1 and 2 below.
2. Once the student is able to identify day and night, introduce the concepts of morning and afternoon. Relate the concept of morning to typical morning activities and to the time after one wakes up on school days. Relate afternoon to the time after lunch and before dusk.

Home

1. Ask the parents to point out the time of the day. Tell them to start with day and night. Tell them to point out clues to such identifiers as darkness, stars, and the moon to indicate that it is nighttime.
2. Ask the parents to read picture books to the child in which day and night are depicted. Tell them to point out the visual clues.

Functional Emphases In designing your own instructional activities and plans, emphasize the following elements:

1. Identification of the time of day in order to keep appointments.
2. Utilization of time of day designations to make appointments.

Specific Objective JJ

The student identifies and names objects in terms of their use.

Functional Settings and Suggested Instructional Activities

School

1. Place functional objects such as a pot, broom, and needle in front of the student. Play a word association game in which you give the student verb clues such as "cook," "sweep," or "sew." Ask the student to point to the object to be used in each case. Repeat the activity and ask him to name the object. Then remove the objects and once again give the verb clues. Ask the student to name each of the objects.

2. Give the student a noun clue such as "needle," "pencil," or "gloves." Ask the student to pantomime an activity for each of the nouns and then to describe what he is pantomiming (e.g., "I am sewing a button on with the needle. I am writing with the pencil. I am wearing gloves to keep my hands warm.").

Home and Community

1. Ask the parents to place various familiar objects in front of the child. Tell them to ask him questions such as "Which one do you eat with?" or "Which one do you play with?"
2. Ask the parents to show the child various familiar objects and equipment used in the home such as a vacuum cleaner, lawnmower, hammer, refrigerator, and needle. Tell them to ask him to demonstrate how to use each item and to describe what he is doing while he is demonstrating it (e.g., "I am cutting the grass with a lawnmower." "A hammer bangs nails into wood.").
3. Take a walk in the community. Ask questions about equipment and machinery you see there (e.g., "Which one tells cars to stop?" "What do you see on the street that takes a lot of people to work?" "Which truck cleans the streets?").

Functional Emphases In designing your own instructional activities and plans, emphasize the following elements:

1. Selection of appliances, equipment, and tools in terms of required or assigned functional tasks.
2. Identification of items to be purchased in terms of required or assigned tasks and responsibilities.

Specific Objective KK

The student uses categorical nouns in his speech.

Functional Settings and Suggested Instructional Activities

School

1. Show the student objects and pictures of animals. Pick up or point to each object or picture and name it. After you have done this, go through them once again and this time say, "Dog—a dog is an animal. Cat—a cat is an animal. Cow—a cow is an animal." After you have named all of the objects and pictures, conclude by saying, "These are all animals."
2. Repeat Activity 1, using objects and pictures of food.
3. Repeat Activity 1, using objects and pictures of clothing.
4. Repeat Activity 1, using objects and pictures of furniture.
5. Repeat Activity 1, using objects and pictures of means of transportation.
6. Give the student pictures of animals and foods. Ask him to separate them into two groups, one of animals and one of foods. Assist him in doing so, if necessary. Once the two groups have been separated, ask the student to give

a name to each of the groups. If necessary, help him by saying, "All of these pictures are pictures of animals and foods."

7. Give the student pictures of clothing and furniture and repeat Activity 6.
8. Give the student pictures of means of transportation and furniture and repeat Activity 6.
9. Give the student pictures of several of the categories and repeat Activity 6.
10. Say a group of words that belong to the same category such as "car," "airplane," "train," and "boat." Ask the student to say the category. Reward her for a correct response.

Home

1. Ask the parents to show the child all the food that is stored in the house. Tell them to name each item and indicate that it is a food.
2. Ask the parents to show the child all the articles of clothing found in the house. Tell them to name each item and indicate that it is an article of clothing.
3. Tell them to do the same as in Activities 1 and 2 with all the categorical items that are found in the home: cooking utensils, eating utensils or silverware, canned goods, spices, china, furniture, medicines, grooming accessories, linen, and knick-knacks.

Functional Emphases In designing your own instructional activities and plans, emphasize the following elements:

1. Identification of categorical nouns so that one is able to comprehend their use in conversational speech and in queries.
2. Identification of a category to which an item belongs so that one may find it in directories and other listings.

Specific Objective LL

The student says her age and the month and date of her birthday.

Functional Settings and Suggested Instructional Activities

School

1. Make a list of the birthdays of the student, his peers, his relatives, and other significant individuals. Obtain a large wall calendar and mark with a marking pen the student's birthday and the birthdays of other individuals. At the beginning of each month, talk about the dates of the coming birthdays. Periodically review the student's birthday with him and show him where his birthday has been marked on the large calendar. Put a star on his birthday to make it stand out.
2. Schedule birthday parties for the student and his peers. Involve the student and his peers in the planning. During the planning sessions, frequently repeat

the person's birthday (month and date) and his new age. Ask the student and his peers to talk about the approaching birthday and the person's new age.
3. Tell the student that there are several important facts that everyone should know about himself. Tell him that you will help him get the right information, but it is up to him to remember it. Tell the student that you will be asking him to tell you this information, so he must try to remember it.
4. Demonstrate ways that help you to remember, such as saying the information over and over again, first out loud and then silently. Help the student to find ways that will assist him in remembering.

Home

1. Ask the parents to plan birthday celebrations with the child. Tell them to say to him frequently, "You are seven now. But on your birthday, this September 23rd, you will be eight. How old are you now? How old will you be on September 23rd?"
2. Ask the parents to sing the song "How Old Are You Now?" to the child. Tell them to encourage the child to respond with the correct answer.

Functional Emphases In designing your own instructional activities and plans, emphasize the following elements:

1. Identification of the student's age and birthdate in response to questions from appropriate people (e.g., teachers, physicians, and prospective employers).
2. Identification of the arithmetic progression of adding one year to an age at each birthday.
3. Comprehension of older and younger.

Specific Objective MM

The student says his home address and telephone number when appropriate.

Functional Settings and Suggested Instructional Activities

School

1. Take a picture of the address plate or numerals found in front of the student's home. Identify the address as his address and keep it in a prominent place along with the student's other personal property. Make a copy of his telephone number and keep that in a prominent place.
2. Tell the student that if he is lost, knowing his address will help him find his way home. Engage in a hand puppet activity in which the puppet is a police officer. Pretend you are lost and ask the hand puppet for help. When it asks you your address and telephone number, give the answers. When the puppet hears the answer, it should respond, "Oh, I know where that is. I will help you get home in no time. Do not worry. I will call home to let them know you are safe."

Home

1. Ask the parents to print the child's address and telephone number on a card that he can carry in his wallet. Tell them to ask him periodically to read these numbers aloud or repeat them from memory.
2. Ask the parents to show the child her address as it appears on the house and on mail addressed to the members of the household.

Functional Emphases In designing your own instructional activities and plans, emphasize the following elements:

1. Commitment of these numbers to memory.
2. Identification of the student's address and telephone number to appropriate persons (e.g., a police officer, a prospective employer, and a teacher).
3. Acquisition of skills in writing these items on appropriate forms.

Specific Objective NN

The student says the days of the week with meaning.

Functional Settings and Suggested Instructional Activities

School

1. Encourage the student to listen to the radio or television news programs to find out what day it is.
2. Use the previous day as a point of reference to indicate the day (e.g., "Since yesterday was Sunday, today must be Monday, and tomorrow will be Tuesday."). Repeat this frequently.

Home

1. Ask the parents to begin by teaching the days of the weeks in order by rote. Tell them to chant the days of the week while encouraging their child to join in.
2. Tell the parents to correlate an activity with each day of the week with the aim of getting the child to associate the day with the specific activity (e.g., "Since we are changing the bed linen, it must be Tuesday.").

Functional Emphases In designing your own instructional activities and plans, emphasize the following elements:

1. Comprehension of the question "What day is it?" and expression of the correct response.
2. Calculation of days left to an approaching day or date from knowledge of today's date and day.

Specific Objective OO

The student says the date by giving the month and the day.

Functional Settings and Suggested Instructional Activities

School

1. Encourage the student to listen to the radio or television to find out the date.
2. Use the previous day's date as a point of reference. "Since yesterday was (month)(date), today must be (month)(date), and tomorrow will be (month)(date)."
3. Show the student the date on a calendar. Say it and encourage him to repeat it. Then ask the question "What is today's date?" Reward the student if he answers correctly.
4. Show the student the key words and numerals on a calendar. Demonstrate using a calendar to find the date.

Home

1. Ask the parents to point out radio and television announcements that specify the month and day.
2. Ask the parents to pose the question "What is today's date?" and to supply the answer. Then ask them to ask the question and urge their child to supply the answer.

Functional Emphases In designing your own instructional activities and plans, emphasize the following elements:

1. Comprehension of the question "What's today's date?" and expression of the correct response.
2. Calculation of the amount of time until an approaching date from knowledge of today's date.

Specific Objective PP

The student describes pictures in detail, using a variety of sentences.

Functional Settings and Suggested Instructional Activities

School

1. Show the student interesting pictures that depict social situations. Encourage him to talk about the relationships in the picture. Discourage the listing of items, and encourage speaking in sentences. If necessary, ask him to make up a story that includes what happened before, during, and after the picture.
2. Show the student a series of pictures that tell a story. Place them in sequential order in front of her. Encourage her to tell the story from the pictures.

Home

1. Ask the parents to read a story from a picture book to the child. Tell them to encourage him to follow along by "reading" the pictures. Tell them that after they have finished the story, they should ask him to retell it by looking at each picture in the story.
2. Ask the parents to show the child pictures cut out of newspapers and magazines that depict scenes involving characters and events. Tell them to ask him to tell a story about the picture. A picture of a family picnic, a baseball game, or a circus will often stimulate interesting stories.

Functional Emphases In designing your own instructional activities and plans, emphasize the following elements:

1. Improvement in conversational and other language skills.
2. Development of social skills.
3. Appreciation for the varieties of leisure, work, and other human experiences and interchanges.

Specific Objective QQ

The student relates the details of stories told or read to him.

Functional Settings and Suggested Instructional Activities

School

1. Schedule on a regular basis a story-telling time during which you read or tell interesting stories and anecdotes. Sometimes ask questions about these stories, but most of the time allow the student to enjoy the story for its own sake.
2. Write a language experience story about a recent experience that you and the student have had. Leave out pertinent facts, read the story to the student and ask him to supply the missing information.

Home

1. Ask the parents to tell or read simple stories to the child. Tell them to ask him detail questions as they read or tell the story and after the story has been completely told or read. Tell them to repeat key elements in the story to help him find details he missed the first time.
2. Ask the parents to read human-interest stories from newspapers and magazines to the child. Tell them to ask him questions designed to test his recall of significant events, persons, places, and things.

Functional Emphases In designing your own instructional activities and plans, emphasize the following elements:

1. Recall of key facts and details as a means of improving conversational skills.

2. Recall of details as a means of building vocabulary and of facilitating oral language comprehension.

Specific Objective RR

The student relates experiences and describes activities.

Functional Settings and Suggested Instructional Activities

School

1. Inquire of parents, guardians, and other significant persons in the student's life whether he has had any recent enjoyable or dramatic experiences. Find out the details and then ask the student to share his experiences (in sequence) with you and/or his peers. Help him by supplying key words such as "first," "second," "next," "then," and "last."
2. Use felt cutouts or pictures of a familiar story. Ask the student to retell the events in the order of their occurrence.
3. Engage the student in activities that require an exact order such as carrying out art activities, recipes, and constructing simple models. Once the activity has been completed, ask the student to describe what he has done in the proper sequence.

Home and Community

1. Ask the parents to share an experience with the child and then "relive" the experience by describing the activity (e.g., a family outing, a baseball game, or a house party).
2. Take the student on an interesting trip (e.g., to a zoo). During the trip, point out and describe the interesting sights and sounds. Immediately upon your return to the classroom, ask the student to tell you what happened and what he saw during the trip. Help him put the events in order by supplying key words such as "first," "second," "next," "then," and "last."

Functional Emphases In designing your own instructional activities and plans, emphasize the following elements:

1. Improvement in conversational skills based upon the relating of details in proper sequence.
2. Observation of sequences in the performance of sequential work and leisure tasks.

Specific Objective SS

The student carries out simple conversations, including telephone conversations, on a one-to-one basis.

Functional Settings and Suggested Instructional Activities

School

1. Show the student interesting filmstrips or movies. After the showing, talk with the student about the movie or filmstrip. Encourage his participation.
2. When appropriate, read human-interest stories from newspapers and magazines. Talk with the student about the story. Encourage his participation.
3. After a trip in the community or into the country, engage the student in a discussion. Encourage her participation.
4. Establish patterns of conversation that are appropriate for given situations: morning greetings, farewell comments, greetings following an absence for illness, greetings following an absence for vacation, greetings for birthdays or special events, and asking for a date.
5. Role play a variety of telephone conversations (e.g., phoning friends, repairmen/women, inviting friends to visit, discussing leisure-time plans, and expressing condolences.

Home

1. Ask the parents to watch television and listen to radio programs of interest with the child. Tell them that after the program is over, they should discuss the program with him while encouraging his active participation.
2. Ask the parents to engage the child in daily discussions of diverse topics designed to improve his ability to participate in conversations and to assume conversational responsibility.

Functional Emphases In designing your own instructional activities and plans, emphasize the following elements:

1. Observation of language and other courtesies.
2. Assumption of communicative responsibility (i.e., the student contributes to the conversation).
3. Avoidance of behaviors that monopolize or limit conversations (e.g., lack of enthusiasm, irrelevant or silly comments, and inattentiveness).
4. Transference of conversational skills to small group conversations and discussions.

Specific Objective TT

The student participates in group conversations and discussions.

Functional Settings and Suggested Instructional Activities

School

1. With the student and several peers, engage in role playing real-life situations. Encourage the student to participate in the discussions and dialogues that ensue.

2. Present problems to the student and ask him and his peers to solve these problems or to think of alternate ways of handling the problems (e.g., "The sink is plugged up; what should you do?" and "Your mother asked you to buy tomatoes at the supermarket, but there are none; what should you do?").
3. Use puppets of family members as props in a role-playing activity. Present the student and his peers with a family situation and encourage them to act out the situation by having a discussion among the members of the family.

Home and Community

1. Ask the parents to set aside times of the day when family members and/or friends can participate in group discussions.
2. Take the student and his peers to a play. Discuss the play while having a snack.

Functional Emphases In designing your own instructional activities and plans, emphasize the following elements:

1. Development of conversational skills.
2. Development of language, including grammatical and syntactical skills.

Specific Objective UU

The student indicates comparative relationships.

Functional Settings and Suggested Instructional Activities

School

1. Review polar adjectives that express opposite characteristics. Give the student pairs of objects and ask him to study and then tell you how they compare (e.g., "This penny is brighter than this one." "This piece of sandpaper is smoother than this one.").
2. If the student masters the comparative form of adjectives, proceed to the use of the superlative form by giving him triplets of objects to describe (e.g., "This book is the largest of the three." "This plant is the tallest one.").

Home

1. Ask the parents to show the child objects that vary in size and other dimensions. Tell them, for example, to refer to the bigger one by saying, "The basketball is bigger than the Ping-Pong ball." Tell them to encourage him to repeat the comparative statement. Once the child expresses the larger, they should voice the other relationship, "The Ping-Pong ball is smaller than the basketball."
2. Ask the parents to show the child the same objects used in Activity 1, this time urging the child to express the relationship first (e.g., "The paperweight is heavier than the feather.").

Functional Emphases In designing your own instructional activities and plans, emphasize the following elements:

1. Comprehension of comparative and superlative adjectives in following directions and instructions.
2. Use of comparative and superlative adjectives in giving directions and instructions.
3. Use of comparative and superlative adjectives in describing objects, persons, and things.

Specific Objective VV

The student asks "how" and "why" questions.

Functional Settings and Suggested Instructional Activities

School

1. Model asking "how" questions to assist the student in describing how to perform school-related tasks. Encourage the student to ask "how" questions when he does not know how to perform a task. Help him analyze whether he can perform a task or whether he needs to ask "how to."
2. Model asking "why" questions to clarify appropriate, safe, healthy, and socially competent behaviors. Assist the student in asking "why" questions that specify ways he should behave.
3. Model asking "why" questions that help explain natural phenomena and cause-and-effect relationships. Assist the student in asking "why" questions of this type.

Home

1. Ask the parents to model the "how" question in asking how to do something (e.g., "How do you play that game?" "How do you open that box?" "How do you sew a button?"). Tell them to encourage the child to ask "how" questions to gain information on a performance activity.
2. Ask the parents to model the "why" question in asking for information (e.g., "Why should we not go into a car with a stranger?" "Why do we have to water the plants?" "Why can I go swimming in an outdoor pool only on a hot day?"). Tell them to encourage the child to ask "why" questions to gain information.

Functional Emphases In designing your own instructional activities and plans, emphasize the following elements:

1. Identification of those occasions when it is necessary to find out how to perform a required or desired task.
2. Identification of those occasions when it is necessary or when he desires to find out why something should be done or why something occurs.

Specific Objective WW

The student uses compound structures and compound sentences in his speech.

Functional Settings and Suggested Instructional Activities

School

1. See Home Activities 1 through 4.
2. Assist the student in differentiating among the "and," "but," "or," and "so" in his connected speech.

Home

1. Ask the parents to demonstrate the use of a compound subject (e.g., "Daddy and I are going to the ballgame tonight." and "The peanut butter and jelly are in the closet."). Tell them to encourage him to use compound subjects when appropriate.
2. Ask the parents to demonstrate the use of a compound object (e.g., "I bought apples and oranges today." "Did you see the boy and girl?").
3. Ask the parents to demonstrate the use of a compound predicate (e.g., "I caught and then threw the ball." and "Mary baked and served the cake.").
4. Ask the parents to demonstrate the use of a compound sentence with the "and" conjunction (e.g., "He made a mistake, and he was very sorry." and "They walked to the park, and then they went to work.").

Functional Emphases In designing your own instructional activities and plans, emphasize the following elements:

1. Comprehension of compound structures to clarify the messages communicated to the student in diverse functional situations, including simple conversations.
2. Use of compound structures to specify his needs and thoughts in simple conversations and in relating and relaying messages.

Specific Objective XX

The student uses complex sentences in his speech.

Functional Settings and Suggested Instructional Activities

School

1. Model the use of the subordinating conjunction "since" and encourage the student to use it in his speech.
2. Model the use of the subordinating conjunction "although" and encourage the student to use it in his speech.
3. Model the use of the subordinating conjunction "until" and encourage the student to use it in his speech.

Home

1. Ask the parents to model the use of the subordinating conjunction "because."
2. Ask the parents to model the use of the subordinating conjunction "if."

Functional Emphases In designing your own instructional activities and plans, emphasize the following elements:

1. Comprehension of complex sentences to clarify the messages communicated to the student in diverse functional settings, including simple conversations.
2. Use of complex sentences to specify his needs and thoughts in simple conversations and in relating and relaying messages.

Specific Objective YY

The student uses idiomatic and figurative expressions in his speech.

Functional Settings and Suggested Instructional Activities

School

1. List some idiomatic expressions found in American English. Use them in your conversations and discussions.
2. Use figurative language such as similes, metaphors, personifications, and hyperbole whenever possible and meaningful in your conversations with the student.
3. Consult your list of idiomatic expressions and review each one with the student. Tell him its idiomatic meaning and use it in your speech. Ask him to use the same expression in his speech. Reward him for using it correctly.

Home and Community

1. Ask the parents to introduce idiomatic expressions to the child on a regular basis since there are so many in our language. Tell them to consult *A Dictionary of Idioms for the Deaf* (see Special Materials List).
2. Visit a sports arena and discuss the figurative language used as part of the "language" of the game.

Functional Emphases In designing your own instructional activities and plans, emphasize the following elements:

1. Facilitation of comprehension of oral language.
2. Stimulation of vocabulary diversity.
3. Improvement of conversational skills.

Specific Objective ZZ

The student speaks in the patterns of acceptable adult speech and does so with intelligible articulation.

Functional Settings and Suggested Instructional Activities

School

1. Make an inventory of all the sounds that the student articulates satisfactorily. Provide the student with a model of a sound that he does not make. Use a mirror. Ask the student to look at you and to listen to you as you say the sound. Then ask him to repeat the sound. Do this several times. If he succeeds, say the sound in a word. Ask him to look at you, to listen to you, and to say what you say. If the student does not succeed in making the sound, show him what he must do to make it. After you have given him instructions, repeat your request that he look at you, listen to you, and repeat what you say.
2. Make sure that you are providing the student with examples of grammatical/syntactical speech that is highly intelligible. Also use a variety of sentence structures in your everyday speech.
3. Provide the student with various sentence patterns. Say the sentence and ask her first to imitate you and then to make up her own sentences with the same linguistic patterns.
4. Show the student pictures of high-interest material. They should be selected specifically because they require a variety of grammatical and syntactical speech patterns. For example, show pictures of a cat who is drinking a bowl of milk and a cat who is licking its whiskers in front of an empty bowl. Collect pictures that require the student to use different tenses, numbers, and cases. Ask him to describe the pictures and program for difficulties evidenced.

Home

1. Ask the parents to serve as models of good speech and language. Tell them to avoid "baby talk" or "talking down" to the child since his speech will be adversely affected.
2. Ask the parents to expose the child to good speech models such as national news commentators.

Functional Emphases In designing your own instructional activities and plans, emphasize the following elements:

1. Articulation of all the sounds of the language.
2. Facilitation of appropriate voice patterns.
3. Facilitation of correct pronunciation and word usage.
4. Development of diverse linguistic structures.
5. Development of syntactical and grammatical skills.

Special Materials List—Verbal Communication Skills

Books/Pamphlets

Excell Experience for Children in Learning. Educators Publishing Service, Inc., 75 Moulton Street, Cambridge, MA, 02238.

Language Stimulation Workbooks. Modern Education Corporation, P.O. Box 721, Tulsa, OK, 74101.

Kits/Games

Oral Language Expansion Resource Kit. Educational Activities, Inc., P.O. Box 392, Freeport, NY, 11520.

Basic Vocabulary Study Cards. Dormac, Inc., P.O. Box 1699, Beaverton, OR, 97075.

Equipment/Materials

Language Master and Cards. Bell & Howell Audiovisual Products Division, 7100 McCormick Road, Lincolnwood, IL, 60645.

Records

Brahm's Lullaby. (Purchase in a local record or department store.)

Dictionary

Dictionary of Idioms for the Deaf. (John Gate, Editor) Barron's Educational Series, Inc., 113 Crossways Park Drive, Woodbury, NY, 11797.

Suggested Readings/References—Verbal Communication Skills

Anderson, M., Boren, N. J., Caniglia, W. H., & Krohn, E. (1980). *The Apple Tree Language Program: A patterned program of linguistic expansion through reinforced experience and evaluations.* Beaverton, OR: DORMAC.

Bear, D. M., & Guess, D. (1973). Teaching productive noun suffixes to severely retarded children. *American Journal of Mental Deficiency, 77,* 498–505.

Bates, E. (1979). *The emergence of symbols: From cognition to communication in infancy.* New York: Academic Press.

Beal, L., & Potter, R. E. (1979). The use of objects and pictures as language stimuli: Influence on response complexity. *Journal of Childhood Communication Disorders, 3,* 47–58.

Bedrosian, J. L., & Prutting, C. A. (1978). Communicative performance of mentally retarded adults in four conversational settings. *Journal of Speech and Hearing Research, 21,* 79–95.

Benedict, H. (1978). Language comprehension in nine 15-month-old children. In R. Campbell & P. Smith (Eds.), *Recent advances in the psychology of language: Language development and mother-child interaction.* New York: Plenum Press.

Berry, P. (Ed.) (1976). *Language and communication in the mentally handicapped.* Baltimore: University Park Press.

Berry, P., & Marshall, B. (1978). Social interactions and communication patterns in mentally retarded children. *American Journal of Mental Deficiency, 83,* 44–51.

Bliss, L., & Allen, D. (1979). *Evaluation of procedures for screening preschool children for signs of impaired language development.* Second Interim Report, Project No. NOI-NS-6-2353. Detroit: Wayne State University.

Bloodstein, O. (1984). *Speech pathology: An introduction.* Boston: Houghton-Mifflin.

Bloom, L., & Lahey, M. (1978). *Language development and language disorders.* New York: John Wiley.

Blumberg, H. M. (1975). *A program of sequential language development.* Springfield, IL: Charles C Thomas.

Boehnlein, M. M., & Ritty, J. M., (1977). Integration of the communication arts curriculum: A review. *Language Arts, 54,* 372–377.

Boynton, K. R., & Henke, L. L., (1978). Conversation expansion in young children. *Communication Education, 27,* 202–211.

Bricker, D. (Ed.) (1980). *New directions for exceptional children, Vol. 2. Language interaction with children.* San Francisco: Jossey-Bass.

Bricker, D. D., Vincent-Smith, L., & Bricker, W. A., (1973). Receptive vocabulary: Performances and selection strategies of delayed and non-delayed toddlers. *American Journal of Mental Deficiency, 77,* 579–584.

Bricker, W. A., & Bricker, D. D., (1976). A program of language training for the severely language handicapped child. In R. Anderson & J. Greer (Eds.), *Educating the severely and profoundly retarded.* Austin: PRO-ED.

Brookshire, R. H., & Nicholas, L. E., (1980). Verification of active and passive sentences by aphasic and nonaphasic subjects. *Journal of Speech and Hearing Research, 23,* 878–893.

Brown, R. (1968). The development of WH questions in child speech. *Journal of Verbal Learning and Verbal Behavior, 7,* 279–290.

Buckhalt, J. A., Rutherford, R. B., & Goldberg, K. F., (1978). Verbal and nonverbal interaction of mothers with their Down syndrome and nonretarded infants. *American Journal of Mental Deficiency, 81,* 1–11.

Buckley, M. H., (1976). A guide for developing an oral language curriculum. *Language Arts, 53,* 621–627.

Cahir, S. R., & Shuy, R. W., (1981). Classroom language learning: What do researchers know? *Language Arts, 58,* 369–374.

Campbell, C. R., & Stremel-Campbell, K. (1982). Programming "loose training" as a strategy to facilitate language generalization. *Journal of Applied Behavior Analysis, 15,* 295–301.

Caramazza, A., & Zurif, E. B., (1978). *Language acquisition and language breakdown.* Baltimore: Johns Hopkins Press.

Carrow-Woolfolk, E., & Lynch, J. I., (1981). *An integrative approach to language disorders in children.* New York: Grune & Stratton.

Casby, M. W., & Ruder, K. F., (1983). Symbolic play and early language development in normal and mentally retarded children. *Journal of Speech and Hearing Research, 26,* 404–411.

Cavallaro, C. C., & Bambra, L. M., (1982). Two strategies for teaching language during free play. *Journal of the Association for the Severely Handicapped, 7,* 80–92.

Cherry, L., & Lewis, M. (1976). Mothers and two year olds: A study of sex differentiated aspects of verbal interaction. *Developmental Psychology, 12,* 278–282.

Cheseldine, S., & McConkey, R. (1979). Parental speech to young Down's Syndrome children: An intervention study. *American Journal of Mental Deficiency, 83,* 612–620.

Chomsky, C. (1969). *The acquisition of syntax in children from five to ten.* Cambridge, MA: M.I.T. Press.

Churchill, D. (1978). *Language of autistic children.* New York: John Wiley & Sons.

Clark, E. V., (1971). On the acquisition of the meaning of before and after. *Journal of Verbal Learning and Verbal Behavior, 10,* 266–275.

Cohen, S. B., (1980). Using learning strategies to teach the language arts. *Exceptional Teacher, 1,* 1–15.

Cole, M. L., & Cole, J. T., (1981). *Effective intervention with the language impaired child.* Rockville, MD: Aspen Systems.

Coleman, R. O., & Anderson, D. E., (1978). Enhancement of language comprehension in developmentally delayed children. *Language, Speech, and Hearing Services in Schools, 9,* 241–253.

Courtright, J. A., & Courtright, I. C., (1979). Imitative modeling as a language intervention strategy: The effects of two mediating variables. *Journal of Speech and Hearing Research, 22,* 389–402.

Crystal, D. (1980). *Introduction to language pathology.* Baltimore: University Park Press.

Culatta, B., & Horn, D. (1982). A program for achieving generalization of grammatical rules to spontaneous discourse. *Journal of Speech and Hearing Disorders, 47,* 178–180.

Cunningham, P. M., (1980). Teaching were, with, what and other "four-letter" words. *Reading Teacher, 34,* 160–163.

Curran, J. S., & Cratty, B. J., (1978). *Speech and language problems in children.* Denver: Love Publishing.

Curtis, J. F., (Ed.) (1978). *Processes and disorders of human communication.* New York: Harper & Row.

Curtiss, S., Prutting, C. A., & Lowell, E. L., (1979). Pragmatic and semantic development in young children with impaired hearing. *Journal of Speech and Hearing Research, 22,* 534–550.

Damico, J., & Oller, J. W., Jr. (1980). Pragmatic versus morphological-syntactic criteria for long-range referral. *Language, Speech, and Hearing Services in Schools, 11,* 85–94.

Denckla, M. B., (1982). Language disorders. In J. A. Downey & N. L., Low (Eds.), *The child with disabling illness: Principles of rehabilitation.* New York: Raven Press.

Dewart, M. H., (1979). Language comprehension processes of mentally retarded children. *American Journal of Mental Deficiency, 84,* 177–183.

Dwinell, M. A., & Connis, R. T., (1979). Reducing inappropriate verbalizations of a retarded adult. *American Journal of Mental Deficiency, 84,* 87–92.

Edelsky, C. (1978). "Teaching" oral language. *Language Arts, 55,* 291–296.

Eisenson, J., & Ogilvie, M. (1983). *Communicative disorders in children* (5th ed.). New York: Macmillan.

Eyde, D. R., & Altman, R. (1979). Communication training in the classroom. A joining of theory and practice. *Education and Training of the Mentally Retarded, 14,* 131–136.

Fay, W., & Schuler, A. (1980). *Emerging language in autistic children.* Baltimore: University Park Press.

Ficociello, C. (Ed.) (1975). *Language development of multihandicapped children.* Dallas: South Central Regional Center for Services to Deaf-Blind Children.

Flowers, D. M., (1974). Expansion and the intelligibility of speech by blind and sighted nonretarded and retarded individuals. *American Journal of Mental Deficiency, 78,* 619–624.

Frederick, H. D. B., McDonnel, J., & Grove, D. (1978). Language programming for the moderately and severely handicapped. *Education and Training of the Mentally Retarded, 13,* 316–322.

French, J. N., (1981). Organizing for comprehension: Strategies for teachers and students. *Education Unlimited, 2,* 33–35.

Gallagher, T. M., & Darnton, B. A., (1978). Conversational aspects of the speech of language disordered children: Revision behavior. *Journal of Speech and Hearing Research, 21,* 118–135.

Goetz, L., Schuler, A., & Sailor, W. (1979). Teaching functional speech to the severely handicapped: Current issues. *Journal of Autism and Developmental Disorders, 9,* 325–344.

Graham, J. T., & Graham, L. W., (1971). Language behavior of the mentally retarded: Syntactic characteristics. *American Journal of Mental Deficiency, 75,* 623–629.

Greer, J. G., Anderson, R. M., & Davis, T. B., (1976). Developing functional language in the severely retarded using standardized vocabulary. In R. Anderson & J. Greer (Eds.), *Educating the severely and profoundly retarded.* Austin: PRO-ED.

Guess, D., & Baer, D. (1973). An analysis of individual differences in generalization between receptive and productive language in retarded children. *Journal of Applied Behavior Analysis, 6,* 311–329.

Guess, D., Sailor, W., & Baer, D. (1978). *Functional speech and language training for the severely handicapped.* Austin: PRO-ED.

Guess, D., Sailor, W., Keogh, B., & Baer, D. (1976). Language development programs for severely handicapped children. In N. Haring & L. Brown (Eds.), *Teaching the severely handicapped* (Vol. 1). New York: Grune & Stratton.

Guttman, A. J., & Rondal, J. A., (1979). Verbal operants in mothers' speech to nonretarded and Down's Syndrome children matched for linguistic level. *American Journal of Mental Deficiency, 83,* 446–452.

Halle, J., Baer, D., & Spradlin, J. (1981). Teacher's generalized use of delay as a stimulus control procedure to increase language use in handicapped children. *Journal of Applied Behavior Analysis, 14,* 389–409.

Halle, J., Marshall, A., & Spradlin, J. (1979). Time delay: A technique to increase language use and facilitate generalization in retarded children. *Journal of Applied Behavior Analysis, 12,* 95–103.

Halliday, M. A. K. (1977). *Learning how to mean: Explorations in the development of language.* New York: American Elsevier.

Hanley-Maxwell, C., Wilcox, B., & Heal, L. W. (1982). A comparison of vocabulary learning by moderately retarded students under direct instruction and incidental presentation. *Education & Training of the Mentally Retarded, 17,* 214–221.

Hart, B., & Risley, T. R. (1981). Grammatical and conceptual growth in the language of psychosocially disadvantaged children. Assessment and intervention. In M. J. Begab, H. C. Haywood, & H. L. Garber (Eds.), *Psychosocial influences in retarded performance.* Austin: PRO-ED.

Haskins, R., Finkelstein, N., & Stedman, D. (1978). Effects of infant and preschool stimulation programs on high-risk children. *American Journal of Mental Deficiency, 83,* 60–68.

Hicks, W. (1980). Communication variables associated with hearing impaired/vision impaired persons: A Pilot Study. *American Annals of the Deaf, 124,* 419–422.

Higginbotham, D., & Yoder, D. (1982). Communication within natural conversational interaction: Implications for severe communicatively impaired persons. *Topics in Language Disorders, 2,* 1–19.

Hillenbrand, J. (1983). Perceptual organization of speech sounds by infants. *Journal of Speech and Hearing Research, 26,* 268–281.

Hubbell, R. (1981). *Children's language disorders—An integrated approach.* Engelwood Cliffs, NJ: Prentice-Hall.

Hurtig, R., Enrud, S., & Tomblin, J. B. (1982). The communicative function of question production in autistic children. *Journal of Autism and Developmental Disorders, 12,* 57–69.

Hutton, B. A. (1980). Moving language around: Helping students become aware of language structure. *Language Arts, 57,* 614–620.

James, S. L., & Seebach, M. A. (1982). The pragmatic function of children's questions. *Journal of Speech and Hearing Research, 25,* 2–11.

Jones, A., & Robson, L. (1979). Language training the severely mentally handicapped. In N. Ellis (Ed.), *Handbook of mental deficiency, psychological theory, and research* (2nd ed.). New York: Lawrence Erlbaum.

Jones, M. L., & Quigley, S. P. (1979). The acquisition of question formation in spoken English and American Sign Language by two hearing children of deaf parents. *Journal of Speech and Hearing Disorders, 44,* 196–208.

Karlan, G. R., & Lloyd, L. L. (1983). Considerations in the planning of communication intervention: Selecting a lexicon. *Journal of the Association for the Severely Handicapped, 8,* 13–25.

Keith, R. W. (1981). *Central auditory and language disorders in children.* San Diego: College-Hill Press.

Kent, R. D. (1981). Articulatory and acoustic perspectives on speech development. In R. E. Stark (Ed.),l *Language behavior in infancy and early childhood.* New York: Elsevier/North-Holland.

Klein, M. L. (1979). Designing a talk environment for the classroom. *Language Arts, 56,* 647–656.

Klein, M. (1977). *Talk in the language arts classroom.* Urbana, IL: National Council of Teachers of English.

Kretschmer, R. R., & Kretschmer, L. W. (1978). *Language development and intervention with the hearing impaired.* Baltimore: University Park Press.

Lackner, J. R. (1976). A developmental study of language behavior in retarded children. In D. M. Morehead & A. E. Morehead (Eds.), *Normal and deficient child language.* Baltimore: University Park Press.

Liles, B. J., & Shulman, M. (1980). The grammaticality task: A tool for language assessment and language intervention. *Language, Speech, and Hearing Services in Schools, 11,* 260–265.

Lodge, D. N., & Leach, E. A. (1975). Children's acquisition of idioms in the English language. *Journal of Speech and Hearing Research, 18,* 521–529.

Lombardino, L., Willems, S., & MacDonald, J. (1981). Critical considerations in total communication and an environmental intervention model for the developmentally delayed. *Exceptional Children, 6,* 455–462.

Lovaas, O. I. (1977). *The autistic child: Language development through behavior modification.* New York: John Wiley.

Lucas, E. V. (1980). *Semantic and pragmatic language disorders: Assessment and remediation.* Rockville, MD: Aspen Systems.

Manson, M. (1982). Explorations in language arts for preschoolers (who happen to be deaf). *Language Arts, 59,* 33–39.

Mayfield, S. A. (1983). Language and speech behaviors of children with undue lead absorption: A review of literature. *Journal of Speech and Hearing Research, 26,* 362–368.

McCarthy, D. (1954). Language development in children. In L. Carmichael (Ed.), *Manual of Child Psychology* (rev. ed.). New York: John Wiley & Sons.

McCormick, L. P., & Elder, P. S. (1978). Instructional strategies for severely language deficient children. *Education and Training of the Mentally Retarded, 13,* 29–36.

McLean, J. E., & Snyder-McLean, L. K. (1978). *A transactional approach to early language training.* Columbus, OH: Charles E. Merrill.

Mecham, M. J., & Willbrand, M. L. (1979). *Language disorders in children: A resource book for speech-language pathologists.* Springfield, IL: Charles C Thomas.

Meline, T. J. (1980). The application of reinforcement in language interaction. *Language, Speech, and Hearing Services in Schools, 11,* 95–101.

Miller, J. F., Chapman, R. S., Branston, M. B., & Reichle, J. (1980). Language comprehension in sensorimotor stages V and VI. *Journal of Speech and Hearing Research, 23,* 284–311.

Minafee, F., & Lloyd, L. (Eds.) (1978). *Communication and cognitive abilities: Early childhood assessment.* Baltimore: University Park Press.

Moerk, E. L. (1977). *Pragmatic and semantic aspects of early language development.* Baltimore: University Park Press.

Morehead, D., & Morehead, A. (Eds.) (1976). *Normal and deficient child language.* Baltimore: University Park Press.

Musselwhite, C. R., & St. Louis, K. W. (1982). *Communication programming for the severely handicapped.* San Diego, CA: College-Hill Press.

Naremore, R. C., & Hipskind, N. M. (1979). Responses to the language of educable mentally retarded and normal children: Stereotypes and judgments. *Language, Speech, and Hearing Services in Schools, 10,* 27–33.

Nietupski, J., Scheutz, G., & Ockwood, L. (1980). The delivery of communication therapy services to severely handicapped students: A plan for change. *Journal of the Association for the Severely Handicapped, 5,* 13–23.

O'Brien, L., & Andresen, J. (1983). A family matter: Stimulating communication in the young cerebral palsied child. *Teaching Exceptional Children, 16,* 47–50.

Oliver, P. R., & Scott, T. L. (1981). Group versus individual training in establishing generalization of language skills with severely handicapped individuals. *Mental Retardation, 19,* 285–289.

Owens, R. E., Jr., & MacDonald, J. D. (1982). Communicative uses of the early speech of nondelayed and Down syndrome children. *American Journal of Mental Deficiency, 86,* 503–510.

Paccia, J., & Curcio, F. (1982). Language processing and forms of immediate echolalia in autistic children. *Journal of Speech and Hearing Disorders, 25,* 42–47.

Piaget, J. (1974). *The language and thought of the child.* New York: New American Library.

Platt, N. G. (1979). Social context: An essential for learning language. *Language Arts, 56,* 620–627.

Prizant, B. M. (1983). Language acquisition and communicative behavior in autism: Toward an understanding of the "whole" of it. *Journal of Speech and Hearing Disorders, 48,* 296–307.

Rees, N. S., & Schulman, M. (1978). I don't understand what you mean by comprehension. *Journal of Speech and Hearing Disorders, 43,* 208–219.

Reichie, J. E., Longhurst, T. M., & Stepanich, L. (1976). Verbal interaction in mother-child dyads. *Developmental Psychology, 12,* 273–277.

Rueda, R., & Chan, K. S. (1980). Referential communication skill levels of moderately mentally retarded adolescents. *American Journal of Mental Deficiency, 85,* 45–52.

Sailor, W., Wilcox, B., & Brown, L. (1980). *Methods of instruction for severely handicapped students.* Baltimore: Paul H. Brookes.

Saltz, R. (1979). Children's interpretations of proverbs. *Language Arts, 56,* 508–513.

Scheuerman, N., Cartwright, S., York, R., Lowry, D., & Brown, L. (1974). Teaching young severely handicapped students to follow verbal directions. *Journal of Special Education, 8,* 223–236.

Schiefelbusch, R. L. (Ed.) (1978). *Bases of language intervention.* Baltimore: University Park Press.

Schuler, A. L. (1979). Echolalia: Issues and clinical applications. *Journal of Speech and Hearing Disorders, 44,* 411–434.

Semel, E., & Wiig, E. (1980). *Clinical evaluation of language functions.* Columbus, OH: Charles E. Merrill.

Shadden, B. B., Asp, C. W., Tonkovich, J. D., & Mason, D. (1980). Imitation of suprasegmental patterns by five-year-old children with adequate and inadequate articulation. *Journal of Speech and Hearing Disorders, 45,* 390–400.

Shuy, R. W., & Griffin, P. (Eds.) (1978). *The study of children's functional language and education in the early years.* Washington, DC: The Center for Applied Linguistics.

Sims-Tucker, B. M., & Jensema, C. K. (1984). Severely and profoundly auditorially/visually impaired students: The deaf-blind population. In P. J. Valletutti and B. M. Sims-Tucker (Eds.), *Severely and profoundly handicapped students: Their nature and needs.* Baltimore: Paul H. Brookes.

Solan, L. (1980). Contrastive stress and children's interpretation of pronouns. *Journal of Speech and Hearing Research, 23,* 688–698.

Spradlin, J. E., & Siegel, G. M. (1982). Language training in natural and clinical environments. *Journal of Speech and Hearing Disorders, 47,* 2–6.

Sternberg, L. (1982). Communication instruction. In I. Sternberg & G. L. Adams (Eds.), *Educating severely and profoundly handicapped students.* Rockville, MD: Aspen Systems.

Sternberg, L., Battle, C., & Hill, J. (1980). Prelanguage communication programming for the severely and profoundly handicapped. *Journal of the Association for the Severely Handicapped, 5,* 224–233.

Stremel-Campbell, K. (1977). Communication skills. In N. G. Haring (Ed.), *Developing effective individualized education programs for severely handicapped children and youth.* Washington, DC: BEH.

Tyack, D. L. (1981). Teaching complex sentences. *Language, Speech, and Hearing Services in Schools, 12,* 49–53.

Van Hattum, R. J. (1979). *Developmental language programming for the retarded.* Boston: Allyn & Bacon.

Webster, B., & Ingram, D. (1972). The comprehension and production of the anaphonic pronouns, he, she, him, her in normal and linguistically deviant children. *Child Language Development, 4,* 55–78.

Weiss, C. E., & Lillywhite, H. S. (1981). *Communicative disorders: Prevention and early intervention* (2nd ed.). St. Louis: C. V. Mosby.

Welch, S. J. (1981). Teaching generative grammar to mentally retarded children: A review and analysis of a decade of behavioral research. *Mental Retardation, 19,* 277–284.

Westby, C. E. (1980). Assessment of cognitive and language abilities through play. *Language, Speech, and Hearing Services in Schools, 11,* 154–168.

Wetherby, A. M., & Gaines, B. H. (1982). Cognition and language development in autism. *Journal of Speech and Hearing Disorders, 47,* 63–70.

Wiig, E. H., & Semel, E. M. (1980). *Language assessment and intervention.* Columbus, OH: Charles E. Merrill.

Wilcox, M. J., & Leonard, L. B. (1978). Experimental acquisition of Wh-questions in language-disordered children. *Journal of Speech and Hearing Research, 21,* 220–239.

Wing, L. (Ed.) (1980). *Early childhood autism.* New York: Pergamon Press.

Winitz, H. (1969). *Articulatory acquisition and behavior.* New York: Appleton-Century-Crofts.

Winkeljohann, Sister R. (1981). How can teachers promote language use? *Language Arts, 58,* 605–606.

Wolf, J. M., & McAlonie, M. L. (1977). A multimodality language program for retarded preschoolers. *Education and Training of the Mentally Retarded, 12,* 197–202.

Wolfus, B., Moscovitch, M., & Kinsbourne, M. (1980). Subgroups of developmental language impairment. *Brain and Language, 10,* 152–171.

Yoder, D. E., & Reichle, J. E. (1978). Some current perspectives on teaching communication functions to mentally retarded children. In P. Mittler (Ed.), *Research to practice in mental retardation: Volume II. Education and Training.* Baltimore: University Park Press.

4 Interpersonal Skills

Functioning as a responsive and responsible person in diverse interpersonal relationships is the bedrock of a functional curriculum. The development of interpersonal skills involves teaching handicapped students those requisite behaviors that will facilitate their acceptance as integrated and participating members of society (Cartledge & Milburn, 1980; Elias & Maher, 1983; Fleming & Fleming, 1982; Mori & Masters, 1980; Vaughan, Ridley, & Cox, 1983).

Emphasis in this curriculum has been placed on identifying instructional objectives that will enhance the ability of handicapped persons to function successfully with others in the home, school, and community. It is hoped that the enhancement of skills in interacting with parents, teachers, and classmates will transfer to other social contexts in a desirable ripple effect (LaGreca & Santogrossi, 1980). Interpersonal skills in interacting with parents (or parent surrogates), teachers, and peers (Davis, 1977; Santomier & Kopczuk, 1981) ought to have a significant impact on other relationships in other natural contexts. Whenever the student comes into contact with people—with prospective mates (Valletutti & Bender, 1982); with coworkers, work supervisors, and employers (Foss & Peterson, 1981; Rusch & Menchetti, 1981); with neighbors, relatives, and siblings; with friends in leisure-time pursuits (Matson & Andrasik, 1982); with colleagues in community living arrangements (Landesman-Dwyer, Berkson, & Romer, 1979) and enterprises; with caregivers; with service personnel who provide needed goods and services (Marholin, O'Toole, Touchette, Berger, & Doyle, 1979; Matson, 1981); and, in the future, with children of his own (Valletutti & Bender, 1982)—the same basic social skills remain consistently and constantly applicable.

The specific interpersonal skills listed in this section should not be taught in isolation because they complement other skills taught throughout the curriculum. It will be necessary to review the curriculum objectives in other areas to ascertain the most appropriate times to include instruction in specific interpersonal skills.

In a functional curriculum, most activities have an interpersonal aspect. For example, the self-care skill of toileting has an interpersonal element in the location and use of sex-appropriate public toilets; in the fine motor area, the manipulation of toys and games is likely to have an interpersonal dimension; and, certainly, communication skills imply a social context.

Interpersonal elements must be considered each time an instructional scenario is envisioned and implemented in classroom action. In carrying out any instructional activity that involves interpersonal aspects, one should be aware of the cognitive dimensions of the desired behavior and especially appreciate the role of cognition training in developing social behaviors (Kneedler, 1980; Valletutti & Bender, 1982). For example, an individual must be able to identify the nature of diverse social situations in order to select behaviors appropriate to a specific social context.

The acquisition and maintenance of positive and supportive relationships with others is the key to enhancing the quality of life for everyone, including those who are handicapped. Too often, however, handicapped individuals do not experience satisfactory and successful relationships since they are shunned by others—largely because they lack those interpersonal skills that make other people seek them out or at least accept them as suitable and desirable companions (Gresham, 1982).

Whenever possible, teachers and parents must provide students with actual experiences in which social behaviors are appropriately and graphically illustrated. When actual experiences are not practical, however, role playing becomes a viable instructional alternative not only to illuminate a behavior but as a means of conflict resolution (Affleck, 1975a, 1975b). Role playing also provides a strategy for reinforcing previous experience and for rehearsing future events.

The Suggested Readings/References and Special Materials List at the end of this chapter provide information on interpersonal skills. The reader should decide which material and information are applicable to a specific student or students being taught.

General Objective of the Unit

The student will function as optimally as possible in social and interpersonal relationships.

Specific Objectives

The student:

A. behaves courteously and uses language courtesies.
B. greets and bids farewell to others in a socially acceptable manner.

C. introduces himself to others at appropriate times.
D. dresses and grooms himself appropriate to the situation.
E. engages in simple conversations and observes the implicit rules of polite conversation.
F. behaves in an acceptable manner in diverse social situations and settings.
G. behaves in an acceptable manner when dealing with people of all ages, of both sexes, and from different racial and ethnic groups.
H. practices sportsmanship.
I. compromises when necessary and "irons out" problems whenever they interfere with interpersonal relationships.
J. asks for help when needed.
K. controls his temper when angry while expressing anger in an appropriate way.
L. expresses his feelings in a socially acceptable way.
M. expresses his beliefs and opinions in a nonthreatening and constructive manner.
N. is reinforcing of others and responds to the reinforcements of others.
O. does not call other people names or otherwise belittle them.
P. ignores being ridiculed or expresses his annoyance, anger, or resentment when he is belittled.
Q. copes with criticism or rejection.
R. accepts responsibility for his actions.
S. works and plays cooperatively with others on a one-to-one basis.
T. works and plays cooperatively with others in a group situation.
U. engages in free-time activities without continual supervision.
V. identifies family members, relatives, friends, neighbors, and acquaintances.
W. distinguishes between significant individuals in his life and strangers and behaves differently with them.
X. participates as a member of a family unit.
Y. shares toys, treats, materials, and games and takes his turn when appropriate.
Z. does not engage in distracting mannerisms and other disconcerting self-stimulatory behaviors.

AA. does not engage in self-destructive behavior.
BB. does not engage in behavior destructive of others, including hitting, scratching, biting, spitting, and pulling hair.
CC. does not engage in behaviors that disturb or distract others or that others find obnoxious.
DD. respects the privacy, property, and civil rights of others.
EE. behaves with others in a mutually supportive and facilitating way and avoids being exploited.
FF. arrives on time to scheduled events and appointments and attends regularly when attendance is required or expected.
GG. completes assigned tasks and otherwise fulfills assigned duties and obligations.

HH. provides help to people, when appropriate, in diverse everyday situations, including emergencies.
II. returns borrowed materials, equipment, money, and other items.
JJ. visits relatives, friends, and neighbors at appropriate times.
KK. communicates with friends, relatives, neighbors, and acquaintances with cards and letters at appropriate times.
LL. communicates with friends, relatives, neighbors, and acquaintances using the telephone whenever appropriate.
MM. invites friends, relatives, neighbors, and acquaintances to socialize with him.
NN. joins friends, relatives, neighbors, and acquaintances in social activities.
OO. joins in projects that provide benefits to the community.
PP. identifies human service persons, community helpers, and other service personnel and interacts with them appropriately.
QQ. obeys all pertinent rules and laws.

Specific Objective A

The student behaves courteously and uses language courtesies.

Functional Settings and Suggested Instructional Activities

School

1. During everyday activities and conversations with the student, say "Please," "Thank you," and "Excuse me" at appropriate times. Tell the student that people with good manners use these words when speaking and working with others. Encourage the student to say "Please," "Thank you," "Excuse me," and other courteous responses at appropriate times.
2. Role play a variety of situations requiring courteous responses. If the student responds courteously, ask her why he said "Please," "Thank you," etc. Discuss courtesy and good manners. Stress the use of good manners and courteous responses as important behavior when meeting new people, seeking employment, during work, and in all activities of daily living.

Home and Community

1. Ask the parents to instruct the child in ways of behaving courteously in various home situations. Tell them to include ways of behaving at mealtimes and when wishing to use the same facilities (e.g., the bathroom) or materials (e.g., the newspaper).
2. Ask the parent to role play situations involving the following language courtesies: "Please," "Thank you," "God bless you," "You're welcome," "Excuse me," "Pardon me," "I beg your pardon," and "I'm sorry."
3. Take the student to crowded places. Show him how to move in crowds by saying "Excuse me" when people are blocking the way. Encourage the student to imitate your actions. Praise his courteous behavior.

4. Take the student on a field trip to a shopping center. Purchase something and point out that the salesperson is courteous (e.g., she says "May I help you?" and "Thank you") when waiting on customers. Encourage the student to use good manners as a consumer (e.g., when asking for help with purchases, tell him to say, "Will you please help me?" and when getting change after paying for something, tell him to say, "Thank you").

Functional Emphases In designing your own instructional activities and plans, emphasize the following elements:

1. Awareness of the relationship of specific language courtesies to specific situations.
2. Realization of the benefits that accrue from behaving courteously to others.

Specific Objective B

The student greets and bids farewell to others in a socially acceptable manner.

Functional Settings and Suggested Instructional Activities

School

1. As the student arrives at the classroom, greet him. Use a variety of greetings (e.g., "Good morning, Stephen," "Hello, John," and "Hi, how are you today?"). Encourage the student to respond appropriately, either by repeating your greeting with "Good morning, Miss Smith" or answering your question with "I'm fine, thank you." For the nonverbal student, a smile or nod to acknowledge the greeting is acceptable. Practice. Also practice farewells.
2. Encourage the student to greet her peers and other individuals who enter the classroom. Explain that "Hi" is an acceptable greeting for peers but not for adults and people they do not know very well. The student should say "Hello," "Good morning," "Good afternoon," or "Good evening" to these people. Practice.

Home and Community

1. Ask the parent to role play and practice greeting and bidding farewell to visitors to the home.
2. Role play walking in the community and greeting people at different times of the day. Practice "Good morning," "Good afternoon," and "Good evening." Practice in real situations.

Functional Emphases In designing your own instructional activities and plans, emphasize the following elements:

1. Avoidance of touching others excessively for routine greetings.
2. Avoidance of handshaking unless appropriate to the situation (e.g., on meeting someone for the first time).
3. Awareness of the relationship between time of day and greeting.
4. Recognition of the different greetings for adults and peers.

Specific Objective C

The student introduces himself to others at appropriate times.

Functional Settings and Suggested Instructional Activities

School

1. On the first day of school or when a new student enters the class, encourage the student to introduce himself. Demonstrate an introduction by introducing yourself to the group (e.g., "Hello, my name is ________, and I'm your teacher."). Encourage the student to imitate your introduction and say, "Hello, my name is ________." Practice.
2. Tell the student that there are times when he should not introduce himself to others. Make a list of these times. Emphasize that he should not introduce himself to strangers and salespeople.

Community

1. At interschool functions (e.g., Special Olympics, sporting events, and dances), encourage the student to meet new people by introducing himself to others (e.g., "Hello, I'm ________. Welcome to our school."). Praise the student for making new acquaintances at supervised events.
2. Explain to the student that if he is ever lost or needs help, he should introduce himself to a policeman and ask for help (e.g., "Hello, my name is ________, and I'm lost."). Discuss a variety of situations that would require the student to ask for help: being lost, losing bus fare, and losing his wallet.

Functional Emphases In designing your own instructional activities and plans, emphasize the following elements:

1. Avoidance of introductions in informal or commercial interactions.
2. Identification of formal situations in which introductions are expected.
3. Avoidance of introductions and other attempts at conversations with strangers unless he is in the company of a responsible adult.

Specific Objective D

The student dresses and grooms himself appropriate to the situation.

Functional Settings and Suggested Instructional Activities

School

1. Show the student pictures of people wearing different clothing. Encourage him to match each picture with an appropriate setting.
2. Show filmstrips and/or movies of people in different social situations. Comment on the clothing worn.

Home and Community

1. Ask the parents to explain to the child why he is dressing the way he is. If he is going to play, tell the parent to explain that he is wearing his play clothes. Tell them to do this for different situations and include recreational clothes (e.g., bathing suits, running shoes, and football helmets), dress clothing (e.g., for church/temple attendance, holiday festivities, and formal parties), and work clothing (e.g., for working in the garden or cleaning house).
2. Go on several visits into the community. In making your plans, discuss the type of clothing to be worn for each occasion.

Functional Emphases In designing your own instructional activities and plans, emphasize the following elements:

1. Recognition of the consequences of inappropriate dress (e.g., embarrassment, ruining good clothing, or not being able to enjoy himself).
2. Identification of the accessories and/or cosmetics to be worn that are consistent with the clothing worn.

Specific Objective E

The student engages in simple conversations and observes the implicit rules of polite conversation.

Functional Settings and Suggested Instructional Activities

School

1. Frequently engage the student in simple conversations as a means of developing oral language skills.
2. Role play conversations as a means of developing oral language skills, examining feelings and attitudes, and developing dialogue for writing scenes and plays.

Home

1. Ask the parents to demonstrate the sharing of interesting experiences as a way of stimulating and maintaining conversations.
2. Ask the parents to demonstrate waiting turns and listening without interrupting as part of conversational etiquette.

Functional Emphases In designing your own instructional activities and plans, emphasize the following elements:

1. Avoidance of monopolizing conversations.
2. Utilization of conversations as a means of exploring feelings and attitudes.
3. Acquisition of the ability to engage in "small talk."
4. Avoidance of controversial topics (e.g., religion, politics, and sex).
5. Development of listening skills.

Specific Objective F

The student behaves in an acceptable manner in diverse social situations and settings.

Functional Settings and Suggested Instructional Activities

School

1. Hold class parties and demonstrate party manners.
2. Simulate telephone conversations using play telephones, teletrainers, or disconnected telephones. Practice good telephone manners, saying "hello" and "goodbye," not speaking too loudly into the telephone, and not banging the receiver down.
3. Set up chairs in the learning area or auditorium to simulate a movie theater. Show a movie or filmstrip and encourage the student to act as he would in a movie theater (paying attention to the movie, speaking in a quiet voice so as not to disturb others, sitting still in his seat, and not getting up and down repeatedly to buy refreshments or to use the bathroom).

Home and Community

1. Tell the parents that when the child is planning to attend a wedding, baptism, bar mitzvah, or other religious event, they should discuss the event with him. Tell them to explain what will happen at the event and the kind of behavior that will be expected of him. Tell them to simulate the occasion through role play, demonstrate appropriate behavior, and encourage him to imitate their actions.
2. Ask the parents to provide the child with experiences in a variety of social situations, including home visits, parties, dances, sports events, picnics, outings, funerals, and wakes. Tell them they should explain the differing nature of these events and should clarify the type of behavior expected.
3. Take the student to a variety of social events offered in the community. Practice suitable behaviors.

Functional Emphases In designing your own instructional activities and plans, emphasize the following elements:

1. Recognition of the impact of the setting on type of behavior (e.g., quiet during religious services, subdued and mournful during a wake or funeral, and happy during a party or celebration).
2. Awareness of manners in face-to-face communication.
3. Sensitivity to telephone manners.

Specific Objective G

The student behaves in an acceptable manner when dealing with people of all ages, of both sexes, and from different racial and ethnic groups.

Functional Settings and Suggested Instructional Activities

School

1. Read stories in which one of the characters is an infant or small child. As you read the story to the student, point out how carefully and gently the characters in the story handle the infant or small child.
2. Call the Red Cross, a hospital, or other community group that offers courses or instruction in child care. Ask the agency to send a trained person to your classroom to demonstrate handling, holding, and carrying infants and young children. Give the student a doll and encourage him to imitate the instructor's actions.
3. Warn the student that rough play with small children may be fun, but it may easily end with the small child getting hurt or crying. Discourage roughhousing and encourage appropriate play activities (e.g., rolling a rubber ball back and forth, playing with soft toys, and singing "Pat-a-Cake").
4. Model appropriate behavior with colleagues of both sexes.
5. Read stories that deal with the cultural diversity of our country. Enjoy the differences and similarities among all people.

Home

1. Ask the parents to show the child pictures of infants and small children. Tell them to include pictures of young sisters, brothers, cousins, and other infants and small children he knows. Tell them to comment on the fact that they are younger and smaller than he is and need special handling.
2. Ask the parents to show the child pictures of aging people who are no longer robust. Tell them to include pictures of the aged members of his family who must be treated gently and/or with whom he cannot play roughly. Tell them to point out that as people get old, they very often become weaker and more susceptible to illness. Tell them to explain that because of these factors, some older people need to be treated with special care and concern.
3. Ask the parents to discuss racial and ethnic groups, to identify the child's group membership, and to emphasize that different groups of people, despite these differences, are all basically the same.
4. Ask the parents to acquaint the child with more enlightened perceptions of the role of males and females. Tell them to discuss socially prevalent differences in relating to male versus female peers and adults.

Functional Emphases In designing your own instructional activities and plans, emphasize the following elements:

1. Identification of the need to relate to a diverse age group in different ways.

2. Awareness of the different treatment required in interacting with senior citizens.
3. Appreciation for the excitement and enrichment that comes from enjoying the ethnic and racial diversity of our nation.

Specific Objective H

The student practices sportsmanship.

Functional Settings and Suggested Instructional Activities

School

1. As the students play and work together, remind them to take turns, share materials, include younger students, help others, and accept winning and losing. Praise the students for behaving in a sportsmanlike manner. Use the expressions "good sport" and "poor sport" whenever appropriate.
2. When the student loses, it is important that he be encouraged to try again. Talk about losing with the student and tell him that losing is as much a part of playing as winning. Once the student recognizes that losing is not a constant condition, he may be better able to cope with losing. Provide opportunities that allow the student to win sometimes, even if it means creating a special game or event to suit the student's particular abilities. Take the time needed to find activities in which the student can be successful. Completing or achieving something is a way of winning.

Home and Community

1. Ask the parents to play table games and other household games. Ask them to model being a gracious winner and an accepting loser.
2. Take the students to a sports event. Point out and praise good sportsmanship. Comment unfavorably when athletes display poor sportsmanship.

Functional Emphases In designing your own instructional activities and plans, emphasize the following elements:

1. Identification of the behaviors that a magnanimous or gracious winner demonstrates.
2. Recognition that being a "sore" loser interferes with establishing and maintaining friendships.

Specific Objective I

The student compromises when necessary and "irons out" problems whenever they interfere with interpersonal relationships.

Functional Settings and Suggested Instructional Activities

School

1. Ask the student what he would like to do during free time. If it is acceptable, let him do it. Explain, however, that he will not always be able to do as he pleases. Tell him that tomorrow someone else may be using some material he wants and that he will have to choose something else with which to work or play. Explain that this is called a compromise.
2. Prepare a list of jobs for the student and his peers to do in the classroom. Ask the student to choose the job he would most like to do. If more than one person chooses a particular job, explain that only one at a time may do the job and that the others will have to compromise. Select one peer to do the job this week. Tell the student and his peers that they may have the job next week or the week after. Praise the student and his peers for being cooperative and accepting the compromise.

Home

1. Ask the parents to help the child differentiate between things that are negotiable (e.g., a choice of activities) and things that are not (e.g., cleaning his room). Tell them to emphasize that negotiable items often require a compromise. Tell them to explain and demonstrate the compromise process.
2. Ask the parents to assist the child in ironing out interpersonal problems that arise. Tell them to make certain that they compromise when compromise is productive.

Functional Emphases In designing your own instructional activities and plans, emphasize the following elements:

1. Differentiation between situations that are negotiable and those that are not.
2. Appreciation for the cumulative pattern of compromise (i.e., an item that is to be negotiated may be influenced by previous negotiations).
3. Appreciation for the negative effects of not compromising.

Specific Objective J

The student asks for help when needed.

Functional Settings and Suggested Instructional Activities

School

1. Discuss and role play a variety of emergency situations (e.g., plumbing clogged up, electricity off, and gas leak). Practice seeking help in each situation by telephoning the appropriate service representative.
2. Set up a buddy system. Explain that buddies help each other when needed.

Home and Community

1. Ask the parents to encourage the child to ask for help when needed. Tell them to discourage her from asking for help by gently reprimanding her and by refusing unnecessary help.
2. Show the student a picture of a police officer. Tell the student that if he is lost or in trouble, he should go to a police officer for help. Role play being lost and asking a police officer for help. Practice.
3. Take the student shopping at a grocery or department store. Point out salespersons to the student, emphasizing the clues that indicate a salesperson (e.g., wearing a name tag, uniform, or smock, and standing beside the cash register). Tell the student that when he is shopping and unsure of what to buy or where items are located, he should seek the help of a salesperson. Role play the situation.

Functional Emphases In designing your own instructional activities and plans, emphasize the following elements:

1. Avoidance of asking for help when it is not needed.
2. Identification of the appropriate way to ask for help.
3. Identification of the appropriate times to ask for help.

Specific Objective K

The student controls his temper when angry while expressing anger in an appropriate way.

Functional Settings and Suggested Instructional Activities

School

1. From magazines, cut pictures of faces showing a variety of expressions (sad, happy, and angry). If you are unable to find magazine pictures suggesting emotions, draw simple faces and put a variety of expressions on them. Show the pictures to the student and ask him to tell you what the people in the pictures are feeling. Practice with the student, using a variety of pictures.
2. Role play a number of situations that might arouse the student's anger. Discuss ways of controlling anger (e.g., counting to ten, thinking of something pleasant, and leaving the situation that is causing the angry feelings). Practice.

Home

1. Tell the parents to encourage the child to verbalize or to indicate his anger. Tell them to discuss the anger-provoking situation and help him control his anger by guiding him into other situations or activities. Stress that fighting and other socially unacceptable behaviors such as biting, kicking, and screaming are not appropriate or productive outlets for his anger.

2. Remind the parents that they must establish a model of the healthy expression of anger.

Functional Emphases In designing your own instructional activities and plans, emphasize the following elements:

1. Differentiation between mature ways of expressing anger and ways that are infantile and counterproductive.
2. Awareness of the consequences of displaying anger in inappropriate ways.

Specific Objective L

The student expresses his feelings in a socially acceptable way.

Functional Settings and Suggested Instructional Activities

School

1. Read newspaper accounts of people who have been subjected to emotional experiences. Discuss the reactions.
2. If a situation arises in the classroom in which feelings run high, encourage their expression in suitable ways.

Home

1. Ask the parents to model the appropriate way of expressing happiness, sadness, fear, and anger. Tell them to accept variations, provided that they are acceptable.
2. Ask the parents to show the child examples of the expression of feelings as depicted in television programs. Tell them to comment on why they are appropriate or inappropriate ways of expressing specific feelings.

Functional Emphases In designing your own instructional activities and plans, emphasize the following elements:

1. Awareness of the possible emotional responses and the situations that stimulate them.
2. Recognition of the range of possible ways of expressing feelings.
3. Identification of the health benefits of expressing feelings instead of keeping them bottled up.

Specific Objective M

The student expresses his beliefs and opinions in a nonthreatening and constructive manner.

Functional Settings and Suggested Instructional Activities

School

1. Discuss problems and issues related to the class routine and to the student's program. Encourage active participation while you model appropriate ways of expressing divergent opinions.
2. Explain to the student that people have different opinions on solving community, national, and international problems. Discuss some of these problems and the ways people have tried to solve or resolve them.

Home and Community

1. Ask the parents to engage the child in discussions of likes and dislikes relevant to foods, activities, toys, games, and clothing. Tell them to encourage reasoned discussion and to discourage heated exchanges and personal attacks.
2. Take the student to a public meeting or meeting of a civic organization. Discuss appropriate ways of expressing opinions.

Functional Emphases In designing your own instructional activities and plans, emphasize the following elements:

1. Awareness that people often disagree about small as well as big issues.
2. Recognition of the diversity of people's taste.
3. Comprehension of the diversity in political opinion and religious beliefs.

Specific Objective N

The student is reinforcing of others and responds to the reinforcement of others.

Functional Settings and Suggested Instructional Activities

School

1. Reward the student for smiling, listening, sharing, and being kind to his peers and to significant others.
2. Point out to the student qualities of his peers that are worthy of being praised. Praise these students and encourage imitation. Reward the student whenever he praises a peer.

Home

1. Ask the parents to review ways that they can be positively reinforcing (see Table 1).
2. Tell the parents that if the child does not respond positively to social reinforcements, they should begin by reinforcing him with tangible rewards such as a nutritionally suitable food he enjoys or a favorite toy. Tell them that they should simultaneously tell him he is doing well (verbal praise). Tell them at first to provide the tangible/social reinforcement at each example of the

Table 1. Forms of praise and reinforcement

Verbal approval	Nonverbal approval	Physical contact
Good	Smiling	Patting on shoulder
Great	Winking	Holding hands
Wow	Nodding	Tousling hair
Fantastic	Gesture	Occasional touching
Good job	Looking interested	Occasional hugging
I'm happy	Laughing	Grasping arm
Excellent	Wrinkling nose	Sitting next to student

desired behavior, then at *fixed intervals* (e.g., every third time the behavior occurs), and next at *intermittent intervals* (i.e., with no fixed pattern of reward). Tell them to continue in this way while sometimes rewarding with the tangible/social reinforcement and sometimes with the social reinforcement alone. Tell them at times to increase the intensity of the social reinforcers (i.e., add smiles, pats, and touches) while occasionally including a tangible reward.

Functional Emphases In designing your own instructional activities and plans, emphasize the following elements:

1. Awareness of the power of reinforcement in that it can modify, change, and control the behavior of others.
2. Recognition of the acceptable ways of providing reinforcement.

Specific Objective O

The student does not call other people names or otherwise belittle them.

Functional Settings and Suggested Instructional Activities

School

1. If the student curses at or calls others derogatory names, try to distract him. Once he has stopped, explain that the word or words he has just said are nasty words that will hurt the feelings of others. Explain that if he really was angry at the person, there are other ways of dealing with his anger. For example,

he can leave the situation; he can stop playing with the person; he can engage in gross motor activities such as pounding clay or calisthenics; and/or he can tell the person he is angry and explain why.

2. Point out that other people have good qualities and should not be called names (e.g., say, "John shares his toys and treats with others; therefore, he is a nice person. He does not deserve to be hurt in any way. He deserves to be treated well. Saying nice words to people is one way of being good.").

Home

1. Remind the parents that calling other people names or belittling others is a modeled behavior. Encourage them not to demonstrate this negative behavior. Tell them to live by the maxim, "If you have nothing good to say about someone, say nothing."
2. Encourage the parents to find nice things to say about others, especially those individuals who are frequently belittled by people in general.

Functional Emphases In designing your own instructional activities and plans, emphasize the following elements:

1. Awareness of the power inherent in saying nice things to others.
2. Recognition of the adverse effects of ridiculing or belittling others.

Specific Objective P

The student ignores being ridiculed or expresses his annoyance, anger, or resentment when he is belittled.

Functional Settings and Suggested Instructional Activities

School

1. During recess or playtime, listen to the students' conversations. If a student calls another student a name, stop the activity immediately and discuss the name calling. Ask the student who was called a name how it made him feel. Explain that when a person is called a name, it usually makes that person feel sad, angry, or hurt. Stress that even though the one who is called a name may want to call the other a name, the best way to behave is to ignore the name calling. Practice ignoring name calling when it occurs and discourage name calling. Reward the student for ignoring name calling.
2. Clarify when it is not possible to ignore being ridiculed. Assist her in clearly and forcibly expressing his resentment and annoyance, especially when it is likely to stop the belittling.

Home and Community

1. Ask the parents to discuss with the child that people often call others names. Tell them to explain that handicapped people are sometimes ridiculed by ignorant or insensitive people. Tell them to explain the nature of the child's handicap in simple terms.
2. While on a trip in the community, if someone ridicules the student, urge the student to ignore the taunt and just enjoy himself.

Functional Emphases In designing your own instructional activities and plans, emphasize the following elements:

1. Awareness of the value of ignoring taunts.
2. Appreciation for those situations when the expression of annoyance or resentment will achieve results and/or enlighten the person who is ridiculing others.

Specific Objective Q

The student copes with criticism or rejection

Functional Settings and Suggested Instructional Activities

School

1. During classroom or sports activities, correct the student if he is behaving unacceptably or doing something incorrectly. Tell him that what he is doing is wrong and help him to correct his behavior. If the student is upset by the correction, explain that correction and criticism are part of life and that he should try not to be upset.
2. When situations in which the student is rejected arise, help the student to cope with the rejection by encouraging him to engage in an activity he likes. Help him enumerate his good points to counteract his feelings of rejection.

Home and Community

1. Ask the parents to explain to the child that they may have to criticize him. Tell them to say that he should listen to the criticism and either discuss his disagreement or change his behavior.
2. Discuss a variety of work situations that are employment possibilities for the student (e.g., sheltered workshop, gardening, or housework). Explain that on a job he will be responsible to a boss or supervisor. Tell the student that if he does not do his job well, his boss will criticize him. Remind the student that, although he might not like being criticized, he must try to accept the criticism and to do a better job. Then role play situations in which the student is criticized by a variety of individuals (e.g., parents, teacher, boss, or friend). Encourage the student to respond positively to constructive criticism. Tell the student to explain to the person if the criticism is not true.

Functional Emphases In designing your own instructional activities and plans, emphasize the following elements:

1. Differentiation between constructive criticism and ridicule.
2. Awareness of the possible steps to be taken in dealing with the stress of criticism.
3. Recognition of his good qualities and positive traits.

Specific Objective R

The student accepts responsibility for his actions.

Functional Settings and Suggested Instructional Activities

School

1. Encourage the student to think about the outcomes of situations before deciding whether or not to do something.
2. When a situation arises in which the student has behaved badly or broken the class rules, discuss the behavior with him. Explain that since he chose to do something against the rules, he must accept the outcome of his actions. Discuss what the student did and decide upon an appropriate punishment or solution to the situation. When possible, involve the student in selecting the punishment.

Home and Community

1. Ask the parents to establish household rules and punishments for breaking them. Tell them that if the child breaks these rules, they should punish her as specified. Remind them to be consistent in applying punishment.
2. Role play a scene in which the student disobeys a community regulation (e.g., he fails to use a trash basket to dispose of litter). Tell him that if he is caught littering, he can be fined. Explain the law and the fine structure.

Functional Emphases In designing your own instructional activities and plans, emphasize the following elements:

1. Awareness of established laws and the possible consequences of disobeying them.
2. Appreciation of the need to establish regulations and the responsibility to observe them.
3. Comprehension of the cause-and-effect relationship of behavior to consequences.

Specific Objective S

The student works and plays cooperatively with others on a one-to-one basis.

Functional Settings and Suggested Instructional Activities

School

1. Involve the student in a two-person dance.
2. Ask the student to gain the help of a peer in carrying a cumbersome box.
3. Involve the student in a game of catch with a peer.
4. Show the student how to ride a seesaw with a peer.

Home

1. Ask the parent to engage the child in two-person games in which the solution is arrived at by working cooperatively (e.g., building a city with building blocks, doing a jigsaw puzzle, and playing statues with the two of them forming a sculpture).
2. Ask the parent to engage the child in a cooperative household chore (e.g., folding sheets, washing and drying dishes, and making a bed).

Functional Emphases In designing your own instructional activities and plans, emphasize the following elements:

1. Awareness that through cooperation, work can be done more effectively and efficiently.
2. Recognition that some activities cannot be easily accomplished without the assistance of another person (e.g., playing on a seesaw or playing catch).

Specific Objective T

The student works and plays cooperatively with others in a group situation.

Functional Settings and Suggested Instructional Activities

School

1. In the classroom, assign the student to a team of three or four peers. Give the team a group activity or chore to complete. Supervise the team as it works, encouraging the student to do his share and to work as a member of the group.
2. Initiate a class project that can be completed on an assembly-line production. Assign each student a specific task and line up the class at a table in the order of assembly. Start the project with the first student. Once the student completes his assigned task, tell him to pass the project to the next person. Continue until the project is completed. Repeat the activity until there are enough completed projects for each person to have one. Tell the student that, by doing his job and working as a part of a group, he has helped to complete each person's project.

Home and Community

1. Encourage the parents to include the child in group projects or activities (e.g., raking and bagging the leaves, folding laundry, and preparing a simple meal).

Tell them to praise him for doing his share and for being a contributing member of a work group. Tell them to practice using a variety of tasks and activities.
2. Ask the parents to set up a housecleaning and maintenance chart that includes chores and chore schedules. Tell them to emphasize that everyone involved is working toward making the home a cleaner and more attractive place to live.
3. Plan a trip to a local or state park. Make planning and preparation a cooperative effort.

Functional Emphases In designing your own instructional activities and plans, emphasize the following elements:

1. Recognition that cooperation is an effective way of achieving a goal that cannot be done by one person alone.
2. Awareness that if he does not cooperate, he cannot enjoy the benefits of group membership.

Specific Objective U

The student engages in free-time activities without continual supervision.

Functional Settings and Suggested Instructional Activities

School

1. Develop a list of free-time activities the student can do while in the classroom. During appropriate times allow the student to have free time and monitor how well he handles the situation. Praise him when appropriate.
2. Ask the student to tell you the free-time activities he likes best. When you wish to reward him for accomplishing a task use one of the free-time activities he has suggested. Monitor him during the free time when necessary.

Home

1. Ask the parents to select activities for their child that require minimal supervision (e.g., watching an educational television program). Tell them to praise the child when he does this appropriately.
2. Ask the parents to make a list of the activities around the home that their child could do that require minimal supervision. Tell them to allow their child to engage in these activities at appropriate times.

Functional Emphases In designing your own instructional activities and plans, emphasize the following elements:

1. Recognition of a variety of free-time activities.
2. Identification of free-time activities the student values.
3. Selection of free-time activities that are safe and appropriate.

Specific Objective V

The student identifies family members, relatives, friends, neighbors, and acquaintances.

Functional Settings and Suggested Instructional Activities

School

1. Show the student pictures of his family members, yourself, and other significant individuals in his life. Place these pictures face down on a desk. Turn each picture over and say, "This is __________ . He is __________ ." Repeat this activity; this time ask the student to turn over each picture and name the person.
2. Make a bulletin board or wall display of the student's "favorite people." Periodically ask the student to name the people whose pictures are on display.

Home

1. Ask the parents to identify people who are favorites of the child. Tell them to review each person's name (or nickname) and relationship to the child (e.g., "This is Michael. He is a friend." or "This is Margaret. She is your aunt. She is Aunt Margaret.").
2. Ask the parents to make a scrapbook of the pictures of relevant people in the child's life. Tell them to set up the scrapbook by relationship categories (i.e., separate sections on relatives, friends, neighbors, acquaintances, and family members).

Functional Emphases In designing your own instructional activities and plans, emphasize the following elements:

1. Recognition of a wide variety of people in the environment and differentiation of these individuals by their relationship to him.
2. Differentiation of family members, relatives, friends, neighbors, and acquaintances and awareness of the differing demands, relationships, and responsibilities involved.
3. Differentiation between significant individuals in her life and strangers.

Specific Objective W

The student distinguishes between significant individuals in his life and strangers and behaves differently with them.

Functional Settings and Suggested Instructional Activities

School

1. Review the behaviors and activities that are suitably engaged in with familiar people and that are not appropriate to do with strangers.

2. Read newspaper accounts of people who have been exploited or hurt by strangers (be cautious about frightening the student). Express the fact that under certain conditions, strangers can become acquaintances and even friends (e.g., meeting someone while with family members, meeting someone at a church or temple function, and being introduced to someone new through a responsible person).

Home

1. Ask the parents to explain the difference between a relative, neighbor, friend, or acquaintance and a stranger. Tell them to show the child pictures of familiar and unfamiliar people. Tell them to ask him to pick out the strangers.
2. Ask the parents to set up a list of rules regarding strangers (e.g., never let a stranger into the house and never accept a ride from a stranger).

Functional Emphases In designing your own instructional activities and plans, emphasize the following elements:

1. Realization that some known adults might hurt or exploit them.
2. Awareness that there are good strangers with whom they might interact under the right circumstances and conditions.

Specific Objective X

The student participates as a member of a family unit.

Functional Settings and Suggested Instructional Activities

School

1. Role play family situations and encourage the student to play the part of each family member.
2. Explain that being a class member is like being a family member in that the members of a class share experiences and responsibilities and care about each other as families do. Encourage the student's group identification by initiating a variety of class activities that include everyone (e.g., assigning cooperative projects and classroom jobs). Praise the student for being a contributing member of the class.

Home

1. Ask the parents to include the child in diverse family activities, including family responsibilities and family social/recreational events. Tell them to involve him in planning and assign him jobs and responsibilities whenever possible. Tell them to praise him for being a contributing family member.
2. Ask the parents to read the child stories about families and family life. Tell them to discuss how the characters interact, share responsibilities and experiences, and care for each other.

Functional Emphases In designing your own instructional activities and plans, emphasize the following elements:

1. Realization that family members have a special bond that can be comforting at times of need.
2. Appreciation for the kinds of responsibilities that a family member has to his family.
3. Recognition of and experience with the kinds of social situations when a family comes together (e.g., weddings, religious observances, holiday celebrations, and reunions).

Specific Objective Y

The student shares toys, treats, materials, and games and takes his turn when appropriate.

Functional Settings and Suggested Instructional Activities

School

1. During opening exercises or a show-and-tell lesson, encourage the student and his peers to tell you something. Remind the student to take turns so that everyone has a chance to speak.
2. Plan an art activity. Pass out enough materials for only half the class to use at one time. Tell the class members to ask each other if they may use or share materials. Encourage the student to share and to take turns using the materials and equipment.

Home and Community

1. Ask the parents to provide the child with many situations in which sharing is an essential social skill. Tell them to make sure he shares. Tell them to help him determine situations in which sharing is not necessary.
2. Ask the parents to play games with the child in which taking turns is an essential part. Tell them to reward her for waiting until it is her turn.
3. While on a field trip, take the student and his peers for a drink at a drinking fountain. Praise him for waiting his turn.

Functional Emphases In designing your own instructional activities and plans, emphasize the following elements:

1. Recognition that sharing is a reciprocal behavior and that he should not share with others who do not share with him.
2. Comprehension of the way to behave when others with him fail to observe the rules of taking turns.

Specific Objective Z

The student does not engage in distracting mannerisms and other disconcerting self-stimulatory behaviors.

Functional Settings and Suggested Instructional Activities

School

1. Show the student a rocking chair. Sit in the chair and demonstrate using it. Explain that rocking is appropriate when in a rocking chair. Also demonstrate rocking from side to side while dancing to suitable music. Discourage back-and-forth rocking.
2. If the student is engaged in repetitive movements, grasp him by the hand and play a circle game such as "The Farmer in the Dell" or "Bluebird."

Home and Community

1. Tell the parents that if the child rocks back and forth, they should show displeasure, stop him immediately, and reward him for not rocking.
2. Tell the parents that if the child engages in repetitive ritualistic movements of the hands and arms, they should stop the behavior immediately. Tell them to use a firm voice and immediately provide him with an alternate activity involving the use of the upper extremities.
3. If the student engages in self-stimulatory behavior while in the community, engage him in an active game or conversation.

Functional Emphases In designing your own instructional activities and plans, emphasize the following elements:

1. Development of interest in relating to others.
2. Development of interest in engaging in constructive or productive activities.

Specific Objective AA

The student does not engage in self-destructive behavior.

Functional Settings and Suggested Instructional Activities

School

1. Indicate that people get angry or frustrated at times and that one way to work it out is by pounding clay. Give the student clay and show him how to pound it vigorously. Indicate in some way that this way of playing or showing anger does not hurt him or the clay. Give him clay or things such as foam rubber that he can pound or twist whenever the need arises.
2. Give the student hard raw carrots or crisp celery. As he chews them, indicate that biting and chewing food are important parts of eating and that is what teeth are for.

3. Whenever the student engages in self-destructive behavior, stop him from doing so and tell him he is a good person and does not deserve to be hurt.
4. Avoid situations that are likely to precipitate self-destructive behavior.

Home

1. Tell the parents that if the child bites his hands or other parts of his body, they should stop him from continuing while telling him he is a nice person and should not be hurt.
2. Tell the parents that if the child engages in head banging, they should remove her from areas near walls, furniture, and other places that might encourage it. Tell them to substitute a suitable activity such as playing percussion-type rhythm instruments. Encourage her to use sticks, cymbals, drums, and tambourines.
3. Tell the parents that if the child scratches and hurts himself, they should stop him immediately. Tell them to hold his hands and quickly substitute a constructive hand activity of high interest to the child.
4. Tell the parents that if the child picks his skin, they should reward him when he is not picking at sores or loose skin.
5. Tell the parents that if the child pulls his hair out, they should reward him for not engaging in hair pulling. Tell them they should comment also on the even head of hair (without bald patches) of others.
6. Tell the parents that if the child uses sharp objects destructively, they should remove them from places easily accessible to him.

Functional Emphases In designing your own instructional activities and plans, emphasize the following elements:

1. Substitution of productive activities for self-destructive ones.
2. Involvement with people and things.
3. Awareness of the appropriate ways of coping with stress, frustration, and anger.

Specific Objective BB

The student does not engage in behavior destructive of others, including hitting, scratching, biting, spitting, and pulling hair.

Functional Settings and Suggested Instructional Activities

School

1. Speak positively about the student's peers. Talk about their good qualities and how they deserve to be treated nicely. Discuss various ways to treat people nicely (e.g., smiling at them and sharing toys, snacks, and experiences). Role play being nice to others. Use as many different ways as possible. Follow up by scheduling a time when each student is expected to say something nice or do something nice for each peer.

2. Try to anticipate destructive behavior toward others by observing behavioral clues that signal an approaching crisis. Intercede by initiating a novel activity.
3. Show the student acceptable ways of attracting attention since destructive behaviors may be an attention-getting strategy. Help the student to imitate these behaviors in simulated situations and then practice them in both simulated and actual situations.

Home

1. Ask the parents to join the child in identifying and discussing the good qualities of others. Ask them to develop the idea of "I'm O.K., and you're O.K."
2. Tell the parents to stop the child if he begins to be destructive, remove him from the situation, and initiate a distracting activity of high interest.

Functional Emphases In designing your own instructional activities and plans, emphasize the following elements:

1. Appreciation for the good qualities in others.
2. Recognition of the appropriate ways to obtain attention.
3. Awareness of the appropriate ways to express anger/frustration/displeasure.
4. Facilitation of a more positive self-image.

Specific Objective CC

The student does not engage in behaviors that disturb or distract others or that others find obnoxious.

Functional Settings and Suggested Instructional Activities

School

1. If the student begins to pick his nose, stop him and tell him he doesn't look good. Tell him he really looks good when he uses a tissue to clean his nose.
2. If the student burps or belches in public, tell him to cover his mouth and indicate in some way that he is sorry.
3. If the student passes wind, take him immediately to a private place, preferably a bathroom, and indicate that he should have passed wind in such a private place.
4. If the student engages in excessive touching, hugging, and/or kissing, gently prevent her from doing so. Say "No" or "Stop." Indicate there are other ways of getting attention without making physical contact.
5. Ignore profanity whenever possible. Do not overreact because it will reinforce the behavior. Whenever profanity cannot be ignored, say, "No, do not say that word (or words). I like to hear you speak, but I like to hear nice words. Those words are not nice, and I do not want to hear them."

Home and Community

1. Ask the parents to make certain that the child:
   a. controls drooling when physically able to do so.
   b. does not pick his nose in public.
   c. eats in a socially acceptable manner.
   d. does not burp, belch, or pass wind in public.
   e. does not pick his scalp.
   f. does not sniff people and objects.
   g. does not fondle himself in public.
   h. does not engage in touching, hugging, kissing, and shaking hands with others unnecessarily or inappropriately.
   i. maintains socially determined distances between himself and others.
   j. avoids using profanities.
2. Take the student to the movies, the theater, and other places requiring quiet. Point out to him that when people are talking too much or too loudly, other people look at them or shush them. Tell the student that if he is somewhere requiring quiet and is talking and people start looking at him or shushing him, he should be quiet because his conversation is disturbing.

Functional Emphases In designing your own instructional activities and plans, emphasize the following elements:

1. Recognition that obnoxious behaviors interfere with being liked.
2. Recognition that disturbing or distracting behaviors reduce the likeliness of social interaction, including acquiring friends and finding a mate.

Specific Objective DD

The student respects the privacy, property, and civil rights of others.

Functional Settings and Suggested Instructional Activities

School

1. Bring games, toys, and books that belong to you into the classroom or learning area. Show them to the student and explain that although the items belong to you, you would like to share them with him. Explain that when he uses things that belong to others, he should be especially careful with them. Encourage the student to use your games, toys, and books and to be especially careful with them.
2. Ask the student and his peers to bring a favorite game, toy, or book into the classroom. Tell each member of the class to show his item to the others. During a supervised play period, encourage them to share their favorite toy, game, or book with the other people. Supervise closely to avoid damage to personal property. Remind the student to be especially careful when using other people's property.

3. Discuss vandalism. Talk about it or read newspaper articles about incidents of vandalism. Explain that vandals harm or ruin other people's property. Tell the student that it is unlawful to harm other people's property and that he must never do it. Use examples of vandalism that the student can understand (e.g., broken windows and graffiti).
4. Review the meaning of civil rights. Enumerate those the student can understand. Review the ways he can behave to ensure the civil rights of others.
5. Discuss personal belongings and school storage areas such as desks and lockers. Explain that these are private materials and areas and should not be disturbed.

Home

1. Ask the parents to discuss privacy with the child. Tell them to model respecting the privacy of others by knocking before entering someone's bedroom, by not eavesdropping on a telephone conversation, and by not going through the drawers, private papers, and closets of another member of the household.
2. Ask the parents to make sure that personal property of each member of the household is carefully identified. Ask them to make certain that borrowed or used property is carefully handled and returned in good condition.

Functional Emphases In designing your own instructional activities and plans, emphasize the following elements:

1. Realization that he should only get involved in private matters when he has been invited *and* wishes to do so.
2. Awareness of the need to return borrowed items promptly and in good condition.
3. Recognition that there are certain behaviors that should be performed in private (e.g., going to the bathroom, engaging in sexual relations, and having private conversations and discussions).

Specific Objective EE

The student behaves with others in a mutually supportive and facilitative way and avoids being exploited.

Functional Settings and Suggested Instructional Activities

School

1. Spend a substantial amount of class time on cooperative endeavors. Throughout these endeavors, make certain that all participants are working and sharing in approximately equal measure.
2. Role play a variety of situations that depict persons being taken advantage of or exploited (e.g., someone taking money from another person, a stranger making sexual advances to a student, and a person giving a student a job but not paying him). Talk about the situations and explain that one person is taking

advantage of another person. Tell the student not to allow people to take advantage of him.

3. Discuss with the student the safety factors involved in carrying money. Tell him to carry money in a wallet in a buttoned pocket, a purse, or a pocket. Remind the student not to give his money away and not to tell strangers that he has money.
4. Show the student pictures and read aloud articles from the newspaper about robberies and muggings. As a safety rule, tell the student that if someone tries to rob him and threatens him, he should give that person his money and may thus avoid injury. Once the robber is gone, the student should seek the assistance of a police officer or other responsible adult.
5. Take the student shopping. As you purchase items, show the student how you check the price on the item against the price you are charged (remember to include tax). Look at the sales slip to see that the price is the same. Check your change closely. Practice with the student.
6. Talk to the student about door-to-door salespeople. Remind the student not to purchase items or to sign any papers unless a responsible person is present to advise him. If the student is interested in purchasing something but no responsible person is present, tell him to ask the salesperson to come back at another specific time when a responsible person will be present.

Home and Community

1. Ask the parents to discuss the various ways he can be exploited. Tell them to include sexual exploitation, flim-flam operations, salary or wage exploitation, and other money, time, and effort activities in which their child contributes substantially more than others.
2. Visit various agencies in the community that provide help to people that have been exploited (e.g., Legal Aid, the police department, Traveler's Aid, Social Services, and the Better Business Bureau).

Functional Emphases In designing your own instructional activities and plans, emphasize the following elements:

1. Appreciation for the fact that most people are well-meaning and helpful.
2. Recognition that there are some people who wish to exploit others, especially in terms of obtaining their money and material goods.
3. Identification of his civil rights.
4. Identification of resource agencies and people who can help him when he has been exploited.

Specific Objective FF

The student arrives on time to scheduled events and appointments and attends regularly when attendance is required or expected.

Functional Settings and Suggested Instructional Activities

School

1. Discuss with the student the time he should wake up in the morning to arrive on time to school. Include in your calculations toileting, washing, dressing, grooming, preparing and eating breakfast, preparing lunch, and collecting needed materials. Check with the parent to arrive at a realistic time. Remember to include leeway time and to check on the time of schoolbus pickup.
2. Whenever the student is absent, discuss the experiences he missed. At these times, emphasize that, if it were a job, he might lose a day's pay or the job itself.

Home and Community

1. Ask the parents to set specific times to engage in previously identified activities. Tell them to urge the child to be on time for these events, or the events will be canceled. Tell the parents to set an alarm clock to a time that will give parents and child enough time to get ready for the next activity.
2. Role play situations in which the student is going to be late because of external, unpredictable factors (e.g., a bus breakdown, a traffic accident, an unexpected storm). Demonstrate how to handle lateness, especially when it involves letting an employer know.

Functional Emphases In designing your own instructional activities and plans, emphasize the following elements:

1. Recognition that lateness and poor attendance can jeopardize a job.
2. Awareness that failure to cancel an appointment in sufficient time might result in a fee being charged.
3. Identification of the best ways to handle lateness and absence when they are unavoidable.

Specific Objective GG

The student completes assigned tasks and otherwise fulfills assigned duties and obligations.

Functional Settings and Suggested Instructional Activities

School

1. Assign a classroom job to the student and his peers. Tell the student to tell you when his job is done. Reward him for finishing his job. If the student says he is finished but he is not, help him to finish his job. Say, "Finished," and reward the student for doing his job.
2. Give the student an assembly project (e.g., folding a pile of towels, inserting papers into envelopes, or stapling notices together). Tell the student to let you know when she is finished.

Home and Community

1. Ask the parents to assign the child various household chores that he is able to complete. Tell them to reward him when he does his chores. If he fails to complete his assignment, encourage them to reprimand him gently and assist him, if necessary, in completing the task.
2. Tell the parents, if the child has difficulty in completing an assigned task at one time, that they may allow him to leave the task and return to it at a later time. (This negotiation must occur before a task is initiated, and the task must always be completed.)
3. Engage in a community clean-up campaign. Give the student a task or tasks. Urge him to finish the task(s) as part of his being a responsible citizen.

Functional Emphases In designing your own instructional activities and plans, emphasize the following elements:

1. Appreciation of the fact that task completion is an important part of dealing with others and of meeting various social roles.
2. Establishment of priorities when several tasks must be completed.
3. Establishment of realistic timelines for completing tasks.
4. Interruption of tasks when rest, relaxation, or a change of pace is required and advisable and when the time constraints permit it.

Specific Objective HH

The student provides help to people, when appropriate, in diverse everyday situations, including emergencies.

Functional Settings and Suggested Instructional Activities

School

1. During dressing and undressing activities, encourage the student to help peers who are unable to do the dressing and undressing activities or who are having difficulty with the activities.
2. After art or physical education activities, tell the student you would like him to help clean up the room. After the student helps you, tell him you appreciate his help.
3. Assign the student and his peers to a work team. Tell the team that they must work together to complete an assigned task (e.g., raking leaves, straightening an art closet, or cleaning up the toy shelf). Explain that if they help each other, the work will be finished more quickly.
4. At recess time, organize group and team games or sports. Encourage the student and her peers who are able to play to help the others who do not know the rules and are unable to play. Play a variety of games so that each person gets a chance to help someone else. Praise the student for being a helpful friend.
5. Explain to the student how he can help in case an emergency situation arises (e.g., a peer is hurt in the shop area or the gym, and he has to seek help).

Home and Community

1. Ask the parents to seek experiences in which the child is able to help others in the completion of a task. Tell them to seek his help in taking care of younger siblings, household plants, household pets, and diverse chores.
2. Ask the parents to describe emergencies that may arise in the household (e.g., a grease fire, someone is hurt, the house has been broken into). Tell them to tell him how he might be of help in solving these emergencies.
3. Role play a situation in which the student calls for an ambulance for someone who has been injured.
4. Role play a situation in which the student calls the police to help someone who has been assaulted or otherwise been a victim of a street crime.
5. Role play a situation in which the student gives directions to someone who is lost.
6. Role play a situation in which the student helps an elderly person or someone who is blind to cross a street.

Functional Emphases In designing your own instructional activities and plans, emphasize the following elements:

1. Awareness of the importance of reciprocity in helping and doing favors for others.
2. Identification of those situations in which it is unwise to do someone a favor (e.g., when he is being exploited).

Specific Objective II

The student returns borrowed materials, equipment, money, and other items.

Functional Settings and Suggested Instructional Activities

School

1. Schedule an activity for which the student must borrow equipment (e.g., a heavy-duty stapler, a hole puncher, or a level). Encourage her to return the tool to its storage area and to thank you for its use. Praise her for being a good borrower.
2. If the student's pencil breaks or he needs a sheet of paper, tell him to borrow it from a peer. Encourage him to return the borrowed item by replacing it.

Home and Community

1. Ask the parents to explain to the child what items belong to him and to other members of the household. Tell the parents to explain which items may be shared by everyone. The parents should ask to borrow something belonging to the child (e.g., "Our radio is broken; may we borrow the one in your room?" or "We'd like to take pictures of the party; may we borrow your new camera?").

They should then return the borrowed item as soon as possible and mention that they have been good borrowers.

2. Role play borrowing from a neighbor an item that is consumed and needs to be replaced (e.g., a cup of flour, two eggs, or some business-size envelopes). Explain that borrowing some items means replacing them in the same amount or quality as the original.

Functional Emphases In designing your own instructional activities and plans, emphasize the following elements:

1. Awareness that some items that are borrowed must be replaced in approximately the same quantity and quality as the original item.
2. Awareness that items that are borrowed must be returned in the same condition as when they were received.
3. Realization that borrowing money is a serious step and requires return payment(s).
4. Identification of people and banks from whom money may be borrowed at good rates or without jeopardizing his budget or credit rating.

Specific Objective JJ

The student visits relatives, friends, and neighbors at appropriate times.

Functional Settings and Suggested Instructional Activities

Home

1. Ask the parents to review with the child when to visit relatives, friends, or neighbors: (a) on a regular basis (e.g., on special occasions and for social events); (b) at times of crisis (e.g., when they are sick, when they are recuperating from surgery or an injury, and when they have lost a loved one).
2. Ask the parents to make visits to relatives, friends, and neighbors. Tell them to tell the child the purpose of the visit.

Functional Emphases In designing your own instructional activities and plans, emphasize the following elements:

1. Identification of those neighbors who would welcome a visit.
2. Identification of those situations when it would be appropriate to visit a neighbor without a formal invitation.
3. Selection of appropriate times to visit someone.
4. Determination of the behavior appropriate to visiting someone.
5. Identification of the locations of relatives' and friends' homes.
6. Identification of the method of transportation and the specific route and type of transportation appropriate to the destination, including estimated costs and time involved.

Specific Objective KK

The student communicates with friends, relatives, neighbors, and acquaintances with cards and letters at appropriate times.

Functional Settings and Suggested Instructional Activities

School

1. Set up a mock card shop. Locate greeting cards by typical categories found in card stores. Send the student on a shopping trip.
2. Help the student compose thank-you notes after he has received gifts (e.g., after Christmas, Hanukkah, or a birthday).

Home and Community

1. Ask the parents to identify different types of greeting cards and the happy occasions when one might send them (e.g., birthdays, anniversaries, graduation, a move to a new apartment or home, a promotion, a religious event or rite, an engagement, marriage, birth, and religious holidays).
2. Ask the parents to identify get-well and sympathy cards and to discuss the occasions when they are sent.
3. Ask the parents to identify thank-you notes and to write thank-you letters on appropriate occasions.
4. Visit a card store and examine the various displays.

Functional Emphases In designing your own instructional activities and plans, emphasize the following elements:

1. Identification of annual special days such as birthdays.
2. Identification of holidays when it is traditional to send greeting cards.
3. Notation of annual special days on a personal or wall calendar.
4. Location of greeting cards appropriate to the situation and to the person.
5. Completion of a greeting or special note and the subsequent identification of the person's address and writing of the envelope.
6. Identification of his own address for writing a return address.
7. Identification of postage and stamps.
8. Location of mailboxes.
9. Identification of mail pickup times.

Specific Objective LL

The student communicates with friends, relatives, neighbors, and acquaintances using the telephone whenever appropriate.

Functional Settings and Suggested Instructional Activities

Home

1. Ask the parents to help the child distinguish when it is appropriate to telephone or write a letter (location and budgetary considerations) to a friend, relative, neighbor, or acquaintance.
2. Ask the parents to assist the verbal child in making telephone calls on appropriate occasions and at appropriate times (e.g., to communicate news of importance or interest, to find out items of importance or interest, and to "touch base" with friends or relatives.

Functional Emphases In designing your own instructional activities and plans, emphasize the following elements:

1. Identification of relevant telephone numbers.
2. Notation of relevant telephone numbers in a personal directory.
3. Identification and execution of a dialing pattern.
4. Awareness of telephone manners.
5. Selection of appropriate times to call.
6. Operation of a pay telephone.
7. Utilization of a telephone directory.

Specific Objective MM

The student invites friends, relatives, neighbors, and acquaintances to socialize with him.

Functional Settings and Suggested Instructional Activities

Home

1. Ask the parents to involve the child in inviting relatives, friends, neighbors, and acquaintances for snacks, meals, and visits.
2. Ask the parents to involve the child in inviting relatives, friends, neighbors, and acquaintances to parties, celebrations, and outings.
3. Ask the parents to involve the child in inviting relatives, friends, neighbors, and acquaintances to participate in recreational and leisure activities.

Functional Emphases In designing your own instructional activities and plans, emphasize the following elements:

1. Identification of the need to reciprocate.
2. Identification of special occasions and holidays.
3. Communication of invitations by telephone, simple notes, or cards.
4. Judgment as to whether he has the time and money to engage in leisure activities.
5. Identification of appropriate snacks and meals to serve to guests.
6. Identification of activities to pursue while entertaining guests.
7. Observation of those behaviors that make one a good host.

Specific Objective NN

The student joins friends, relatives, neighbors, and acquaintances in social activities.

Functional Settings and Suggested Instructional Activities

School

1. At various times during the day, give the student a break. Encourage the student to stop what he is doing and to visit with his peers.
2. Arrange to visit another classroom or learning area. Introduce the students to each other and encourage them to talk and to get to know each other.
3. Plan a dance or small party in the gymnasium or classroom. Assign the student the job of host or hostess. Encourage her to make the guests feel welcome by speaking with them and introducing them to her peers.

Home

1. Ask the parents to set a model of involvement in joining others for recreational and leisure activities and for holidays.
2. Ask the parents to set a model of involvement by joining others in events that are of mutual interest.

Functional Emphases In designing your own instructional activities and plans, emphasize the following elements:

1. Identification of holidays that are traditionally celebrated by relatives, friends, neighbors, and acquaintances.
2. Identification of holidays as they appear on calendars.
3. Identification of the day, date, and time of parties, outings, picnics, and celebrations.
4. Determination of the costs involved in participation.
5. Determination of any special requirements (e.g., wearing costumes to a Halloween party, bringing food to a Labor Day picnic, and bringing gifts).
6. Judgment as to whether he has the time to participate.
7. Identification of leisure pursuits in which he is interested and has the necessary skills.

Specific Objective OO

The student joins in projects that provide benefits to the community.

Functional Settings and Suggested Instructional Activities

School

1. Involve the student in activities designed to keep the classrooms as neat and attractive as possible.

2. Involve the student in activities designed to make the outside of the school and its grounds as neat and attractive as possible.

Home and Community

1. Ask the parents to involve the child in neighborhood clean-up campaigns and other efforts to conserve and beautify the environment.
2. Ask the parents to interest the child in maintaining the exterior and grounds of the home so that they are neat and attractive.
3. If there are tree- and shrubbery-planting campaigns in the community, join the student in being responsible citizens.

Functional Emphases In designing your own instructional activities and plans, emphasize the following elements:

1. Identification of materials that are no longer needed or usable and should be discarded.
2. Identification of public litter receptacles, including the differentiation of public receptacles from privately owned ones.
3. Identification of when a receptacle is filled and should not be used.
4. Identification of material that is no longer usable but can be recycled.
5. Identification of the directions for planting trees, shrubs, and bulbs.
6. Identification of the condition of lawns, shrubs, and trees as well as the steps involved in keeping them healthy and attractive.

Specific Objective PP

The student identifies human service persons, community helpers, and other service personnel and interacts with them appropriately.

Functional Settings and Suggested Instructional Activities

School

1. Show the student pictures of people at the barber shop, beauty parlor, doctor's office, department store, bank, or any other public place the student uses or may need to use in the future. Discuss what the people in the pictures are doing (e.g., sitting quietly, looking at magazines, conversing quietly while waiting their turn in line, and politely requesting help from a salesman). Ask the student if he has been to any of the places shown in the pictures. If he has, tell him to describe how he behaved. Talk about whether or not the student acted in an acceptable manner.
2. On a bulletin board, place pictures of community helpers. Discuss each one, their function in the community, and situations in which the student might interact with them.
3. Role play situations involving community helpers and the student (e.g., a lost student and a police officer, a student talking to a teacher, a student visiting

a fire station and speaking with the firefighter, a student at the doctor's having a checkup). Include situations the student is likely to experience. Repeat the activity frequently to give the student a chance to role play himself as well as each community helper.

4. For the younger student, make "community helper" costumes from brown paper grocery bags. Cut out arm and neck holes, and slit the bags down the front so the student can wear them. Paint the bag to simulate community helper uniforms (e.g., blue for a police officer, white for a doctor or nurse, and yellow or whatever color the firefighters in the community wear). Assist the student as he adds details such as brass buttons, badges, and name tags. Once the student has completed his costume, encourage him to use it in play situations. Tell the student to exchange costumes with his peers and to play the parts of different community helpers.
5. Invite community helpers to come to the classroom or learning area and speak with the student. Encourage them to discuss their jobs and responsibilities within the community.
6. Show filmstrips and read stories in which some of the characters are community helpers. Stories such as *Make Way for Ducklings* portray warm and unusual situations involving community helpers. Choose films and stories representing a variety of situations and characters.

Home and Community

1. Ask the parents to take the child with them to a variety of public places to interact with service people. Tell them to model appropriate interactions.
2. Take the student on field trips to the places where the community workers do their jobs (e.g., a police station, fire station, hospital, doctor's or dentist's office). After each visit and field trip, assist the student in preparing a language experience chart or story. Encourage him to draw pictures of the things he saw on the field trips. Add the language experience charts and pictures to the community helpers' bulletin board.
3. Take walks into the community. Point out community helpers and talk about situations in which the student might seek help from these individuals (e.g., "There is a police officer. A police officer will help you if you are lost or in some sort of trouble." "There is a hospital. Doctors and nurses at the hospital will help keep you well and make you well if you are sick.").

Functional Emphases In designing your own instructional activities and plans, emphasize the following elements:

1. Identification of community helpers by uniforms and accessories.
2. Identification of service professionals by their titles.
3. Identification of service personnel by their job titles.
4. Association of an occupation with the service provided.
5. Comprehension of the different behaviors appropriate to different settings.

Specific Objective QQ

The student obeys all pertinent rules and laws.

Functional Settings and Suggested Instructional Activities

School

1. Ask the student if he can tell you any classroom rules. Review the classroom rules and explain their purposes (e.g., "There is no ball playing allowed in the classroom because the balls could break something or hurt people."). Stress that rules are to be obeyed and that anyone who does not obey them must be willing to accept the consequences.
2. When the student breaks a rule, sit down with him and discuss it. Review the rule and its purpose with him. Explain that by breaking the rule, he may have hurt himself or someone else. Between the two of you, determine an appropriate punishment if necessary. Remind the student that rules are for everyone's protection and should be obeyed.
3. Discuss job safety. Explain that following the rules when working on a job is essential to the student's safety as well as the safety of his coworkers. Remind the student that, as a worker or employee, it is part of her job to be aware of on-the-job rules and to obey them at all times.
4. Ask a police officer or other law enforcement officer to speak to the student. Encourage the speaker to remind the student that it is his responsibility as a member of the community to be aware of the laws and to obey them. Stress that, although laws may seem restrictive, they are for our protection and well-being and should be obeyed.
5. Read stories or show filmstrips in which people break laws and are held responsible for their actions; *Curious George Rides a Bike* might be appropriate for your students. Discuss the events and their outcomes. Ask the student what he thinks he would have done in a similar situation.

Home and Community

1. Ask the parents to establish rules governing the child's behavior. Ask them to involve him in making the list of rules he is to follow. Tell them to discuss the rules with him. Tell them to try to make him aware that a person who breaks rules or laws must accept the consequences which usually are punishment of some sort. Tell them to explain the term *consequences*.
2. Show the student pictures of transportation vehicles (e.g., car, bus, taxi, train, airplane, and subway). Identify and name each picture. Ask the student which transportation vehicles he has ridden in. Explain that when using cars, buses, trains, taxis, airplanes, and subways, we must observe safety rules and be considerate of other riders. Then take the student on field trips. Use a variety of transportation vehicles. Before the trip, review the safety and social rules for the vehicle. School bus rules may include: (a) stay in your seat, (b) no shouting or loud conversation, (c) no pushing or shoving. Public transportation

bus rules may include: (a) stay in your seat, (b) do not start conversations with strangers, (c) say, "Next stop, please" to the driver when you want to get off the bus. Reward the student for behaving in an acceptable manner when using public or private transportation.

Functional Emphases In designing your own instructional activities and plans, emphasize the following elements:

1. Identification of relevant laws that apply to the student.
2. Awareness of the relationship between cause and effect and between his behavior and effects/consequences.
3. Provision of experience with a wide range of social settings.

Special Materials List—Interpersonal Skills

Books/Pamphlets

Explore Social Concepts. Communication Skill Builders, 3130 N. Dodge Blvd., P. O. Box 42050-E, Tucson, AZ 85733.

Kits

Me and Others (Multimedia Program). Chaselle, Inc., 9645 Gerwig La., Columbia, MD 21046.

Personal, Social, Occupational Basic Survival Skills. EBSCO Curriculum Materials, 1230 1st Ave. North, Box 1943, Birmingham, AL 35201.

Films/Filmstrips

How Do I See Myself? Chaselle, Inc., 9645 Gerwig La., Columbia, MD 21046.

Suggested Readings/References—Interpersonal Skills

Adkins, J., & Matson, J. L. (1980). Teaching institutionalized mentally retarded adults socially appropriate leisure skills. *Mental Retardation, 18,* 249–252.

Affleck, G. G. (1975a). Role-taking ability and interpersonal conflict resolution among retarded young adults. *American Journal of Mental Deficiency, 80,* 233–236.

Affleck, G. G. (1975b). Role-taking ability and the interpersonal competencies of retarded children. *American Journal of Mental Deficiency, 80,* 312–316.

Allen, R. M., Loeffler, F. J., Levine, M. N. & Alker, L. N. (1976). Social adaptation assessment as a tool for prescriptive remediation. *Mental Retardation, 14,* 36–37.

Barton, L. E., Brulle, A. R., & Repp, A. C. (1982). The social validation of programs for mentally retarded children. *Mental Retardation, 20,* 260–265.
Bates, J. E. (1980). The concept of difficult temperament. *Merrill–Palmer Quarterly, 26,* 299–319.
Bates, P. (1980). The effectiveness of interpersonal skills training on the social skill acquisition of moderately and mildly retarded adults. *Journal of Applied Behavior Analysis, 13,* 237–248.
Bates, P., & Harvey, J. (1978). Social skills training with the mentally retarded. In: O. C. Karan (Ed.), *Habilitation practices with the severely developmentally disabled, Vol. 2.* Madison, WI: Waisman Center.
Bernstein, G. S. (1981). Research issues in training interpersonal skills for the mentally retarded. *Education and Training of the Mentally Retarded, 16,* 70–73.
Berry, P., & Marshall, B. (1978). Social interactions and communication patterns in mentally retarded children. *American Journal of Mental Deficiency, 83,* 44–51.
Blacher, J. (1982). Assessing social cognition in young mentally retarded and nonretarded children. *American Journal of Mental Deficiency, 86,* 473–484.
Boruchow, A. W., & Espenshade, M. E. (1976). A socialization program for mentally retarded young adults. *Mental Retardation, 14,* 40–42.
Cartledge, G., & Milburn, J. F. (Eds.). (1980). *Teaching social skills to children: Innovative approaches.* New York: Pergamon Press.
Cuvo, A. J., & Davis, P. K. (1980). Teaching community living skills to mentally retarded persons: An examination of discriminative stimuli. *Gedrag, 1,* 14–33.
Davis, D. E. (1977). *My friends and me—A program to promote the personal and social development of young children.* Circle Pines, MN: American Guidance Service.
Day, R. M., Powell, T. H., Dy-Lin, E. B., & Stowitscher, J. J. (1982). An evaluation of the effects of a social interaction training package on mentally handicapped preschool children. *Education and Training of the Mentally Retarded, 17,* 125–130.
Dunlop, K. H., Stoneman, Z., & Cantrell, M. L. (1980). Social interaction of exceptional and other children in a mainstreamed preschool classroom. *Exceptional Children, 47,* 132–141.
Elias, M. J., & Maher, C. A. (1983). Social and affective development of children: A programmatic perspective. *Exceptional Children, 49,* 339–346.
Elias-Burger, S. F., Sigelman, C. K., Burger, D. L., & Danely, W. E. (1981). Teaching interview skills to mentally retarded persons. *American Journal of Mental Deficiency, 85,* 655–657.
Farina, A., Thaw, J., Felner, R. D., & Hust, B. E. (1976). Some interpersonal consequences of being mentally ill or mentally retarded. *American Journal of Mental Deficiency, 80,* 414–422.
Fleming, E. R., & Fleming, D. C. (1982). Social skill training for educable mentally retarded children. *Education and Training of the Mentally Retarded, 17,* 44–50.
Forness, S. R., Thornton, R. L., & Horton, A. A. (1981). Assessment of applied academic and social skills. *Education and Training of the Mentally Retarded, 16,* 104–109.
Foss, G., & Peterson, S. L. (1981). Social-interpersonal skills relevant to job tenure for mentally retarded adults. *Mental Retardation, 19,* 103–106.
Fredericks, H. D. (1977). Social skills. In N. Haring (Ed.), *Developing effective individualized education programs for severely handicapped children and youth.* Washington, DC: Bureau of Education for the Handicapped.
Gentile, C., & Jenkins, J. O. (1980). Assertive training with mildly mentally retarded persons. *Mental Retardation, 18,* 315–317.
Gibson, F. W., Lawrence, P. S., & Nelson, R. O. (1976). Comparison of three training

procedures for teaching social responses to developmentally disabled adults. *American Journal of Mental Deficiency, 81,* 379–387.

Goldstein, H. (1972). Construction of a social learning curriculum. In E. Meyen, G. Vergason, & R. Whelen (Eds.), *Strategies for teaching exceptional children.* Denver: Love Publishing Company.

Goldstein, H. (1977). *Merrill's social learning curriculum.* Columbia, OH: Charles E. Merrill.

Gresham, F. M. (1982). Misguided mainstreaming: The case for social skills training with handicapped children. *Exceptional Children, 48,* 422–433.

Gresham, F. M. (1983). Social skills assessment as a component of mainstreaming placement decisions. *Exceptional Children, 49,* 331–338.

Gresham, F. M. (1981). Social skills training with handicapped children: A review. *Review of Educational Research, 51,* 139–176.

Hayes, C. S., & Prinz, R. J. (1976). Affective reactions of retarded and nonretarded children to success and failure. *American Journal of Mental Deficiency, 81,* 100–102.

Heiny, R. W., & Stachowiak, R. J. (1976). Real matching of socialization activities with individual needs. *Mental Retardation, 14,* 12–15.

Irvin, L. K., Halpern, A. S., & Reynolds, W. M. (1977). Assessing social and prevocational awareness in mild and moderately retarded individuals. *American Journal of Mental Deficiency, 82,* 266–272.

Kirkland, K., & Laughlin-Carver, J. (1982). Maintenance and generalization of assertive skills. *Education and Training of the Mentally Retarded, 17,* 313–318.

Klein, N. K., & Babcock, D. (1979). Assertiveness training for moderately retarded adults: A position. *Education and Training of the Mentally Retarded, 14,* 232–234.

Kneedler, R. D. (1980). The use of cognitive training to change social behaviors. *Exceptional Education Quarterly, 1,* 65–73.

Konczak, L. J., & Johnson, C. M. (1983). Reducing inappropriate verbalizations in a sheltered workshop through differential reinforcement of other behavior. *Education and Training of the Mentally Retarded, 18,* 120–124.

LaGreca, A. M., & Santogrossi, D. A. (1980). Social skills training: A behavioral group approach. *Journal of Consulting and Clinical Psychology, 48,* 220–227.

Landesman-Dwyer, S., Berkson, G., & Romer, D. (1979). Affiliation and friendship of mentally retarded residents in group homes. *American Journal of Mental Deficiency, 83,* 571–580.

Lupin, M. (1979). *Peace, harmony, awareness: A relaxation program for children.* Boston: Teaching Resources Corporation.

Marholin, D., O'Toole, K. M., Touchette, P. E., Berger, P. L., & Doyle, D. A. (1979). I'll have a big mac, large fries, large coke, and apple pie . . . or teaching adaptive community skills. *Behavior Therapy, 10,* 236–248.

Marlowe, M. (1979). The games analysis intervention: A procedure to increase the peer acceptance and social adjustment of a retarded child. *Education and Training of the Mentally Retarded, 14,* 262–268.

Matson, J. L. (1981). Use of independence training to teach shopping skills to mildly mentally retarded adults. *American Journal of Mental Deficiency, 86,* 178–183.

Matson, J. L., & Adkins, J. (1980). A self-instruction social skills training program for mentally retarded persons. *Mental Retardation, 18,* 245–248.

Matson, J. L., & Andrasik, F. (1982). Training leisure-time social interaction skills to mentally retarded adults. *American Journal of Mental Deficiency, 86,* 533–542.

Mayhew, G. L., Enyart, P., & Anderson, J. (1979). Social reinforcement and the naturally occurring social responses of severely and profoundly retarded adolescents. *American*

Journal of Mental Deficiency, 83, 164–170.

Monson, L. B., Greenspan, S., & Simeonsson, R. J. (1979). Correlates of social competence in retarded children. *American Journal of Mental Deficiency, 83,* 627–630.

Mori, A. A., & Masters, L. F. (1980). *Teaching the severely mentally retarded: Adaptive skills training.* Gaithersburg, MD: Aspen Systems Corporation.

Morse, W. C., Ardizzone, J., MacDonald, C., & Pasick, P. (1980). *Affective education for special children and youth.* Reston, VA: Council for Exceptional Children.

Moxley, D., Nevil, N., & Edmonson, B. (1981). *Socialization games for mentally retarded adolescents and adults.* Springfield, IL: Charles C Thomas.

Nietupski, J., & Williams, W. (1976). Teaching selected telephone related social skills to severely handicapped students. *Child Study Journal, 6,* 139–153.

Perry, M. A., & Cerreto, M. C. (1977). Structured learning training of social skills for the retarded. *Mental Retardation, 15,* 31–34.

Peterson, G. A., Austin, G. J., & Lang, R. P. (1979). Use of teacher prompts to increase social behavior: Generalization effects with severely and profoundly retarded adolescents. *American Journal of Mental Deficiency, 84,* 82–86.

Richardson, S. A. (1978). Careers of mentally retarded young persons: Services, jobs and interpersonal relations. *American Journal of Mental Deficiency, 82,* 349–358.

Richey, J. (1978). *Restaurant language: A survival vocabulary.* Haywood, CA: Janus Book Publishers.

Ridley, C. A., & Vaughn, S. R. (1982). Interpersonal problem solving: An intervention program for preschool children. *Journal of Applied Developmental Psychology, 3,* 177–190.

Rusch, F. R. (1979). Toward the validation of social/vocational survival skills. *Mental Retardation, 17,* 143–144.

Rusch, F. R., & Menchetti, B. M. (1981). Increasing compliant work behaviors in a non-sheltered work setting. *Mental Retardation, 19,* 107–111.

Sailor, W., Wilcox, B., & Brown, L. (1980). (Eds.). *Methods of instruction for severely handicapped students.* Baltimore: Paul H. Brookes.

Santomier, J., & Kopczuk, W. (1981). Facilitation of interaction between retarded and nonretarded students in a physical education setting. *Education and Training of the Mentally Retarded, 16,* 20–23.

Sigelman, C. K., & Davis, P. J. (1978). Making good impressions in job interviews: Verbal and nonverbal predictors. *Education and Training of the Mentally Retarded, 13,* 71–77.

Smith, I. L., & Greenberg, S. (1979). Hierarchial assessment of social competence. *American Journal of Mental Deficiency, 83,* 551–555.

Sowers, J., Rusch, F., & Hudson, C. (1979). Training a severely retarded young adult to ride the city bus to and from work. *AAESPH Review, 4,* 15–22.

Sternberg, L., Pegnatore, L., & Hill, C. (1983). Establishing interactive communication behaviors with profoundly mentally handicapped students. *The Journal of the Association for the Severely Handicapped, 8,* 39–46.

Valletutti, P. J., & Bender, M. (1982). *Teaching interpersonal and community living skills to handicapped adolescents and adults.* Austin: PRO-ED.

Van Hasselt, V. B., Hersen, M., Whitehall, M. B., & Bellack, A. S. (1979). Social skills assessment and training for children: An evaluative review. *Behavioral Research and Therapy, 17,* 413–437.

Vaughn, S. R., Ridley, C. A., & Cox, J. (1983). Evaluating the efficacy of an interpersonal skills training program with children who are mentally retarded. *Education and Training of the Mentally Retarded, 18,* 191–196.

Williams, W., Pumpian, P., McDaniel, J., Hamre-Nietupski, S., & Wheeler, J. (1975). Teaching social interaction skills to severely handicapped students. In L. Brown, T. Crowner, W. Williams, & R. York (Eds.), *Madison's alternative for zero exclusion: A book of readings.* (Vol. 5). Madison, WI: Madison Public Schools.

Young, C. C., & Kerr, M. M. (1979). The effects of a retarded child's social initiations on the behavior of severely retarded school-aged peers. *Education and Training of the Mentally Retarded, 14,* 185–190.

5 Sex Education

The inclusion of sex education in a comprehensive curriculum for handicapped individuals has become an increasingly acceptable procedure (Bass, 1972a; Craft, 1982; Fischer, Krajicek, & Borthick, 1973, 1974; Hamre-Nietupski & Williams, 1977; Johnson & Kempton, 1981; Kempton & Forman, 1976; Kempton, Gordon, & Bass, 1971; Monat, 1982). Ironically, there currently appears to be less resistance to incorporating sex education into programs for handicapped populations than there is for including it in programs for nonhandicapped students. Controversy still abounds when programs on human sexuality are planned for nonhandicapped students. Attitudes run the gamut from curricula excluding sex education altogether to the more liberal attitude of a comprehensive curriculum including all significant aspects of human sexuality: biological, psychological, and social (Gimarl, 1979; Gordon, 1979).

While community values and standards vary widely relevant to nonhandicapped populations, the need for educating handicapped populations has achieved greater consensus. Perhaps this greater acceptance is a by-product of the deinstitutionalization/normalization process which highlights the need for the sexual education of the handicapped as they attempt increasingly to integrate into community life (Flynn & Nitsch, 1980). One wonders whether this greater acceptance reflects the desire to diminish feared public displays of sexual interest and arousal, to reduce an imagined increase in sexual exploitation, and/or to foster eugenic birth control programs (Adams, Tallon, & Alcorn, 1982; Brantlinger, 1983; Heshusius, 1982). Indeed, increasing acceptance of sex education programs for disabled populations may be viewed as a tacit means of inhibiting, through education, the mythic sexual freedom/hypersexuality of handicapped people. Certainly educational programming is a more enlightened response to the situation than that demonstrated in the past (Haavik & Menninger, 1981, 1982). Whatever the motivation for including sex education for handicapped persons, professionals and lay people alike have become increasingly aware of the sexual rights of this population (Bass, 1972b; Gordon & Bilken, 1979). Early programs of sex education for the handicapped emphasized basic health and hygiene factors. Management issues assumed hegemony as teachers, parents, and other caregivers became absorbed with basic issues such as the satisfactory handling of cleanliness and menstruation and the avoidance of public masturbation and sexual exploitation. While health and hygiene areas have been included in the curriculum objectives, they are only minor aspects of sex education for the moderately and severely handicapped. Health- and hygiene-oriented skills are treated as simply the initial phase of a total program that also addresses sexual feelings and emotions; the sexual aspects of interpersonal communication, including dating and courtship; the avoidance of sexual exploitation; awareness of the changing perceptions of sex roles; the communication of sexual feelings, attitudes, and needs; and the development of a personal value system.

For the successful teaching of the sex education objectives, it is essential that teachers and parents be sensitive to the needs and feelings of the student. Not all students will respond to every activity, and many should not be exposed to some of the objectives and activities. Parents should be continuously consulted and continually informed of the programming considerations and plans as well as their child's progress.

It is advisable for teachers and parents to share the teaching of sex education and to use the same information and activities at home and in the classroom to avoid confusing the student with too much or conflicting information.

The Suggested Readings/References and Special Materials List at the end of this chapter provide information on sex education. The reader should decide which material and information are applicable to a specific student or students being taught.

General Objective of the Unit

The student will function as a sexual being in ways that will bring him acceptance, love, and pleasure.

Specific Objectives

The student:

A. reacts to elimination processes as normal bodily functions.
B. practices good health habits (including cleanliness) and maintains a healthy attitude toward his body.
C. undresses only in private.
D. respects the privacy of others.

E. identifies body parts, including sexual organs, and refers to sexual organs by their correct names.
F. identifies sex differences between males and females.
G. (female) prepares and cares for her body during menstruation and reacts to it as a normal bodily function.
H. (female) practices sanitary behaviors that reduce the likelihood of vaginal infections.
I. (female) carries out prescriptive practices for vaginitis.
J. (female) carries out a self-examination of her breasts.
K. (female) describes the several steps involved in a gynecological examination.
L. (male) reacts to erections and ejaculations as normal bodily functions.
M. does not fondle or handle his genitals in public.
N. masturbates in private and in a safe manner.
O. copes with and accepts feelings arising from an awareness of his sexuality.
P. practices socially acceptable behavior with members of both sexes, including engaging in acceptable dating and courtship customs.
Q. discriminates among and responds appropriately to friends, family members, acquaintances, and strangers.
R. identifies the changing sex roles involved in male-female interactions.
S. describes the relationship of sex to love.
T. identifies family, cultural, religious, and personal values relevant to sexual behavior.
U. engages in responsible decision making about his own sexual behaviors and practices, including the avoidance of provocative or flirtatious behaviors.
V. avoids sexual exploitation or victimization and does not sexually exploit or victimize others.
W. identifies and reacts appropriately to physical changes occurring during the maturation process.
X. discusses elementary facts of reproduction, including pregnancy and birth, as normal bodily functions.
Y. discusses the role the mother can play in breast-feeding babies.
Z. discusses venereal diseases: their transmission, prevention, symptoms, treatments, and consequences.
AA. discusses the nature and purpose of marriage and the family unit and the roles that each member plays in a family.
BB. discusses and prepares for the role of a parent.
CC. practices birth control when appropriate.

Specific Objective A

The student reacts to elimination processes as normal bodily functions.

Functional Settings and Suggested Instructional Activities

School

1. Show the student a picture of a boy urinating into a urinal or toilet. Ask the student to tell you what the boy is doing. The student may say, "Pee, pee," "Wee, wee," or some other infantile or slang expression. Encourage him to say that he is going to the bathroom rather than to permit him to use these slang terms. Repeat the activity, using a picture of a girl sitting on a toilet urinating. You may wish to introduce a discussion of the sexual organs at this time as a part of explaining why boys urinate while standing or sitting whereas girls urinate sitting on the toilet.
2. Show the student a picture of a boy sitting on a toilet seat. Ask the student to explain what the boy is doing. Discourage the use of slang terms by substituting correct terminology. Tell him that the grown-up term for what the boy is doing is called a B.M. or bowel movement. Tell the student to use this term when he has to go to the bathroom for a bowel movement.

Home and Community

1. Ask the parents to discuss urination and defecation as ways the body gets rid of waste products. If possible, ask them to draw an analogy with waste products of industry and the problems of their removal. Tell them to emphasize that these are normal and important bodily functions.
2. Ask the parents to refer to the sexual organs by their correct names.
3. Take trips in the community. Point out restrooms in public buildings, in sports arenas, and in diverse recreational and business settings. Say that these facilities are needed because everyone needs to urinate and defecate.
4. Point out the different names and symbols on restroom doors. Help the student locate the the correct-sex restrooms as they are found throughout the community.

Functional Emphases In designing your own instructional activities and plans, emphasize the following elements:

1. Identification of the sex organs by their appropriate names.
2. Identification of restrooms by names, symbols, and rebuses.

Specific Objective B

The student practices good health habits (including cleanliness) and maintains a healthy attitude toward his body.

Functional Settings and Suggested Instructional Activities

School

1. Show the film *Questions about Health* (see Special Materials List) and discuss with the student what it means to be clean and to have a clean body and clean clothes.

2. Play the Hap Palmer record *Take a Bath* (see Special Materials List) and pantomime the actions.
3. Play the Sesame Street record *Everybody Wash* (see Special Materials List) and ask the student to role play washing her hands and face as the song is playing.
4. Encourage the student to practice good health habits. Present him with pictures showing students practicing good and poor health habits; ask him to differentiate between them. For example, show him a picture of a boy who obviously looks tired and exhausted staying up late at night watching television. Contrast this with a picture of a boy who has gone to bed on time, sleeping peacefully in his bed. Ask the student which picture portrays a good health habit. Praise him if he selects the appropriate picture.
5. Show the film *Learning About Neatness* (see Special Materials List). After reviewing the film, ask him what he might do to look neater. Each morning, as the student arrives at the classroom or learning area, tell him how nice he looks and praise him when he is neat and clean.
6. Show the Harris County filmstrip *Teaching Good Conduct and Personal Hygiene to Retarded Teenagers* (see Special Materials List). Follow the suggestions in the filmstrip to develop grooming and hygiene activities.

Home and Community

1. Ask the parents to tell the child that it is very important that he always be clean and in good health. Encourage them to tell him that good health will help him feel well. Tell them to help him practice good health habits by encouraging him to wash his hands and body following activities that cause him to perspire or become dirty. Tell them to praise the student when he washes himself on his own.
2. Ask the parents to work with the child so that he seeks to keep his body as sound as possible. Explain the idea of a sound body and a sound mind. Then tell them to assist the child in keeping his body as healthy and attractive as possible within the limits of his physical potential. Whenever there is a physical condition that cannot be corrected, ask the parents to help him capitalize on his good features. Tell them that proper dressing, grooming, and the use of cosmetics, when appropriate, can be aids in achieving a more attractive look.
3. Show the student recreational centers, spas, and health clubs in the community. Explain that people use these places to keep their bodies healthy and attractive. Explain that being as attractive as possible is an important social skill.

Functional Emphases In designing your own instructional activities and plans, emphasize the following elements:

1. Identification of ways he can improve his physical health.
2. Identification of ways he can prevent illness.
3. Identification of ways he can improve his attractiveness.
4. Recognition of the physical and social value of cleanliness.

Specific Objective C

The student undresses only in private.

Functional Settings and Suggested Instructional Activities

School

1. Plan an activity in school (class play or Halloween party) that requires the student to dress up in an outfit or costume. Give him the outfit or costume and tell him to change his clothes. If the student requests to go to the bathroom or another room for privacy while changing, praise him and allow him to do so. If the student starts to disrobe in front of the class, stop him. Remind him that changing clothes should be done in private.
2. If the school has a locker room where the students change before and after gym and/or swimming classes, explain that he may undress there because all those undressing are the same sex. Point out that locker rooms are private places used to change clothing.

Home and Community

1. Ask the parents to explain to the child that he should undress only in private or if a family member, doctor, or other responsible adult requests him to do so. Tell them to list times when he should disrobe in private that parallel his daily or weekly routine, such as taking a bath, getting dressed in the morning or undressed in the evening, and putting on gym suits. Tell them to review the list. Also make sure they tell him that if situations not on his list arise in which he is asked to disrobe, he should seek their advice before disrobing.
2. When the student needs to purchase clothing, accompany him to a large department store that has individual dressing rooms. Tell him you want him to try on an article of clothing to see how it fits and looks. Help the student to select a suitable article of clothing and tell him to go into the dressing room to change. Watch the student closely and praise him if he closes the dressing-room door or curtain and undresses and changes his clothes in private.

Functional Emphases In designing your own instructional activities and plans, emphasize the following elements:

1. Identification of those actions that are considered to be appropriate to demonstrate one's modesty.
2. Identification of situations and places where it is appropriate to undress.
3. Awareness of the possibility of sexual exploitation as it involves undressing and exposing one's body to others.

Specific Objective D

The student respects the privacy of others.

Functional Settings and Suggested Instructional Activities

School

1. Role play taking a nap or going to sleep. Tell the student that he should not disturb people who are sleeping. At nap time or other quiet times during the day, reward the student for not disturbing his peers. Emphasize how pleased you are that he is respecting the privacy of others.
2. Point out to the student several lunch boxes that his classmates have brought in. Tell him that what is in other people's lunch boxes belongs to them and that he should not open up or handle packages, notes, or other objects that belong to other students. During the day, place the student in a situation that allows him free access to his peers' lunch boxes. Praise him if he respects the privacy of others and does not open or handle their property. If he does open or handle his peers' lunches or property, remind him that they are not his and that he should leave them alone.

Home

1. Ask the parents to tell the child that he should not walk into bathrooms, bedrooms, or other rooms whose doors are closed without getting permission to enter. Tell them to role play situations in which he must seek permission to enter a room.
2. Ask the parents to explain that one's drawers, closets, and personal belongings are private. Tell them to respect his privacy so he has a model of respecting the personal property of others.

Functional Emphases In designing your own instructional activities and plans, emphasize the following elements:

1. Identification of personal property, the personal property of others, and the property that is shared by all.
2. Awareness of when someone wishes to share personal property.
3. Recognition of verbal and nonverbal clues that someone wishes to be left alone.

Specific Objective E

The student identifies body parts, including sexual organs, and refers to sexual organs by their correct names. (Note: The student may give a variety of answers in identifying the sexual organs. Do not respond negatively to any of these words, but always substitute the correct name if he uses slang or an infantile expression.)

Functional Settings and Suggested Instructional Activities

School

1. Listen to the Sesame Street record *I've Got Two* (two eyes, ears, etc.). (See Special Materials List.) Tell the student to act out the song as it plays.
2. Play Hap Palmer's record *Let's Dance* (see Special Materials List) and touch and identify the parts of the body named in the song.

3. Give the student anatomically correct dolls. Tell him to point to and name the body parts that he sees. Praise the student for identifying the parts of the doll. If he misses any, tell him what they are. At this time, point out the sexual organs or genitals on the doll. Use the correct names to identify them. Encourage the student to identify the sexual organs as you name them. Then point to a part and encourage the student to name it.
4. Bring in plastic scale models of a male and of a female. Explain that these male and female models are called men and women. Point out the different parts on the models to the student. At a later time in the day, call the student over and ask him to identify the body parts you point to. Reward him if he does this correctly. Both male and female students should be shown male and female models.
5. Bring in large pictures of a nude male and a nude female. Show the student one of the pictures and ask him if it is a male or a female. If he answers correctly, ask him what makes the pictures look like a male or a female. If his answer is not correct, explain why it is not. If it is correct, praise him.
6. Bring into the classroom large pictures of a male and a female that show the sexual organs. Point out the body parts, including the sexual organs, and call them by their correct names. Tell the student that the penis should be called a penis, the breasts, breasts, and the vagina, a vagina. It is important that the explanation of terminology be coordinated with the student's understanding of the topic and with the permission of the parents who will be working with the student at home.

Home

1. Ask the parents to read the pamphlet *Love, Sex, and Birth Control for the Mentally Retarded* (see Special Materials List). Then tell them to show him pictures of the nude male and female and name the sexual organs. Tell them to ask their child to point to the bodily parts when named and then, if possible, to name them. Tell them to use the words "penis," "testicles," "breasts," and "vagina."
2. Tell the parents that they should explain to the child at the time of bathing that certain parts of the body need special attention in cleaning. Tell them to emphasize that the genital areas require special attention. Tell them to call the sexual organs by their correct names when describing the bathing operation (e.g., "Make sure you are cleaning your penis and the area around your testicles.").

Functional Emphases In designing your own instructional activities and plans, emphasize the following elements:

1. Utilization of the appropriate adult terms in referring to the sexual organs.
2. Discretion in referring to the sexual organs and using these terms only in appropriate situations.

Specific Objective F

The student identifies sex differences between males and females.

Functional Settings and Suggested Instructional Activities

School

1. Show the student a picture of clothed adult males and females. Ask the student to tell you if it is a female or male. Encourage her to describe the parts of the picture that differentiate the male from the female (e.g., "The woman is wearing a dress. She has a feminine figure. She is wearing makeup. She is female.").
2. Show the student a picture or drawing of a nude adult male and then of a nude adult female. Ask the student to tell you which one is the male and to indicate why. Be aware that this may cause some embarrassment and that the student may not be willing to respond. It is important that the explanation for why a picture is a male or a female be made in a serious but casual manner and at a level that the student can comprehend.
3. Show the film *Boy to Man* and *Girl to Woman* (see Special Materials List) to the student. Discuss the body changes that are shown in the films.

Home

1. Ask the parents to discuss the significant people in the life of the child. Tell them to point out if they are male or female. Tell them to equate the words "boy" and "man" with "male," and "girl" and "woman" with "female."
2. Ask the parents to discuss the distinguishing external features that generally point to the sex of people (e.g., clothing, bodily types, hair styles, and cosmetics). Tell them to make sure that they also deal with ambiguous features (e.g., long hair on males or short hair and slacks/jeans on women).

Functional Emphases In designing your own instructional activities and plans, emphasize the following elements:

1. Awareness that sometimes external features are not clear, especially when there are unisexual hair and clothing styles.
2. Recognition that, while there are obvious physical differences between the sexes, both sexes have the same basic needs and are equal.

Specific Objective G

The female student prepares and cares for her body during menstruation and reacts to it as a normal bodily function.

Functional Settings and Suggested Instructional Activities

School

1. For the female who has not yet begun to menstruate, prepare her for its eventuality by showing the Harris County film on menstruation (see Special Materials List), showing her pictures, reading about it, demonstrating with a mannequin or science model, and discussing it.
2. Write to companies that sell feminine hygiene products and ask them for any brochures, films, or educational materials on menstruation (e.g., Kimberly-Clark Corporation). Discuss and use these materials with the student.
3. Tell the student she should tell an appropriate person (mother, teacher, or responsible adult) when she has begun to menstruate. Praise the student if she tells you she is beginning to menstruate and has taken appropriate precautions.
4. Put the student on a napkin-changing schedule, perhaps every other time she goes to the bathroom to urinate. Check to see if this is being done until you are sure she can take care of her needs on her own.
5. Tell the student she should dispose of used sanitary napkins by rolling up the soiled napkin (soiled side inside) and wrapping it in toilet paper, a paper towel, or a small paper bag and discarding it in the proper receptacle. When the student is having her period, check to see that she is disposing of sanitary napkins properly. Remind the student not to flush the sanitary napkins down the toilet.
6. Discuss the need to be prepared by keeping a napkin with her at all times. Check at regular intervals to see that the student has one in her handbag.
7. Tell the student that she should not announce her period or discuss it with everyone. Help her to select someone with whom she should discuss it in case she needs help and for record-keeping purposes.
8. Stress the importance of cleanliness during menstruation. The student should wash, bathe, or shower daily because of the added glandular activity.
9. Tell the student who menstruates to notify her mother if she has not had her period during the time she expected it.
10. Explain the menstrual process to male students.

Home and Community

1. Ask the parents to prepare their daughter for menstruation before it has begun. Tell them to tell their daughter that when menstruation begins, it is something to feel good about because it means that she is growing up and becoming a woman. Tell the parents to make certain they communicate the idea that menstruation is nothing to be afraid or ashamed of since it happens to all women, and being a woman is a wonderful thing.
2. Ask the parents to explain the process of menstruation. Tell them to be sure to stress that the menstrual flow is blood that is meant to be lost and is not like bleeding after being hurt.
3. Ask the mother to discuss the purpose of the sanitary napkin or pad and explain that the sanitary napkin or pad is used to absorb the blood from the vagina.

Tell the mother to explain that it absorbs the blood so that it will not stain the woman's clothing.

4. Tell the mother to practice putting on a sanitary napkin. Tell the mother that it is usually preferable to use the kind of sanitary napkin that sticks to the panties since it is the easiest to handle and requires no belt. Ask the mother to show the child how to determine which is the sticky side by feeling both sides with her fingers; then assist her in sticking the sticky side to her panties. Show her how to wrap up the used sanitary napkin and dispose of it.
5. Ask the mother to assist the child in identifying signs that menstruation is beginning and to help her put on a napkin, if necessary.
6. Show the student how to use a vending machine that dispenses sanitary napkins.
7. Take a trip to a supermarket or pharmacy. Show her the section where sanitary napkins and belts are stocked. Discuss the purchasing of these supplies and buy appropriate supplies when necessary.

Functional Emphases In designing your own instructional activities and plans, emphasize the following elements:

1. Skill in using sanitary napkins.
2. Identification of problems in menstruation.
3. Appreciation for the role of a woman and pride in menstruating.
4. Awareness of the proper procedures for disposing of sanitary napkins.
5. Awareness of the private nature of menstruation.
6. Recognition of the need to be prepared for an approaching period.
7. Education of male students so that they view menstruation as a healthy and necessary process.
8. Use of panty liners or shields and mini-pads as needed before and after menstruation.

Specific Objective H

The female student practices sanitary behaviors that reduce the likelihood of vaginal infections.

Functional Settings and Suggested Instructional Activities

School

1. Review the need with the female student to wipe herself from front to back after urinating or having a bowel movement.
2. Emphasize the need to clean the genital area regularly to prevent infection.

Home

1. Ask the mother to show her daughter how to wipe herself from front to back after voiding and eliminating.

2. Ask the mother to show her daughter how to wash and keep her genital area clean. Tell her to encourage her daughter to wash her genital area at least once a day.

Functional Emphases In designing your own instructional activities and plans, emphasize the following elements:

1. Establishment of a regular washing schedule with particular attention paid to the genital area.
2. Recognition of the signs of vaginitis.

Specific Objective I

The female carries out prescriptive practices for vaginitis.

Functional Settings and Suggested Instructional Activities

Home

1. Ask the mother to help her daughter identify signs of vaginitis (e.g., itching, burning, and vaginal discharge).
2. Ask the mother to demonstrate the use of a warm water/vinegar solution for douching.
3. Ask the mother to select a physician to call in case the vaginitis does not clear up quickly.

Functional Emphases In designing your own instructional activities and plans, emphasize the following elements:

1. Recognition of signs of vaginitis.
2. Preparation of a warm water/vinegar solution.
3. Development of the skills involved in notifying a physician, in setting up an appointment, in filling a prescription, and in carrying out the prescribed treatment.

Specific Objective J

The female student carries out a self-examination of her breasts.

Functional Settings and Suggested Instructional Activities

Home

1. Ask the mother to demonstrate how to carry out an examination of the breasts. Tell her to encourage this self-examination once a month.
2. Ask the mother to point out other possible signs (beside the tactile) that might indicate the possibility of a problem (e.g., pain or itching of the breasts or visual

changes). Tell her to encourage making an appointment with a physician if lumps are detected or other unusual changes occur.

Functional Emphases In designing your own instructional activities and plans, emphasize the following elements:

1. Awareness of signs that suggest the existence of a problem.
2. Identification of the steps involved in palpating the breasts.
3. Awareness of the need to contact a physician when necessary.

Specific Objective K

The female describes the several steps involved in a gynecological examination. (*Note*: This objective is designed to prepare the female for a gynecological examination so that she does not become alarmed or frightened.)

Functional Settings and Suggested Instructional Activities

Home

1. Ask the mother to discuss the various steps involved in a gynecological examination. Tell the mother to discuss that it is all right for a physician to examine her private parts, although she has been warned in the past about allowing other people to touch her or fondle her genitals. (It is recommended that male physicians have a female nurse or other female medical person present for this examination.)
2. Ask the mother to explain the need for gynecological examinations as a preventive medical procedure.

Functional Emphases In designing your own instructional activities and plans, emphasize the following elements:

1. Appreciation for the need to schedule regular gynecological examinations.
2. Awareness of the steps involved in arranging or setting up an appointment.
3. Identification of the steps involved in the examination.

Specific Objective L

The male student reacts to erections and ejaculations as normal bodily functions.

Functional Settings and Suggested Instructional Activities

School

1. If there is reason to believe the student has ejaculated, explain to the student what has happened. Stress that what has happened is a private and personal

thing. If necessary, take him to the bathroom and tell him to wash himself. When appropriate and if it is feasible, ask him to change his underwear.

2. Discuss with the student who has an erection that it is something that should not be joked about or drawn attention to. Remind the student that erections and ejaculations are private bodily functions that should not be discussed except, perhaps, with a parent or physician.
3. Write to SIECUS (Sex Information and Education Council of the United States) for information or educational materials. (See Special Materials List for the address of SIECUS.)

Home

1. Ask the parents to explain to their son that having erections is a normal body function, that all boys have erections, and that he should not be ashamed when he has one. Have them tell him that he should not draw attention to his erection because it is a private thing. Tell them to tell him to think about something else when he has an erection and that then the erection should soon go away.
2. Ask the parents to explain nocturnal emissions and ejaculations when the boy enters puberty. Tell them they should emphasize that these are normal and should not frighten him because they are a sign that he is becoming a man, which is a wonderful thing.

Functional Emphases In designing your own instructional activities and plans, emphasize the following elements:

1. Awareness of the normalcy of erections and ejaculations.
2. Recognition of the need to inhibit erections when in public.
3. Identification of the need to wash and change underwear or pajamas when ejaculations have occurred.

Specific Objective M

The student does not fondle or handle his genitals in public.

Functional Settings and Suggested Instructional Activities

School

1. Discuss obnoxious behaviors as well as those behaviors that annoy or embarrass others. Explain that while fondling the genitals can bring pleasure, it is annoying to others and should be done in private.
2. During the day, notice if the student is fondling any part of his body. If he appears to be grasping his groin as if he needs to go to the bathroom, ask him if he has to go to the bathroom. If he says "Yes," give him permission to go. If he says "No," provide him with an activity that will require him to use his hands.

Home and Community

1. Ask the parents to make sure the child washes his genitals carefully and thoroughly on a regular basis. Tell them to make certain that the child is wearing the proper clothing since irritations caused by ill-fitting garments (underwear that is too tight or trousers that bind and chafe) sometimes cause the child to scratch and fondle the genital area.
2. Take the student to public places and point out appropriate public behavior.

Functional Emphases In designing your own instructional activities and plans, emphasize the following elements:

1. Awareness of the difference between public and private behaviors.
2. Identification of private places where it is okay to fondle himself.

Specific Objective N

The student masturbates in private and in a safe manner.

Functional Settings and Suggested Instructional Activities

School

1. Stress that masturbation is a private and personal experience. Tell the student that when he feels the need to masturbate, he should go to a private place.
2. Tell the student that masturbation should not be discussed with her peers, as it is a private subject. Tell the student to ask you about masturbation if she has any questions. Make sure your answers are short and simple.
3. Write to SIECUS (see Special Materials List) and obtain and read the Study Guide (No. 3) on masturbation. Use this information as a resource when discussing masturbation with the student.

Home

1. Ask the parents to discuss masturbation with the child. (Some children may not be familiar with this term, so they may have to tell him it is the proper word to use instead of any slang words.) Tell them to emphasize that masturbation is a normal part of sexual development and that people do it because it is pleasurable. Tell them to emphasize that masturbation is an acceptable practice as long as it is done safely, in moderation, and in private.
2. Tell the parents to stress that masturbation is acceptable as discussed in Activity 1 and review with him where he may find privacy in the home.

Functional Emphases In designing your own instructional activities and plans, emphasize the following elements:

1. Awareness that masturbation is a normal sexual behavior.
2. Recognition that masturbation should be done in private, in moderation, and in a safe manner to avoid injury or infection.

Specific Objective O

The student copes with and accepts feelings arising from an awareness of his sexuality.

Functional Settings and Suggested Instructional Activities

School

1. Discuss jealousy, crushes, and infatuations with the student. Tell the student that these feelings may occur throughout his life. Ask the student if he has ever experienced any of the specific feelings discussed or if he has any of these feelings now. Listen to the student and encourage him to express his feelings. Try to explain why he feels the way he does.
2. Read the pamphlet *Techniques in Leading Group Discussions on Human Sexuality* (see Special Materials List) for additional information.
3. Read the Guide for Parents pamphlet *Love, Sex, and Birth Control for the Mentally Retarded* (see Special Materials List). This offers suggestions that may be helpful for discussion sessions with the student as well as his parent, guardian, or other responsible person with whom he lives.
4. Show the film *Mental Retardation and Sexuality* (see Special Materials List) and use it as a basis for discussing sexuality with the student. You may also wish to show the film to the parents of the student to help them understand the student's sexuality.

Home

1. Ask the parents to discuss the process of physically and emotionally growing up. Tell them to emphasize bodily changes and the feelings associated with these changes.
2. Ask the parents to discuss with the child if there are times or situations that sexually excite or arouse her. Tell them to listen carefully to her explanations, being careful not to make value judgments. Ask them to help her with suggestions on how to make these situations easier to handle (e.g., turn away from what is arousing him, think of other things, or begin an interesting, unrelated activity).

Functional Emphases In designing your own instructional activities and plans, emphasize the following elements:

1. Identification of physical changes that occur during puberty and the emotional concomitants.
2. Awareness of changes that occur during sexual arousal and after sexual release.
3. Development of control over sexual impulses.

Specific Objective P

The student practices socially acceptable behavior with members of both sexes, including engaging in acceptable dating and courtship customs.

Functional Settings and Suggested Instructional Activities

School

1. Ask the student to help you make a list of rules for the classroom. Include among these rules those involving acceptable sexual behaviors. For example, one of the rules might be not to hug, kiss, or touch people who walk into the room. Another might be to knock on the bathroom door before entering to be sure it is unoccupied. Reinforce the student as he observes these rules during the day.
2. Tell the student that he should not touch people, kiss them, or disturb their clothing because this may upset them. If the student participates in any of these acts, immediately stop him. Repeat your explanation of why he should not engage in these behaviors.
3. Stress to the student that specific areas of his body should not be discussed in public. For example, tell the female student that she should not discuss her menstrual period with others. Tell the student that when he has questions of a sexual or personal nature, he should discuss them with his parents or other responsible adults.
4. Discuss dating practices. Role play making dates and planning the activities for a date, including estimating costs and determining budgetary factors.

Home and Community

1. Ask the parents to explain appropriate ways to behave with members of both sexes (e.g., he may roughhouse with a male but not with a female, and he may hug and kiss a female if she invites this behavior while it is not appropriate to kiss and hug a fellow male).
2. Ask the parent to explain acceptable dating and courtship practices. Ask them to role play different practices, including asking for, planning, and behaving on a date.
3. Ask the parents to discuss strategies for successful courtship (e.g., putting his best foot forward, showing consideration, and exchanging flowers and gifts).
4. When the student is out in the community with a special friend of the opposite sex, remind him to behave in a manner acceptable to others. Tell the student that although he and his friend are especially fond of each other, they should not kiss, touch, or fondle each other in public because it might be offensive or embarrassing to others. Remind him that some emotions and feelings are personal things and should be displayed and expressed in private.

Functional Emphases In designing your own instructional activities and plans, emphasize the following elements:

1. Identification of appropriate behaviors with members of both sexes, in public and in private.
2. Identification of prevailing dating and courtship practices.
3. Determination of behaviors appropriate on a date.
4. Identification of suitable places and activities for dates.
5. Estimation of the costs of dating and courtship.
6. Identification of behaviors that will lead to successful courtships, including the giving of flowers and gifts.

Specific Objective Q

The student discriminates among and responds appropriately to friends, family members, acquaintances, and strangers.

Functional Settings and Suggested Instructional Activities

School

1. Discuss the different types of relationships the student may have with friends, family members, acquaintances, etc. For each specific type of relationship, explain to him the feelings that may be associated with such a relationship. For example, tell the student that we may love our friends one way and love our family members another way. Repeat this with all of the relationships the student may have. Discuss love relationships with a mate or prospective mate. Discuss the relationship between love for a mate and sex as one expression of that love.
2. Discuss living arrangements that are possible with families, friends, and mates. It is extremely important that the mores of the student and his sociocultural and age group be taken into consideration. Stress traditional relationships since handicapped people have enough acceptance problems. However, do not treat all other life styles as bad or sinful.
3. Discuss the relationship between husbands and wives. Explain that their love, unlike the love between a mother and child or between good friends, includes sexual love. Answer any questions the student may have regarding different types of relationships.
4. View the film *Like Other People* (see Special Materials List). When appropriate, show it to the student and discuss what the film is about. (The film shows the loving relationships between physically handicapped people and how they love and help each other.)

Home

1. Ask the parents to collect pictures of family members, friends, and acquaintances. Tell them to assist the child in identifying each one by name and relationship. Ask them to ask the child to point to and/or name each one and give the relationship.

2. Ask the parents to point out strangers met while in the community. Tell them to explain that he must be especially careful if strangers ask him to engage in behaviors that might endanger him. Ask the parents to make certain that they explain that not all strangers may cause trouble and that friends, family members, and acquaintances may also ask him to do something that may endanger or exploit him.

Functional Emphases In designing your own instructional activities and plans, emphasize the following elements:

1. Identification of people and their relationship to the student.
2. Awareness of behaviors that are acceptable with others regardless of relationship.
3. Recognition of behaviors that are acceptable with only some categories of people.
4. Awareness of behaviors that should be avoided.
5. Identification of the relationship between love and sex.

Specific Objective R

The student identifies the changing sex roles in male-female interactions.

Functional Settings and Suggested Instructional Activities

School

1. Check instructional materials to see if they are sexist and remove them from the classroom.
2. Discuss the jobs that women are now performing that were once restricted to men or thought of as men's jobs. Invite a female police officer, physician, or construction worker to class.

Home

1. Ask the parents to make certain that they explain to the child that work assignments and jobs are available to and done by people of both sexes. Ask them to point out examples of people who are performing roles that were previously stereotypically assigned to one sex.
2. Ask the parents to identify sexist words and behaviors practiced by members of the household and then take steps to change them. Tell the parents to involve the child in eliminating sexist language and behavior.

Functional Emphases In designing your own instructional activities and plans, emphasize the following elements:

1. Realization that men and women are expected to share household chores.
2. Appreciation for the role that men should play in child rearing and child care.
3. Elimination of sexist language and behavior.

Specific Objective S

The student describes the relationship of sex to love.

Functional Settings and Suggested Instructional Activities

School

1. Discuss the various ways of sharing love with family members, relatives, and friends.
2. Discuss the various ways of expressing love with a mate. Discuss the multitude of ways that demonstrate respect, valuing, and caring. Do not overemphasize or underemphasize the role of sex in a loving relationship.
3. Discuss the exploitative and unrewarding aspects of sex without love and the enriching and fulfilling pleasure of sexual intercourse when it is part of a love relationship.

Home

1. Ask the parents to explain the different kinds of love: love of a mother or father for a child, love of a family member for another member, love in a friendship, and love for a mate or prospective mate.
2. Ask the parents to discuss the different ways people express love. Tell them to describe sexual expression as a way of sharing love with a mate.

Functional Emphases In designing your own instructional activities and plans, emphasize the following elements:

1. Identification of the various types of love.
2. Identification of the various ways to express love.
3. Recognition of the need to express love for a mate in diverse ways, including sex.
4. Appreciation for the lasting pleasure of sex in a loving relationship.

Specific Objective T

The student identifies family, cultural, religious, and personal values relevant to sexual behaviors.

Functional Settings and Suggested Instructional Activities

Home

1. Ask the parents to discuss family values relevant to sexual behaviors.
2. Ask the parents to discuss cultural and religious values when pertinent to sexual behaviors.
3. Ask the parents to explain to the child that while he should be governed by family, cultural, and religious values, he must arrive at his own value system.

Ask them to explicate the problems, social and legal, that might arise from nontraditional values.

Functional Emphases In designing your own instructional activities and plans, emphasize the following elements:

1. Development of awareness in parents that they are essentially responsible for instilling appropriate values in their children.
2. Identification of the possible social and legal consequences of nontraditional values relevant to sexual behavior.

Specific Objective U

The student engages in responsible decision making about his own sexual behaviors and practices, including the avoidance of provocative or flirtatious behaviors.

Functional Settings and Suggested Instructional Activities

School

1. Tell the student that sexual exploitation may be encouraged if she wears inappropriate clothing. Point out the importance of buying clothing that fits and is not overly revealing.
2. Discuss teasing with the student. Give examples of teasing such as teasing a friend or someone younger than he is. Point out that this type of behavior is not acceptable and can lead him to trouble. Explain that teasing often starts as a joke but ends up causing problems. During the day, if teasing is observed, stop the student from doing it. Ask him to explain why he should not tease anyone.
3. During times when the student may be in close physical contact with his peers (i.e., lining-up time, game time, or sitting in circles for specific activities), point out that it is not acceptable to rub or to sit too closely to someone else. Tell the student that this may upset or embarrass a peer. Emphasize that this type of behavior can be avoided by sitting a specified distance away from the peer. Praise the student if he engages in appropriate behavior during the next activity that requires him to sit close to someone.

Home

1. Ask the parents to discuss what constitutes provocative or flirtatious behavior. Tell them to point out that these behaviors are not acceptable and can lead to trouble.
2. Ask the parents to explain to the child that he must assume responsibility for making decisions about his total behaviors, including his sexual behavior.

Functional Emphases In designing your own instructional activities and plans, emphasize the following elements:

1. Awareness of the possible problems that may arise from flirtatious or provocative behavior.
2. Recognition of the need for the student to evolve his own model of acceptable behavior.
3. Awareness of appropriate ways to behave in courtship and dating relationships.

Specific Objective V

The student avoids sexual exploitation or victimization and does not sexually exploit or victimize others.

Functional Settings and Suggested Instructional Activities

School

1. Tell the student not to take off his clothes except at appropriate times. Review situations in which it is appropriate to remove his clothing in front of others. Tell the student that "playing doctor" or "nurse" by removing his clothes and allowing someone to touch or fondle his body is not an acceptable thing to do. If a stranger approaches the student and asks him to remove his clothing or to "play doctor," tell the student to ignore the request and to report the incident to his parent or another responsible adult.
2. Warn the student that he must never get into a car with a stranger or accompany a stranger anywhere. Discuss the dangers of this type of behavior. Tell the student that if a stranger attempts to get him into a car or tries to get him to go someplace, he should try to run away from the stranger. Tell him to report such incidents to a parent or other responsible adults.
3. Stress the emotional aspects of intercourse and explain to her what promiscuity is. Explain and discuss rape. Invite doctors or members of the Rape Crisis Center to speak to the student about rape and the ways women and men can protect themselves against rape. If someone attempts to have sexual intercourse by force with the student, tell her to report the incident to a parent or other responsible adults.
4. Discuss the fondling and touching of the student's body by another person. Explain that while this may be pleasurable, the student should never allow a stranger to fondle or to touch his body. If the stranger tries to touch the student, the student should tell his parent or a responsible adult. Tell the student that it is his right to decide whether or not he wants his body fondled. Explain that on dates his partner may want to fondle or touch his body. Tell the student that he does not have to let anyone do this. It is his choice.
5. Explain to the student that he should not exploit others. Give him examples of exploitative behavior and discuss each one. If the student is observed exploiting another student, he should be told to stop what he is doing.

Home

1. Ask the parents to discuss sexual exploitation with their child and explain what it is (i.e., allowing someone to touch or to fondle his body when he does not want them to, having sexual intercourse when he does not want to, taking off his clothes because someone tells him to, and being asked to perform sexual acts in which the student does not want to participate). Tell them to use simple terms when discussing these situations. Tell them to explain that if someone tries to exploit him sexually he should try to walk away from the situation, and that if he is unable to leave the situation he should report the incident to a parent or other responsible adult who will help him decide what to do about the incident.
2. Ask the parents to explain that the child should avoid exploiting others. Tell them to point out actions that are exploitative of others.

Functional Emphases In designing your own instructional activities and plans, emphasize the following elements:

1. Identification of situations that increase the likelihood of his being victimized or exploited.
2. Identification of behaviors that increase the likelihood that he will be sexually victimized.
3. Recognition that he must act responsibly in relating to others so that he does not sexually exploit or victimize others.

Specific Objective W

The student identifies and reacts appropriately to physical changes during the maturation process.

Functional Settings and Suggested Instructional Activities

School

1. Discuss the changes that occur to people as they go from infancy to childhood to adolescence to young adulthood to the middle years and to late adulthood.
2. Show the student pictures of people at different stages in the life cycle. Associate each stage with someone he knows, if possible.

Home

1. Ask the parents to describe the physical changes that occur during puberty to both sexes. Tell them to schedule this discussion when there are signs that he is entering puberty.
2. Ask the parents to discuss the ways he must behave at different times in his life (e.g., while it was appropriate to greet adults with hugs as a child, it is not appropriate to hug them indiscriminately when he is a teenager).

Functional Emphases In designing your own instructional activities and plans, emphasize the following elements:

1. Identification of physical changes that occur during the major subdivisions of the life cycle.
2. Recognition that different maturational levels require different behaviors based upon people's expectations.
3. Awareness of the physical changes that take place in the total body as well as the development of secondary sex characteristics.

Specific Objective X

The student discusses elementary facts of reproduction, including pregnancy and birth, as normal bodily functions.

Functional Settings and Suggested Instructional Activities

School

1. Read stories to the student on how young children grow up and how the female gives birth. Be careful not to explain details in a technical manner. When questions arise, answer only those specific questions, using the simplest terms possible. Do not add information or answer questions that the student does not ask.
2. Discuss the changes that occur in the female body during pregnancy. Show pictures of a pregnant woman at various stages of pregnancy. Explain that the baby grows in a specific place inside the woman's body. Discuss the ways she looks and dresses in the initial stages of her pregnancy compared to the way she looks just before giving birth.
3. Tell the student that pregnancy and birth are normal bodily functions. Encourage the student to express her feelings about birth and pregnancy. If she expresses fear about pregnancy, discuss these fears with her. Answer all questions as simply and as accurately as possible.
4. Read *Sex Education of the Mentally Retarded Child in the Home* (see Special Materials List).
5. Show the film *Labor of Love* (see Special Materials List). This film emphasizes the total experience of maternity and childbirth and shows the actual birth of a baby.

Home

1. Ask the parents to read the books *How Babies Are Made* and *A Baby Is Born* (see Special Materials List) to the child. Discuss the information found in these books. Answer all questions simply and accurately.
2. Ask the parents to read the Guide for Parents pamphlet *Love, Sex, and Birth Control for the Mentally Retarded* (see Special Materials List). Show pictures of the birth of a baby to the child as they discuss the topic with him.

Functional Emphases In designing your own instructional activities and plans, emphasize the following elements:

1. Identification of the elementary facts of reproduction.
2. Identification of the signs of pregnancy, the ways a woman can determine if she is pregnant, and the changes that take place in a woman during pregnancy.
3. Identification of the stages of pregnancy, labor, and birth.

Specific Objective Y

The student discusses the role the mother can play in breast feeding babies.

Functional Settings and Suggested Instructional Activities

School

1. Show the student movies or slides of animals feeding their young.
2. Discuss the reasons why some women wish to breast feed their babies.

Home

1. Ask the mother to discuss how mother animals feed their young. Ask her to show pictures of baby animals suckling.
2. Ask the mother to explain the purpose of a woman's breasts and to explain that when a woman has a baby, she may want to feed the baby the milk her body makes for that purpose.

Functional Emphases In designing your own instructional activities and plans, emphasize the following elements:

1. Recognition that breast feeding an infant is a natural behavior.
2. Awareness that breast feeding is a private behavior that, in American society, is done in private or in a private way.

Specific Objective Z

The student discusses venereal diseases: their transmission, prevention, symptoms, treatments, and consequences.

Functional Settings and Suggested Instructional Activities

School

1. Consult a public health nurse or doctor for information that has been specifically developed for the handicapped about venereal diseases. Invite these people into your class and arrange a question-and-answer period. Tape record the information and play it back at a later date.

2. Obtain booklets and pamphlets published by Planned Parenthood that discuss venereal diseases and their causes. Discuss these pamphlets with the student. You may want to share the information with the student's parents, guardians, or other responsible adults with whom the student resides.
3. Explain to the student that venereal disease comes from having sexual relations with someone who has been infected. Read the section on venereal diseases in the Guide for Parents pamphlet *Love, Sex, and Birth Control for the Mentally Retarded* (see Special Materials List). Stress that if he thinks he may have a venereal disease, he should seek medical help.
4. View the film *Mental Retardation and Sexuality* (see Special Materials List). Use it as a reference for group discussions with the parents of the students.

Home

1. Ask the parents to discuss the way venereal diseases are transmitted and the ways they can be prevented, including abstinence, fidelity to a mate, and the use of condoms.
2. Ask the parents to describe the symptoms of venereal diseases without unduly alarming the child. Tell the parents to make certain that the child is mentally, emotionally, and physically ready for this discussion.

Functional Emphases In designing your own instructional activities and plans, emphasize the following elements:

1. Prevention of venereal diseases.
2. Early detection and prompt treatment.
3. Recognition of the need to refrain from sexual activity when infected to avoid transmitting the disease to others.

Specific Objective AA

The student discusses the nature and purpose of marriage and the family unit and the roles that each member plays in a family.

Functional Settings and Suggested Instructional Activities

School

1. Discuss the family unit with the student. Be sure to stress that all family units are not the same (i.e., some are large, some small, some have two parents, others only one, and some have grandparents, stepparents, aunts, or uncles living with them).
2. Read the stories *Grandmother Dear* and *Grandfather and I* (see Special Materials List). Ask the student to talk about his grandparents and parents and the things they do together. Role play situations based on the stories in these books.

3. Play the Sesame Street record *Five People In My Family* (see Special Materials List). Tell the student to pantomime the song. Compare the family on the record to the student's family when appropriate.
4. Read the story *The Littlest House* (see Special Materials List). Discuss different types of houses, such as tenements, apartments, one-family houses, and trailers. Then ask the student to discuss the type of house or home in which he lives.
5. Discuss with the student being a member of a family. Talk about family responsibilities—for example, mother and father may have jobs, and the student may have household chores to perform. Ask the student what responsibilities are and what he does to help his family. Talk about the importance of being a contributing member of the family unit.
6. Show the film *Family Fun* (see Special Materials List). This specific film stresses fun things families can do together. Talk about the trips and vacations they have viewed on the film and ask the student what he does for fun with his family.

Home

1. Ask the parent to make certain the nature of the particular family unit is clear to the child.
2. Ask the parent to make sure the child understands the role he is to play in the family unit.
3. Ask the parent to explain the marriage customs of the family, cultural group, and the religious affiliation, if pertinent.

Functional Emphases In designing your own instructional activities and plans, emphasize the following elements:

1. Identification of the need to communicate with family members.
2. Identification of the need to cooperate with family members to ensure the most effective operation of the family unit.
3. Awareness of the changing sex roles.
4. Appreciation for the behaviors necessary to maintain a successful marriage.

Specific Objective BB

The student discusses and prepares for the role of a parent.

Functional Settings and Suggested Instructional Activities

School

1. Identify the various parenting duties expected of a parent. Design instructional experiences to practice specific skills (e.g., bathing a baby, feeding a baby, and dressing a young child).
2. Read stories to the student in which parental duties are clearly demonstrated (e.g., *Little House on the Prairie*).

Home

1. Ask the parent to explain what she has done to prepare for the role of the parent.
2. Ask the parent to discuss the various dimensions of her and the father's role as parents.

Functional Emphases In designing your own instructional activities and plans, emphasize the following elements:

1. Identification of parenting skills.
2. Development of specific skills related to the total range of skills, including caregiving, counseling, and training skills.

Specific Objective CC

The student practices birth control when appropriate.

Functional Settings and Suggested Instructional Activities

School

1. Read the pamphlet *Questions and Answers About Birth Control* (see Special Materials List). Discuss these questions and answers with the student.
2. Discuss with the student ways of preventing pregnancy. Show him examples of birth control devices such as an IUD, a condom, etc. Discuss each device and how it is used. Explain that some devices may be put on by the male student and others may be taken or used by his female partner, while others may require insertion by a doctor. Show him pictures of various birth control devices and ask him to identify them and describe their use.
3. Read the pamphlet *Questions and Answers about Intrauterine Devices* (see Special Materials List). Discuss the questions and answers with the student.
4. Discuss vasectomies and other surgical forms of birth control with students who require this information. Read the section on vasectomy or tubal ligation in the Guide for Parents *Love, Sex, and Birth Control for the Mentally Retarded* (see Special Materials List) for additional information on this topic.

Home

1. Ask the parents to discuss the family, cultural, and religious attitudes toward birth control. Tell the parents to discuss specific methods of birth control if they believe their child is able to understand the concept and if she should practice birth control.
2. If the parents believe that birth control should be practiced, ask them to help the child decide on the method to be used if he is sexually active.

Functional Emphases In designing your own instructional activities and plans, emphasize the following elements:

1. Examination of the issues involved in birth control, including religious views and the advantages of family planning.
2. Identification of the efficiency of typical methods.
3. Identification of the health factors relevant to specific methods.
4. Calculation of the costs of different methods.
5. Identification and implementation of procedures to be followed.

Special Materials List—Sex Education

Books/Pamphlets

Love, Sex and Birth Control for the Mentally Retarded; Questions and Answers About Birth Control; Questions and Answers About Intrauterine Devices; Techniques in Leading Group Discussions on Human Sexuality. Planned Parenthood Association of Southeastern Pennsylvania, 1220 Samson St., Philadelphia, PA 19107.

Study Guide No. 3, Masturbation. SIECUS, 1855 Broadway, New York, NY 10023.

How Babies Are Made. Time-Life Books, 777 Duke St., Alexandria, VA 22314.

A Baby Is Born. Maternity Center Association, 48 E. 92nd St., New York, NY 10028.

Sex Education of the Mentally Retarded Child in the Home. National Association for Retarded Citizens, 2709 Avenue E East, Box 6109, Arlington, TX 76005.

Grandmother Dear. Follett Publishing Co., 1010 W. Washington Blvd., Chicago, IL 60607.

Grandfather and I. Lothrop, Lee, and Shepard Co., 105 Madison Ave., New York, NY 10016.

The Littlest House. Bowmar/Noble Publishing Corp., 4563 Colorado Blvd., Los Angeles, CA 90039.

Films/Filmstrips

Family Fun; Learning About Health; Learning About Neatness; Questions About Health—Learning About Health. Encyclopedia Britannica Educational Corp., 425 N. Michigan Ave., Chicago, IL 60602.

Boy to Man; Girl to Woman. Churchill Films, 662 N. Robertson Blvd., Los Angeles, CA 90069.

Labor of Love. Leonard J. Abbey, Md., 683 Beacon St., Newton Centre, MA 02109.

Like Other People. Society for Mentally Handicapped Children, 86 Newman St., London, W.I., England.

Mental Retardation and Sexuality. Planned Parenthood Association of Southeastern Pennsylvania, 1220 Samson St., Philadelphia, PA 19107.

Menstruation; Teaching Good Conduct and Personal Hygiene to Retarded Teenagers. Harris County Center for the Retarded, Inc., 3550 W. Dallas St., Houston, TX 77019.

Records

Everybody Wash (Sesame Street); Five People in My Family; I've Got To. Columbia Book and Record Library, 51 W. 52nd St., New York, NY 10019.

Let's Dance; Take a Bath. Hap Palmer Record Library, Educational Activities, Inc., P. O. Box 392, Freeport, NY 11520.

Suggested Readings/References

Adams, G. L., Tallon, R. J., & Alcorn, D. A., (1982). Attitudes toward the sexuality of mentally retarded and nonretarded persons. *Education and Training of the Mentally Retarded, 17*, 307–312.

Amary, I. B., (1980). *Social awareness, hygiene, and sex education for the mentally retarded-developmentally disabled.* Springfield, IL: Charles C Thomas.

Andry, A. C., & Schepp, S. (1969). *How babies are made.* New York: Time–Life Books.

A resource guide in sex education for the mentally retarded. (1971). Washington, DC: American Association for Health, Physical Education and Recreation and Sex Information and Education Council of the United States.

Atwell, A. A., & Jamison, C. B., (1977). *The mentally retarded: Answers to questions about sex.* Los Angeles: Western Psychological Services.

Bass, M. (1972a). *Developing community acceptance of sex education for the mentally retarded.* New York: SIECUS.

Bass, M. (Ed.). (1972b). *Sexual rights and responsibilities of the mentally retarded: Proceedings of AAMD Conference, Region IX.* Ardmore, PA: American Association on Mental Deficiency.

Brantlinger, E. (1983). Measuring variation and change in attitudes of residential care staff toward the sexuality of mentally retarded persons. *Mental Retardation, 21*, 17–22.

Calderwood, D. (1972). *About your sexuality.* Boston: Beacon Press.

Caplan, F. (1972). *The first twelve months.* New York: Grosset and Dunlap.

Craft, A. (1982). *Sex educational counseling of the mentally handicapped.* Baltimore: University Park Press.

Craft, M., & Craft, A. (1978). *Sex and the mentally retarded.* Boston: Routledge and Kegan Paul, Ltd.

Demarest, R. J., & Sciarra, S. J., (1969). *Conception, birth, and contraception.* New York: McGraw–Hill.

Dupras, A., & Tremblay, R. (1976). Path analysis of parents' conversation toward sex education of their mentally retarded children. *American Journal of Mental Deficiency, 81*, 162–166.

Durana, L., & Cuvo, A. J., (1980). A comparison of procedures for decreasing public disrobing of an institutionalized profoundly mentally retarded woman. *Mental Retardation, 18*, 185–188.

Edmonson, B., McCombs, K., & Wish, J. (1979). What retarded adults believe about sex. *American Journal of Mental Deficiency, 84*, 11–18.

Edmonson, B., & Wish, J. (1975). Sex knowledge and attitudes of moderately retarded males. *American Journal of Mental Deficiency, 80*, 172–179.

Family planning services for disabled people: A manual for service providers. (1980). Rockville, MD: National Clearinghouse for Family Planning Information.

Fischer, H. L., Krajicek, M. J., & Borthick, W. A., (1974). *Sex education for the developmentally disabled.* Baltimore: University Park Press.

Fischer, H. L., Krajicek, M. J., & Borthick, W. A., (1973). *Teaching concepts of sexual development to the developmentally disabled.* Denver: JFK Child Development Center, University of Colorado Medical Center.

Fleming, M. A., (1979). Teaching sex to institutionalized retarded people: What society says is accepted behavior. *Disabled USA, 3*, 7–10.

Flynn, R. J., & Nitsch, K. (Eds.). (1980). *Normalization, social integration, and community services.* Austin: PRO-ED.

Gimarl, J. D., (1979). *Social/sexual living skills.* Columbia, SC: University of South Carolina Press.

Gordon, S. (1979). *Facts about sex for today's youth.* New York: Ed-U Press.

Gordon, S. (1974). *Girls are girls and boys are boys: So what's the difference?* New York: John Day.

Gordon, S., & Bilken, D. (1979). *Sexual rights for the people who happen to be handicapped.* New York: Ed-U Press.

Growing up young and how to tell the retarded girl about menstruation. (1971). Neenah, WI: Kimberly-Clark.

Haavik, S. F., & Menninger, K. A., II. (1982). Sexuality, law, and the developmentally disabled person: Legal and clinical aspects of marriage, parenthood, and sterilization. *Education and Training of the Mentally Retarded, 17,* 76–77.

Haavik, S. F., & Menninger, K. A., II. (1981). *Sexuality, law, and the developmentally disabled person: Legal and clinical aspects of marriage, parenthood, and sterilization.* Baltimore: Paul H. Brookes.

Hamre-Nietupski, S., & Williams, W. (1977). Implementation of selected sex education and social skills to severely handicapped students. *Education and Training of the Mentally Retarded, 12,* 364–372.

Hatcher, R., Stewart, G., Stewart, F., Guest, F., Schwartz, D., & Jones, S. (1980). *Contraceptive technology* (10th Rev. Ed.). New York: Irvington Publishers.

Heshusius, L. (1982). Sexuality, intimacy, and persons we label mentally retarded: What they think—what we think. *Mental Retardation, 20,* 164–168.

Johnson, W. R., (1972). *Masturbation. Siecus study guide No. 3.* New York: SIECUS.

Johnson, W. R., & Kempton, W. (1981). *Sex education and counseling of special groups: The mentally and physically handicapped, ill and elderly.* Springfield, IL: Charles C Thomas.

Kempton, W. (1979). *Sex education for persons with disabilities that hinder learning: A teacher's guide.* Philadelphia: Planned Parenthood of Southeastern Pennsylvania.

Kempton, W., & Forman, R. (1976). *Guidelines for training on sexuality and the mentally handicapped.* Philadelphia: Planned Parenthood Association of Southeastern Pennsylvania.

Kempton, W., Gordon, S., & Bass, M. (1971). *Love, sex, and birth control for the mentally retarded—A guide for parents.* Philadelphia: Planned Parenthood Association of Southeastern Pennsylvania.

Mitchell, L., Doctor, R. M., & Butler, D. C. (1978). Attitudes of caretakers toward the sexual behavior of mentally retarded persons. *American Journal of Mental Deficiency, 83,* 289–296.

Monat, R. K. (1982). *Sexuality and the mentally retarded.* San Diego: College-Hill Press.

Perske, R. (1973). About sexual development. *Mental Retardation, 11,* 6–8.

Russell, T., & Hardin, P. (1980). Sex education for the mentally retarded. *Education and Training of the Mentally Retarded, 15,* 312–318.

Thinesen, P. J., & Bryan, A. J., (1981). The use of sequential pictorial cues in the initiation and maintenance of grooming behaviors with mentally retarded adults. *Mental Retardation, 19,* 247–250.

Wilbur, C., & Aug, R. (1973). Sex education. *American Journal of Nursing, 73,* 88–91.

6 Drug Education

A curriculum unit concerned with drug education is particularly pertinent considering the society-wide fascination with and social acceptance of both licit and illicit drugs. Its inclusion in a holistic, functional curriculum for moderately to severely handicapped students is particularly critical, considering the fact that many of these individuals are placed early in their lives on drug regimens of various kinds to ameliorate symptoms and to control and modify behavior (Gadow & Kalachnik, 1981; Silva, 1979; Singh & Aman, 1981). The situation is further compounded when one considers the psychological impact on moderately and severely handicapped individuals resulting from the increasing attention directed to the use of vitamin and mineral supplements in attempts to reverse atypical physiological and behavioral states (Harrell, Capp, Davis, Peerless, & Raritz, 1981).

In this curricular section, emphasis is placed on reducing the use of medicines and medications unless they are absolutely necessary to the general well-being and overall health of the student (LaMendola, Zaharia, & Carver, 1980) and unless they have been prescribed, recommended, administered, and/or supervised by a responsible person or by an interdisciplinary treatment team (Vankrevelen & Harvey, 1982).

The major thrust is to help moderately and severely handicapped students to act responsibly in their use of over-the-counter medications, prescribed medicines, and nutritional supplements. The implicit goal, as in all other curricular areas, is the enhancement of skills, the acquisition of knowledge, and the development of a value system that will lead to independent and judicious self-medication (Brickley, 1978; Richey, 1978). The skills and knowledge necessary to the reasoned and reasonable use of medicines, medications, and nutritional supplements not only involves the act of ingesting or applying them but, in addition, the purchase and storage of these substances in economically wise as well as in healthy and safe ways.

The curriculum objectives and activities attempt also to reduce the likelihood that moderately and severely handicapped students will become abusers of illicit drugs. Handicapped individuals are subject to the same personal stresses and social pressures that lead to drug dependency and addiction whether they live in the institutional setting or have been integrated into the mainstream of a community life where drugs are, too often, a peer-sanctioned leisure activity (Davis, Cullari, & Breuning, 1982; Fielding, Murphy, Reagan, & Peterson, 1980).

Teachers and other professionals working with moderately and severely handicapped persons must not only be sophisticated about pharmacotherapy (Gadow, 1979 & 1983) and its behavioral manifestations (Gadow, 1982), but they must also be alert to those behaviors that suggest that students are possibly abusing drugs (Craig, 1975).

Further, this curriculum is meant to assist teachers and other concerned professionals in helping prevent physical and social addiction to the ubiquitously abused drugs: alcohol and nicotine. The hazards of smoking are of particular concern, especially because of the undeniable evidence of its deadly effects on health, its lethal contribution to fires, and its use in ingesting other harmful drugs. The emphasis is placed on stopping the student before he begins smoking, since once a person has become addicted to nicotine, it is extremely difficult for him to refrain from smoking. The dangers of alcohol addiction are also incontrovertible, and major efforts should be taken to dissuade students from drinking alcoholic beverages since alcohol is the most rapidly physically damaging drug and is highly physically and socially addictive.

The Suggested Readings/References and Special Materials List at the end of this chapter provide information on drug education. The reader should decide which material and information are applicable to a specific student or students being taught.

General Objectives of the Unit

I. The student will act as responsibly and as independently as possible in using medicines, vitamins, and minerals.

II. The student will act as responsibly as possible in relation to smoking.

III. The student will act as responsibly as possible in relation to drinking alcoholic beverages.

General Objective I

The student will act as responsibly and as independently as possible in using medicines, vitamins, and minerals.

Specific Objectives

The student:

A. differentiates between foods (including beverages) and nonfoods.
B. differentiates nonfoods that never should be ingested from nonfoods that are oral medications, vitamins, or minerals.
C. eats foods and avoids eating or ingesting nonfoods that are harmful.
D. who is not mature enough to self-administer vitamins, minerals, and medications accepts these substances only from responsible people.
E. who is mature enough self-administers vitamins and minerals according to an established regimen in specified amounts and at established times.
F. identifies signs of illness in himself.
G. indicates in some way to a responsible person that he is feeling ill, including those occasions when he might require medicine.
H. who is functioning in an independent or semi-independent situation, self-administers medications and medicines under appropriate conditions in specified amounts and at established times, including the identification of normal dosages and differentiation between those that are orally taken and those that are externally applied.
I. does not abuse or misuse drugs.

Specific Objective A

The student differentiates between foods (including beverages) and nonfoods.

Functional Settings and Suggested Instructional Activities

School

1. Make a list of the foods that the student regularly eats and drinks. Purchase these foods and show the student the food packages. Before you open each package, point to pictures of the food found on the label, and compare these pictures to actual samples of the food. Open each package and match its contents to the picture on the label and to the previously shown sample. Eat the food (ready-to-eat) or cook the food and eat it. Just before eating the food, say, "I am going to eat (or drink) some ____________ because it is a food that is good for me. We eat food to keep us healthy. Would you like some?" Encourage the student to join you and to sample the foods.

2. If the student begins to eat something that is not a food, immediately stop him. If it is a toxic substance, you may have to remove it forcibly from his mouth. Say, "Stop eating (or drinking) that; it is not a food. Stop." After he has stopped, explain the actual purpose of that substance (e.g., "This is paste. Paste is not a food. It is used to make paper and other materials stick together. It is not to be eaten!"). Make a list of the nonfood substances that the student attempts to eat or drink; from this list, construct a chart—written or pictorial—"Objects and Their Purposes," which gives the function of each of these substances. Periodically review the chart with the student (see Figure 1). If possible, use each substance for the purpose stated in the chart as you review the chart with the student.

Home and Community

1. Ask the parents to make a food chart of the foods the child eats and drinks. Tell them to include pictures of the foods and labels taken from their packages.
2. Once the child is skilled at using his own chart, ask the parents to identify foods and to make a new chart of foods that he does not eat but with which he may come in contact. This chart may be called "Foods Other People Eat" and should be set up in the same way as his own chart. It is meant to familiarize the student with other food possibilities because as he grows and his experiences change, his food tastes may vary.
3. Tell the parents to make sure that only food is stored in food storage areas (e.g., never put medicine in the refrigerator unless it must be kept there). Tell them to wrap it up and point it out to the child as a nonfood that must be stored in the refrigerator. Tell them to put a picture of a person eating and/or drinking on all cabinet doors in which food is stored and to show these signs to the child and ask her to explain, through word or gesture, what they mean.
4. Take a trip to a supermarket. Walk through the market and identify all the substances that are foods. Say "No" and shake your head when you come to something that is not food. Explain and/or pantomime the function of that nonfood. Walk through the supermarket again; this time ask the student to conduct the tour of foods and nonfoods.
5. Take another trip to a food store or supermarket. Pay particular attention to nonfood items that have pictures of food on them (e.g., detergents, shaving creams, and polishes with pictures of lemons). Encourage the purchase of fresh lemons and limes.

Functional Emphases In designing your own instructional activities and plans, emphasize the following elements:

1. Identification of common objects and their purposes.
2. Experiences with a wide range of common objects that are nonfoods.

3. Experiences with a wide range of foods.
4. Identification of food storage areas as opposed to storage areas for non-foods.

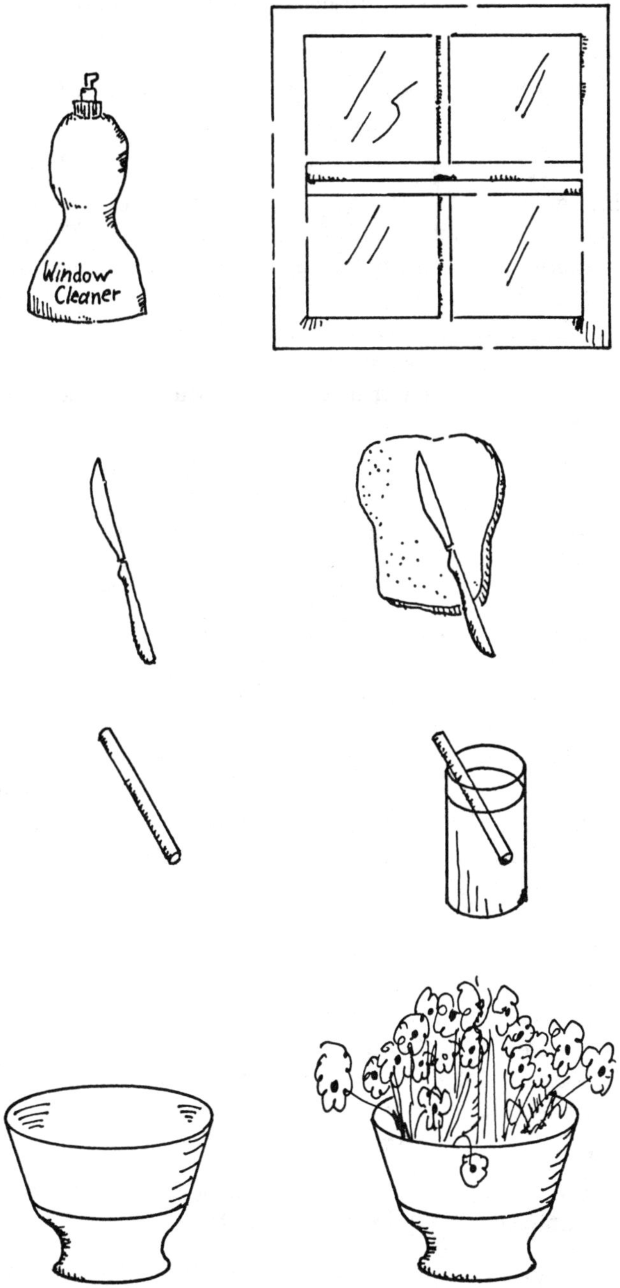

Figure 1. Objects and their purposes chart.

Specific Objective B

The student differentiates nonfoods that never should be ingested from nonfoods that are oral medications, vitamins, or minerals.

Functional Settings and Suggested Instructional Activities

School

1. Simulate a kitchen and a bathroom area if a housekeeping unit is not available in the school. Then play the game of "Put It Away." Give the student a variety of items to put away. Reward the student for putting food in the food cabinets, refrigerator, or freezer. Praise him for putting his medicines, vitamins, and minerals in his special medicine cabinet.
2. Collect sample packages of oral medications. Discuss each item and explain its uses. Pay particular attention to safety packaging and explain why such packaging is necessary.

Home

1. Ask the parents to explain to the child that there are special nonfoods that people take into their mouths and swallow to keep them healthy and/or to make them feel better when they are ill. Tell them to show the child sample bottles of vitamins and minerals that are taken by people living in the home. Tell them to make a chart of the vitamins and minerals prescribed by a physician for the student so that she can match the bottles with their pictures (Figure 2).
2. Tell the parents to repeat Activity 1. This time, they should show him samples of prescribed drugs taken by people (including himself) living in his residence. Tell them to point out the typed labels that appear on these bottles and boxes and encourage him to identify the containers that hold medicine prescribed for him. Tell them then to point out his name on these labels and make a chart of his medicines and show the prescribed dosages pictorially on his chart of medicines.
3. Tell the parent to make sure that only prescribed and over-the-counter drugs taken internally are stored in medicine cabinets and to set up a separate storage area for medicines that are to be used externally. It may be necessary to set up a separate storage area where the student can keep his own medicines and vitamins or minerals. If this is done, tell the parent to paste his picture and name on the door of this cabinet.

Functional Emphases In designing your own instructional activities and plans, emphasize the following elements:

1. Awareness that there are a variety of over-the-counter medications that may be ingested if recommended by physicians and other significant adults.

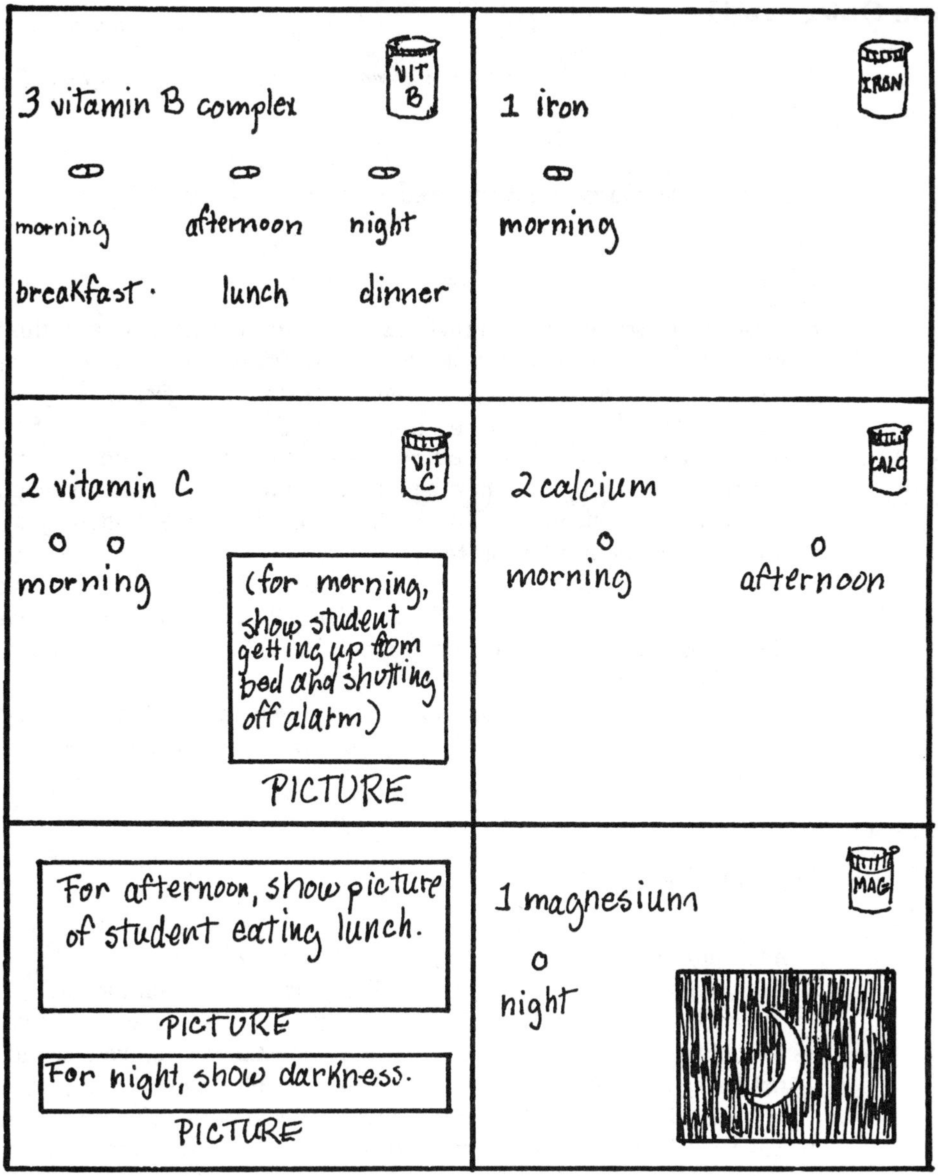

Figure 2. Vitamins and minerals chart.

2. Identification of safety packaging elements and verification that they are intact.
3. Awareness of over-the-counter medications that must not be taken orally.
4. Appreciation for the potential need for vitamin and mineral supplements as recommended by physicians, nutritionists, and other informed adults.

Specific Objective C

The student eats foods and avoids eating or ingesting nonfoods that are harmful.

Functional Settings and Suggested Instructional Activities

School

1. Observe the student as he functions in his environment. If he begins to play with or attempts to ingest a harmful substance, immediately stop him. Explain the dangers involved, shake a warning finger, shake your head, and say "No." Then show the student how the substance is used. Say, "This is a window cleaner. It is used for washing windows. Watch as I wash the window." Then remind him to put the window cleaner away until the windows need cleaning. Do this for each item the student plays with inappropriately or attempts to ingest.
2. Read the brochure *Poison Perils in the Home* (see Special Materials List), distributed by the National Safety Council. This brochure explains the poison perils that exist in every room of a house. Discuss this information with the student.
3. Show the slide presentation *Poison Perils* (see Special Materials List), distributed by the National Safety Council. Discuss the slides with the student.

Home and Community

1. Tell the parents to put nonfood, toxic items on high shelves, away from heat sources, and in locked cabinets.
2. Ask the parents to put "Mr. Yuk" stickers or other poison-indicating stickers on bottles of harmful nonfood substances. Tell them to show the sticker to the child and explain that this means the substance is dangerous and should not be eaten or played with. Tell them to praise him for not playing with or attempting to eat substances that are labeled with "Mr. Yuk" stickers.
3. Take a trip to a supermarket and a hardware store. Point out poisonous substances to the student (Figure 3). When you return to the classroom or learning area, make an experience chart describing the poisons you saw.

Functional Emphases In designing your own instructional activities and plans, emphasize the following elements:

1. Identification of nonfoods that are poisonous substances.
2. Utilization of poisonous substances appropriately.
3. Storage of poisonous substances in appropriate places.

Figure 3. Example of poisonous substances.

Specific Objective D

The student who is not mature enough to self-administer vitamins, minerals, and medications accepts these substances only from responsible people.

Functional Settings and Suggested Instructional Activities

School

1. Ask the student to help you make a chart and identify responsible people from whom he could receive medicine and vitamins or minerals (e.g., family members, teacher, doctor, and school nurse). See Figure 4.
2. Explain to the student that he might receive medication from a nurse. Tell him that a nurse's job (like the doctor's) is to help people stay or get well and that this is why the nurse may give him medicine. Tell him that he should only take medicines from the nurse on the job or at school, at the residential center, in the doctor's office, or at the hospital.
3. Play the "Commercial" game. Use a hard-sell approach and try to sell the student some medicine. Reward the student for refusing to buy the substance.

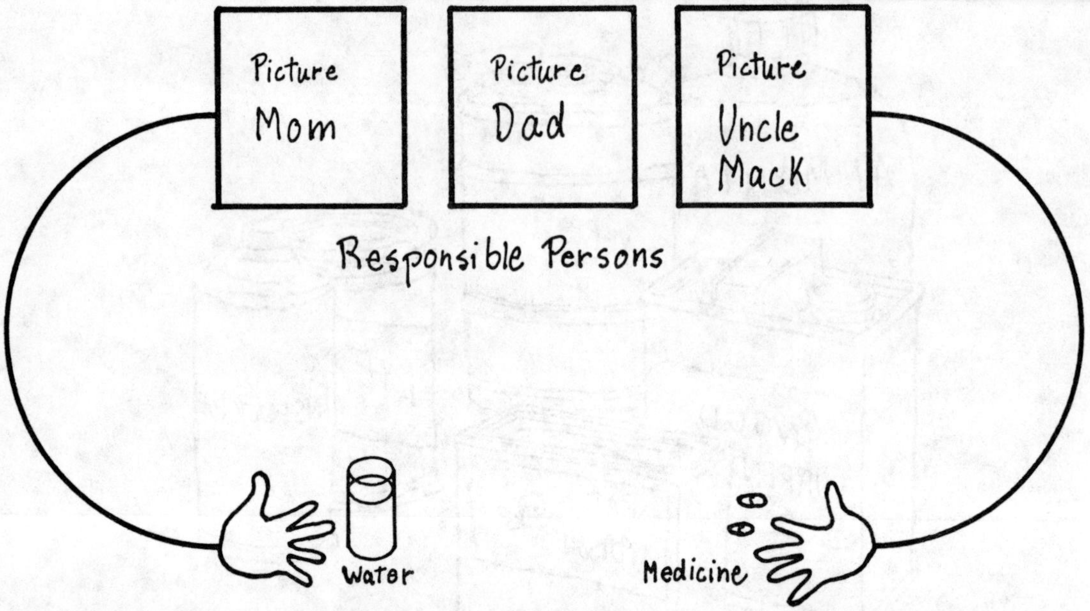

Figure 4. Chart of persons authorized to dispense medicines.

4. Play the "Pusher" game. Use a soft-sell approach and offer to give the student medicine (pills or capsules) for little or no money. Reward the student for refusing and for indicating in some way that he must check with someone special before buying and/or using any drugs or medicines offered him.
5. Role play situations in which people who have been coached attempt to give or sell the student pills, capsules, liquid medicines, and drugs. Reward the student for rejecting these offers.

Home and Community

1. Ask the parents to identify people in the home from whom the child can accept medicines, minerals, and vitamins.
2. Tell the parents to explain to the child that he might have to visit the doctor's office and that the doctor might want to give him medicine. Tell them to explain that a doctor's job is to keep people healthy and to make sick people better. For these reasons, the doctor might give him medicine, and it is alright to take medicines from a doctor.

Functional Emphases In designing your own instructional activities and plans, emphasize the following elements:

1. Awareness that there are individuals from whom she should not accept drugs, medications, vitamins, and minerals.
2. Identification of the times and dosages of medicines, vitamins, and minerals.

Specific Objective E

The student who is mature enough self-administers vitamins and minerals according to an established regimen in specified amounts and at established times.

Functional Settings and Suggested Instructional Activities

School

1. Periodically role play a situation in which a new medication has been prescribed for the student. Play the part of the physician and explain to the student the dosage and the times when the medicine should be taken. Reward the student for pretending to take the "pills" in the prescribed amounts at the appropriate times (see Figure 5).

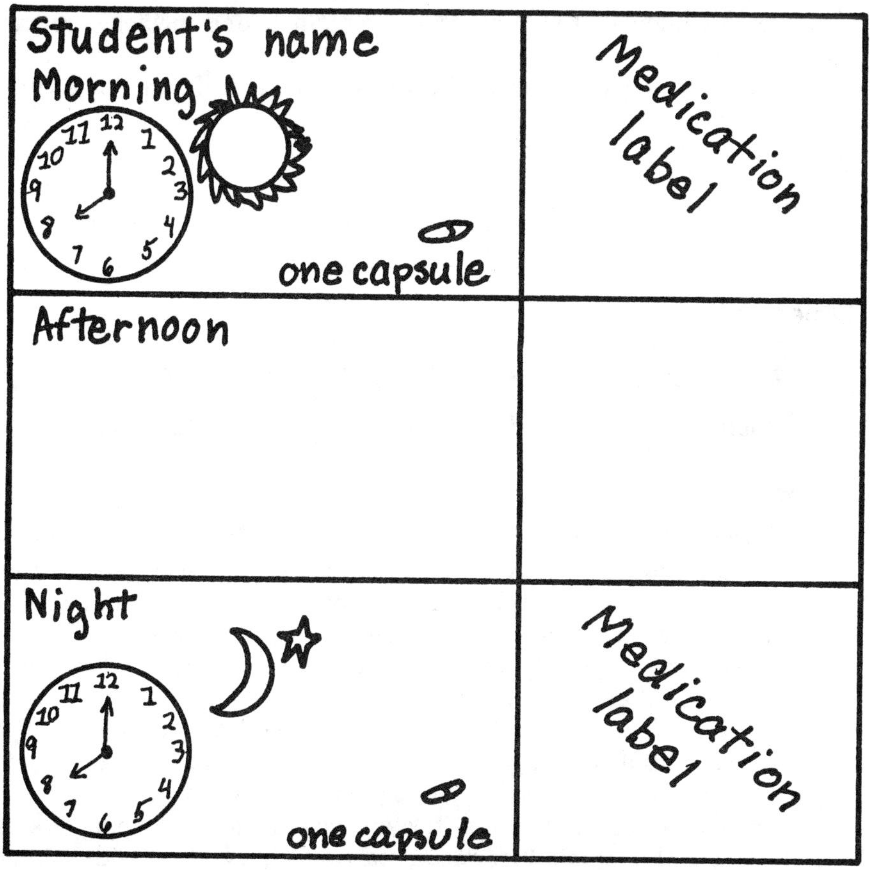

Figure 5. Medication chart. (For the student who is unable to identify time on a clock, use pictures representing the time of day.

2. Assist the student in establishing a regimen for taking vitamins, minerals, and medicines. Remind him to update his schedule whenever changes are necessary.

Home

1. Tell the parents only to allow the child to self-administer after they have observed that he has behaved responsibly toward medicine and vitamins over a sustained period of time.
2. Tell the parents to check periodically to determine whether the child is continuing to behave responsibly in this matter.

Functional Emphases In designing your own instructional activities and plans, emphasize the following elements:

1. Importance of not deviating from the prescribed regimen.
2. Awareness of expiration dates on vitamins, minerals, and medications.
3. Recognition of the dangers inherent in taking medicines prescribed for others.
4. Awareness of the dangers of taking overdoses, including some vitamins.

Specific Objective F

The student identifies signs of illness in himself.

Functional Settings and Suggested Instructional Activities

School

1. Explain that when we become ill, we feel different than when we are well. This is our body's way of telling us that we are sick. Ask the student if he has ever had a cold. If he indicates yes, review the signs of a cold (i.e., running nose, stuffed nose, sore throat, sneezing, and coughing). Tell him that these signs, especially when more than one occurs, are the body's ways of telling us that something is wrong.
2. Reward the student for bringing to the attention of a responsible person the signs of his illness. If you suspect he is faking as an attention-getting device, review acceptable ways of getting someone's attention.
3. Explain to the student that doctors have the job of helping sick people get better. Also explain that doctors cannot help everyone with an illness to get better. Tell him that medicines have been developed to help doctors make people better. Explain that the sooner he tells someone that he is sick, the sooner he will get help.

Home

1. Ask the parents to make a list of symptoms of illness that the child should be able to identify in himself. Tell them to include pain, fever and chills, nausea, upset stomach, vomiting, dizziness, bleeding and discharges from areas other than cuts, sores and other skin eruptions, sores that do not heal, abrupt changes in functioning such as of the bladder and/or bowel, a wart or mole that starts growing, a lump forming or the skin thickening, swelling, persistent cough or hoarseness, difficulty in breathing and/or swallowing, and fatigue. Tell them to review each of the symptoms and explain that, if he experiences any of them, he should let his parents or some other responsible person know.
2. Tell the parents that whenever the child is ill, they should draw her attention to the symptoms (e.g., they should say, "You are very tired. You have a red rash all over your body. Your body feels very warm. You are nauseous and dizzy. All these things are happening to you because you are sick. You have ______________________." Then tell the parents to reassure her that with medicine, bed rest, and whatever other treatment has been prescribed she will get well.

Functional Emphases In designing your own instructional activities and plans, emphasize the following elements:

1. Identification of signs that are mild variations of wellness and do not require sharing with others, differentiating these signs from more serious states.
2. Identification of multiple or extreme symptoms that require consultation with a physician.

Specific Objective G

The student indicates in some way to a responsible person that he is feeling ill, including those occasions when he might require medicine.

Functional Settings and Suggested Instructional Activities

School

1. Role play a situation in which the student pretends he is sick and tells a responsible person he is sick.
2. Review the signs of illness (see Objective F, Home Activity 1). For each symptom, practice describing it to another person.

Home

1. Tell the parents that when the child is ill, they should encourage him to point to the area of pain or discomfort (e.g., putting his hand on his head and making a pained facial expression to indicate a headache and pointing

to his stomach or holding his hands against his stomach while grimacing to indicate stomach cramps.

2. Tell the parents that if the child has sufficient speech, they should encourage him to tell them when he is sick and to describe his symptoms (e.g., "I don't feel well. My stomach hurts. I feel dizzy, and I just threw up.").

Functional Emphases In designing your own instructional activities and plans, emphasize the following elements:

1. Identification of people in his environment to whom he should confide signs of illness.
2. Development of descriptive skills in order to explicate diverse symptoms.

Specific Objective H

The student, who is functioning in an independent or semi-independent situation, self-administers medications and medicines under appropriate conditions in specified amounts and at established times, including the identification of normal dosages and differentiation between those that are orally taken and those that are externally applied.

Functional Settings and Suggested Instructional Activities

School

1. Bring in samples of bottles and boxes that contain medication prescribed for you. Show the student your name and the doctor's name on the label. Explain that these medicines have been prescribed just for you by your doctor. Ask him if he has any medicine that has been prescribed just for him. If so, ask the student's parent to send in empty bottles with their labels. Ask the student to identify his name and his doctor's name on the label. Assist him if necessary.
2. Put various bottles in front of the student; include bottles containing food, beverage, vitamins, poisons, over-the-counter drugs, and prescribed drugs. Ask the student to identify those bottles that have prescription drugs in them. Tell him to make two groups, one of the prescription drugs and the other of the remaining bottles. Assist him when necessary.
3. Place a variety of bottles containing different substances in front of the student. Ask her to identify all of the bottles of vitamins. Tell her to put the bottles not containing vitamins to one side.
4. Send the student to the store to purchase vitamins and/or minerals. Give him a note on which you have written the specific vitamin name and the desired dosage. Remind him to check his note against the label. Tell him to seek the help of the pharmacist or a store clerk if he has difficulty. Reward him for returning with the correct purchase.
5. Make a list of the over-the-counter drugs that are found in the student's home or living quarters. Pay particular attention to those over-the-counter

drugs that are given to the student to treat minor illnesses. Assemble these drugs in their packages and place them before him. Introduce each item by its most commonly used identifying name (i.e., use the term "nonaspirin pain reliever" rather than a brand name, and use a brand name such as Tylenol when the product is closely associated with its brand name). In introducing each item, say its name, point to its name as it appears on the package, tell the medicine's purpose, and mention that the student has taken this medication in the past (when applicable).

6. Show the student dosage information and time designations that appear on the labels of prescribed drugs. Help him to identify the information on the label of each of his prescribed drugs. Review the information periodically. If he is unable to identify the dosage and time interval information, stress that he should seek help from a responsible adult before taking the medicine.
7. Help the student identify when he should stop taking drugs. Explain that when his symptoms have disappeared, he should stop taking the medication. In cases where the medication has been prescribed by the physician, his/her directions should be followed for stopping use of the drug. Tell the student that it is his responsibility to let the responsible persons in his environment know when he is feeling better again.
8. Make a list of the externally applied medications that are found in the student's home or living area. Begin by showing her those medications, over-the-counter and prescribed, that are packaged in tubes. Explain that substances that are medicines are found in the drug departments of stores or are prepared by a pharmacist from a doctor's prescription. Medicines that are packaged in tubes, however, are never to be swallowed but rather are to be applied to the body surface. Show the student how to apply various ointments to the body. Tell her that toothpaste is a special material packaged in a tube that is safe to put in the mouth.
9. Collect other externally applied medicines such as iodine and Mercurochrome that have applicators attached to the cap. Show the student how to use the applicator. Explain that the applicator is part of the cap so that the user can apply the medicine to his body. Warn the student never to drink anything from a bottle that has an applicator.
10. Point out the words FOR EXTERNAL USE ONLY and NOT FOR INTERNAL USE as they appear on bottles, cans, tubes, and other containers. Explain the meaning of these words. When necessary, put "Mr. Yuk" labels on these containers. Also underline or circle warning words that appear on containers.
11. Remind the parent or other significant persons living with the student to keep externally applied medicines separate from internally used ones. Although this practice may create the need for extra storage space, the safety benefits more than justify it. Encourage the student to store externally applied and internally applied medication in separate places. Remind him to return these products to their separate storage areas after their use.

On containers of externally applied medicines, draw a mouth with an X over it to indicate that it should not be taken by mouth.

12. Pay particular attention to the identification and use of eye and nose drops, because the student may confuse droppers with applicators. Encourage the student to check with a responsible adult before using eye or nose drops to avoid application errors (e.g., eye drops into the nose or vice versa). Discourage the student from applying medications near the eyes and nose and tell him to seek help from a responsible person when medications need to be applied in the facial area. Alert the student to other sensitive body areas besides the eyes and nose (e.g. warn him to be especially careful when applying medicine in the area of the genitals and anus unless the medication is especially for these specific areas).

Home and Community

1. Ask the parents to remind the child to keep all medicines in their original bottles. Also tell them to urge him never to put medicine in an unmarked container.
2. Tell the parents to advise the child to seek the opinion of a responsible person before purchasing and using over-the-counter drugs. This is particularly necessary because of the high volume of advertising of over-the-counter drugs.
3. Take the student on trips to pharmacies and supermarkets and ask him to find the section and shelves where over-the-counter drugs are displayed. Request him to point to over-the-counter drugs that he might need to purchase in the future (e.g., cough medicine, laxatives, and headache remedies).

Functional Emphases In designing your own instructional activities and plans, emphasize the following elements:

1. Identification of dosage information.
2. Identification of contraindications to taking specific medications, including adversive side effects.
3. Awareness of the synergistic effects of taking several medicines at once.
4. Awareness of safety packaging and identification that such features are intact.

Specific Objective I

The student does not abuse or misuse drugs.

Functional Settings and Suggested Instructional Activities

School

1. Be alert to those behaviors that suggest the possibility that the student is abusing drugs. If one or more of the behaviors listed below occurs, investigate further. Behaviors to be concerned about include:
   a. Sudden or unexpected behavioral change
   b. Dissocial or antisocial behavior
   c. Seclusive or withdrawn behavior
   d. A flushed face
   e. Weight loss and emaciation
   f. Sleepiness
   g. Tremor or shakiness
   h. Hunger
   i. Abcesses, needle marks, and tracks in the vein
   j. Reddening of the eyes and chronic conjunctivitis
   k. Dilated or contracted pupils
   l. Double vision and temporary blindness
   m. Increased blood pressure and abnormal heart rhythm
   n. Increased blood pressure and normal heart rhythm
   o. Confused and slurred speech (when it had been satisfactory previously)
   p. Unsteady gait and impaired coordination (when it had been satisfactory previously).
2. If direct evidence is available that the student is abusing drugs (e.g., you observe him actively doing so), immediately stop him and confiscate the drugs. Express your disapproval of his drug abuse, but assist him in any way possible (your help, a physician's, or a counselor's) to deal with any emotional or physical problem that may be contributing to the drug abuse. Disapproval of the behavior, combined with support for the student abusing drugs, is recommended. If there is any question of withdrawal and/or other problems associated with discontinuance of a drug, consult a physician about steps to be taken.

Functional Emphases In designing your own instructional activities and plans, emphasize the following elements:

1. Provision of sufficient information to guard against the misuse and abuse of drugs.
2. Provision of a supportive and responsive environment in the home and in school that fosters a positive self-image in the student.
3. Provision of a wide variety of leisure experiences that keep the student occupied, stimulated, and interested.

General Objective II

The student will act as responsibly as possible in relation to smoking.

Specific Objectives

The student:

A. identifies the dangers of smoking.
B. does not smoke.
C. who does smoke does not accept cigarettes or tobacco from strangers.
D. who does smoke does not smoke when lying in bed or on upholstered furniture.
E. who does smoke obeys laws and rules governing smoking.

Specific Objective A

The student identifies the dangers of smoking.

Functional Settings and Suggested Instructional Activities

School

1. If you smoke, never smoke in front of the student or in places where he is likely to see you.
2. Show the student movies on fires and fire prevention that emphasize the dangers from lit cigarettes and matches.
3. Show the student movies that depict safety hazards involving smoking on the job (e.g., smoking in an area where dangerous vapors, gases, and other volatile substances are present). Stress the dangers of smoking in restricted places ("No Smoking" areas).
4. Invite someone from the fire department, an insurance company, a labor union, or the Occupational Safety and Health Agency to discuss the dangers of smoking on the job.
5. Ask someone from an organization such as Smokers Anonymous or the American Cancer Society to speak to the student and his peers. Inform the speaker of the functioning level of the student so that he or she can provide the student with information he will be able to understand.
6. Whenever new information becomes available on the hazards of smoking, share it with the student.
7. Obtain from the Children's Bureau its booklets on smoking (see Special Materials List). Read *A Light on the Subject of Smoking* and *You Can Quit*

Smoking—Young Smokers Aren't Really Hooked. Discuss with the student the information found in these booklets.

Home and Community

1. Ask the parents to inform the child that smoking definitely causes serious illnesses that often lead to death. Tell them to cite cases of familiar and prominent people whose smoking habits led to their death from lung cancer, heart attack, and emphysema.
2. Tell the parents to attempt to stop the child from beginning to smoke because once it becomes a habit, it is difficult to break.
3. Ask the parents to consider stopping smoking if they smoke.
4. When you are with the student and you see someone smoking, say, "That person is smoking a cigarette (cigar or pipe). It is not healthy to smoke." At other times say, "It is not safe to smoke. A lit cigarette (cigar or pipe) can cause fires."
5. Go on trips in the community. Point out sections of restaurants and other facilities that are for nonsmokers. Discuss the reason for this.

Functional Emphases In designing your own instructional activities and plans, emphasize the following elements:

1. Prevention of smoking since it is easier never to start than to stop once someone becomes addicted.
2. Exploration of the overwhelming evidence of the deleterious effects of smoking.
3. Awareness that each of us is responsible for his/her own behavior.

Specific Objective B

The student does not smoke.

Functional Settings and Suggested Instructional Activities

School

1. Tell the student that many people who do not smoke dislike being near people who are smoking. Explain that cigarette, cigar, and pipe smoke often make people who are nearby feel ill.
2. Praise the student's peers who do not smoke.
3. If the student has begun to smoke, comment on the changes it is making in his appearance (e.g., he now has yellow-brown stains on his teeth and fingers).
4. If the student has begun to smoke, comment on changes that may have occurred in his health (e.g., say, "Now that you have started smoking, you are coughing all the time.").

5. Point out the warning statement on cigarette packages and advertisements. Explain that cigarettes are so dangerous that the government has forced cigarette manufacturers to put warning labels on the packages and advertisements. Ask the student to talk about the other warning signs that are in his environment.
6. Send for the booklet *You Can Quit Smoking—Young Smokers Aren't Really Hooked* from the Children's Bureau (see Special Materials List). Discuss with the student the information found in this booklet.

Home

1. Tell the parent to reward the child for ignoring pressure (peer and otherwise) to smoke.
2. Tell the parents to reprimand the child if he starts to smoke. Remind him of the health and safety dangers involved. Tell them to indicate displeasure in his behavior.

Functional Emphases In designing your own instructional activities and plans, emphasize the following elements:

1. Exploration of the various diseases that are clearly related to smoking.
2. Discussion and explication of the rights of nonsmokers.

Specific Objective C

The student who does smoke does not accept cigarettes or tobacco from strangers.

Functional Settings and Suggested Instructional Activities

Home

1. Ask the parents to explain the dangers of accepting food and other substances from strangers. Tell them to warn of the possible adulteration of tobacco.
2. Tell the student that if his peers or others offer him a cigarette or tobacco-like substances from other than a standard package, he should refuse it. Explain that there are cigarettes and tobacco-like substances that look and smell different from normal cigarettes. Tell him that many people think that these cigarettes and tobacco-like substances are even worse to smoke than regular cigarettes and tobacco. Again, remind him that not smoking is the best, i.e., the healthiest and the safest thing to do.

Functional Emphases In designing your own instructional activities and plans, emphasize the following elements:

1. Avoidance of smoking and exploration of the axiom "An ounce of prevention is worth a pound of cure."

2. Exploration of the idea that there are people who might wish to hurt him and the realization that there are sometimes "friends" who might offer him a "tainted" cigarette.
3. Discrimination between friendly and unfriendly behaviors, independent of *who* is behaving in these ways.

Specific Objective D

The student who does smoke does not smoke when lying in bed or on upholstered furniture.

Functional Settings and Suggested Instructional Activities

School

1. Discuss the dangers of smoking in bed and while sitting or lying on upholstered furniture. Discuss the danger from smoke as well as fire. Smoke is likely to be more of a problem than fire.
2. Ask a representative from a fire department to visit the class and to talk on the dangers of smoking in bed.

Home

1. Ask the parents to point out any upholstered furniture in the home. Tell them to stop the student from smoking while sitting on upholstered furniture.
2. Tell the parents to observe the child. Tell them to stop him from smoking in bed and assist him in locating a safe place to smoke. Tell them not to forget to remind him that while he is smoking in a safe place, he is still behaving in an unhealthy way.

Functional Emphases In designing your own instructional activities and plans, emphasize the following elements:

1. Identification of upholstered furniture.
2. Awareness of the dangers of smoke inhalation and poisoning.

Specific Objective E

The student who does smoke obeys laws and rules governing smoking.

Functional Settings and Suggested Instructional Activities

School

1. Tell the student there are many public places where smoking is not allowed. Depending on the community in which the student lives, smoking

may not be allowed in schools, libraries, movie houses and theaters, department stores, supermarkets, buses, subways, cable cars, museums, or elevators.

2. Make certain that the student understands that the school is off-limits to smoking. Explain why the school is considered an inappropriate place to smoke. If the student observes teachers smoking, explain that once smoking becomes a habit, it is difficult to stop.

Home and Community

1. Ask the parents to review with the child those places they are likely to visit where smoking is not allowed.
2. Ask the parents to assist the child in identifying ashtrays.
3. Take a trip to each of the places identified in School Activities 1. Point out "No Smoking" signs. Explain the reasons for the regulations.
4. Observe the student when he is in places where smoking is prohibited. If he does not smoke in these places, reward him. Encourage him to find an area where he is allowed to smoke (e.g., leave the store and smoke on the sidewalk).
5. Show your displeasure at other people who disobey the laws governing smoking.

Functional Emphases In designing your own instructional activities and plans, emphasize the following elements:

1. Avoidance of smoking.
2. Avoidance of smoking in restricted areas.
3. Awareness of the rights of nonsmokers.
4. Recognition that others may be allergic to cigarette or cigar smoke.

General Objective III

The student will act as responsibly as possible in relation to drinking alcoholic beverages.

Specific Objectives

The student:

A. identities the dangers of drinking alcoholic beverages.
B. does not drink alcoholic beverages or does so in moderation.
C. who does drink does so only under the supervision of a responsible adult.
D. obeys laws governing the drinking of alcoholic beverages.

Specific Objective A

The student identifies the dangers of drinking alcoholic beverages.

Functional Settings and Suggested Instructional Activities

School

1. Tell the student that many highway deaths and car accidents are caused by drunk drivers. Discuss why drunk drivers have more accidents. Invite someone from MADD (Mothers Against Drunk Driving) to talk to the class.
2. Explain that when people are drunk over an extended period of time, they may become very sick when they stop drinking. Describe and discuss, at the student's level of understanding, withdrawal symptoms resulting from alcohol addiction.
3. Emphasize how the family unit and friends of people who drink excessively also suffer. Describe and discuss, at the student's level of understanding, the sociological/psychological impact of alcoholism.
4. Obtain the book *Learning about Alcohol—A Resource Book for Teachers* (see Special Materials List). Discuss the information found in the resource book and modify it according to the level of understanding of the student.

Home

1. Ask the parents to discuss with the child the physical, mental, and social dangers of misusing or abusing alcohol.
2. Tell the parents to warn the child that alcohol must never be taken with drugs. Tell them to explain that taking alcohol and medicine (or other drugs) at the same time can make a person very ill or be fatal.

Functional Emphases In designing your own instructional activities and plans, emphasize the following elements:

1. Avoidance of alcohol except in moderation.
2. Awareness of the ethnic use of wine as an adjunct to meals.
3. Awareness of the impact of alcohol misuse and abuse on various functions, especially in relation to driving.
4. Recognition of the impact of a person's abuse of alcohol on others, especially family members.

Specific Objective B

The student does not drink alcoholic beverages or does so in moderation.

Functional Settings and Suggested Instructional Activities

School

1. If someone is placing pressure on the student to drink alcoholic beverages, speak to that individual and attempt to persuade him to stop.
2. Reward peers who do not drink alcoholic beverages.
3. If the student has begun to drink excessively, comment negatively on the change it is making in his appearance, health, and behavior.

Home

1. Tell the parents that if they or some other member of the household drinks excessively, they should attempt to obtain help so that they can serve as a positive model rather than a negative one.
2. Ask the parents to reprimand the child if he begins to abuse alcohol. Tell them to remind him of the health dangers involved.

Functional Emphases In designing your own instructional activities and plans, emphasize the following elements:

1. Recognition that abstinence is preferable for most people, especially those who are alcoholics.
2. Awareness of the various programs available to alcoholics, recovering alcoholics, and their family members.

Specific Objective C

The student who does drink does so only under the supervision of a responsible adult.

Functional Settings and Suggested Instructional Activities

School

1. When the student does drink, explain that he should drink in small amounts and only when a responsible adult is present. Wine taken with meals and as part of religious ceremonies may be such an integral part of social, cultural, and religious patterns that the student will be under great pressure to indulge in the drinking of wine. Tell the student that he may drink wine when he is with responsible adults and when he can stop after he has had a moderate amount.
2. Explain that if he drinks when he is with a responsible person, he is less likely to drink to excess. Explain that many people when they drink become annoying to others and that this is why he should drink only when he is with a responsible person who can help him.

Home

1. Ask the parents to make it clear to the child from whom he might accept a drink. Tell them also to delineate the occasions and situations when and where he might take a drink.
2. Tell the parents to explain any cultural patterns that involve the drinking of wine. Also tell them to explain the drinking of wine as part of religious observances (e.g., at Passover and as part of Communion). Tell them to limit the number of drinks and restrict the drinking to one area of the house such as the dining room or television room.
3. Tell the parents to observe the legal age requirements of the community in allowing the child to drink in the home.

Functional Emphases In designing your own instructional activities and plans, emphasize the following elements:

1. Identification of responsible persons.
2. Identification of cultural and religious patterns of alcohol consumption.
3. Development of self-monitoring in the consumption of alcoholic beverages.
4. Avoidance of all alcoholic beverages when he responds adversely to even small amounts.

Specific Objective D

The student obeys laws governing the drinking of alcoholic beverages.

Functional Settings and Suggested Instructional Activities

School

1. Find out the laws that govern the consumption of alcoholic beverages in the student's community. Explain each of the laws to the student. Most of the laws are concerned with the age of the drinker, places where drinking is permissible, and restrictions on behavior after a person has been drinking, such as driving.
2. Show dissatisfaction with any behavior that runs counter to community standards as well as its rules and regulations.
3. Reward the student's peers when they obey standards and laws relative to the drinking of alcoholic beverages.

Home

1. Tell the parents to observe the child as he functions in life. Tell them that if he begins to break a law relative to drinking, they should stop him.
2. Tell them to establish specific rules for alcohol consumption in the home. Tell them to make certain all members of the household observe the rules. If there are different rules for different age groups, tell them to make these various rules as clear as possible.

Functional Emphases In designing your own instructional activities and plans, emphasize the following elements:

1. Awareness of the laws of the community.
2. Awareness of the impact of these laws on his behavior.
3. Comprehension of the differences in the types of alcoholic beverages and the differences in laws related to their purchase and consumption.

Special Materials List

Books/Pamphlets

Poison Perils in the Home. (599.73). National Safety Council, 425 N. Michigan Ave., Chicago, IL 60602.

A Light on the Subject of Smoking; You Can Quit Smoking—Young Smokers Aren't Really Hooked. Children's Bureau, U.S. Government Printing Office, Washington, DC 20036.

Learning About Alcohol—A Resource Book for Teachers. AAHPER Publications, 1201 16th St. N.W., Washington, DC 20036.

Films/Filmstrips

Poison Perils. (576.04). (slides). National Safety Council, 425 N. Michigan Ave., Chicago, IL 60602.

Epidemic: Kids, Drugs, Alcohol. Correctional Service of Minnesota, 1427 Washington Ave. South, Minneapolis, MN 55454.

Cassettes

Drug Abuse Cassettes. ESP, Inc., 1201 E. Johnson Ave., P. O. Box Drawer 5037, Jonesboro, AR 72401.

Suggested Readings/References

Agran, M., & Martin, J. E. (1982). Use of psychotropic drugs by mentally retarded adults in community programs. *The Journal of the Association for the Severely Handicapped, 7*, 54–59.

Brickley, M. (1978). A behavioral procedure for teaching self-medication. *Mental Retardation, 16*, 29–32.

Craig, T. J. (1975). Teacher awareness of drug abuse problems. In R. H. A. Haslam & P. J. Valletutti (Eds.), *Medical problems in the classroom: The teacher's role in diagnosis and management.* Baltimore: University Park Press.

Davis, V. J., Cullari, S., & Breuning, S. E. (1982). Drug use in community foster-group homes. In S. E. Breuning & A. D. Poling (Eds.), *Drugs and mental retardation.* Springfield, IL: Charles C. Thomas.

Fielding, L. T., Murphy, R. J., Reagan, M. W., & Peterson, T. L. (1980). An assessment program to reduce drug use with the mentally retarded. *Hospital and Community Psychiatry, 31,* 771–773.

Gadow, K. D. (1979). *Children on medication: A primer for school personnel.* Reston, VA: Council for Exceptional Children.

Gadow, K. D. (1978). *Drug therapy with trainable mentally retarded children in public schools.* Paper presented at the annual meeting of the Council for Exceptional Children, Kansas City, MO.

Gadow, K. D. (1983). Educating teachers about pharmacotherapy. *Education and Training of the Mentally Retarded, 18,* 69–73.

Gadow, K. D., & Kalachnik, J. (1981). Prevalence and pattern of drug treatment for behavior and seizure disorders of TMR students. *American Journal of Mental Deficiency, 85,* 588–595.

Gadow, K. D. (1982). Problems with students on medication. *Exceptional Children, 49,* 20–27.

Harrell, R. F., Capp, R. H., Davis, D. R., Peerless, J., & Rarirtz, R. E. (1981). Can nutritional supplements help mentally retarded children? An exploratory study, *Proceedings of the National Academy of Science, 78,* 574–578.

Inoue, F. (1982). A clinical pharmacy service to reduce psychotropic medication use in an institution for mentally handicapped persons. *Mental Retardation, 20,* 70–74.

Inoue, F. (1981). Psychotropic drug history chart. *Drug Intelligence and Clinical Pharmacy, 15,* 134–135.

LaMendola, W., Zaharia, E. S., & Carver, M. (1980). Reducing psychotropic drug use in an institution for the retarded. *Hospital & Community Psychiatry, 31,* 271–272.

Richey, J. (1978). *Drugstore language: A survival vocabulary.* Hayward, CA: Janus Book Publishers.

Silva, D. A. (1979). The use of medication in a residential institution for mentally retarded persons. *Mental Retardation, 17,* 285–288.

Singh, N. N., & Aman, M. G. (1981). Effects of thioridazine dosage on the behavior of severely mentally retarded persons. *American Journal of Mental Deficiency, 85,* 580–587.

VanKrevelen, N. D., & Harvey, E. R. (1982). Integrating clinical pharmacy services into the interdisciplinary team structure. *Mental Retardation, 20,* 64–68.

7 Leisure Skills

Traditionally, leisure experiences have been viewed as sports-related, competitive activities that are secondary to more basic curricular areas. When programs emphasized education for leisure, they typically were provided by parks and recreation agencies or by specialists working in the areas of recreation and physical education. Methodology and approaches to teaching the area of leisure have either been narrowly defined or absent altogether from educational programs. In part, this phenomenon can be attributed to the attitude held by many professionals and parents that leisure activities are of secondary importance in planning programs of instruction.

Leisure experiences are a positive and valuable resource to people as they function on a daily basis in society (Wehman & Schleien, 1980). Leisure experiences facilitate learning, adapting, and adjusting during nonwork hours; combat negative stress; develop physical fitness; enhance the work experience (McCarron, Kern, & Wolf, 1979); and foster relaxation.

Leisure, in a comprehensive educational context, offers an innovative channel that:

1. Allows an individual to know himself in relation to others.
2. Enhances the quality of his life.
3. Addresses his specific needs, capabilities, and values through the self-selection of meaningful experiences.
4. Enables an individual to evaluate his use of time and behaviors in situations ranging from the simple to complex.
5. Teaches critical social and interpersonal skills (Matthews, 1977).

The handicapped student's leisure time, especially for the student who is no longer eligible for educational programs, has increased rapidly. Lack of adequate facilities, age limits, eligibility restrictions, and limited summer and after-school programs have added to the need for leisure-time programming. This section of the curriculum is intended to provide objectives and activities to help meet this critical need. It is important to underscore that this chapter does not stress skill development because the authors believe that leisure-time activities should be primarily for enjoyment (Voeltz, Wuerch, & Wilcox, 1982), fitness (Beasley, 1982), and social experiences (Adkins & Matson, 1980). If skills are incidentally learned while these primary objectives are being attained, they should be utilized to enhance the program.

The activities presented in this chapter will enable the handicapped student to participate in a variety of leisure experiences at home (Hanley, 1979) and in the community (Brannan, 1979) and will afford the student opportunities to learn the rules of games, participate as a player and as a spectator in a variety of sports and games (Marchant, 1979), meet people with whom he may make friends (Kingsley, Viggiano, & Tout, 1981), actively engage in hobbies (Giangreco, 1983) and arts and crafts experiences (Frith & Mitchell, 1983), and use community facilities in his leisure time.

Providing a handicapped student with ways of using leisure time in a satisfying manner is also a way of enhancing the student's self-esteem and emotional well-being (Allen, 1980). The student who is able to initiate or join in activities during his leisure time may become more self-confident than the student who has much leisure time and few ideas about how to utilize it.

Because leisure time is a major part of the handicapped student's daily routine, parents, teachers, and other significant persons must encourage him to seek a variety of interesting leisure-time activities (Joswiak, 1979) and discourage the nonproductive ones such as watching television without regard to programming.

The growing number of older handicapped students who have completed their formal school programming represents a large population that must be considered (Salzberg & Langford, 1981). The integration of handicapped persons into the mainstream of community life is greatly facilitated by the development of leisure and leisure-related skills. It is recommended that the teacher review the materials developed by the American Alliance for Health, Physical Education, and Recreation for additional ideas concerning leisure-time programming.

For many people, social encounters are largely a direct result of participating in leisure experiences (Nietupski & Svoboda, 1982). Because of this, the integration of leisure experiences is a *sine qua non* of functional educational programming. An organized instructional program designed to develop a repertoire of leisure time interests and skills is essential for preparing handicapped students for a life that is as satisfying, pleasurable, stimulating, and enriching as possible (Sternlight & Hurwitz, 1981). Leisure offers all individuals the opportunity to experience new and creative avenues for fulfilling their lives.

Toys and games mentioned throughout this chapter can be found in most toy stores or ordered through toy or educational catalogs. The Suggested Readings/References and Special Materials List at the end of this chapter provide information on leisure skills. The reviewer should decide which material and information are applicable to a specific student or students being taught.

General Objective of the Unit

The student will function in leisure experiences as independently and as skillfully as possible and will gain physically and emotionally from these experiences.

(*Note:* In all games, sports, and other activities requiring strength, endurance, and agility, attention must be given to any physical limitations of the individual. The emphasis should be on enjoyment and fitness rather than on winning and competing with others. Further, emphasis should be placed on establishing a wide repertoire of leisure-time possibilities so that the individual does not engage in the same activities all the time.)

Specific Objectives—Play and Games

The student:

A. participates in games of make-believe and role playing.
B. selects durable and safe toys and games.
C. engages in water play.
D. plays low-activity games.
E. plays high-activity games.
F. plays target games.
G. plays balance games.
H. plays table games.
I. plays card games.
J. plays games of chance.
K. plays strategy games.
L. plays real-life games.
M. plays knowledge and word games.
N. chooses a variety of toys and games.

Specific Objective A

The student participates in games of make-believe and role playing.

Functional Settings and Suggested Instructional Activities

School

1. Read the student an interesting story. Add extra details to the story as you read it. Once you have finished reading the story, assign the student a part as a character in the story. Reread the story slowly and encourage the student to act out the story. Repeat the activity, using a variety of stories or rhymes. Praise the student.
2. Set up a "pretend house" in the classroom. This may be a large appliance box or "rooms" marked out by masking tape lines. Talk about things that happen at home, meals, bedtime, a family party, holiday get-together, or when people visit. Assign roles or let the student choose the roles he wants to play. Act out a variety of family situations. Switch roles so that the student has the opportunity to pretend to be a variety of family members.
3. At recess or playtime encourage the younger student to play games of make-believe (e.g., a tea party, kings and queens, and community helpers).

Home

1. Ask the parents to read simple rhymes or nursery rhymes to their child. Tell them to pantomime the rhyme and encourage him to imitate their actions. Repeat the activity, using a variety of rhymes.
2. Ask the parents to play school with their child. Tell them to play the part of a kind, helpful teacher.

Functional Emphases In designing your own instructional activities and plans, emphasize the following elements:

1. Awareness of the difference between fantasy and reality.
2. Utilization of make-believe as a means of practicing role-related skills.
3. Utilization of role play to examine feelings and attitudes.
4. Utilization of make-believe and role playing games as exploration of themes for creative dramatics.

Specific Objective B

The student selects durable and safe toys and games.

Functional Settings and Suggested Instructional Activities

School

1. Go to the toy shelf or game storage area. Take out each toy or game and show it to the student. Comment on each one (e.g., "This is a wooden puzzle and will last a long time if it's taken care of." "This is an unbreakable plastic truck and has no removable or sharp parts that could hurt you."). Encourage the student to comment on the toys and games verbally or through gesture.

2. Show the student a variety of games that are appropriate to her functional level and interests. Point out the small parts (marbles, dice, place markers) and explain that they are to be used only with the game. Remind the student never to put the pieces in her mouth, ear, or nose and to keep the pieces out of the reach of others who might swallow them.

Home and Community

1. Ask the parents to be cautious in selecting toys and games. Tell them to pay particular attention to the functioning level of the child. For example, if the child puts objects in his mouth, parents should not purchase miniature toys, toys with removable parts, or games with small game pieces.
2. Take the student on a field trip to a toy store. Purchase items for the classroom or the student, or just browse. Point out safe, durable games and toys to the student. Also point out dangerous toys (e.g., anything with small, loose parts, toys with sharp or pointed edges, games with darts or arrows, and toys with chemicals or toxic paints). Stress to the student that he should purchase and use safe, durable toys rather than dangerous ones.

Functional Emphases In designing your own instructional activities and plans, emphasize the following elements:

1. Judgment as to appropriate places to store toys.
2. Awareness of the need to put toys and games away after their use.
3. Attention to media accounts that point out unsafe toys.

Specific Objective C

The student engages in water play.

Functional Settings and Suggested Instructional Activities

School

1. Show the student how to fill various containers with water at a water table. Assist him as he does this and provide opportunities for water play.
2. Show the student how to pour water from one container to another while playing at a water table, a sink, or a dishpan. Give the student a variety of different-size containers and encourage him to use them as he plays with the water.
3. Bring a sieve, small colander, or tea strainer into the classroom. Show the sieve to the student and demonstrate pouring water through it.
4. Bring into the classroom empty plastic detergent bottles or plastic spray window cleaner bottles. Demonstrate filling the bottles with water (add a little dishwashing detergent to make bubbles), screwing on the tops, and squeezing or pumping the water out of the bottles and into the water table.

5. Give the student a variety of plastic containers (e.g., margarine containers, plastic Jello molds, and plastic cups). Put the containers in the water and demonstrate how they float. Put weights into the containers and comment on how the weight sinks the containers.

Home

1. Ask the parents to give their child plastic toy dishes, pots, pans, silverware, a sponge, and soap. Tell them to demonstrate washing the dishes while encouraging him to imitate their actions and to wash the dishes. Tell them to provide him with opportunities to wash the play dishes and to allow older or more able students to wash real dishes and silverware.
2. Ask the parents to encourage their child to use bathtub toys (Busy Bath Toy or Weebles Tub Sub) at bath time. Tell them to make certain to remind him to wash himself as well as play.

Functional Emphases In designing your own instructional activities and plans, emphasize the following elements:

1. Avoidance of playing with water when using electrical equipment.
2. Identification of the places where it is appropriate to engage in water play.
3. Recognition of the need to clean and wipe up after water play.
4. Awareness of the need to put away materials used during water play.

Specific Objective D

The student plays low-activity games.

Functional Settings and Suggested Instructional Activities

School

1. Teach the student jumping rope games.
2. Show the student how to play hopscotch.
3. Play the game of musical chairs.

Home and Community

1. Take the student to a miniature golf course.
2. Ask the parents to set up a croquet set on the lawn or garden area and teach him to play croquet.

Functional Emphases In designing your own instructional activities and plans, emphasize the following elements:

1. Observation of safety rules while playing low-activity games.
2. Selection of low-activity games when low-activity is preferable to high-activity games because of recent illness, physical discomfort, and other relevant factors.

3. Calculation of the cost of equipment or admission charges as appropriate.
4. Awareness of the time and space requirements of specific games.
5. Comprehension of diagrams and written instructions found in instructional booklets and on game boxes.
6. Comprehension of scoring rules and procedures.

Specific Objective E

The student plays high-activity games.

Functional Settings and Suggested Instructional Activities

School and Community

1. In appropriate weather, take the student to the school yard to play dodgeball, four square, Greek dodge, and tetherball.
2. Go to the gym and engage in a variety of racing games, including relays and slow racing.
3. Take a trip to a neighborhood recreation center and play Keep Away and Elimination.
4. Visit a neighborhood playground and play tetherball or a modified version of tag or hide-and-seek in which there are limited playing boundaries.

Functional Emphases In designing your own instructional activities and plans, emphasize the following elements:

1. Observation of safety rules.
2. Avoidance of high-activity games when he is tired, ill, or in physical discomfort.
3. Selection of high-activity games when he requires strenuous exercise.
4. Calculation of the cost of equipment as appropriate.
5. Awareness of the time and space requirements of specific activities.
6. Awareness of steps to follow if an injury occurs.

Specific Objective F

The student plays target games.

Functional Settings and Suggested Instructional Activities

School

1. Show the student how to play ring toss.
2. Show the student how to play marbles.

Home and Community

1. Ask the parents to show their child how to play tiddlywinks.
2. Take the student to a playground facility where there is a horseshoe court. Observe for awhile and, when possible, play the game.
3. Take the student to a playground where there is a shuffleboard court. Observe for awhile and, when possible, play the game.

Functional Emphases In designing your own instructional activities and plans, emphasize the following elements:

1. Observation of safety rules.
2. Calculation of the cost of equipment as appropriate.
3. Awareness of the time and space requirements of specific target games.
4. Estimation of distances and the amount of energy needed to arrive at a target.
5. Coordination of hand and arm movements through visual monitoring.
6. Comprehension of diagrams and written instructions found in instructional booklets and on game boxes.
7. Comprehension of scoring rules and procedures.

Specific Objective G

The student plays balance games.

Functional Settings and Suggested Instructional Activities

School

1. Play Bash, Twister, and Operation with the student.
2. Engage the student in playing Tip-It, Blockhead, and Jack Straws.
3. Play the game Barrel of Monkeys.

Home

1. Ask the parents to show their child how to play dominoes.
2. Ask the parents to demonstrate playing Pick Up Sticks.

Functional Emphases In designing your own instructional activities and plans, emphasize the following elements:

1. Comprehension of diagrams and written instructions found in instructional booklets and on game boxes.
2. Avoidance of balancing activities where danger is involved (e.g., balancing on an outside wall or railroad track).

Specific Objective H

The student plays table games.

Functional Settings and Suggested Instructional Activities

School

1. Show the student how to play air hockey, football, and Ping-Pong.
2. Set up a Ping-Pong tournament between you and the student. Keep a running record of games won.

Home and Community

1. Ask the parents to show their child how to play table hockey, shuffleboard, or Ping-Pong if they can afford the equipment and have space in the home for its storage and use.
2. Take the student to a recreation center where there are Ping-Pong tables and equipment.

Functional Emphases In designing your own instructional activities and plans, emphasize the following elements:

1. Observation of safety rules.
2. Calculation of the cost of equipment.
3. Awareness of the space and time requirements of specific activities.
4. Comprehension of the scoring rules and procedures.

Specific Objective I

The student plays card games.

Functional Settings and Suggested Instructional Activities

School

1. Show the student how to play card games he can play when he is alone (e.g., solitaire and double solitaire).
2. Encourage her to play simple card games with peers during free play.

Home

1. Ask the parents to purchase card games that require special cards (e.g., Mille Borne and Uno) and teach the games to their child.
2. Ask the parents to teach their child simple card games that use a regular 52-card deck (e.g., War, Go Fish, hearts, Concentration, Fan Tan, I Doubt It, poker, rummy, twenty-one, and cassino).

Functional Emphases In designing your own instructional activities and plans, emphasize the following elements:

1. Avoidance of using cards as a means of gambling.
2. Awareness that there are people who might exploit him by playing cards for money.
3. Identification of the face value of cards (numerals, letters, and pictures).
4. Identification of the suit to which a card belongs.
5. Placement of cards in rank order.
6. Designation of point value of cards when points are assigned in scoring.
7. Designation of winning values when different hands have different value or power.
8. Identification of the value of a trump suit.
9. Identification of the ranking order of suits when suits possess different values.

Specific Objective J

The student plays games of chance.

Functional Settings and Suggested Instructional Activities

School

1. Show the student how to play Yahtzee and Double Yahtzee.
2. Engage the student in real-life games that are also games of chance (e.g., Easy Money).
3. Show the student how to play dice as part of games in which the throw of the dice determines the order of play and/or the spaces moved.

Home

1. Ask the parents to show their child how to play games such as bingo and lotto.
2. Ask the parents to purchase specially designed lotto games (such as Zoo Lotto) that are educational and fun.

Functional Emphases In designing your own instructional activities and plans, emphasize the following elements:

1. Calculation of the costs of purchasing games of chance.
2. Estimation of the effect of purchasing these games on his or his family's budget.
3. Comprehension of diagrams and written instructions found in instructional booklets and on game boxes.
4. Comprehension of the scoring rules and procedures.

Specific Objective K

The student plays strategy games.

Functional Settings and Suggested Instructional Activities

School

1. Show the student how to play Sorry, Parcheesi, Trouble, Whosit, and other strategy games. Play these games at appropriate times.
2. When there is a moderately or severely physically handicapped student who is able to play a complex or advanced game such as backgammon, chess, Scrabble, or Master Mind, engage him in these games.

Home

1. Ask the parents to show their child how to play checkers, Chinese checkers, and Rummy-Q.
2. Ask the parents to purchase strategy games such as Battleship, Stratego, Brainwaves, and Monopoly and engage their child in these games at appropriate times.

Functional Emphases In designing your own instructional activities and plans, emphasize the following elements:

1. Calculation of the costs of purchasing games of chance.
2. Estimation of the effect of purchasing these games on his or his family's budget.
3. Comprehension of diagrams and written instructions found in instructional booklets and on game boxes.
4. Comprehension of the scoring rules and procedures.

Specific Objective L

The student plays real-life games.

Functional Settings and Suggested Instructional Activities

School

1. Show the student how to play Monopoly and the Game of Life.
2. Engage in simulation games that reflect the problems or issues of contemporary life (e.g., Careers and Pay Day).

Home

1. Ask the parents to play real-life games such as Easy Money, Careers, and Pay Day.

2. Tell the parents to spend sufficient time working with play paper money when the exchange of money is an integral part of a game.

Functional Emphases In designing your own instructional activities and plans, emphasize the following elements:

1. Calculation of the costs of purchasing games.
2. Estimation of the effect of purchasing these games on his or his family's budget.
3. Comprehension of diagrams and written instructions found in instructional booklets and on game boxes.
4. Comprehension of the scoring rules and procedures.

Specific Objective M

The student plays knowledge and word games.

Functional Settings and Suggested Instructional Activities

School

1. Play the game Go to the Head of the Class if it is within the student's ability.
2. Play academic games such as Game of the States, Categories (Guggenheim), and Read Around.

Home

1. Ask the parents to purchase games such as Concentration, Password, and Twenty Questions if their child is able to play these games. Tell them to engage in these games during leisure time.
2. Ask the parents to play word games such as Scrabble, Word Squares, Spill and Spell, and Alphabet Game if their child is able to play these games.

Functional Emphases In designing your own instructional activities and plans, emphasize the following elements:

1. Calculation of the costs of purchasing knowledge and word games.
2. Estimation of the effect of purchasing these games on her or her family's budget.
3. Comprehension of diagrams and written instructions found in instructional booklets and on game boxes.
4. Comprehension of the scoring rules and procedures.

Specific Objective N

The student chooses a variety of toys and games.

Functional Settings and Suggested Instructional Activities

School

1. Designate specific times of the day as free play periods. Encourage the student to play with a variety of toys and games. If the student chooses the same toy or game each time, take the toy or game away and encourage him to choose a different one.
2. On the toy shelf, place a check-out chart. At playtime, mark down which toys or games the student chooses. If you notice that the student is using the same toys and games all the time, encourage him to choose different ones.

Home and Community

1. Ask the parents to encourage the child to play with different toys. Tell them that while it is natural to play with a new toy or game for a long period of time, they should encourage returning to former games and toys whose novelty has worn off.
2. Discuss with the student places in the community where you can go for fun. Suggest new places or places that you have not been to recently.

Functional Emphases In designing your own instructional activities and plans, emphasize the following elements:

1. Exploration of new toys and activities.
2. Selection of toys and games to play with that were once favorite playthings but have lost their novelty.
3. Selection of safe toys and games.

Specific Objectives—Sports and Physical Fitness

The student:

A. rides a tricycle or bicycle.
B. participates in skating activities individually, with friends, and/or as part of a team.
C. participates as a spectator or active participant in water sports.
D. participates in boating activities.
E. participates in snow sports.
F. participates in mountain sports activities.
G. participates in exercise and physical fitness activities.
H. participates as a spectator at sports events.

I. participates in two-person sports.
J. participates in team sports.

Specific Objective A

The student rides a tricycle or bicycle.

Functional Settings and Suggested Instructional Activities

School

1. Schedule bicycle or tricycle riding during play period in an appropriate schoolyard area.
2. Discuss safety rules for riding. Discourage riding at night. If necessary, however, review the rules to follow when bicycle riding at night.

Home and Community

1. Tell the parents to set aside time for bicycle riding on a regularly scheduled basis depending on weather conditions and the child's health.
2. Locate a bicycle path in a natural setting. Take the student for a ride to enjoy the physical activity and the beauty of the environment.
3. Join a bicycle ride that raises money for a community charity. Explain the need to help others as part of the responsibility of good citizenship.

Functional Emphases In designing your own instructional activities and plans, emphasize the following elements:

1. Observation of safety rules.
2. Knowledge of maintenance procedures and skill in their application.
3. Awareness of the physical and mental benefits of bicycle riding.
4. Awareness of traffic patterns and regulations.
5. Experience in different locations (i.e., bicycle paths and routes, rural routes, and city streets) as appropriate to the student's level of functioning.
6. Calculation of the cost of buying, maintaining, and renting bicycles.
7. Development of psychomotor skills.

Specific Objective B

The student participates in skating activities individually, with friends, and/or as part of a team.

Functional Settings and Suggested Instructional Activities

Home and Community

1. Ask the parents, if appropriate, to purchase training roller and/or ice skates and to assist the child in acquiring skating skills.

2. Take the student to a roller-skating rink.
3. Take the student to an ice-skating rink.

Functional Emphases In designing your own instructional activities and plans, emphasize the following elements:

1. Observation of safety rules.
2. Judgment as to appropriate places and times to skate.
3. Calculation of the cost of equipment and admission and rental fees as appropriate.
4. Estimation of the time requirements for skating activities.
5. Determination of whether he should participate in skating activities alone or whether he needs supervision.
6. Development of psychomotor skills.

Specific Objective C

The student participates as a spectator or active participant in water sports.

Functional Settings and Suggested Instructional Activities

School

1. Ask a lifeguard or Red Cross worker to come to the classroom to speak to the student. Review with the person the functioning level of the student to whom he will be talking. Ask him or her to stress water safety and responsible behavior in pools and other swimming areas.
2. Refer to the book *Practical Guide for Teaching the Mentally Retarded to Swim* (see Special Materials List) for a variety of ideas involving swimming activities and instruction for the mentally retarded.

Community

1. Contact the personnel of a local indoor pool. Ask if they will provide free swimming lessons to the student. Ask a civic group or local organization to sponsor the student. Get permission from the student's parents or other responsible person with whom he resides before taking him to a pool. Take the student for swimming lessons. Practice.
2. Once the student is able to swim, take the student to a pool on a regular basis. Form teams for water relay races, water volleyball, or a simplified version of water polo. Practice.

Functional Emphases In designing your own instructional activities and plans, emphasize the following elements:

1. Observation of safety rules.
2. Awareness of the physical and mental benefits of water sports.
3. Calculation of the cost of special clothing (bathing suits) and equipment.

4. Avoidance of swimming or diving activities where there are no lifeguards.
5. Avoidance of unsafe places (quarries) or unhealthy places (polluted) to engage in water sports.
6. Awareness of steps to follow in case of injury.
7. Awareness of the special problems involved in swimming in lakes, rivers, and at ocean beaches.
8. Development of psychomotor skills.

Specific Objective D

The student participates in boating activities.

Functional Settings and Suggested Instructional Activities

Community

1. Take the student on a trip to a place where rowboats may be rented. Demonstrate how to row a boat.
2. If there are paddle boats for rent somewhere in the community, take the student for a ride. Enjoy the sights of the harbor or lake.
3. If appropriate, take the student sailing and/or canoeing or for a ride on a motorboat.

Functional Emphases In designing your own instructional activities and plans, emphasize the following elements:

1. Observation of safety rules.
2. Calculation of the costs of renting different kinds of boats.
3. Awareness of the time when boats are rented by the hour.
4. Appreciation for the steps to take if an accident or injury occurs.
5. Realization of the need to properly maintain boats when they are owned by the individual.
6. Appreciation for the paddling movements necessary to move the boat in the desired path.
7. Development of psychomotor skills.

Specific Objective E

The student participates in snow sports.

Functional Settings and Suggested Instructional Activities

Community

1. If appropriate, demonstrate how to use a sled safely.
2. On a snowy day, join the student in building a snowman, an igloo, or a snow castle.

Functional Emphases In designing your own instructional activities and plans, emphasize the following elements:

1. Observation of safety rules.
2. Identification of the proper way to dress when playing in the snow.
3. Identification of the procedures to follow when returning indoors after engaging in snow sports (e.g., drinking hot chocolate, changing wet socks, and drying off wet feet).
4. Avoidance of those snow sports in which he is not able to safely participate.
5. Avoidance of participating in snowball fights.
6. Awareness of special ways to walk when walking on snow and ice.

Specific Objective F

The student participates in mountain sports activities.

Functional Settings and Suggested Instructional Activities

Community

1. Take the student for a walk or hike on mountain paths.
2. If available, take a ski lift, a funicular, or cable car to a mountain or hilltop. Walk down to the bottom.

Functional Emphases In designing your own instructional activities and plans, emphasize the following elements:

1. Observation of safety rules.
2. Selection of appropriate clothing and footwear.
3. Appreciation of the need to use skin creams, sunscreens, and sunglasses for walking on mountains when there is ice and snow on the mountains.
4. Avoidance of mountain sports such as rappeling or mountain climbing unless she is able to perform these difficult sports.

Specific Objective G

The student participates in exercise and physical fitness activities.

Functional Settings and Suggested Instructional Activities

School

1. Initiate a program of calisthenics. Each morning or afternoon, ask the student to do a series of calisthenics or exercises. Chart the number of each exercise the student can do. Make weekly checks for improvement. Praise the student for taking an active part in keeping physically fit.
2. Play Simon Says. Include calisthenics and exercises as part of the game.

3. Use the manual *Programming for the Mentally Retarded in Physical Education and Recreation* (see Special Materials List) to develop physical education and recreation curricula for the student.
4. Obtain the *Special Olympics Manual* (see Special Materials List) and use it as a guide for physical fitness activities.
5. Engage the student in tumbling, weight lifting, yoga, rope jumping, and isometric activities appropriate to his functioning level.

Home and Community

1. Ask the parents to begin a program of calisthenics with the child after consultation with his physician.
2. Ask the parent to play music and to encourage the child to exercise in time with the music.
3. Go for a fast walking hike.
4. Encourage the student to join an exercise, aerobic, or other physical-fitness class sponsored by a community group such as the local YMCA or YWCA.

Functional Emphases In designing your own instructional activities and plans, emphasize the following elements:

1. Identification of one or more activities of interest that contribute to physical fitness and mental health.
2. Avoidance of overindulgence in any activity (*Note:* compulsive physical activity may be as or more dangerous than abstinence from exercise).
3. Calculation of costs of special clothing.
4. Calculation of costs of classes.
5. Determination as to whether particular clothing or classes can be afforded.
6. Estimation of time and space requirements.
7. Observation of safety rules.

Specific Objective H

The student participates as a spectator at sports events.

Functional Settings and Suggested Instructional Activities

School

1. Read the student simple books about sports. Comment on the sports and the spectators. Ask the student if he or his family attend sporting events. Encourage the student to describe, through words and/or gestures, any sporting events he has attended.
2. Bring the recreation or amusement section of the newspaper into the classroom. Point out to the student the various sporting events (professional, amature, or college) that are going to take place. Encourage the student's interest in sports.

Home and Community

1. Encourage the parents to provide the student with opportunities to watch major sporting events on television (e.g., the World Series, the Stanley Cup playoffs, and the Super Bowl).
2. Ask the student to make a recreation calendar of events. Encourage him to place sports events (professional, college, high school, and little league) on his calendar.

Functional Emphases In designing your own instructional activities and plans, emphasize the following elements:

1. Comprehension of announcements of sports events made over the radio and television.
2. Comprehension of printed announcements and advertisements concerning sports events.
3. Location of seats within an arena or stadium.
4. Calculation of cost of tickets and transportation as appropriate.
5. Comprehension of the rules of the game.
6. Identification of players.

Specific Objective I

The student participates in two-person sports.

Functional Settings and Suggested Instructional Activities

Community

1. Take the student to public recreation centers where he can participate in two-person sports.
2. Take the student to parks and playgrounds where he can participate in two-person sports.
3. Interest him in one or more of the following: badminton, handball, racquetball, tetherball, squash, table tennis, golf, tennis, or bowling.

Functional Emphases In designing your own instructional activities and plans, emphasize the following elements:

1. Observation of safety rules.
2. Location of places and centers where two-person sports can be played.
3. Identification of special clothing and equipment needed.
4. Calculation of the cost of special clothing, equipment, and admission or other playing fees.
5. Knowledge of the rules of the game and scoring procedures.
6. Development of psychomotor skills.
7. Development of sportsmanship.

Specific Objective J

The student participates in team sports.

Functional Settings and Suggested Instructional Activities

School

1. Form teams for sports in their appropriate seasons (e.g., soccer, football, and lacrosse in the fall; basketball and indoor volleyball in the winter; tennis, baseball, and softball in the spring; swimming and aquatic team games in the summer). If indoor facilities are available year round, any team sports can be played throughout the year regardless of the season.
2. Start an intramural sports program between classes. Play a variety of team sports; plan tournaments and award prizes. Include sportsmanship awards so that everyone, losers as well as winners, gets an award.
3. Encourage the student to join, in his leisure time, bowling, swimming, or other teams that are sponsored by school or community groups. Many associations for retarded citizens provide such activities in the summer, after school, and/or on weekends. If such programs are not available, contact community groups or parent organizations and try to develop one.
4. As a part of your school recreation or field trip program, arrange for the student to swim or bowl once a week. Form teams in both of these sports and encourage competition between class teams as well as individuals.

Community

1. Encourage the student to join bowling, baseball, softball, and other teams. Visit one of his games as one of his "fans."
2. Encourage the student to join social and other groups that include team sports as one of their activities. Urge him to join at least one team, if appropriate.

Functional Emphases In designing your own instructional activities and plans, emphasize the following elements:

1. Observation of safety rules.
2. Development of psychomotor skills.
3. Development of sportsmanship.
4. Knowledge of the rules of each game and scoring procedures.
5. Awareness of procedures to follow in case of accident or injury.
6. Location of places where team sports can be played.
7. Identification of special clothing and equipment needed.
8. Calculation of the cost of special clothing, equipment, and admission fees.

Specific Objectives—Camping and Outdoor Activities

The student:

A. engages in a variety of activities, using park and playground facilities and equipment.
B. goes fishing and/or catches shellfish.
C. goes camping.
D. engages in outdoor cooking activities.
E. engages in diverse outdoor activities, including operating a lantern and camp stove; using utensils, a knife, an ax, and compass; and tying ropes.

Specific Objective A

The student engages in a variety of activities, using park and playground facilities and equipment.

Functional Settings and Suggested Instructional Activities

School

1. During recess, encourage the student to use the play equipment on the playground. If the student uses play equipment unsafely or in a manner dangerous to others, stop him immediately and demonstrate the safe way to use the equipment.
2. Set up obstacle courses on the playground. As part of the course, include swinging on a swing, climbing on a jungle gym, and other relevant activities. Lead the student through the obstacle course a few times. Leave the obstacle course set up and encourage the student to use it as a recess or play activity.

Community

1. Take the student to a park or playground. Point out and name the play equipment in the park or playground. Demonstrate the use of each one and encourage the student to imitate your actions. Practice playing on the playground equipment.
2. Go to a park or playground. Play Follow the Leader with the student. As part of the game, stop at each piece of playground equipment and use it correctly (e.g., climb on the jungle gym, swing on a swing, and slide down a sliding board). Encourage the student to imitate your actions and to use the play equipment safely and correctly. Switch leaders and encourage the student to lead you and his peers and to use the play equipment correctly as part of the game.

Functional Emphases In designing your own instructional activities and plans, emphasize the following elements:

1. Observation of safety rules.
2. Development of gross motor skills.
3. Development of cooperative play in the use of the seesaw and the swings.
4. Awareness of the physical and mental benefits of outdoor play.
5. Recognition of the time requirements for traveling to and for utilizing playground equipment.
6. Determination of the locations and the ways to travel to parks and playgrounds.

Specific Objective B

The student goes fishing and/or catches shellfish.

Functional Settings and Suggested Instructional Activities

Community

1. If it is geographically feasible, plan and take a saltwater fishing trip to a nearby beach area.
2. If it is geographically feasible, plan and take a freshwater fishing trip to a nearby stream, lake, or river area.
3. If it is geographically feasible, plan and take a trip to catch shellfish (crabs, lobsters, and other seafood).
4. If it is geographically feasible, plan and take a fishing trip to nearby bodies of water to catch live bait as part of fishing plans.
5. If it is geographically feasible, plan and take an ice-fishing trip.

Functional Emphases In designing your own instructional activities and plans, emphasize the following elements:

1. Observation of safety rules.
2. Identification of special equipment and clothing needs.
3. Operation of fishing equipment.
4. Identification of fish and shellfish.
5. Preparation of fish and shellfish for cooking.
6. Identification of fish and shellfish recipes and cooking fish and shellfish dishes.

Specific Objective C

The student goes camping.

Functional Settings and Suggested Instructional Activities

School

1. Review safety rules for campers (e.g., never wander into the woods alone, extinguish all campfires, and do not eat plants or berries unless a responsible adult has said it is safe to do so). Ask a forest ranger or experienced camper (the United States Park Service will provide speakers) to speak to the student about camping safely.
2. Plan and go on daytime nature walks or hikes. Collect plant or leaf specimens. In the classroom compile a scrapbook of the plants and leaves the student has collected.

Home and Community

1. Ask the parents to take the child on weekend or overnight camping trips and nature walks or hikes.
2. Take the student to a sporting goods store. Point out the various camping equipment and explain the function of each piece of equipment.
3. Contact the National Safety Council and obtain the *Family Camping Booklet* (see Special Materials List). This is a basic camping guide, and it contains a list of agencies that provide camping information.
4. Contact the local Boy Scouts or Girl Scouts council in your area. Ask if the council will provide speakers and/or guides to go with you on camping trips. Some scouting organizations will do this as a troop project or for merit badges.

Functional Emphases In designing your own instructional activities and plans, emphasize the following elements:

1. Identification of the costs involved in going on a camping trip or in attending a camp.
2. Identification of safe, accessible, and otherwise suitable locations for camping activities.
3. Identification and purchasing of camping equipment and clothing.
4. Development of camping-related skills.
5. Development of plans and a schedule for camping activities.

Specific Objective D

The student engages in outdoor cooking activities.

Functional Settings and Suggested Instructional Activities

Home and Community

1. Ask the parents to invite relatives and friends for a holiday party. Tell them to include a barbecue as part of the food preparation process. Tell them to make their child responsible, if feasible, for part of the outdoor cooking, even if it is just toasting marshmallows.

2. Take the student on a camping trip. Demonstrate how to build, use, and extinguish a campfire safely.

Functional Emphases In designing your own instructional activities and plans, emphasize the following elements:

1. Identification and purchasing of appropriate foods and beverages.
2. Preparation of foods and beverages.
3. Identification and purchasing of supplies (e.g., paper plates, cups, charcoal, napkins, and plastic utensils).
4. Organization and packing of food, beverages, and supplies.
5. Identification of the procedures and practicing of the process of starting and maintaining a campfire.
6. Identification of the procedures and practicing of the process of extinguishing a campfire.
7. Identification of steps to follow in building a fireplace.
8. Implementation of gathering and chopping wood.
9. Implementation of cleaning up and garbage disposal procedures.

Specific Objective E

The student engages in diverse outdoor activities, including operating a lantern and camp stove; using utensils, a knife, an ax, and compass; and tying ropes.

Functional Settings and Suggested Instructional Activities

School

1. Schedule a knot-tying activity; especially practice those knots used in camping activities. Invite a Boy Scout or Girl Scout for a demonstration.
2. Show the student how to set up a tent on the school playground.

Community

1. Take the student on a camping trip and demonstrate how to operate a camp light and a camp stove.
2. Take the student on a camping trip and demonstrate the use of a compass and other techniques to avoid getting lost.
3. Take the student on a camping trip and demonstrate how to use a knife and ax safely to gather wood and to carry out diverse camping tasks.

Functional Emphases In designing your own instructional activities and plans, emphasize the following elements:

1. Observation of safety rules.
2. Identification of steps to take to avoid getting lost.
3. Identification of steps to be taken to avoid dangerous animals and plants.

4. Identification of steps to be taken to establish and secure shelter areas.
5. Identification of steps to be taken to establish food and beverage storage and preparation areas.
6. Identification and scheduling of recreational activities.

Specific Objectives—Nature Study

The student:

A. plans and goes on walks and hiking trips.
B. participates in nature exploration activities.
C. raises and cares for plants.
D. raises and cares for pets.
E. collects leaves, rocks, and shells for a collection, crafts, and/or decorating projects.
F. engages in photography and other art experiences based upon natural themes.

Specific Objective A

The student plans and goes on walks and hiking trips.

Functional Settings and Suggested Instructional Activities

School

1. Take the student on a walking trip around the school. Point out natural and other landmarks and sights.
2. Plan a field trip to a nearby park, arboretum, or wildlife preserve. Discuss the safety factors and the plants and animals he might see there. Show him a nature film.

Home and Community

1. Ask the parents to plan a hiking trip and to prepare the child for the activities and to review safety practices with the child.
2. Take the student to a state park or nature preserve. Plan a nature walk. Collect leaves and flowers. Remind the student not to eat or to touch plants unless he recognizes them or a responsible person tells him they are safe to handle. Upon returning to the classroom, press the plants, leaves, and flowers and compile a nature scrapbook.

Functional Emphases In designing your own instructional activities and plans, emphasize the following elements:

1. Observation of safety rules.
2. Identification of area plants and animals, including dangerous ones.

3. Location of parks, aboreta, wildlife preserves, and other locations where there are interesting walk or hiking possibilities.
4. Implementation of procedures to avoid getting lost.
5. Recognition of appropriate clothing and footwear to use on walks and hikes.
6. Awareness of the health benefits.
7. Appreciation for the aesthetic benefits of walks and hikes.

Specific Objective B

The student participates in nature exploration activities.

Functional Settings and Suggested Instructional Activities

Community

1. If geographically feasible, take the student on a beachcombing trip.
2. Arrange a bird-watching trip. Check to see whether there is a bird sanctuary nearby or a place where birds stop as part of migratory patterns.
3. If applicable and safe, take the student on a cave-exploring trip. Check to see there are caves or caverns in the area that are open to public view.
4. Take the student on a rock-finding trip and start a class and/or an individual rock collection.

Functional Emphases In designing your own instructional activities and plans, emphasize the following elements:

1. Observation of safety rules.
2. Selection of appropriate sites for nature exploration.
3. Appreciation for the variety of exploration activities.
4. Calculation of the time and money requirements for nature exploration activities.
5. Development of collections.
6. Identification of situations in which he should not collect specimens ("Do Not Pick the Flowers").
7. Identification of unsafe places.

Specific Objective C

The student raises and cares for plants.

Functional Settings and Suggested Instructional Activities

School

1. Bring into the classroom plants that are easy to care for (e.g., philodendron, snake plant, and coleus). Give the student a plant and tell him it is his respon-

sibility to care for it. Encourage the student to add other plants to the one you gave him.

2. Make a plant care chart (Figure 6). Draw a picture of the plant or plants the student has. Next to the picture of the plant, indicate how often to water it and what conditions it needs to thrive. Put the chart on the wall and encourage the student to use it as a plant care guide.
3. Plant a vegetable or victory garden near the school, if possible. Use the vegetables for class salads and snacks.

Home and Community

1. Ask the parents to encourage the child to keep plants in the home and assume responsibility for their care.
2. If the student's residence has a yard or gardening area, encourage the parents to encourage the child to plant a vegetable or flower garden. Tell them to help him in planting and caring for his garden and to praise him for his efforts and his finished product (i.e., flowers or vegetables).
3. Take a trip to a botanical garden and identify the foliage and plants found there.
4. Take a trip to a farm. Ask the farmer to describe his or her planting and other agricultural activities.

Functional Emphases In designing your own instructional activities and plans, emphasize the following elements:

1. Recognition of steps to be taken in raising and caring for houseplants, flowers, garden, and a lawn.
2. Selection of plants appropriate to climatic factors and the individual procedures to follow.
3. Calculation of the costs of raising and caring for plants.

Specific Objective D

The student raises and cares for pets.

Functional Settings and Suggested Instructional Activities

School

1. Set up a five- or ten-gallon aquarium in the classroom. Set up a schedule for the care and feeding of the fish. Praise the student if he follows the schedule.
2. Bring into the classroom small pets such as fish, birds, hamsters, and guinea pigs. Demonstrate how to care for each pet. Encourage the student to imitate your actions and to help you as you care for and handle the pets. Practice.

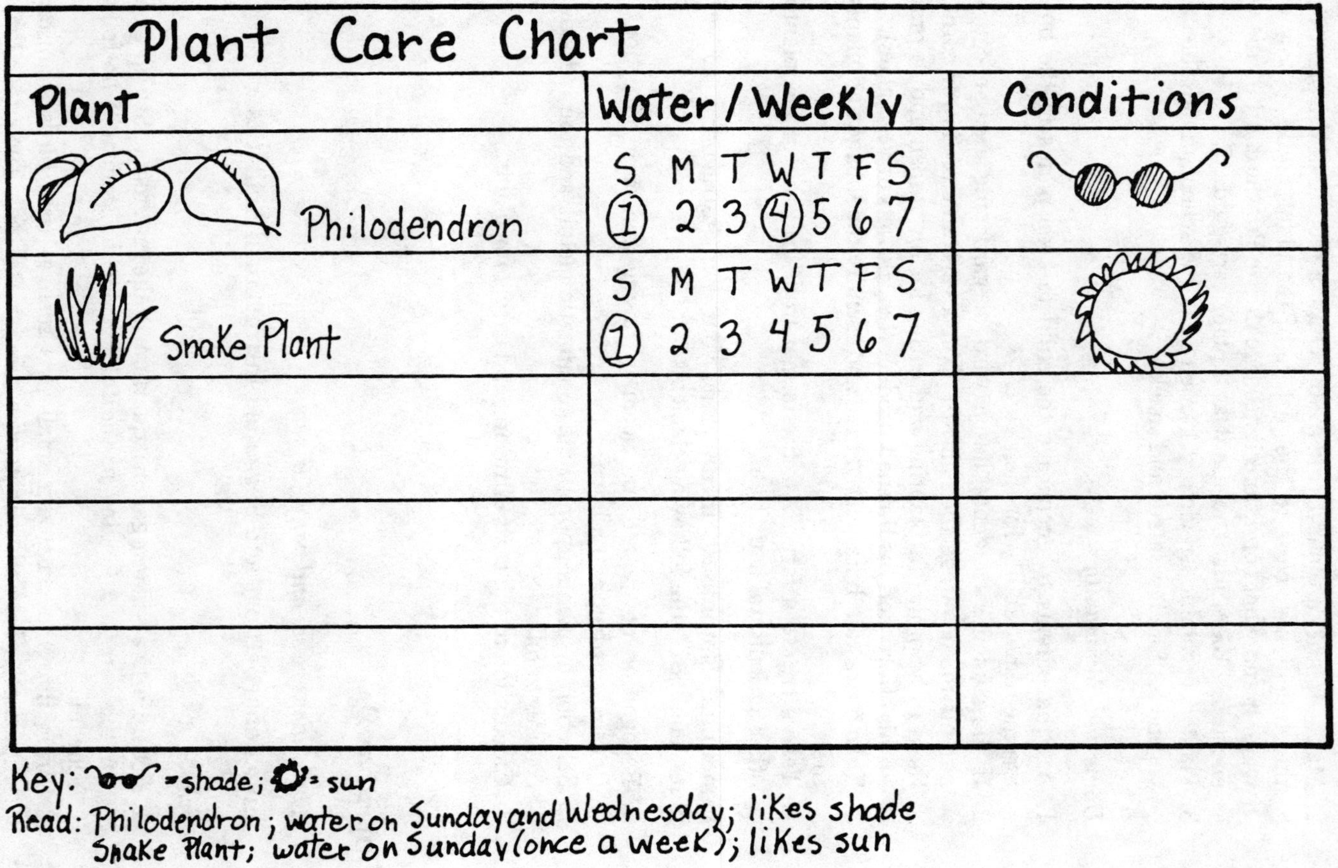
Plant Care Chart
Plant
Water / Weekly
Conditions
Philodendron
S M T W T F S
1 2 3 4 5 6 7
Snake Plant
S M T W T F S
1 2 3 4 5 6 7
Key: = shade; = sun
Read: Philodendron; water on Sunday and Wednesday; likes shade
Snake Plant; water on Sunday (once a week); likes sun

Figure 6. Plant care chart.

3. Make a pet care chart (Figure 7) and assign the student the job of caring for a pet or doing a specific part of the pet's care (e.g., cleaning a bird cage and feeding the fish).

Home and Community

1. Ask the parents to consider getting the child a small pet. Tell them to remind him that he is responsible for his pet's welfare and must take proper care of it.
2. Take the student to a pet store to view the pets found there. Discuss their care.
3. Take the student to a zoo. Discuss the difference between zoo animals and household pets.
4. Take the student to an aquarium if there is one in the community or in a nearby town.
5. Take the student to an aquarium store and ask him to select two or three fish for the class aquarium. Supervise him so that he purchases fish that are healthy, easy to care for, and not too expensive.

Functional Emphases In designing your own instructional activities and plans, emphasize the following elements:

1. Observation of health and safety rules.
2. Calculation of the costs involved in purchasing and caring for pets.
3. Identification of an appropriate pet for his situation (space, costs, interests, and parental likes and dislikes).
4. Awareness of the variety of pet possibilities, including fish and other aquatic pets; birds; reptiles; cats, dogs, and other small mammals; and large domestic animals (e.g., horses, cows, and goats).

Specific Objective E

The student collects leaves, rocks, and shells for a collection, crafts, and/or decorating projects.

Functional Settings and Suggested Instructional Activities

School

1. Show the student how to make a seed, nutshell, seashell, and leaf collage.
2. Set up a collection display table. Encourage the student to start a natural collection.

Home and Community

1. Ask the parents to encourage the child to start a collection of natural objects. Tell them to assist him in starting or making a collection.

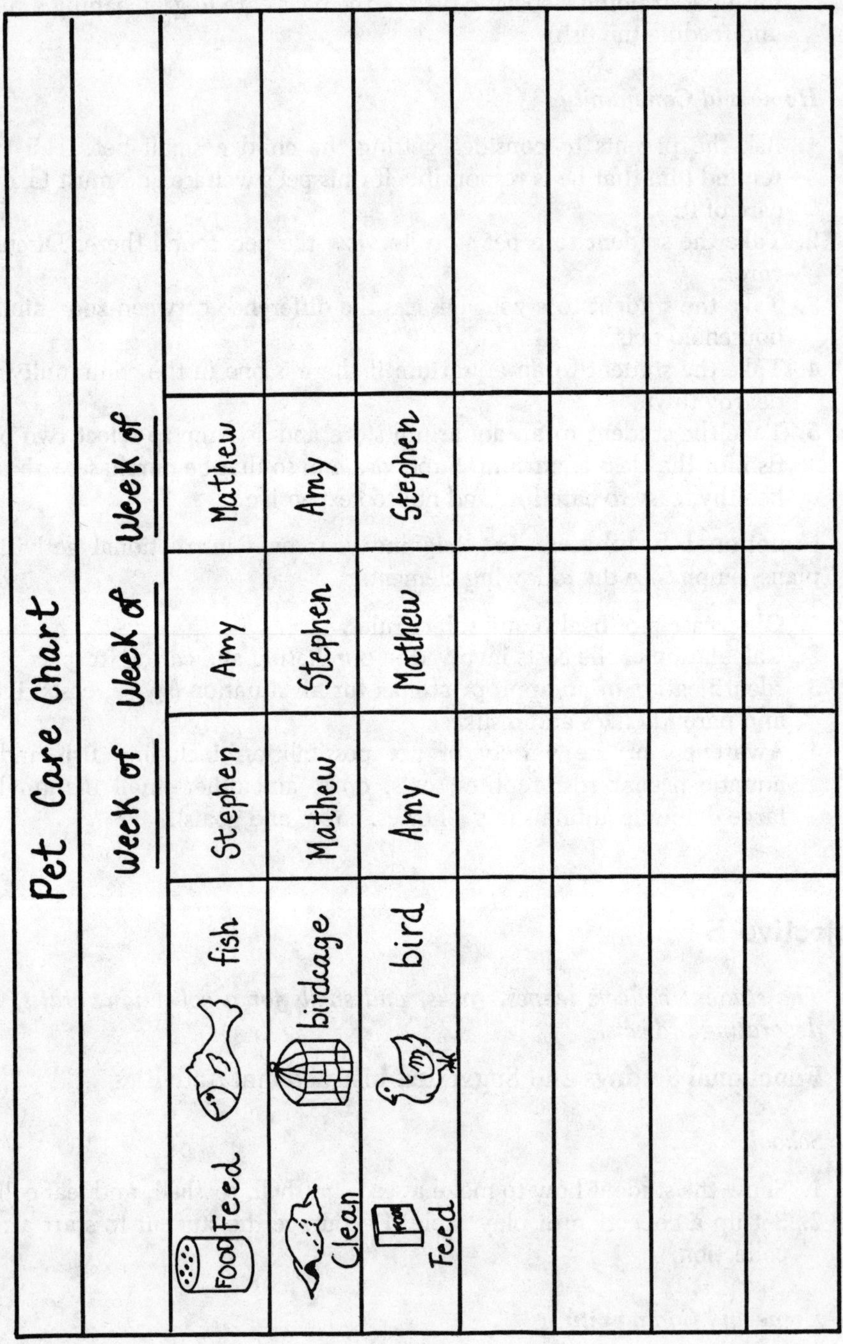
Pet Care Chart
Week of
Week of
Week of
FOOD Feed fish
Stephen
Amy
Mathew
Clean birdcage
Mathew
Stephen
Amy
FOOD Feed bird
Amy
Mathew
Stephen

Figure 7. Pet care chart.

2. Take the student on a nature walk to a nearby park where he might obtain natural samples.
3. If practical, ask the parent to show the child how to use natural objects as a decorative item (e.g., shells placed in a bowl as a table display or a natural collage framed and displayed).

Functional Emphases In designing your own instructional activities and plans, emphasize the following elements:

1. Avoidance of collecting specimens that are poisonous or dangerous.
2. Avoidance of specimens that should not be picked because they are part of plant or flower displays.
3. Calculation of the time and money requirements for engaging in collecting trips.
4. Observation of safety rules.

Specific Objective F

The student engages in photography and other art experiences based upon natural themes.

Functional Settings and Suggested Instructional Activities

School

1. Show the student slides of famous paintings of landscapes and seascapes.
2. Set up a bulletin board of photographs you and he have taken of natural themes.

Home and Community

1. Ask the parents to show the child pictures of land and seascapes found in magazines and newspapers.
2. Take the student on a photographic trip to beautiful sites in his community or in a nearby one.
3. Arrange a sketching or painting trip.

Functional Emphases In designing your own instructional activities and plans, emphasize the following elements:

1. Utilization of a camera in various light and weather conditions in outdoor settings.
2. Selection and purchase of film.
3. Identification of the steps involved in loading and unloading a camera.
4. Utilization of charcoal and sketching pads.
5. Utilization of paints, brushes, easels, and canvas.
6. Selection of sights to photograph, sketch, or paint.

Specific Objectives—Hobby Activities

The student:

A. selects and pursues a hobby.
B. collects "collectibles" and antiques.

Specific Objective A

The student selects and pursues a hobby.

Functional Settings and Suggested Instructional Activities

School

1. Bring a variety of hobby and craft magazines into the classroom. Look through the magazines with the student. If he expresses an interest in a particular craft or hobby and it is appropriate to his functioning level, encourage his interest.
2. Set up a craft or hobby corner in the classroom. Encourage the student to use a variety of craft materials (e.g., paints, decoupage, clay modeling, jewelry making, and leathercraft). Supervise and praise the student for his efforts.
3. As the student expresses an interest in a hobby or craft, offer assistance if needed. Provide opportunities for crafts and hobby work at school. Plan a hobby or craft show. Display items the student has made or collected and invite other classes or parents to view the hobby display.

Home and Community

1. Take the student on a field trip to a hobby or craft store or exhibit. Encourage the student to look at the variety of craft and hobby materials. Explain that pursuing a hobby or craft is a good way to use leisure time.
2. Ask the parents to share any hobbies they have with their child. If there is a sibling with a hobby, tell them to encourage the sibling to share his or her hobby with the child.

Functional Emphases In designing your own instructional activities and plans, emphasize the following elements:

1. Experience with a wide variety of hobbies.
2. Calculation of the costs involved in pursuing a hobby.
3. Determination of the ways of acquiring collections.
4. Appreciation for the time and space requirements.
5. Review of catalogs, brochures, and specialty magazines.
6. Observation of safety rules.

Specific Objective B

The student collects "collectibles" and antiques.

Functional Settings and Suggested Instructional Activities

School

1. Share, if appropriate, any collections you or peers have with the student.
2. Review the wide range of possible "collectibles." Include in your discussion natural objects; models; dolls and doll clothing; antique toys; art objects; low-cost objects such as buttons and matchbook covers; coins, stamps, and medals; magazines, sheet music, and comic books; and pictures, autographs, and other memorabilia of athletes, movie stars, and other celebrities.

Home and Community

1. Ask the parents, if appropriate, to share any collections they have with their child. If there is a sibling with a hobby, tell them to encourage the sibling to share his or her collection with the child.
2. Take the student to a flea market.
3. Take the student to an antique show.
4. Take the student to a specialty show (e.g., a stamp store, a mineral and gem exhibit, and a stamp show).

Functional Emphases In designing your own instructional activities and plans, emphasize the following elements:

1. Review of specialty magazines, brochures, and catalogs.
2. Calculation of the costs involved in collecting.
3. Determination of the time and space requirements.
4. Location of hobby sections in libraries.
5. Location of hobby magazines in stores.
6. Location of flea markets, shows, and relevant exhibits.

Specific Objectives—Craft Activities

The student:

A. engages in food crafts.
B. engages in craft activities involving fibers and fabrics.
C. engages in craft activities for gift making and/or for home decorating.
D. engages in model and craft making involving the use of kit materials.

Specific Objective A

The student engages in food crafts.

Functional Settings and Suggested Instructional Activities

School

1. Demonstrate making a gingerbread house for display or for a gift for the student to take home to his family.
2. Bring pasta of different shapes and sizes into the classroom. Using food dyes, dye the pasta different colors. Demonstrate stringing macaroni to make single-strand bracelets, necklaces, belts, and headbands. Create simple designs by alternating and mixing macaroni shapes and colors. Encourage the student to imitate your actions and to make jewelry of his own.
3. Make popcorn with the students and bring cranberries into the classroom. Demonstrate how to string cranberries and popcorn, using a large needle and heavy thread. Encourage the student to imitate your actions and to make cranberry and popcorn garlands. Supervise closely. Use the garlands as Christmas tree or holiday decorations.

Home

1. Ask the parents to assist the child in making a dried-food collage using beans, seeds, lentils, and uncooked pasta.
2. Ask the parents to assist the child in making a bread sculpture.

Functional Emphases In designing your own instructional activities and plans, emphasize the following elements:

1. Utilization of foods for crafts activities only when they are not needed for consumption.
2. Use of food crafts for decorative purposes, especially when it is less expensive than buying decorations.
3. Use of food crafts for making gifts, especially when it is less expensive than buying a gift and/or when a personal touch is desired.

Specific Objective B

The student engages in craft activities involving fibers and fabrics.

Functional Settings and Suggested Instructional Activities

School

1. Demonstrate the use of sewing to create simple items such as aprons.
2. Show the student how to crochet a simple pot holder.

Home and Community

1. Ask the parents to demonstrate basic sewing skills.
2. If the parents engage in knitting, crocheting, macramé, quilting, and/or braiding activities, encourage them to demonstrate one of these crafts to their child, if he realistically can develop skill in any of these areas.
3. Attend a city, town, or state fair where home crafts are on display.

Functional Emphases In designing your own instructional activities and plans, emphasize the following elements:

1. Development of fine-motor skills.
2. Calculation of the costs involved.
3. Selection of appropriate-level activities within a skill area.
4. Use of those crafts to make gifts, especially when a personal gift is intended and the item is more expensive to purchase.

Specific Objective C

The student engages in craft activities for gift making and/or for home decorating.

Functional Settings and Suggested Instructional Activities

School

1. Show the student how to make snowflakes and other decorations by folding and cutting paper.
2. Demonstrate the making of collages and decoupage (see Figure 8).
3. Demonstrate candle and soap making.
4. Demonstrate the antiquing process.
5. Demonstrate string art.
6. Show the student how to engage in the batiking process.

Functional Emphases In designing your own instructional activities and plans, emphasize the following elements:

1. Provision of a wide range of experiences so that the student develops a repertoire of craft skills and interests.
2. Calculation of the costs involved in a specific project.
3. Use of crafts for decorative purposes.
4. Use of crafts for gift making.

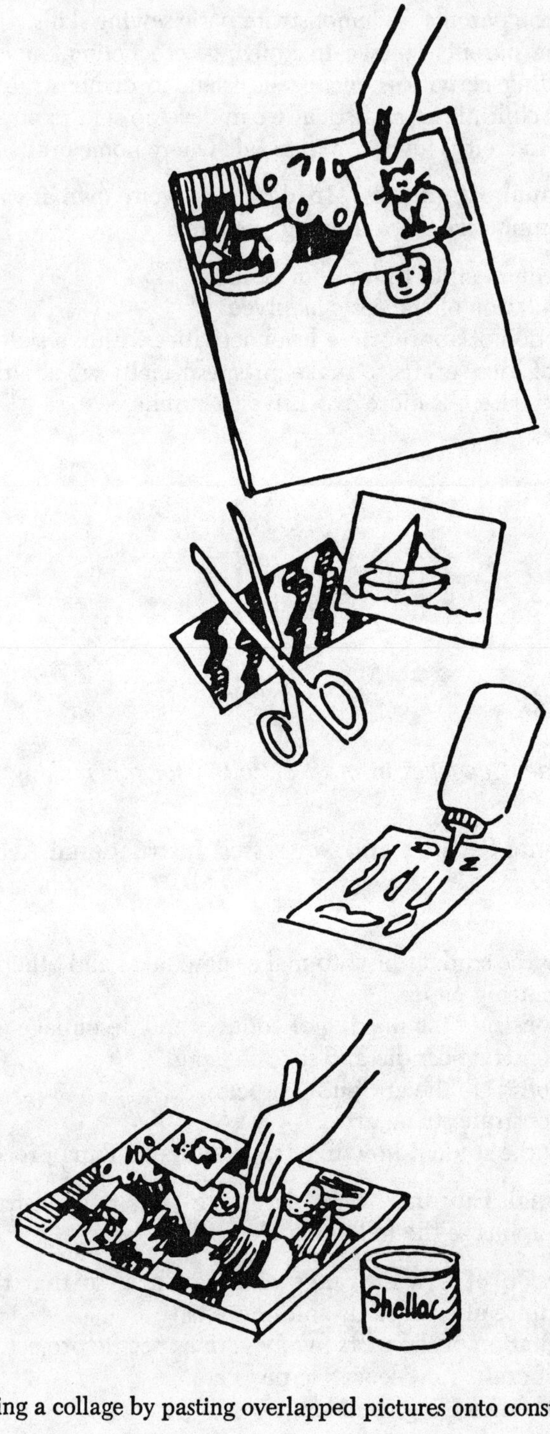

Figure 8. Making a collage by pasting overlapped pictures onto construction paper.

Specific Objective D

The student engages in model and craft making involving the use of kit materials.

Functional Settings and Suggested Instructional Activities

School

1. Ask other students or teachers to bring in models and crafts made from kits. Ask these classroom visitors to discuss their work.
2. Provide experiences in making models and in engaging in paper crafts, leather crafts, textile crafts, wood crafts, and metal crafts, as appropriate to the student's functioning level.

Home

1. Ask the parents to determine if the child has any interests in a crafts or model making activity involving the use of a kit.
2. If the child evidences interest in a model or crafts activity and is functionally able to participate, urge the parents to purchase the necessary kit(s) and assist him in making the model or product.

Functional Emphases In designing your own instructional activities and plans, emphasize the following elements:

1. Provision of a wide range of experiences.
2. Selection of skill appropriate kits.
3. Calculation of the costs involved.
4. Observation of safety rules.

Specific Objectives—Art Activities

The student:

A. engages in fine-arts activities.
B. engages in musical activities as a participant.
C. engages in musical activities as a listener/spectator.
D. participates in creative dramatics and in plays and play productions.

Specific Objective A

The student engages in fine-arts activities.

Functional Settings and Suggested Instructional Activities

School

1. Give the student paint brushes and water-soluble, nontoxic tempera or watercolor paints. Demonstrate using paints and brushes to paint washes, designs, and pictures. Ask the student to imitate your actions and to use paints and brushes to create washes, designs, and pictures.
2. Give the student paints and sponges cut into a variety of shapes. Demonstrate dipping the sponges into the paints and pressing them onto construction paper to create designs and pictures.
3. Give the student Play-Doh, clay, and plasticene. Demonstrate modeling the substances. Encourage the student to imitate your actions.
4. Demonstrate the use of tempera, watercolor, oil, paint (acrylic and other types), pastels, charcoal, crayon, and pencil.
5. Demonstrate various sculpting activities, including the use of wood, soap, ceramics, metal, fabrics, string, paper, junk, and clay.
6. Demonstrate the following graphic art activities: photography (still and movie), silk-screening, stenciling, etching, block printing, offset printing, lithographing, and modeling.

Home and Community

1. Ask the parents to show the child how to use all parts of his hands such as his fingertips, fingernails, knuckles, palms and sides, and heels to create linear shapes and patterns with fingerpaint.
2. Tell the parents to give their child crayons and paper. Depending upon the student's functioning level, they should encourage him to scribble, draw designs, or draw pictures on the paper with the crayons. Tell them to play music, and ask him to draw to the music.
3. Take the student to an art museum.

Functional Emphases In designing your own instructional activities and plans, emphasize the following elements:

1. Provision of experience in a wide range of fine and graphic arts, including exploring, creating, and appreciating.
2. Determination of the supplies needed to participate in these arts.
3. Calculation of the costs and the purchase of supplies.
4. Appreciation for the time constraints of participating in fine and graphic art activities.

Specific Objective B

The student engages in musical activities as a participant.

Functional Settings and Suggested Instructional Activities

School

1. Bring a variety of rhythm band instruments into the classroom or learning area. Show each instrument to the student and demonstrate its use. Encourage the student to handle and to play the instrument.
2. Play marching music on a record player, tape recorder, or piano. Play rhythm band instruments to the beat of the music. Give the student a rhythm band instrument and ask him to imitate your actions. Once you have established a steady beat with the instruments, begin to march around the room. Encourage the student to march and to play his rhythm band instrument to the music. Practice.
3. Play popular music that the student enjoys listening to. Encourage the student to play rhythm band instruments to the music. Praise the student for playing a good accompaniment to the music.
4. As you engage in daily activities, use music and singing as part of the activities. For example, in activities involving washing hands and face, sing "This is the Way We Wash Our Clothes," changing the words to "wash our face" or "wash our hands." Make up a simple melody and sing "Johnny, get in line, get in line" when you want the student to line up.
5. Sing songs that have accompanying hand actions (e.g., "This Old Man" and "Where Is Thumbkin?"). Sing the songs and demonstrate the hand movement. Encourage the student to sing along and to do the hand movements.

Home

1. Tell the parents to use music or singing as part of their daily household activities. Tell them to assign him chores and to encourage their performance to music or singing, when appropriate.
2. Ask the parents to do exercises to music and to encourage her to exercise to music.
3. Encourage the parents to dance with the child. If they know ethnic dances or special dances (e.g., square dances), tell them to teach them to their child.
4. Encourage the parents to sing nursery rhymes, commercials and other simple tunes to the child.

Functional Emphases In designing your own instructional activities and plans, emphasize the following elements:

1. Awareness of the range of musical activity possibilities.
2. Participation in a wide range of activities, including singing, dancing, and the playing of instruments.

Specific Objective C

The student engages in musical activities as a listener/spectator.

Functional Settings and Suggested Instructional Activities

School

1. Show the student interesting album covers and play records of a variety of musical styles.
2. Attend a school dance recital, a chorus production, and a band concert, if available.

Home and Community

1. Ask the parents to play records and the radio and demonstrate listening to music as a form of relaxation.
2. If the parents or a sibling plays a musical instrument or sings, tell the person to do so for the student and family's pleasure.
3. Attend various concert and recitals, including operas, concerts, ballets, dance performances, recitals, musical theater, symphonies, and popular performers in concert.

Functional Emphases In designing your own instructional activities and plans, emphasize the following elements:

1. Provision of experiences with a wide variety of musical performances.
2. Calculation of the costs involved in attending musical performances.
3. Determination of time requirements and travel arrangements.
4. Location of seats in a theater or concert hall.

Specific Objective D

The student participates in creative dramatics and in plays and play productions.

Functional Settings and Suggested Instructional Activities

School

1. Obtain simple one-act plays or write them yourself. Encourage the student and his peers to play the various parts in the play and to be responsible for the technical aspects of the play production (e.g., props and scenery). If the student is verbal and the lines are simple, he may want to learn the lines and say them. If the student is nonverbal, you may record the lines on a tape recorder and ask the student to lip-sync the lines. Practice the play, and build or obtain the props and scenery (keep it simple). Invite another class or parents to view the production of your class play. Praise the student for his efforts.
2. Engage in a variety of creative dramatics and pantomime activities.

Home and Community

1. Encourage the parents to engage in creative dramatic activities. Demonstrate creative dramatics techniques. Observe the parents interacting with their child, if possible.
2. Take the student to children's theater productions and to puppet shows.

Functional Emphases In designing your own instructional activities and plans, emphasize the following elements:

1. Participation in a wide range of drama activities, including creative dramatics, pantomimes, and story-telling activities.
2. Attendance at a variety of dramatic performances.
3. Calculation of costs involved in performing and attending dramatic productions.
4. Participation in all the diverse aspects of play production.
5. Location of seats in a theater.

Specific Objectives—Entertainment and Cultural Activities

The student:

A. engages in quiet activities such as looking at picture books and magazines and listening to the radio and stereo.
B. watches television.
C. visits relatives and friends.
D. plans and conducts a party.
E. goes to restaurants.
F. attends movies, puppet shows, concerts, and plays.
G. plans and participates in picnics, outings, and excursions.
H. participates in special events such as holiday parties, programs, dances, and the Special Olympics.
I. locates and participates in clubs, classes, and events sponsored by community groups such as scouts, 4-H, and garden clubs.
J. attends programs, workshops, classes, and other educational events offered in the community.
K. takes vacations and goes on other trips.

Specific Objective A

The student engages in quiet activities such as looking at picture books and magazines and listening to the radio and stereo.

Functional Settings and Suggested Instructional Activities

School

1. Keep a variety of puzzles in the classroom. When the student has completed his work but other students have not, tell him that he may do a quiet activity such as a puzzle. Tell the student that when others are working and he wants to play, he should select a puzzle because it is quiet and will not disturb those who are working.
2. Plan an art activity. When the student completes his art project, give him permission to listen to the radio or play records quietly. Encourage the student to choose the records or radio station he wants to listen to. Remind him to keep the volume low so the noise does not disturb others in the room. Praise the student for engaging in an activity that is not distracting or disturbing to others.
3. Schedule quiet activities while the student rests as pleasant music is played.

Home

1. Tell the parents to encourage their child to participate in quiet activities during his leisure time, especially late at night, early in the morning, or when others are involved in other activities. Such activities might be solitaire, puzzles, coloring, craftwork, or looking through magazines.
2. Tell the parents if a situation arises when they and other family members are engaged in an activity in which the child does not wish to participate, they should encourage him to initiate a quiet activity that will not disturb others.

Functional Emphases In designing your own instructional activities and plans, emphasize the following elements:

1. Selection of appropriate music to play for relaxation purposes.
2. Determination of an inappropriate sound level so that he does not disturb others.
3. Determination of when it is healthy and appropriate to engage in quiet activities.

Specific Objective B

The student watches television.

Functional Settings and Suggested Instructional Activities

School

1. Bring the television section of the newspaper into the classroom. Talk about a variety of television programs and help the student to select programs suitable for viewing. Encourage the student to watch suitable television programs during his leisure time or in the evening when he is unable

to play outside. Remember to stress educationally oriented and nonviolent programming.

2. Put on television programs in the classroom that are educational and good fun.

Home

1. Ask the parents to monitor the child's television watching, controlling the hours, amount, and programs watched.
2. Tell the parents to review television listings with their child.

Functional Emphases In designing your own instructional activities and plans, emphasize the following elements:

1. Substitution of other leisure activities for television watching.
2. Avoidance of programs that are overly violent.

Specific Objective C

The student visits relatives and friends.

Functional Settings and Suggested Instructional Activities

School

1. Read the student stories about visiting friends or relatives. Encourage the student to talk about his visits to friends or relatives.
2. Make the experience chart "Good Manners for Visitors" (Figure 9). Review the chart with the student and remind him to observe the rules when he is a visitor.
3. Role play a variety of visiting situations (e.g., calling before visiting and arriving after mealtimes). Assist the student in role playing the situations. Switch roles so that the student has the opportunity to be the visitor as well as the host or hostess.

Home and Community

1. Encourage the student's parents or other responsible adults to take her along when they visit relatives and friends.
2. Encourage parents or other responsible adults with whom he lives to arrange for him to visit his friends and peers during vacations and on weekends.

Functional Emphases In designing your own instructional activities and plans, emphasize the following elements:

1. Reciprocity in visiting friends and relatives.
2. Determination of the times and ways to travel to the homes of friends and relatives.

1. Call for permission to visit before visiting.
2. Be courteous and polite.
3. Do not visit at mealtimes unless invited to do so.
4. Do not overstay your welcome.

Figure 9. Good manners for visitors chart.

3. Observation of the ways to behave in arranging visits.
4. Observation of the ways to behave while visiting friends and relatives.

Specific Objective D

The student plans and conducts a party.

Functional Settings and Suggested Instructional Activities

School

1. Talk about parties to the student. Recall parties you have been to and encourage the student to tell his peers about parties he has been to.
2. Plan a holiday or birthday party. Include the student in all planning stages of the party: menu planning, guest list, shopping decorations, clean-up, and cooking or baking. As you carry out each stage of planning for the party, take the student with you.

Home

1. At birthday and holiday times, ask the parents to plan small parties. Remind them to include him in the planning and preparation for the party.
2. Once the student has helped to plan and prepare for a number of parties, encourage him to plan a small party for four or five people on his own.

Functional Emphases In designing your own instructional activities and plans, emphasize the following elements:

1. Determination of whom to invite to parties.
2. Comprehension of the need to reciprocate.

3. Calculation of the costs involved.
4. Determination as to whether he can afford the party.
5. Determination of a menu.
6. Purchase and preparation of foods.
7. Purchase and use of decorations.
8. Purchase and utilization of supplies.
9. Determination of party activities.
10. Arrangements for clean-up and removal of garbage.

Specific Objective E

The student goes to restaurants.

Functional Settings and Suggested Instructional Activities

School

1. Review restaurant listings found in newspapers, magazines, and the Yellow Pages. Discuss restaurants he has been to.
2. Role play making a telephone reservation.
3. Collect representative menus and review items and prices.
4. Draw up sample checks. Match the prices to menu listings. Calculate taxes and tips.

Community

1. Take the student to a fast-food restaurant, cafeteria, lunchroom, or diner.
2. Take the student to a more formal restaurant.
3. Take the student to a place where family-style dinners are served.

Functional Emphases In designing your own instructional activities and plans, emphasize the following elements:

1. Determination of the location of restaurants.
2. Identification of the type or types of food served.
3. Identification of days and hours of operation.
4. Determination of payment policies (i.e., cash, check, and/or credit cards).
5. Comprehension of menus and food directories, including food items and costs.
6. Calculation of taxes and tips.
7. Verification of checks.
8. Understanding of reservation policies and procedures.

Specific Objective F

The student attends movies, puppet shows, concerts, and plays.

Functional Settings and Suggested Instructional Activities

School

1. Plan a field trip to the movies. Include the student in planning when to go and what movie to see. Use the ratings as a guide.
2. Plan field trips to concerts. Most symphonies offer special reduced rates to students. Before going to the concert, play a record of the music the student will be hearing. Review the rules for concert-goers (e.g., no loud talking during the performance, allowing the usher to lead you to your seat, and staying in your seat until intermission or the end of the concert). Go to the concert. Compliment the student on his responsible behavior.
3. Put on a puppet show. Use a story the student particularly enjoys. Invite parents or other classes to come to see your puppet show.

Home and Community

1. Ask the parents to take him to movies, theaters, concerts, and plays. Ask them to include their child in the planning.
2. Contact a theater (amateur, repertory, or professional) and arrange to attend a performance. Before attending the performance, acquaint the student with the play and the characters. Attend the theater performance. Upon returning home or to the classroom, ask the student if he enjoyed the play and encourage him to comment on it.
3. Arrange to visit local puppet theater performances. Take the student to the puppet show. After the performance, encourage the student to comment on it.
4. Go to the movies with the student. Remind him to observe the rules of the movie theater (e.g., no smoking in the theater, no loud talking during the movie, etc.).

Functional Emphases In designing your own instructional activities and plans, emphasize the following elements:

1. Selection of shows of interest.
2. Selection of shows appropriate for his viewing.
3. Calculation of the costs involved.
4. Determination of travel costs and traveling patterns.
5. Location of seats in theaters.

Specific Objective G

The student plans and participates in picnics, outings, and excursions.

Functional Settings and Suggested Instructional Activities

School

1. Plan a class picnic. Consult the student as to where the picnic should be held, what should be on the menu, what play and sports equipment to take along, and the type of transportation needed to get to the picnic area. Make a shopping list, written or pictorial, and accompany the student to the grocery store. Assist the student as he chooses and purchases the items for the picnic.
2. Bring the amusement section of the newspaper into the classroom. Point out various functions of interest to the student (e.g., a walking tour of an historical section of the city or a bus trip to a nearby spot of interest). Help the student to plan to attend one of these functions. Remind her to check the price of the excursion, to see if it is open to the public at large or if there is an age limit (whether anyone under eighteen must be accompanied by an adult), to find the date and time of the excursion, and to determine how and when to make reservations and purchase tickets. Go on the excursion with the student.

Home and Community

1. Ask the parents to plan weekend trips and overnight camping trips and to include him in the planning of these outings. For example, they may make him responsible for shopping for the food for the trip, planning the menu, or checking the camping equipment. Tell them to praise him for being a responsible and contributing member of the family.
2. Encourage the student and a friend (or family member) to go on an outing to a place of interest.
3. Plan an outing by public bus to a local shopping center. Point out to the student that you are checking the bus schedule to see what time the bus leaves to go to the shopping center and returns to school. Go on the outing to the shopping center. Window shop.

Functional Emphases In designing your own instructional activities and plans, emphasize the following elements:

1. Selection of appropriate places to go to on outings, picnics, and excursions.
2. Calculation of the costs involved in participating in these events.
3. Determination of the time and space requirements.
4. Observation of safety rules.

Specific Objective H

The student participates in special events such as holiday parties, programs, dances, and the Special Olympics.

Functional Settings and Suggested Instructional Activities

School

1. In the classroom, include the student in planning and preparing for holiday parties. Encourage him to help in menu planning, food shopping, decorations, food preparation, and making invitations. Once each step has been completed by the student as independently as possible, praise him for his efforts. Give the party and stress that the student did most of the planning and work involved. Comment on what a nice party it is.
2. Ask the physical education instructor to arrange for the student to participate in the Special Olympics. Help with the activities and training necessary to prepare the student for the Special Olympics.

Home and Community

1. Ask the parents to discuss community special events such as Fourth of July and Labor Day celebrations with the child. Tell them to plan attending these events.
2. Take the student to a local parade (e.g., Patriot's Day, Columbus Day, and Thanksgiving).
3. Attend the Special Olympics.
4. Attend an arts festival sponsored by the National Committee Arts for the Handicapped.

Functional Emphases In designing your own instructional activities and plans, emphasize the following elements:

1. Comprehension of reports over the media that announce special events.
2. Comprehension of advertisements and notices in newspapers, magazines, and brochures that announce special events.
3. Determination of travel plans and costs.
4. Determination of all costs, above and beyond transportation.
5. Observation of safety rules.

Specific Objective I

The student locates and participates in clubs, classes, and events sponsored by community groups such as scouts, 4-H, and garden clubs.

Functional Settings and Suggested Instructional Activities

School

1. Compile a list of organizations that sponsor events in which the student may wish to participate (e.g., scouts, YMCA, YWCA, garden clubs, 4-H, and Association for Retarded Citizens). Encourage the student to call the organizations for information concerning the activities they sponsor and to ask to be put on the organizations' mailing lists.
2. Encourage the student to join the YMCA, YWCA, or Association for Retarded Citizens and to attend the events the organization sponsors (e.g., swimming lessons, exercise or dance classes, summer camps, bazaars, or fairs). Remind the student that these are good ways to spend leisure time.
3. Encourage the student who is interested in gardening to join a garden club.
4. Encourage the student to join a scout troop. You may want to contact the scout council to see if your group can participate. You may want to form your own troop for handicapped students.

Home and Community

1. Encourage the parents, if it is at all possible, to arrange for the child to join community groups, especially when they engage in recreational events.
2. Tell the parents to seek out community groups that include programs for the handicapped. Urge them to be advocates for the handicapped by encouraging community groups to include activities for the handicapped.
3. Take the students to special events sponsored by community groups.

Functional Emphases In designing your own instructional activities and plans, emphasize the following elements:

1. Identification of groups functioning in the community.
2. Calculation of the costs involved in participating in such groups.
3. Determination of eligibility and membership criteria.

Specific Objective J

The student attends programs, workshops, classes, and other educational events offered in the community.

Functional Settings and Suggested Instructional Activities

School

1. Visit the school library and media center. Discuss and demonstrate their use.
2. Discuss the educational/cultural resources available in the community and in nearby areas.

Home and Community

1. Tell the parents to try to determine the child's interests so that they can arrange for his participation in these events.
2. Take the student to some of the following: art galleries, science, natural history, and other special museums, music and folk festivals, libraries, city/county/state fairs, parks and playgrounds, parades, botanical and zoological gardens, spectator sports, community education classes, special courses, self-improvement workshops, meetings of civic organizations, religious services, and church- or temple-sponsored activities and events.

Functional Emphases In designing your own instructional activities and plans, emphasize the following elements:

1. Provision of a wide range of educational/cultural experiences.
2. Calculation of costs involved.
3. Arrangements for traveling to events, including estimating travel times, costs, and most efficient means.
4. Determination of the impact on his budget of these events.

Specific Objective K

The student takes vacations and goes on other trips.

Functional Settings and Suggested Instructional Activities

School

1. Involve the student in planning field trips.
2. Obtain travel brochures and review them. Discuss all dimensions of travel, including costs.
3. Role play making telephone reservations.
4. Review the travel or living section of newspapers.

Home and Community

1. Encourage the parents to involve the child in vacation and other travel plans.
2. Take a trip to a visitors bureau or tourist agency. Review travel possibilities.

Functional Emphases In designing your own instructional activities and plans, emphasize the following elements:

1. Determination of places of interest.
2. Identification of the time available for taking trips.
3. Calculation of the costs involved.
4. Identification of the luggage and clothing needs.
5. Provision of experiences in packing and unpacking.

6. Provision of experiences in making reservations.
7. Identification of special needs such as passports.

Special Materials List

Books/Pamphlets

Practical Guide for Teaching the Mentally Retarded to Swim; Programming for the Mentally Retarded in Physical Education and Recreation; Special Olympics Instructional Manual. AAHPER Publications, 1201 16th St. N.W., Washington, DC 20036.

Family Camping Booklet. (083.01); *All About Bikes.* National Safety Council, 425 N. Michigan Ave., Chicago, IL 60602.

Camping Adventure. National Geographic Educational Services, 17th and M Streets, Washington, DC 20036.

Kits

Learning Through Art. Teaching Resources Corp., 50 Pond Park Rd., Hingham, MA 02043.

Films

Watching Animals. National Geographic Educational Services, 17th and M Streets, Washington, DC 20036.

Suggested Readings/References

Adkins, J., & Matson, J. L. (1980). Teaching institutionalized mentally retarded adults socially appropriate leisure skills. *Mental Retardation, 18*, 249–252.

Allen, J. I. (1980). Jogging can modify disruptive behaviors. *Teaching Exceptional Children, 2*, 63–70.

Amary, I. (1975). *Creative recreation for the mentally retarded.* Springfield, IL: Charles C. Thomas.

Beasley, C. R. (1982). Effects of a jogging program on cardiovascular fitness and work performance of mentally retarded adults. *American Journal of Mental Deficiency, 86*, 609–613.

Bohm, H. (1972). *Making simple constructions.* New York: Watson-Guptill.

Brannan, S. (1979). *Project Explore: Expanding programs and learning in outdoor recreation/education for the handicapped.* Washington, DC: Hawkins and Associates.

Brannan, S. (1975). Trends and issues in leisure education for the handicapped. In E. Fairchild & L. Neal (Eds.), *Common-unity in the community—A forward looking program of recreation and leisure services for the handicapped.* Eugene, OR: University of Oregon, Center of Leisure Studies.

Breuning, S. E., Davis, V. J., & Lewis, J. R. (1981). Examination of methods of selecting goal-directed activities for institutionalized retarded adults. *Education and Training of the Mentally Retarded, 16*, 5–12.

Byers, E. S. (1979). Wilderness camping as a therapy for emotionally disturbed children: A critical review. *Exceptional Children, 45*, 628–635.

Crawley, S. B., & Chan, K. S. (1982). Developmental changes in free-play behavior of mildly and moderately retarded preschool-aged children. *Education and Training of the Mentally Retarded, 17*, 234–239.

Day, R., & Day, H. M. (1977). Leisure skills instruction for the moderately and severely retarded: A demonstration program. *Education and Training of the Mentally Retarded, 12*, 128–131.

Davis, P. (Ed.). (1975). *NAGWS: Aquatics guide.* Washington, DC: AAHPER.

Deyrup, A. (1972). *The complete book of tie dyeing.* New York: Lancer Books.

Elium, M. D., & Evans, B. (1982). A model camping program for college students and handicapped learners. *Education and Training of the Mentally Retarded, 17*, 241–242.

Evans, J., & Moore, J. E. (1979). *Art moves the basics along vehicle units.* Hollywood, CA: Evan-Moor Corporation.

Farina, A. M. (1976). Implementing play activities for the mentally retarded. *Physical Education, 33*, 180–185.

Fairchild, E., & Neal, L. (1975). *Common-unity in the community—A forward looking program of recreation and leisure services for the handicapped.* Eugene, OR: University of Oregon, Center of Leisure Studies.

Favell, J. E., & Cannon, P. R. (1976). Evaluation of entertainment materials for severely retarded persons. *American Journal of Mental Deficiency, 81*, 357–361.

Frith, G. H., & Mitchell, J. W. (1983). Art education for mildly retarded students: A significant component of the special education curriculum. *Education and Training of the Mentally Retarded, 18*, 138–140.

Funk, D. (1980). *Guidelines for planning travel for the physically handicapped. A handbook for travel agents, tour wholesalers, and recreation/travel personnel.* Washington, DC: Hawkins and Associates.

Giangreco, M. F. (1983). Teaching basic photography skills to a severely handicapped young adult using simulated materials. *Journal of the Association for the Severely Handicapped, 8*, 43–49.

Gould, E., & Gould, L. (1978). *Arts & Crafts for physically and mentally disabled: The how, what and why of it.* Springfield, IL: Charles C Thomas.

Halle, J. W., Silverman, N. A., & Regan, L. (1983). The effects of a data-based exercise program on physical fitness of retarded children. *Education and Training of the Mentally Retarded, 18*, 221–225.

Hanley, P. E. (1979). Handmade games for home and school. *Day Care and Early Education, 7*, 38–40.

Harvey, J. R. (1979). The potential of relaxation training for the mentally retarded. *Mental Retardation, 17*, 71–76.

Hedberg, S. (1980). Outdoor education can help the handicapped. *Today's Education, 2*, 54–56.

Hill, J. W., Wehman, P., & Horst, G. (1982). Toward generalization of appropriate leisure and social behavior in severely handicapped youth: Pinball machine use. *Journal of the Association for the Severely Handicapped, 6*, 38–44.

Hopper, C., & Wambold, C. (1978). Improving the independent play of severely mentally retarded children. *Education and Training of the Mentally Retarded, 13*, 42–46.

Joswiak, K. F. (1979). *Leisure counseling program materials for the developmentally disabled.* Washington, DC: Hawkins and Associates.

Kingsley, R. F., Viggiano, R. A., & Tout, L. (1981). Social perception of friendship, leadership, and game playing among EMR special and regular class boys. *Education and Training of the Mentally Retarded, 16*, 201–206.

Leisure today. Selected readings. (1975). Washington, DC: AAHPER.

Let's play to grow. (1980). Washington, DC: Joseph P. Kennedy, Jr. Foundation.

Li, A. K. F. (1981). Play and the mentally retarded child. *Mental Retardation, 19*, 121–126.

Marchant, J. A. (1979). Teaching games and hobbies. In P. Wehman (Ed.), *Recreation programming for developmentally disabled persons.* Austin: PRO-ED.

Marion, R. L. (1979). Leisure time activities for trainable mentally retarded adolescents. *Teaching Exceptional Children, 11*, 158–160.

Mathews, P. (1977). Recreation and normalization of the mentally retarded. *Therapeutic Recreation Journal, 11*, 17–21.

Matson, J. L., & Marchetti, A. (1980). A comparison of leisure skills training procedures for the mentally retarded. *Applied Research in Mental Retardation, 1*, 113–122.

Maynard, M. (1976). The value of creative arts for the developmentally disabled child. Implications for recreation therapists in community day service programs. *Therapeutic Recreation Journal, 10*, 10–13.

McCarron, L., Kern, W., & Wolf, C. S. (1979). Use of leisure time activities for work adjustment training. *Mental Retardation, 17*, 159–160.

Museums and handicapped students—Guidelines for educators. (1977). Washington, DC: Smithsonian Institution.

Moon, M. S., & Renzaglia, A. (1982). Physical fitness and the mentally retarded: A critical review of the literature. *Journal of Special Education, 16*, 269–287.

Nietupski, J., & Svoboda, R. (1982). Teaching a cooperative leisure skill to severely handicapped adults. *Education and Training of the Mentally Retarded, 17*, 38–43.

Odom, S. L. (1981). The relationship of play to developmental level in mentally retarded preschool children. *Education and Training of the Mentally Retarded, 16*, 136–141.

Pope, L., Edel, D., & Hakley, A. (1979). *Special needs: Special answers: A resource of reproducible exercises and activities for special education and early childhood programs.* New York: Book-Lab, Inc.

Salzberg, C. L., & Langford, C. A. (1981). Community integration of mentally retarded adults through leisure activity. *Mental Retardation, 19*, 127–131.

Santomier, J., & Kopczuk, W. (1981). Facilitation of interactions between retarded and nonretarded students in a physical education setting. *Education and Training of the Mentally Retarded, 16*, 20–23.

Schleien, S. J., Kiernan, J., & Wehman, P. (1981). Evaluation of an age-appropriate leisure skills program for moderately retarded adults. *Education and Training of the Mentally Retarded, 16*, 13–19.

Schleien, S., Wehman, P., & Kiernan, J. (1981). Teaching leisure skills to severely handicapped adults: An age-appropriate darts game. *Journal of Applied Behavior Analysis, 14*, 513–520.

Sengstock, W., & Jens, K. G. (1974). Recreation for the handicapped: Suggestions for program adaptations. *Therapeutic Recreation Journal*, 8, 172–178.

Shea, T. M. (1977). *Camping for special children*. St. Louis: C. V. Mosby Company.

Shields, E. W. (1979). Intramurals: An avenue for developing leisure values. *Journal of Physical Education and Recreation, 50*, 75–77.

Sliney, M. A., & Geelen, K. E. (1977). *Manual of alternative procedures: Recreational activities*. Medford, MA: Massachusetts Center for Program Development and Education.

Sports skills instructional program. (1980). Washington, DC: Special Olympics.

Stein, A., & Sessoms, H. D. (1977). *Recreation and special populations*. Boston: Holbrook Press.

Sternlight, M., & Hurwitz, R. (1981). *Games children play: Instructive and creative play activities for the mentally retarded and developmentally disabled child*. New York: Van Nostrand-Reinhold.

Sussman, E. J. (1976). *Art projects for the mentally retarded child*. Springfield, IL: Charles C. Thomas.

Switzky, H. N., Ludwig, L., & Haywood, H. C. (1979). Exploration and play in retarded and nonretarded preschool children. Effects of object complexity and age. *American Journal of Mental Deficiency, 83*, 637–644.

Verhoven, P., & Goldstein, J. (1976). *Leisure activity participation and handicapped populations: An assessment of research needs*. Arlington, VA: National Recreation and Park Association.

Voeltz, L. M., Wuerch, B. B., & Bockhaut, C. H. (1982). Social validation of leisure activity training with severely handicapped youth. *The Journal of the Association for the Severely Handicapped, 7*, 3–13.

Voeltz, L. M., Wuerch, B. B., & Wilcox, B. (1982). Leisure/recreation: Preparation for independence, integration and self-fulfillment. In B. Wilcox & G. T. Bellamy (Eds.), *Design of high school programs for severely handicapped students*. Baltimore: Paul H. Brookes.

Wahler, R. G., & Fox, J. J. (1980). Solitary toy play and time out: A family treatment package for children with aggressive and oppositional behavior. *Journal of Applied Behavior Analysis, 13*, 23–29.

Wambold, C., & Bailey, R. (1979). Improving leisure-time behaviors of severely/profoundly mentally retarded children through toy play. *AAESPH Review, 4*, 237–250.

Wehman, P. (1976). A leisure time activities curriculum for the developmentally disabled. *Education and Training of the Mentally Retarded, 11*, 309–313.

Wehman, P. (1977). *Helping the mentally retarded acquire play skills*. Springfield, IL: Charles C Thomas.

Wehman, P. (1979). Instructional strategies for improving toy play skills of severely handicapped children. *AAESPH Review, 4*, 125–135.

Wehman, P. (Ed.). (1978). *Recreation programming for developmentally disabled persons*. Baltimore: University Park Press.

Wehman, P. (1979). Teaching table games to severely retarded children. *Mental Retardation, 17*, 150–151.

Wehman, P., & Schleien, S. (1980). Assessment and selection of leisure skills for severely handicapped individuals. *Education and Training of the Mentally Retarded, 15*, 50–57.

Wehman, P., & Schleien, S. (1979). *Leisure skills curriculum for the severely handicapped*, Books I, II, III, & IV. Richmond, VA: Virginia Commonwealth University.

Wuerch, B., & Voeltz, L. (1982). *Longitudinal leisure skills for severely handicapped learners: The Ho'onanea curriculum component.* Baltimore: Paul H. Brookes.